Lost Teams
of the South

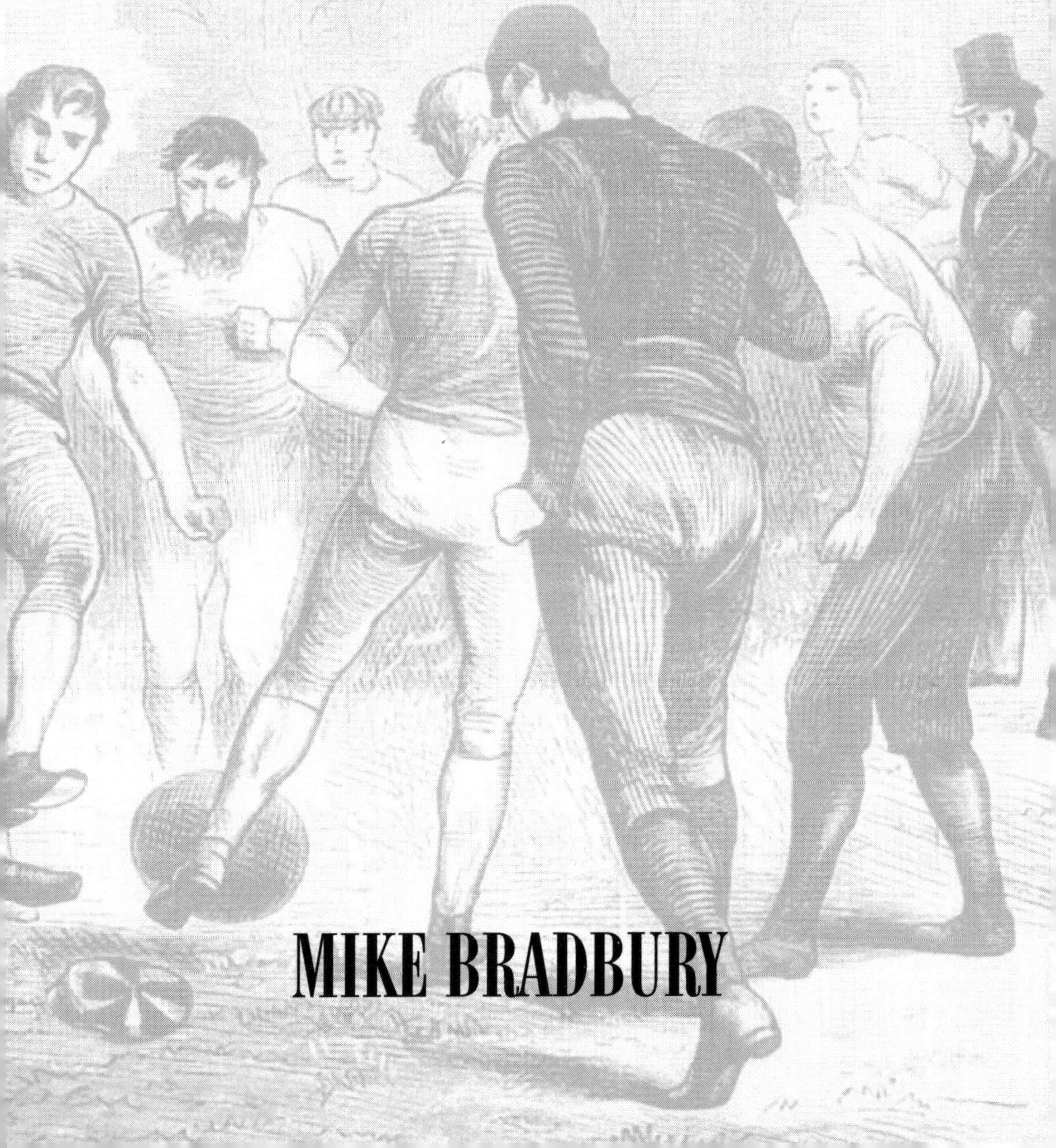

MIKE BRADBURY

Published by
Black Country Research
Willenhall, West Midlands, WV12 4TG

ISBN 978-1-9160595-0-4

Designed and produced by John Griffiths. Printed in the UK.

Contents

Dedication 5

Introduction 6

The Teams

ABERDARE ATHLETIC 21

BARNES 25

BEDMINSTER 31

BOURNEMOUTH GASWORKS ATHLETIC 35

CHESHAM GENERALS 38

CLAPHAM ROVERS 43

CROYDON COMMON 54

CRUSADERS 59

CRYSTAL PALACE 63

FOREST 70

GITANOS 80

GREY FRIARS 85

HAMSTEAD HEATHENS 90

HANOVER UNITED 94

HARROW CHEQUERS 99

HENDON 104

HERTS RANGERS 112

HIGH WYCOMBE 121

HITCHIN 125

HOTSPUR 130

ILFORD 135

LAUSANNE 140

LEYTON 144

LEYTONSTONE 150

LONDON CALEDONIANS 153

LOVELLS ATHLETIC 160

MERTHYR TOWN 164

MINERVA. 167

NEW CRUSADERS. 171

NO-NAMES KILBURN 175

NUNHEAD 181

OLD BRIGHTONIANS. 185

OLD CASTLE SWIFTS. 190

OLD ST. STEPHENS 193

OLYMPIC FC (LONDON) 196

PANTHERS 199

PEGASUS. 208

PILGRIMS 213

READING MINSTER/ SOUTH READING 222

REMNANTS. 229

SOUTHILL PARK. 235

SURREY RIFLES. 238

THAMES 241

THAMES IRONWORKS. 244

THE CASUALS. 249

THE SWIFTS 253

THE WANDERERS. 270

TROJANS. 289

TUFNELL PARK. 292

UPTON PARK 295

WALTHAMSTOW AVENUE. 303

WEST END (LONDON). 307

WEST HAMPSTEAD 310

WEST KENT 316

WEST/ SOUTH NORWOOD 319

WINDSOR HOME PARK 324

WOODFORD WELLS 330

Acknowledgements 333

Bibliography. 334

References 335

Other titles 336

This book is dedicated to my brother,
Carl Bradbury (1958-2015)

Introduction

Few books were read in the compiling of this one, except those which list the results and scorers' details of the F.A. and Amateur Cups. Experience has shown me that it is far better to rely on authentic Victorian and Edwardian newspaper reports, and thus the compounding of modern day factual errors is eliminated. Despite match reports from the 1870s and 1880s frequently giving players names as they were phonetically pronounced, it soon becomes clear which are the correct spellings. Wikipedia can be a useful starting point, but caution must be used, and often, dates, scores and names are found to be in error, when the 19th century newspapers are instead consulted. One early London Cup final, reported as 4-1 on the Internet, was in fact, 1-0, and the real truth of why, and when a club disbanded, is revealed when more than one newspaper is consulted. Ordnance Survey maps have also been cross referenced with the modern tool of Google Earth to pinpoint 'lost' football grounds, to be able to say what is there today, and sadly all too often, the answer is a school or a cul-de-sac. I have no desire to plagiarize another's work (especially a modern one) as I know all too well the thousands of hours of research which have been put into them, but where I have found a vital clue to something which I could not discover for myself, I have always acknowledged the work of others, and expect that other researchers using my work would do the same courtesy. In this matter, I am indebted to Dave Twydell who instructed me to freely extract additional information from his well-known *Gone But Not Forgotten* series, and also to Robin Horton, who allowed me to access his club colours database to fill in a few gaps in my own, which now runs to 600 teams.

This book is intended to be a sister book to my earlier works, *Lost Teams Of The Midlands,* and *Lost Teams Of The North,* which were well received by libraries, football historians and casual readers alike. I believe that the typical reader of these books already had a fair knowledge of the history of the development of football in Britain, from its medieval street brawls, day-long inter-village versions of 'violence with a ball in there somewhere' type of game, through to the split into the two versions of those who wanted the eliminate handling, running with the ball, and general violence (association football), and those who enjoyed the mauling and sweaty struggling in the rucks of the rugby game. Such month by month details, and how the public schools and universities ironed out the rules over two decades is not only well enough known, but readily available both on the internet, and in the myriad of books on the subject written across the twentieth century. I shall therefore, not pad out the book by giving great lists of all the matches ever played in the F.A. Cup, Home Internationals, or Football League tables, as these may readily be looked up in the great brain in the sky.

As a hater of lists, let me get this one out of the way at the start of the book: here you will see the names of all those pioneering young men who attended some or all of the first six meetings of the newly founded Football Association between October and Christmas

1863. Most records only talk about Charles Alcock, Ebenezer Cobb, Francis Marindin, Arthur Pember, Arthur Kinnaird, but these were only the men at the top, the president, secretary, treasurer and so on. Any member club who paid their guinea (one pound, one shilling) was entitled to send two representatives to each meeting, and thus, rules were hammered out taking into account the opinions of about a dozen clubs. Having said that, you will notice an almost complete absence of representatives from the public school teams and universities, although many of those below had enjoyed (or endured) such privileged education. This was not because they were snubbed; far from it, after all Charles Alcock and Morton Betts had been to Harrow, Arthur Kinnaird and Arthur Dunn to Eton College, Reginald Birkett and Charles Woollaston to Lancing College (claimed birthplace of the passing game), Edgar Parry and James Princep to Charterhouse, and Herbert Rawson and R.Walpole Vidal to Westminster. No, it was their insular protectionism which kept the away the very establishments which had nurtured the boys into the young men who sat around the long table at the Sportsman office in London, attempting to formulate a set of universal laws. Throughout the 1850s and into the 1860s, all the principal public schools had, because of peculiarities of their playing arena, developed their own individual type of football. Quite simply, the different public schools had got so used to their own version of rules, honed down over perhaps fifteen or more years, that none of them was willing to let go and concede a single point to the others.

Some schools allowed handling, catching and running with the ball, or patting high balls down to the ground with the hand; others almost encouraged shin-kicking and 'tackling' so dangerous that some were almost throttled. Scrimmages, still recognisable in modern rugby, gave every boy his chance to 'get his own back' on any bully or disliked boy. Indeed, if you *were* the school bully, then where better to get away with half maiming someone in full view without anyone raising an eyebrow. Eton had expansive playing fields, whilst other schools such as Westminster had narrow cloisters which meant no room for passing, only dribbling. Goals varied widely, some no more than a yard apart, whilst at Uppingham in tiny county Rutland (once absorbed into Leicestershire, now returned to its former status) goals were a remarkable 24 yards wide. Almost no school had a height limit between the posts, and punts aimed at the clouds would count as a score, and thus, today in the rugby game, we see fifty feet high posts reminding us of this. Incidentally, the Wednesbury rugby club near Walsall claim to posses the tallest rugby posts in the world, at a staggering 115 feet ! Made from tubular steel, they are intended to demonstrate the prowess of Wednesbury's heritage as the Midland's leading steel fabricating town.

By 1853, Shrewsbury public school had reduced its football team numbers to eleven a side; in the same year, in London, a certain George Bambridge placed an advert in *Bell's Life* asking for all interested parties concerned with forming a football team to write to him at 22 Brunswick Terrace, Windsor. Such activity proved that football, in its rawest sense, was already going on in schools and colleges two decades before the start of the F.A. Cup. A generation later, Bambridge's sons would become famous footballers with The Swifts and the Corinthians. By 1856, eleven a side was now the favoured number at Charterhouse, Eton, Winchester and Charterhouse, whilst at Rugby school, a match under their mauling code lasted for four days. In 1856, the Cambridge Etonians football club came into being on November 7th, and football was in full swing at all the major public schools and college. In 1858, Westminster started playing eleven a side and Harrow school's inter-house matches were being reported in Bell's Life newspaper. Keen students had sent in some brief match reports, mostly simply saying who had won, and to their amazement, they were duly published, leading to weekly insertions thereafter. However, the editor of that paper felt sufficiently knowledgeable a year later to make a statement to the effect that he thought it would be best all round, "if public schools did not play each other".

Thus, the public schools had spent many decades perfecting their own kind of game, and the general ruling was that when two schools met, they would each use the prevailing home rules, although for a long time, public schools simply played in-house matches, or annual fixtures against their own old boys. Public schools by their class intake would have produced young men who were highly opinionated and strung; they would not take one single step backwards to concede an inch in order to protect what they knew so well. Thus, when invited by letter from Charles Alcock of the newly-created Football Association to attend a meeting at the Sportsman office in London, they already knew that they were dinosaurs, simply unable to embrace change. Unshackled from their alma mater the following young men got on with the business of creating a unified code, despite the fact that their body represented only a small fraction of football teams around the country.

The names of those representatives who met in committee at the earliest meetings of the Football Association in 1863 and the clubs they represented were-

Arthur Pember and George Lawson (N.N.); Ebenezer Cobb Morley and Thomas Dyson Gregory (Barnes FC); Charles Frederick Hawker, George Twizel Wawn, George Marriette and Horace William Gray (Civil Service); Herbert Thomas Steward (Crusaders); Francis Day, James Turner, Henry Lloyd, Theodore Lloyd, John Louis Siordet, Lawrence Vivian Desborough and Frederick Urwick (Crystal Palace); John Forster Alcock, Alfred Westwood McKenzie, and Cowper Donne Jackson (Forest Club); Theodore Bell (Surbiton); George William Shillingford, Arthur Christian Tawke, Alexander Rose Stenning, Walter Russell Brackenbury (Percival House school); Bertram Foulke Hartshorne (Charterhouse); William John Mackintosh, Lewis McIver, Jasper Alexander Redgrave, Eyre Burton Powell (Kensington School); William Henry Gordon, Thomas Percy Fox, John Barwick Sams (Blackheath); Ferdinand Brand, William Pears Johnson, (Royal Navy); Fletcher Haynes Cruickshank, Archibald Edward Duthy (Wimbledon school); David John Morgan, John Bouche (Forest school); and five members of the Blackheath Club: Francis and Lorne Campbell, Frederick Moore, John Cooper, and Alfred Poynder.

Don't you just love those amazing Victorian Christian and middle names, often passed down through the generations. You will come across many of those names later on in the section on the clubs for which they played.

Football as played around 1870 was still violent, dangerous and disorganised although gentlemen footballers would at least apologize profusely if they broke your leg.

Pember, Morley and Gregory attended all of the first six meetings, held across October to December

1863. Attending the last meeting in December was the sports outfitter and newspaper reporter John Lillywhite, who had a business in Seymour Street, Eaton Square. By 1870, Lillywhites was the premier sports outfitters, and its prominent advertisements in the sporting press proclaimed that from their warehouse at 10 Seymour Street, Euston, they could supply " football caps made in silk or velvet or flannel; jerseys in any colour made to order; india-rubber ball made by Mackintosh & Co., and football rules at sixpence", and a few years later, goals, flags and football pumps.

Football of one sort or another had been played in-house and between the public schools and universities throughout the 1850s, but there was rarely any continuation of these teams, which were formed and disbanded at a whim, and dictated by school and term holidays, and whether the best players had gone home at Easter and Christmas-time. However, the general opinion of old boys of the various schools at the end of the 1850s was that no school would give up its own rules, especially Harrow and Eton, whose fierce rivalry meant that they were never likely to play each other, even if a common set of rules could be agreed. It was this entrenchment by the very establishments which had made football popular which was holding back the unification and progress of the game, to the national detriment. As will always be the case, there will always be those who are good sports and those who are not, and then there are those who even detest it. It was only natural in school playgrounds and playing fields, that the best players would always be 'showing off' and trying to catch the eye, and thus, imagine in the highly-strung confines of those 1850 public school matches, where good footballers would become almost demi-gods when their long mazy dribbles resulted in a goal. Not only would house-fellows suddenly find a new friend in the boy who was academically weaker, suddenly in favour because he shone on the football pitch, but fags could impress their prefects, and prefects could impress their house-masters or even the headmaster. Later, when they left school and formed new teams, passers-by and young ladies were there to be impressed too. Football in the 1850s and 1860s was played purely for personal enjoyment and glory : even as late as 1877, the Hon. Alfred Lyttleton was chastised in an International match for constantly failing to pass the ball or lay it on to a better placed colleague. When asked afterwards for an explanation, he said " my dear fellow, I play purely for my own enjoyment!" So much for old boy combination play then.

At first, no thought was given to spectators, and in an age before pitch markings and boundaries, they would often get caught up in the play, and sometimes even injured. Some old boys teams had no desire to be watched by the general public, and their audience was restricted to boys and masters from their old schools or colleges. Even at venues like the Kennington Oval, what the public school men thought of as an affordable entry fee was often quite beyond the means of the ordinary working class man. When the first F.A. Cup final was played in 1872, the shilling admission price was half a day's wages for a general labourer, but pin money for those who played the match (*Cassells Household Guide for 1880*). After a while, spectators would be permitted and expected to stay behind the now roped off arena (sometimes flag markers), although in places like Wednesbury and Leek in Staffordshire, home crowds would deliberately encroach in order to prevent shots crossing the goal-line, or worse, attempt to assault the visiting players! As teams began to rent their own fields, if they were enclosed or defined by hedges, they would be able to start asking a small admittance fee, usually two or three (old) pence. In the case of public schools or colleges, the charging of an admittance would not be allowed, and the Old Boys teams who played their matches back on the school playing fields had no reason to ask for an entry fee. Coming from middle or upper class families, those footballers would hardly be interested in collecting a few shillings when they were already well-off. Games played in public parks or public open spaces were also free to watch even when several thousand spectators lined the field, such as at West Ham park in London. In the natural order of things, spectators would go to watch the more successful teams, and in areas where there were perhaps five or six teams in a square mile, then only the best one or two would survive. Attendances in the South were generally much smaller than in the Midlands and the North, where rapid progress towards professionalism was being made in the 1880s. Even so, few teams ever got more than about 2,000 spectators in the 1870s, and much less than that in the amateur South. Even after the Football League was established, some League clubs got by on crowds of 4,000. Those tales from your granddad about 'sixty thousand crowds at every First Division match' never happened until after the country settled back down after the end of the Second World War, when the male population flocked to football as an indication of the nation's huge sigh of relief.

And what of the spectator? Did his attitude change over the years, from watching gentlemen amateur teams 'playing for their own pleasure' through to fully-involved professionals who by 1890, virtually lived at the club premises? Well it certainly did, and like the footballer, it was indirectly proportionate to money. Generally, the paid player was expected to put more effort into his game than the unpaid player, although it seems, from watching some recent Premiership matches, some players seem to stop trying once they are paid far in excess of their true worth. When spectators were first allowed to watch, in the 1860s and 1870s, no-one would have dared shout out " what a load of rubbish - I could do better!" simply because he was likely to have been invited (or even forced) to go on the pitch and put his feet where his mouth was, quite literally. Even today, no passer-by watching a Sunday team would bad-mouth the genuine efforts of the casual player. However, as soon as people are asked to pay to spectate, then this empowers them with a right to comment, if not criticize. Couple this with the knowledge that the players are also paid to perform, then the £100 a minute player is expected to perform better than the £100 a week player. More is demanded from the highest paid players, and rightly so; but the spectator's entitlement to be a critic rises with the player's perceived value. If a part-timer misses an open goal, the full wrath of the spectator is withheld due an unspoken understanding of his limitations; should an international pampered pet miss such a sitter, he gets the full vocal 'treatment'.

There is, in every occupation, the right price for the right job. Pay a man a pound for every item he can produce, and he will make as many as he can in the available hours; pay a man a fixed sum, and he will make as few as he can. Thus, even in these inflated times, there should still be the right salary for a top footballer. Until recent decades, top players got paid an amount broadly equal to three or four times the typical salary of someone in a professional occupation, such as a headmaster, solicitor, or police inspector. Today, some well-known players are paid a nurses' annual salary *per day*. Unless this madness stops, the game will shrink down to one league of a dozen clubs, with all remaining others playing each other on an amateur basis in regional leagues and cups. Just like it was in 1888. A frightening thought, but even the dinosaurs died out, and until the Premier League shares its vast fortunes from the likes of BT and Sky TV with smaller clubs, and makes across the board hand-outs to the hundreds of failing lower pyramid clubs, then Association will no longer be Rex.

As the cost of watching increases, such as between watching a lower pyramid team at a cost of say six pounds, and going to a Premiership game, where a good seat might cost you a day's wages, then the entitlement of the spectator to vent his displeasure and exasperation increases in proportion to the cost of admission. I recently got wound up at the inability of one of my local semi-professional teams to manage to win at home, when a fellow sufferer, some ten seats away, reminded me that 'big Baz' the centre-forward who had just missed an open goal, was in fact a delivery driver for Amazon in the week. There are no such excuses at Premiership grounds. What 'locks' together the crowd at a football match, is that we all suffer or rejoice together, and as such, surrounded by perhaps thirty thousand people we have never met, all become one single family. The football spectator has been almost completely overlooked in the story of the game, but yet I doubt if even the Corinthians would have played any better if the crowd had been 100,000 instead of 10,000, although there was no doubt that the Amateur Cup Final, in front of a full house bought the best out of both sets of players on the day.

And what of that anonymous figure in black, who has to fulfil both requirements of making himself invisible on the field of play, yet make himself constantly available to the players with his decisions? Has the referee himself altered or become treated differently over the years? Well certainly, for in the early days -1860s to 1880s - he was certainly inconspicuous, as he did not yet exist! The field of play was, when available, controlled by two umpires, one supplied by each side, who patrolled their own half of the pitch and made decisions when appealed to by the players, as in cricket. Decisions were not volunteered, so if a team failed to appeal for a goal or free kick, it was not given. The umpire was like a 12th man, who turned out with his club both home and away. Often he was a retired or injured player, or an elderly administrator, and he would wear either his day clothes, or some type of sporting version, often looking like Sherlock Holmes, or with a raincoat down to the floor and waving an umbrella to signal his decisions. A goal would be signalled by the raising of the umbrella, or the waiving of a white hankie. In the Midlands in the 1880s, Aston Villa were often umpired by retired founder George Ramsay, who was effectively their manager, and he would use the opportunity to spy on opposing teams, and put a mental marker of future players they could sign up! Many umpires could not match the fitness of the footballers, and so 'parked' themselves in one spot from where they thought that they could see everything. Which of course, they couldn't. The two umpires were supposed to agree on major claims, such as goals, and off-sides, although I cannot see how a man standing in the other half can make such decisions. Some were lazy, and simply stood in the middle of the pitch all through the match. It was as if they were a spectator allowed on to the pitch, rather than a component of the event. When the two umpires could not agree, they *referred* the point to a third independent man standing off the pitch, and in time, he became the sole referee, with the two umpires relegated to running the touchline waving their flags or hankies to signal off-sides and balls out of play. Some umpires were known to be lazy and of poor judgement, and frequently got in the way of the action, with balls bouncing off them, and players getting accidentally poked by wayward umbrellas. Some men were well-known as wise and fair referees, such as Francis Marindin, the Royal Engineer, Charles Alcock, and Alfred Stair from the Upton Park club, or that man whose name may have started all the chants- Segar Bastard, the London solicitor who also played cricket for the MCC and Essex. He was, according to the 1881 census, the only man in the country with that name. It was the start of the Football

11

League in 1888-89 which began the downfall of the reputation of the referee. Before the legalisation of professionalism in 1885-6, referees and umpires were seen as merely mortal, with associated frailties, and thus although there were many times when a captain led his team off the pitch in a sulk at having a perfectly good goal disallowed, by and large they were not the target for the fan for the failure of his team. Teams could not be led of the pitch in a sulk after 1888 in the Football League. Not in front of 10,000 spectators anyway. When the instant success of the professional Football League grabbed the nation in a new football fever, suddenly the result of every match mattered far more than ever before. The future of entire football clubs was at stake, careers were on the line, and for the owners and directors, thousands of pounds could go down the drain if their team was relegated, or knocked out of the Cup. Suddenly, everything that went wrong was the fault of the referee; if he awarded your team two penalties, he was only doing his job; if he awarded two against your team, he was every name you could think of. In today's game where managers live from week to week on their team's results, technology is beginning to help referees 'see' what the armchair TV fan is able to see over and over with multi-angle camera and slow motion replays, and we now have 'goal-line technology' a set of sensors arrayed inside the goal-frame to decide whether the ball has completely crossed the line. But didn't it take a long time in coming? How long now, until the referee gets sent a bleep message to a wristband to confirm the ball is 'over' ? The modern-day referee at the top level, is slowly getting more respect, because frequently the TV pundits, who review and analyse the match to bits, frequently proclaim that the referee was right after all. All that is left in order to eliminate all possible referee errors, is for referees to watch instant replays on a wrist-screen and make a perfect decision, as now happens in top class rugby. If he blows up for a foul, and he is shown to be wrong, he could then simply award the free-kick to the other team. He might also never again show the red card to the wrong man, or to an innocent defender following a 'dive' by the forward. I hope it never happens but I predict that in the future, the football referee will actually be removed from the pitch, and placed in a viewing box, where he watches the game on multi screen monitors, and VR technology gives him instant decision making capabilities. I would also not be surprised if infra-red VR lasers detecting offsides did away with the linesmen – sorry 'assistant referees' – too.

Despite the interest generated by the creation of the Football Association in 1863, it was not for a while, judged as a success. Indeed, after the six clubs who broke away (led by the Richmond club) to play the handling Rugby game, there remained only nine member clubs, and this number was not added to for some months afterwards. Letters began to appear in the sporting press criticizing the new F.A., saying that it was failing to show the way to the nation, and that it was too slow to formulate a national set of playing rules which were acceptable to all parties in all regions. Some even suggested that the early meetings had been deliberately held at a time which precluded the attendance of representatives of the leading old boys clubs, particularly Charterhouse, whose 'gentle' rules were closer to what became the 1870 rules. Indeed, Hartshorne, captain of the Charterhouse school XI, sent in a letter to the F.A. saying that " I am directed to say that as yet Charterhouse cannot be included amongst the clubs who form the Football Association".

The response from Harrow was equally stonewall; in his letter, Harrow school captain Charles Gordon Browne enquired what benefits might arise from becoming a member, and stated that the headmaster had not given permission for any Harrow boys to attend F.A. meetings should they occur in term-time. Winchester, Eton and Rugby remained silent.

One correspondent making the valid point that until the F.A. had substantially increased its membership, it had no real right to attempt to formulate and force upon the country a unified code, when only a handful of London clubs were at the table. It would take a while before everyone settled down. Meanwhile, a hundred miles north, the well organised Sheffield Association of some twenty clubs, was forging ahead with pioneering inventions, such as corner flags and wooden crossbars.

In 1863, the Civil Service cricket club started up a football team which still plays to this day; Cambridge University re-formed their football team as a club and played on Parker's Piece, and published the club rules in *Bell's Life*. Flags defined the 150 x 100 yard field, and the goals were two poles, only 15 feet apart, with no height limit, and thus, a high punt thirty feet in the air still counted as a Cambridge goal! Any player in front of the ball was 'out of play' and hands and tripping were forbidden. Cambridge and Oxford met on the last day of November 1863, at of all venues, Eton College. A large crowd formed a rectangle, and the match was played inside them. No reference was made as to differing sets of rules, and a harmonious match ended with Oxford declared winners by one rouge to nil. Interestingly, Oxford were in blue, and Cambridge wore red.

By the mid-1860s, dedicated sports papers such as the *Sportsman* and *Sporting Life*, were being joined by *The Graphic, London Standard, Sheffield Telegraph, Sheffield Independent,* and *Sport & Play* in giving results (if not descriptions) of many football matches, of all codes. Despite matches taking place the length and breadth of the country (but principally in London and Sheffield until the mid 1870s) to a variety of local rules, with 'touchdowns', 'rouges', 'points', 'bases' and goals all being mixed up together, it was nonetheless possible to read about the fortunes of about fifty clubs by the end of the 1860s, although few of them belonged to the FA. By 1867, the Sportsman was providing a wonderful service of listing all the fixtures yet to be played in the season, giving dates and venues; additionally it would also give all known results during the season, although it was clear that rugby and football was all being mixed together. Unsurprisingly, several clubs played both the handling code and the non-handling codes, particularly Clapham Rovers, Flamingos, C.C.C., Civil Service, and many of the hospital and college teams. Even by 1870, many London hospitals competed in their own hospitals cup, although the favoured rules were rugby.

On January 8th 1867, a most outrageous football match took place at Harrow school, which I must tell you about. It seems that by then, the Eton and Harrow lot were beginning to have some fun with their football, not always taking it seriously. A match audaciously billed as 'Eton & Harrow versus The World'! caused *The Sportsman* paper to treat the match in the same outlandish fashion, with much 'mickey-taking' from the newspaper reporter who went along to observe the proceedings. Played as an 5-a-side match, the home side included young Arthur Kinnaird and G.G. Kennedy, both future Wanderers, and on the 'World' team, we had Charles Alcock and the football-mad Muir-Mackenzie brothers (who played the next day for the Wanderers against Westminsters). *The Sportsman*, entering into the spirit, jokingly apologised for the weak teams, as apologies of absence had been received from the various heads of state of Europe and the Far East! The match finished a 2-2 draw. Incidentally, Arthur Kinnaird's last ever game of football after a 300 game 'career' was in a 5-0 win for Wanderers against Harrow School in 1884. Traceable games for one of the game's greatest ever legendary players show that he played 92 games for the Old Etonians, 88 for Wanderers, 15 for Gitanos, 8 for West Kent, 2 for Hanover United, and 2 for the Flying Dutchman, and many other random or unreported matches took his total to beyond 300, in an age of twenty game seasons.

The newspapers were keeping a keen eye on the way the game of football was being unified, although of course, only one side of the social divide was having its say. The well-heeled leisured London set were frequently writing to the papers, each one making a case for the rules as played at his public school or college, and the rugby chaps equally vocal about their belief in the importance of retaining the mauls, rucks and charging features of the ball-carrying version, which had made just as strong a foothold in the capital as had the 'feet only' version. It was hard to tell what was happening in the Midlands and the North, even though London papers often reported on games in those regions. There was no doubt that apart from in the well self-organised 'bubble' of Sheffield football, that consistency of both rules, playing duration, and size of teams, was still subject to regional variations even beyond the crucial year of 1871, when all who entered the Cup were compelled to play the 'London F.A. Rules'. What the press did offer, was well-judged criticism and encouragement, as the February 16th 1869 edition of the *Penny Illustrated* had this to say:-
" there are still a few good old English sports which demand pluck, courage, strength and agility, as well as mutual forbearance and good temper, and assuredly, football is one of them. This manly and athletic game which may be said to divide the year between cricket and rowing, is one that cannot be undertaken by people with weak limbs, short breath, or irascible tempers, with knocks and falls being commonplace". Yet another broken leg, this time to a player in the St. Barts v Clapton rugby match in the same month, caused the *London Morning Post* to remark that " it advocates doing away with this style of football in favour of the association game as played by Wanderers and The Old Westminsters".

By 1870, there were said to be 3,000 footballers in the London area alone, (of both codes) and everywhere you looked, schools, colleges, hospitals and old boys were forming football teams, if not clubs. Football was now a big topic of general conversation; how to play it, the best way to play it, which rules were best, and the sporting press was full of letters both in support and against the two codes. Most people did seem to want to see the dangerous element of rough play to be eliminated, and letters claiming to be by old boys of schools such as Rugby were talking about having seen 'maiming, gouging and strangling' on the field of play, probably in an effort to alienate and discredit the rugby version. However, retorts from supporters of clubs such as Blackheath and Richmond, vehemently denied that such excesses were happening, and that the rugby game, was 'calming down' from the violent stuff, whilst still retaining the essential ball carrying aspects. The public schools however, were not required to adopt the F.A. rules, unless competing in the cup, and at 1870, they still retained their own features. Harrow school allowed the ball to be brought under control with the hand, and a mark on the ground would obtain a 'free kick'; Charterhouse and Westminster allowed 'hands' under limited circumstances, but Eton no longer permitted any contact of hand to ball, unless being thrown back into play from touch. 1870s throw-ins could be done with one or both hands, and under or over arm style, and some players could throw a ball into the goalmouth from the half-way line.

Once again, the headmasters of Westminster and Charterhouse schools put their foot down, when in April 1871, they forbade older boys to take part in the Wanderers' sports day on Saturday 8th April on the Amateur Athletic Association grounds at Lillie Bridge. By the early 1870s, there was a clear distinction between the rugby and association codes, and unlike in the north, both codes flourished side by side, with public parks such as Battersea and Richmond home to up to a dozen teams of both persuasions. Spectators, watching for free, could stroll around the London parks and watch many different matches should they wish, with even lacrosse on offer in the winter. London in the 1870s still had enough farmland within a mile or two of the city to enable football teams to find a field to rent: places like Hampstead Heath, Hackney Marshes, Kentish Town and Kilburn were almost out in the countryside. To the south of the Thames, Clapham, Sydenham, Dulwich and Norwood still had plenty of undeveloped open spaces, and soon, the London area was peppered with association and rugby teams, and as public school men returned to their homes at holiday times, they took with them the spirit and excitement of forming an eleven in their home town too. Oxford football, already based around its separate college teams, increased in popularity when, in 1870, the game 'was removed to The Parks', exposing it to both the public, and acting as a visible catalyst for other college teams to be formed.

As 'late' as the commencement of the 1871-72 season, several years after the formation of the Football Association (1863) and the forbidding of handling (1870), there was still no universally accepted standardisation of rules. The *London Standard* of October 1871 was particularly scathing about the state of affairs, when it said *"we are aware there exists a so-called Football Association, which is supposed to govern the game,... but it does nothing of the kind...and its authority is of the most shadowy and vague kind"*. At the start of every match, it was still the first thing to come to an agreement on what would and would not be allowed during the game. Eleven a side or fourteen? Two hours, or ninety minutes? Hacking and tripping or not? Patting high balls down to the ground, or no hands at all? All these matters needed ironing out very quickly, as football teams were springing up all over the country, and it was already the nation's second most popular participatory sport behind cricket.

In terms of what even the more advanced teams were doing in the 1870s, with a formation which was basically two backs and everyone else as a forward, games would have been pretty much kick-and-rush, with the occasional breakaway dribble backed up by other forwards who formed a scrimmage around the ball when it broke loose. Until around 1877, some old boys teams were still playing seven forwards, two backs and a goalkeeper. The seven forwards comprised a pair of men on each wing, who worked together to get the ball past the full back on their side, and three centres, awaiting crosses in the goalmouth. The goalkeeper was an open target for one or more of the centres to charge him out if the way when the cross came over, and even force him into his own goal even if he was holding the ball! Scrimmages in front of goal were a frequent method of scoring until the mid 1880s, when a more 'scientific' approach was developed, thanks to teams like Lancing College, Cambridge, Royal Engineers, and in the north, Queens Park and Sheffield FC. By pulling back one of the two centre forwards to fill the large gap between the backs and the forwards, the new centre-half position was born by 1883. Some teams by the late 1870s had already realised that even seven forwards was just too many, and the half-back line was starting to appear, created by withdrawing the two 'inside' wing men to partner the new centre half. This gave the advantage that instead of the two backs just hoofing the ball up-field (however accurate), that it was better and more controlled to pass the ball forward to the half backs who could either run forward or 'feed' the wingers of both flanks. With more thought now being put into the way the game was played, teams would meet in pubs and committee-rooms to discuss plans and new ideas. It soon became apparent that the centre half position was best allocated to the captain, who could marshal his men, calling them back if they wandered too far up field, and reminding his half backs to stay with the men they were told to mark.

Even by 1880 the old fashioned star dribbler was a thing of the past, and both spectators, newspapers, and teams had begun to realise that all eleven men in the team needed to learn their positions, and stick to them during the game, and not simply roam all over the field randomly, as implied by the phrase of the day "leather-chasers". I believe that Alcock's F.A. Cup snapped the country into focus, by forcing every team who took part to use the F.A.'s 'London' rules. The winning of the English Cup, as it was then known, permitted for the first time, the universally accepted crown of the national champion to be worn, and this became the ultimate achievement to which every club in the land aspired. It may have, at first been a small acorn with less than twenty, mostly London area clubs taking part, but it would soon become the nation's newest drug, and every team in the land wanted a taste of it. In the Midlands, the early pioneering clubs - Calthorpe, Burton, Shrewsbury, Saltley College, Stafford Road, West Bromwich FC, had all been founded by educated middle class men who had been through the local colleges and grammar schools. Soon, these would be replaced and overtaken in numbers by working-class teams, formed out of churches, factories, and cricket clubs. There was no real example of 'old-boys' teams or network, (apart from the clergy) unlike in the south, where even well beyond the introduction of professionalism, teams like the Old Harrovians, Old Etonians, Old Cathusians, Old Westminsters, Old Foresters and Upton Park, all carried on regardless into the twentieth century. Such teams still held sway in 1888 in the south, by which time professional teams headed the lists in the rest of the country, and thus, professionalism was late arriving in this region. Indeed, with four London Cup wins in a six year period at the end of the 1880s and start of the 1890s, the Old Westminster had a good claim for being the best team in the South. They strolled onto the pitch for the 1890 London Cup final against unbeaten Royal Arsenal with an air of coolness which they kept during the match, and let Arsenal do all the nervous football, and they were despatched 1-0 *(Pall Mall Gazette)*.When the F.A. instructed all county associations to affiliate all professional clubs in their region, the Surrey and Middlesex County F.A.s refused to do so. Arsenal (then Woolwich Arsenal) were the first team in the South to turn professional, doing so in 1891, five years after their formation as Royal Arsenal. Millwall (1893), Tottenham Hotspur (1895) and both Fulham and West Ham (1898) all followed, but the London F.A weren't happy about this trend, which shifted the balance away from long-established old boy's teams. This led to them being boycotted by the London Football Association, formed nine years earlier. This late southern professionalism didn't kill off the amateurs, but they were soon left behind. Some of the early amateur sides are still alive today, such as Uxbridge (f.1871) who play in the Southern League Division 1 Central Division.

There are many other aspects of the development of the game, but as I covered them in *"Lost Teams Of The Midlands"* which included an impression of what a spectator would see if he went to games across the decades, I do not feel it is necessary here to go over the same ground again. By the very nature of this book's title, I have hoisted myself on my own petard; of the early 'greats' of Victorian football, the Wanderers, Swifts, and perhaps Clapham Rovers, and the Caledonians are the only ones which are extinct. Institutionally-based teams, such as Old Etonians, Old Harrovians, Old Westminsters, Oxford & Cambridge Universities, Old Foresters, Old Carthusians and even the Royal Engineers (who claim continuous existence from 1863) are still alive today, mostly playing in the

Arthurian League and Arthur Dunn Cup. Perhaps one day I will write a book about the Old Boys FC; until then, I will take any opportunity to give them a mention in this one, where appropriate. As for the Casuals, and the Corinthians, I had to decide whether, in the usual sense, they were defunct. Both giants of the amateur game, they amalgamated in 1939 and shared a joint name, and thus it could be argued that from that moment *neither club* existed. The delightful colours of the Casuals, chocolate and pink halves, navy shorts were drawn from the horse racing colours of their patron, the (Winston) Churchill family, and are worn today by Corinthian-Casuals FC. I could not possibly even scratch the surface of the history and achievements of the Corinthians, and thus I chose to leave them out, rather than do them an injustice. At least three ex-Corinthian players have written club histories, and it is still said that you need all three to secure the full story of what they gave to the game. I shall instead, delve into the histories of many of the clubs in the south of England which have not previously been written about, and for those that have, I will grasp the opportunity to furnish new facts and trace their old grounds and colours to assist both the amateur historian and general reader alike.

Whilst researching the teams in this book, I came across hundreds of 'lesser' teams, who played in public parks or untraceable fields, but the two most important football grounds in early (1850-1890) football in London, I am happy to say are still there to be seen today. Westminster School and their old boys side entertained virtually every team of any note at their Vincent Square ground in the heart of the city of London. Properly described as a rhombus, it is approximately 220 yards square, and tree-lines on all four sides. Today, hemmed in by hospitals, exclusive properties and the buildings of the Royal Horticultural Society (f.1804), it sits off Rochester Row, its large black and white pavilion suggesting the halcyon days of Victorian gentleman amateur football and cricket. A 'pilgrimage' would be well worthwhile on your next London trip, as here played the Wanderers, Old Harrovians, Swifts, Forest, Old Etonians, Clapham Rovers, and Oxford University and many others.

Long since only thought of as the cricket ground of Surrey, the Kennington Oval today bears no resemblance as the Cup Final venue of 1872-1892, hemmed in now on all four sides with five storey flats, although the ever-present Gasworks has been a reference point since the first Cup Final, with teams either kicking off towards the gasometer or the Hayleford Street ends.

The 160 yard diameter cricket oval, now the beneficiary of untold millions of pounds of improvements, now bears little resemblance to that of the Cup Final years, when there were no permanent grandstands, only a moveable one on rollers, and sheep were still allowed to graze on the field. To put football in context of Victorian cricket, in 1868, 20,000 people filled the ground for its first important cricket match; four years later, only a tenth of that number paid a shilling to watch the first Cup Final.

Having said at the start of the book, that I do not favour 'lists', then here is another one! I soon began to realise that the keenest early footballers loved the game so much that that played for up to half a dozen clubs. Not consecutively, like today's oft-transferred player, but *concurrently* which must have taken some stamina. Charles Alcock, when in later life, explaining how he had kept a reasonably proportionate figure, said that he used football as a means of getting and staying fit, and tried to play *every day*. In his Wanderers days, it was not rare for players like him to play four or five times a week. Here then, is what I think is an *interesting* list, of the leading Victorian amateur players of the South, and the clubs for which they played, mostly, as I said, at the same time -

Player	Lifetime	Clubs know to have played for
Alcock, Charles W	1842-1907	Wanderers, Harrow Pilgrims, Old Westminsters, Forest, Gitanos, Civil Service, Barnes, Flying Dutchmen, West Kent,
Alcock, John Foster	1841-1910	Forest, Wanderers, Harrow Pilgrims
Baker, Alfred	1846-1900	Forest, Wanderers, No-Names
Barker, Robert	1847-1915	Old Westminsters, Herts Rangers, Wanderers
Bailey, Norman	1857-1923	Old Westminsters, Clapham Rovers, Corinthians, Swifts, Wanderers
Bambridge, Charlie	1858-1935	Windsor Home Park, Swifts, Corinthians
Bastard, Segar	1854-1921	Upton Park, Trojans, Leyton, Corinthians
Betts, Morton Peto	1847-1914	Wanderers, Old Harrovians, Harrow Chequers, West Kent
Birley, Francis	1850-1910	Oxford University, Wanderers (32)
Bonsor, Alexander	1851-1907	Wanderers, Old Etonians
Chenery, Charlie	1850-1928	Wanderers, Barnes, Crystal Palace
Cotterill, George M	1868-1950	Old Brightonians, Corinthians, Swifts
Crake, William Parry	1852-1921	Barnes, Wanderers, Harrow
Cutbill, R		Forest, Wanderers, Crystal Palace
Cutbill, J		Forest, Wanderers, Crystal Palace
Dixon, Harold B		Wanderers, Flying Dutchmen, Oxford University
Dunn, Arthur	1869-1902	Wanderers, Casuals, Corinthians, Cambridge University, Old Etonians.
Field, Edgar	1854-1934	Reading, Clapham Rovers, Gitanos, Wanderers
Fry, Charles B	1872-1956	Corinthians, Casuals, Southampton
Green, Frederick	1851-1928	Oxford University, Wanderers, Old Wykehamists
Greig, W.D.O	1851-1942	Old Brightonians, Wanderers (23), Herts Rangers, Farningham
Haygarth, Edward	1854-1915	Wanderers, Reading, Swifts
Hawtrey, Edward.M	1847-1916	Remnants, Old Etonians, Swifts

Hawtrey, John Purvis	1850-1925	Windsor, Remnants, Swifts.
Hogg, Quintin	1845-1903	Gitanos, Polytechnic,Wanderers, Old Etonians
Jarrett, Beaumont	1855-1905	Wanderers, Old Harrovians, Grantham, Cambridge University
Kinnaird, Arthur	1847-1923	Wanderers, Old Etonians, Gitanos, West Kent, Flying Dutchmen
Lloyd-Jones, Clopton	1858-1918	Nottingham Trent, Shropshire Wanderers, The Wanderers, Clapham Rovers
Lubbock, Edgar	1847-1907	Wanderers, Old Etonians, West Kent, Gitanos, Civil Service
Kirkpatrick, Sir James	1841-1899	Wanderers, Civil Service, Gitanos
Mersey-Thompson, Albert	1848-1894	Cambridge Etonians, Wanderers, Old Etonians
Morice, Charles	1850-1932	Wanderers, Harrow Chequers, Barnes
Morton, Alex	1831-1900	Crystal Palace, Wanderers, No-Names
Ottoway, Cuthbert	1850-1878	Crystal Palace, Oxford University, Old Etonians
Parry, Edgar Hubert	1855-1931	Old Carthusians, Wanderers, Swifts, Remnants, Windsor, Stoke Poges, Oxford University.
Pember, Arthur	1835-1886	No-Names, Wanderers
Princep, James	1861-1895	Oxford University, Old Carthusians, Clapham R
Rawson, William	1854-1932	Oxford University, Wanderers, Old Westminsters
Rawlinson, John F	1860-1926	Wanderers, Cambridge University, Old Etonians, Corinthians
Sparks, Francis	1855-1934	Brondesbury, St.Albans, Pilgrims, the Swifts, Clapham Rovers, Herts Rangers,
Stair, Alfred	1845-1914	Civil Service, Upton Park, Wanderers
Spreckley, Tom	1850-1927	Forest, Upton Park, Crystal Palace
Stephenson, Charles	1853-1924	Civil Service, Wanderers, Old Westminsters
Swepstone, Harry	1859-1907	Pilgrims, Corinthians, Ramblers, Swifts
Tebbut, Charles Goodman	1860-1944	Forest, Wanderers, Flying Dutchmen, No-Names
Tebbut, M		Forest, Herts Rangers, No-Names

Todd, Arthur H		Oxford University, Clapham Rovers, Old Carthusians
Vidal, R.W.S	1853-1914	Remnants, Old Westminsters, Oxford University, Wanderers, Flying Dutchmen,
Wace, Henry	1853-1947	Cambridge University, Clapham Rovers, Wanderers, Shropshire Wanderers, Shrewsbury.
Walters, Arthur M	1865-1941	Cambridge University, Corinthians, Swifts, Old Carthusians
Walters, Percy M	1863-1936	Cambridge University, Corinthians, Swifts, Old Carthusians
deWelch, Reginald C	1851-1939	Harrow Chequers, Wanderers, Old Harrovians

And so, finally, to the near-sixty extinct football clubs featured in this book. I have chosen them for a variety of reasons, such as having a famous or successful history, or because they were a pioneering team, but mostly for the reason that few of them have previously been written about, and thus I hope even collectors of the numerous football history books will find new material here to add to the interest and fascination of a bygone age, where players wore knee length trousers, chased a waterlogged leather ball across uneven and bumpy fields, with moustaches and egos flying in the breeze. Virtually all the teams I have chosen have FA Cup history, and this final book in the "Lost Teams" series bring to almost 200, the number of teams covered.

Even at 1900, some of the Old Boys teams were able to give the professional sides a good game, particularly Cambridge University, the Old Malvernians and the Old Carthusians, and of course the composite 'super teams' like the Corinthians and the Casuals.

Cambridge University v Old Etonians, a corner to Cambridge.

The Teams

ABERDARE ATHLETIC

Founded - 1893
Folded - 1928
Ground - Ynys Meadow
Colours - 1. Maroon shirts   1892-1898
        2. Navy and gold stripes   1898-1921
        3. Claret and blue shirts 1921-1923
        4. Navy and gold stripes   1923-1924
        5. Black and amber stripes 1924-1927

It seems hard to believe that a small town in the south welsh valleys with a population of less than 20,000 could host a Football League team. Due to the rise of the coal industry in south Wales in the 1860s, people began to move to the area and the population of the village of Aberdare went from a thousand to over 10,000 in a couple of decades. Sadly, it was to be the economic slump of the 'twenties which also led to their demise. The quality of Aberdare coal created a boom town, with new houses, pubs and shops. There had been a cricket club in the town since before 1870, and athletic events had also taken place for amusement. The founding of the football team was followed two year later by the death of Lord Aberavon, who was buried in Mountain Ash with a service in Westminster. Rugby so dominated the region, that when the Western Gazette did a whole page feature (with sketches of leading men) in September 1895, there was no mention of association football at all!

No reports for the club could be found until 1900, and then, it was a sad one, reporting the sudden death of Aberdare player Ben Gibbons. At the end of the 1899-1900 season, the *Western Gazette* thought that Aberdare had claim to being south Wales' premier club that season on the basis of winning the Welsh League and taking the Leominster cup. Never drawn at home, they had to beat holders Leominster on their own ground in the final. Only the 3rd round of the Welsh Cup was reached, however, going out to Rhyl. Scorers that season were Steve Jones, Leo Tubb, F.I. Caldicott, Woolnacott, Webster, and A. Jones, H. Williams and S. Parker. A remarkable 32 victories included wins over Cardiff University (7-0), Sheffield United (2-1), Crewe (6-1), Aberaman (7-0), Pontyprydd (5-0), and Leominster (6-2). Their usual team for 1900-01 was -

			W. Stone			
		Hugh Jones		Shenton		
	G. Davies		F. Davies		F. Stone	
A. Jones	Steve Jones		Webster	Packer		Hugh Williams

In 1904 and 1905, Aberdare were beaten finalists in the Welsh Cup (no reports found) and these early successes prompted their decision in 1909 Aberdare to turn professional, and, along with Merthry Town and Ton Pentre, joined the expanding Southern League, who were trying to build up their empire to rival the Football League, which at that time still only had two divisions. Later, when the Southern League's First Division was embraced as the new Third Division (South) of the Football League, several Welsh clubs, including Aderdare, found themselves in the top league in the land. In the Edwardian era, Aberdare won the Welsh League in 1905, 1909, 1912 and 1921

I spotted that the *London Gazette* reported on 9th January 1914, that there had been an extraordinary meeting of members of the Aberdare FC at 2 Cannon Street, where it was agreed that the club would be voluntarily wound up, with James Salmon appointed liquidator. I could not determine whether this was the rugby club or not.

In 1914, Aberdare played Ton Pentre four times in four weeks in different competitions, their home Welsh League match finishing 2-0 with goals from Smith and Hatton. The press seemed to be calling them the 'Darrians' at this time. With poor timing by departing in June 1914, trainer George Rowlands moved on to unknown club Bramsley. However, when they beat Mid-Rhonda 2-0 in February 1914, it was their first win in the Welsh League since the previous October, so this seems to have been a poor season. Aberdare got elected into the Football League's Division Three South in 1921, but never really made a mark, and when they finished bottom in 1927, were voted out again.

Aberdare's finest season was their Football League debut one in 1921-22 when they finished 8th in Division 2 South, above rivals, Swansea, Merthyr and Newport County by which time they had added the 'Athletic' tag. One of their players that season was Robert Barnshaw (1889-1974). Signed from Watford at the end of his career, the centre half had spent four years with both the leading Sheffield clubs, but only in their reserves. Another man with a lot of Sheffield experience was later manager Frank Bradshaw, who played 87 games for The Wednesday, 66 times for Everton and 132 times for the Arsenal before retiring into managership. He also scored a hat-trick for England in their remarkable 11-1 away win over Austria in 1908.

Meadows lying between two converging railway lines of the Great Western and Taff Vale Railway became used for the town's recreation, and the football field lay adjacent to the GWR line, and both the Taff Vale and GWR stations were only 200 yards away. Unfortunately, spectators coming from the two bridges on Abernant Road would have had to walk past the town abattoir to get to the six acre ground. The site of the old ground is now the Astropitch of the Michael Sorbell Sports Centre. Sorbell was a remarkable character; a fleeing Jew from the old Austria-Hungarian empire, his family left behind factories in Europe to escape from anti-Semitism. Soon, with his father, they set up businesses in London, including leather and electronics, where their company Allied Radio Industries became a major part of the G.E.C conglomerate. He later became a well known successful horse race owner, and with legend Gordon Richards at the reins, his horses won many famous races. In later life, he began to set up foundations and funded many pioneering industries. The sports centre in Aberdare is only one of several to carry his name, with others in London.

Their Ynys Stadium was gradually improved during the 1920s, with a large grandstand on the 'town' side, and banked terracing behind the goals replaced the earlier cycle track, bringing the capacity up to around 23,000 which ambitiously was about the same as the

Aberdare Athletic circa 1910
Courtesy of Rhondda Cynon Taff Library Service

entire population of the town ! However, a late bonfire on 7th November 1923 burned the main stand and dressing room down, and the club had to borrow a set of kit (probably from Newport, since it was black and amber stripes) for their home game against Brighton on the following Saturday. Only twisted girders of the insured £11,000 stand remained the following morning. On the previous night, the F.A. had made the 2nd round Cup draw, which paired Aberdare away to either Torquay or Yeovil. (*Gloucester Echo*) The Aberdare Stadium seems to have remained until the 1960s when the site was redeveloped.

For the period in which Aberdare were in the League, they got through a lot of managers! During 1920-22 it was William Lot, followed by Frank Bradshaw 1923-4, then Sydney Beaumont from 1924-7, and then Harry Hadley for the 1927-8 season. Beaumont (1884-1939) was previously the manager of Barry Town, and moved on to manage Blackpool after leaving Aberdare. As a player, Syd had been a wing-half at Watford and Lincoln, but ended his playing days with various minor south Welsh clubs.

After their promising 1922 finish, Aberdare fell back into a lowly position, finishing 21st, 12th, 18th and 9th and the next four seasons. League opposition at this time included Brentford, Reading, Charlton, Southend, Norwich, Millwall, Watford, none of which were exactly on the doorstep, leading to high expenses, although fixtures against Swansea, Bristol, Merthyr, and Newport would have brought the 'derby' crowds in.

In season 1925-6, Aberdare managed to reach round 3 of the F.A. Cup. Beating Bristol Rovers 4-1 in round 1, they then overcame Luton Town 1-0, before meeting powerful Newcastle United who comfortably beat them 4-1. 74 League goals only got them to 9th place in the Third Division, and the season produced their biggest league win, an 8-1 score against Watford, and also the 'double' over Q.P.R. By this time however, gates were falling from the thousands into the hundreds. In 1926-7, they finished in 22nd place, and had to apply for re-election, but it was by then tradition that almost no club had ever been re-elected, and Aberdare's place was given to Torquay United, winners of the Western

Division of the Southern League. A low point of the season was a 0-7 home drubbing by Coventry on Easter Monday. Their final ever league game was a 2-2 draw with Brighton. At the annual Football League meeting they polled 21 votes, the same as Torquay. In a re-ballot, Torquay were elected by a 26-19 majority.

After losing their League place, Aberdare went into free-fall. Returned to the Southern League, no longer the status of yore, they were forced to amalgamate with Aberaman Athletic, and within a year, had effectively disappeared altogether, as the new club continued on, only called Aberaman Athletic. On August 28th 1928, the *Derby Telegraph* announced 'the death of Aberdare FC'. Unable to fulfil a fixture against Torquay the following week, the Forthlith Bank called in their debts and told the club to 'realise its assets' (i.e. sell up). Two other clubs, Mid-Rhondda and Llanhilleth also folded in the same week, illustrating the continued economic depression of the region.

BARNES FC

Founded   -   1858 (possibly much earlier)
Folded   -   Circa 1912
Colours   -   Broad navy and white hoops
Ground   -   1. Barnes Green from 1862
                   2. White Hart Inn ground
Headquarters -   White Hart Inn

Barnes football team were an off-shoot of the Barnes Rowing Club, who were, naturally, based on the Thames near to Barnes bridge itself. Early matches were played on Barnes Green, and a couple of years later they rented a large field from Sir W. Johnstone at the rear of the White Hart Inn, which still exists, although of course, that field was long ago built over with splendid grand Victorian terraces which now command millionaire prices. Rowing was the primary interest of the oarsmen who started the football team up as a winter activity, with Johnstone, Ebenezer Morley and R.G. Graham all on the Barnes Rowing Club committee, who were based at the White Hart, which at the end of the 1860s was run by a Mr. Wilcox. A famous Thames landmark, the square four storey building was erected in 1662 and rebuilt in 1899, and today features a room named after E.C. Morley. From its rear terraced three floors, it offers wonderful views of the river and its renowned sunsets.

Their football shirts were probably their rowing costume, which returned to its original use when winter turned into spring for the rowing season. Being low lying land under the bend of the Thames which forms a loop around the Barnes area, they would have got used to much of the eastern side lying under flood water, and perhaps that was a factor in moving from Barnes Green over to the White Hart field by Barnes bridge and church. Barnes FC were a well-connected club, illustrated by the fact that H.R.H. The Prince of Teck was its president, and the Earl of Lonsdale, R. Inchbald, and Cannon Melville were amongst their patrons in 1866. The site of that football field is now occupied by rows of very expensive four storey houses in First and Second Avenues at the rear of Mortlake High Street.

No-one knows exactly when the Barnes Football Club was formed, but certainly well before 1865, as they appear on the Wanderers' fixture list for that season, and they were still going in 1900 as I found a result from that year when they were demolished 8-0 by the Charterhouse School XI. The Barnes Football Club held its annual athletic sports day on 25th March 1865, "on a field belonging to Mr Marsh Nelson by the White Hart Inn" (Bells Life).

Indeed, it has been suggested that 'the Barnes foot-ball club' was started as far back as 1838, playing the singular rugby-style game prevalent at the time, in which a modern day spectator would believe he was watching a street brawl loosely based on rugby or 'street football'. Barnes were involved in the creation of the Football Association and sent two representatives, Ebenezer Cobb Morley and Thomas Dyson Gregory to the embryonic meetings. In 1862, the Barnes FC issued a statement saying that all equipment would be kept at the White Hart Inn, and that "Barnes Green shall be the place to play football".

Their first recorded match, played to rugby rules, was in November 1862, against the Richmond RFC, the venue being Barn Elms park, later home to Fulham in 1886-8 (Sporting Life) which became home to the famous Ranelagh Polo Club during 1878 to

1938, which by 1913 had a massive 3,000 members of the highest classes. I think the truth lies somewhere between the lines of different stories; perhaps a Barnes club was started as a rowing club on the Thames, later trying out the various codes of football during the 1850s and 1860s. Today, the Barnes RFC play in green and yellow hoops. Barn Elms ground briefly became home to Queens Park Rangers in 1891 before returning to polo use, and was eventually destroyed by fire in 1954.

The most well known name associated with the Barnes FC is Ebenezer Cobb Morley. Born in Hull in 1831, he came to London when he was 27, and "threw himself into the life of the community with great energy" (Barnes-history.org). He qualified as a solicitor and kept chambers at 3 Bench Walk, E.C., and would often be seen trotting his horse along the Thames embankment, resplendent in top hat and morning dress. In 1862 he founded the Barnes & Mortlake Regatta, and rowed in the Henley Regatta of 1864. Founder-captain of the Barnes FC, it was his letter to *Bells Life* paper in early 1863 that proposed that football needed a standardised set of laws and a national association based on that of the Marylebone Cricket Club. He wrote to the leading public schools with his proposals, but their insular response was disappointing. He then organised the first meeting at the Freemasons Tavern, from which, the Football Association was born, and he was duly elected its first Secretary. He held the post for four years when he took over from Arthur Pember to become President. He died in 1924 at the grand old age of 94, and is buried in Barnes old cemetery. Another Barnes founder was Thomas Dyson Gregory. Born Wakefield in 1835, he had a corn merchants business with his two brothers George and Frederick. Along with Willis and Morley, he was a member of the London Rowing Club, and treasurer of the Barnes & Mortlake rowing club.

When Barnes played the ball-carrying Blackheath club in March 1863, the weather was unusually warm which tired the players, no goals resulting after a game which began at three o'clock concluded two hours later. No wonder players of both sides were run out of steam! Interestingly, there was no mention of the ball being carried, or scrimmages, suggesting perhaps that Blackheath agreed not to do so. Their playing rules for 1862-63 season stated " if the ball is kicked out of the ground, it is dead, and the first player who can pick it up shall be entitled to bring it back to the place where it left the ground, and kick it (back into play) as he sees fit". The rules of the Forest FC were different on this point, and said " the ball is 'out' when it has passed the line of flags on either sides of the ground, in which case it shall be thrown (back) in straight". In other words, Forest had created the modern throw-in, whilst Barnes were doing a free-kick style ball return. There were many such differences at the various early clubs, and it was clear that if everyone could iron out their differences and agree to the same set of laws, then it would be an accelerant for the game and clubs alike.

Bells Life reported on a match on Saturday 20th February 1864, between Barnes and an eleven brought by a Mr. Burnett. Three goals behind after an hour, Barnes walked off the pitch refusing to play on when the visitors disputed a possible Barnes score. Barnes had also played at home on the previous Saturday, when after a close game with the usual disputed goal, Crystal Palace were beaten 2-1 on a pitch which was described as perfectly level. Such tiny snippets of information, added together, eventually help historians to piece together a visual representation of these lost football grounds, the Barnes field being one of the very few without a slope.

Their status as a rowing club indicates a middle-class background for their membership, if not upper-class. In May 1866, two of their members, K.T. Digby and the Count de Montagu no less, competed in the sports day of the Sheffield football club, with Digby winning the 150 yards open race. This indicates men with time and money on their hands. Barnes' own sports day of Saturday 17th March 1866, as reported in *Bells Life* drew a large attendance and was a great success. Interestingly, at a time when I would have thought that shirts for football, rugby or rowing would have been limited to perhaps half a dozen colour options, the identifying tops worn by the competitors makes for interesting reading. B.C. Molloy (Barnes) wore mauve and black hoops, the Count de Montagu wore blue and yellow, E.G. Farquarson (Panthers & West London Rowing Club) wore chocolate, James Kirkpatrick (Civil Service) wore blue and gold, F.W. Smith (Civil Service) wore violet and crimson, F.W. Gouldsmith wore black and gold stripes, F. Moore (Barnes) wore blue and brown, C.W. Roney (Barnes) cherry and black stripes, and J. Muir (Wanderers) wore pink and white. Those were just a selection of the dozens of keen athletes who each wore a distinctive top or shirt. One athlete wore a top of orange, a colour I was surprised to read for the times. Thus, the whole affair must have been one of a rainbow of colours, as athletes contested and mingled with one another and the spectators. Barnes football club members competing included the Honourable Robert Villiers, Count de Montagu, B.C. Molloy, K.T. Digby, F.T. Moore, R.G. Graham, J.K. Barnes, J.W. Blunt, C.H. Tebbs, G. Montgomery, C.H. Farhall, G. Ryan, William Crake, and G.M. O'Leary.

The *Sportsman* paper reporting on the 1868 Barnes sports day, remarked that the club could be contacted through their secretary R.W. Willis via the club headquarters of the White Hart Inn, Barnes. The Hanover FC (f.1873) also shared the Limes ground with Barnes during the mid-1870s.

William Parry Crake (1852-1921) was born in Madras, as were many of the children of the militia men who were serving in the British Army when India was under British rule. Brought to England for his education, he attended Harrow during 1866-70 where he played for the school team. Crake, sometimes known as Parry, also turned out for the Wanderers and Harrow Chequers clubs. He was one of England's first International footballers, and played in the annual matches against Scotland (the only opponents) in 1870,71 and 72. The *1873 Alcock Annual* describes him as "a neat dribbler, slow but certain, a useful asset to a side".

He was introduced into the Wanderers side in January 1870 for the away match with Crystal Palace, by his headmaster E.E. Bowen, who was already a Wanderers player. By 1879, Crake had returned to India for a career as a tea merchant, but retired back to London in 1892. Both his sons Ralph and Eric, were county cricketers.

In the early 1870s, Barnes were copying many other football clubs, who found that by hosting an all-day general athletics meeting with an entry fee, not only would it attract large numbers of spectators who would not otherwise attend a football match, it also proved an annual source of income to keep the club going. Barnes, however, seemed to be plagued with bad luck as their 1869 sports day was held under a torrential downpour, and the following year saw a snowstorm at Easter! These events were grand affairs, often with the 1st Surrey militia band playing nationalistic tunes to the assembly which included many local dignitaries such as Members of Parliament and Justices of the Peace. So well connected were the Barnes club, that their 1875 sports day was reported 200 miles away in the *York Herald*. Their 1877 sports day was unfortunately planned for the same day as the Cup Final between the Wanderers and Oxford University which may have hampered attendances (*Lloyds Weekly* paper). Prizes at these events lavishly reflected their social sphere, with many silver cups and gilt watches and medals being awarded, no doubt by exquisitely-attired ladies who had full dance cards to the evening ball. For Barnes, as an early club, their 'time' was in the 1860s and 1870s. Star player Charles Chinnery, (or Chenery) described by the *Surrey Mirror* as a very fast runner, was capped for England in March 1870, and another Barnes player, their captain Percy Weston, was capped for England against Scotland in February 1872.

This was the usual Barnes team of 1871-

A. Adams, A.C. Highton, G. DeCastro, William G. Butler, C.R. Etherington, F.C. Clerkson, W. Page, E.O. Edwars, Charles Chinnery, C.H. Mason, A.E. Ball, J. Powell.

The rules of etiquette went out of the window when Barnes went over to play the 1st Surrey Rifles FC on their Camberwell ground on Saturday 5th January 1878. Barnes kicked off with only eight militia-men on the field, and proceeded to score two goals in the opening five minutes, after which, three more 'Rifle-men' turned up to make theirs a full compliment. A 'very fast game' was drawn to an end after only an hour with Barnes 2-0 winners. (*Lloyds Weekly* newspaper). Two teams were certainly going in different directions when Barnes played host to the powerful Clapham Rovers for the opening match of the 1880 season, played on Saturday 9th October. Played under a torrential downpour, Rovers thrashed the Oarsmen by 10-0, with goals from Pollock (3), Scott (2), Sparks (2), Lloyd-Jones, Stanley and White.

Famously, Barnes were one of the original entrants of the first ever F.A. Cup in 1871, then known as the English Cup. A 1st round win by 2-0 over the Civil Service FC saw them go out to the Hampstead Heathens in round 2 by the same score. The following year saw a quick exit when they were beaten 1-0 at South Norwood. 1873 saw them edge past the 1st Surrey Rifles with the only goal of the game, but had the bad luck to be drawn against eventual cup winners, the powerful Oxford University in round 2, where they narrowly lost 1-2. Barnes had a clear 3-0 win over Upton Park in round 1 of the 1874-5 English Cup, but once more, lady luck abandoned them when they were pitched against the 'celebrated' Wanderers in round 2. The Wanderers beat them comfortably by 4-0 at the Oval on a bitterly cold day which did not prevent 'a large attendance' from assembling around the ropes. 1875 saw another early exit from the Cup, as Reigate Priory scored the only goal of the game, but in 1876 a curious thing happened at the same stage. Barnes were drawn against previous year's cup finalists, the Old Etonians, and strangely, the old boys gave them a walkover. I can only think that they could not raise a team, as a letter in the London press in 1878 said that "the Old Etonians football club had been resurrected yet again", and indeed, they went on to win the Cup in 1879. Once more, the 2nd round proved their stumbling block as Upton Park got revenge on them with a 1-0 victory which saw them reach the 4th round themselves. Finally, in 1877-8, Barnes made it through to round 3. A walkover against St. Marks and a 3-1 win over Great Marlow saw them draw the name of Wanderers yet again out of the hat. A spirited effort saw Barnes hold them to a 1-1 draw thanks to a goal from Ainslie but Wanderers 'proved too strong' in the replay at the Oval, where they were beaten 4-1. Wanderers were probably at their peak in 1878, as they went on the defeat the Royal Engineers to lift the Cup for the third time. December 1878 saw Barnes once again safely through the 1st round of the Cup as they beat Maidenhead by 4-0, and they turned the tables on bogey side Upton Park in round 2 to enter the 3rd round, where strangely eleven teams remained. Even though the competition had been going for nearly a decade, and notwithstanding the Eton and Harrow-educated men in charge of the F.A., the concept of arranging byes in the early rounds to arrive at a perfect 8 at the 4th round had not yet dawned on them. They were not alone in this; the Birmingham Cup continued to be 'organised' on this haphazard style for many years, with 11, 13 or 17 teams left in knockout cups when there should have been 16. None of this would matter to Barnes, as once again, Oxford University beat them 2-1 to reach the 4th round before bowing out to Nottingham Forest. For the third year running, there were three sides left in the semi-finals, and there was the ridiculous situation of one team getting a free passage into the final. Far better to have all the byes done with in round 1. Barnes must have been fed up with being drawn against a side they knew they could not beat, so when they heard that it was Oxford University yet again in the 1879-80 cup draw, they withdrew. 1880 saw another straight exit for Barnes, who were trounced 6-0 by a side in the ascendancy, Herts Rangers. In the following year - the season which saw the English Cup celebrate a decade of existence- Barnes got past Kent side Rochester 3-0 only to receive a beating to the tune of 7-1 by the Old Carthusians. By this time, the Cup, once almost composed entirely of London area clubs, now had a national balance, with at least half the entries coming from the Midlands and the North, many of whom were 'shamateurs' secretly paying star players behind the scenes either in cash, or with easy or even non-existent jobs provided by the club's backers, often breweries or factory owners. Another 1st round exit in 1882-3 to Brentwood by 4-2 seemed to have dampened their interest, as they did not enter for 1883-4. They returned to the competition for 1884-5 only go out again to Brentwood. At this time, the Cup was swamped out with entries from the resurgent North, as village teams from all over Lancashire, south Yorkshire and Staffordshire almost took over the national cup. Barnes' final appearance in the national cup came at the end of 1885 when they took another battering by 7-1 to the old boys of Lancing College.

Successes were few and far between for Barnes, but they did win the Surrey County Cup in 1884. Defeating Reigate Priory 3-2 in the final, the game was played at the Oval cricket ground. Reigate appeared in all the first five Surrey finals, and another six during the 1890s, when it was held at Woodbridge Road, Guildford. In 1888, for some unknown reason, Barnes failed to show for the Surrey Cup final replay after drawing 1-1 with Lyndhurst at Walton-on-Thames, an attendance of about 300 would have been likely. The Surrey Cup, a rather squat but large silver trophy, seems to have been the basis for the modern F.A. Cup in terms of appearance.

However, their position in the changing football world was demonstrated when they were humiliated 10-0 by Clapham Rovers on Saturday 9th October 1880, a side to which they would have provided decent opposition a decade earlier. However, the odd Barnes player still got picked for the various representative teams. In 1878 W. Dorking played for the London FA versus the Sheffield FA, and a year later, W.S. Burmester played in goal for the Surrey FA side. In 1884, J.O. Ferns was elected treasurer to the Surrey County Association.

A small reward came Barnes' way when they won the Surrey Easter Tournament of 1885. They defeated Reigate Priory 5-0, East Sheen 3-2, Brixton 3-1, and Dorking 4-1 to win the competition. However, by the 1890s, Barnes' position in the London football world had fallen down several ladders, and by then typical opponents included hospital and college teams. Two clubs from different eras met in the 3rd round of the 1887 London Cup, when Barnes travelled to the Oval ground to meet the London Caledonians, and were well beaten by 6-0. Multi-sports club Clapham Rovers trounced them 7-2 in the London Senior Cup in October 1893, suggesting that only their previous stature in the early years of the Football Association, and E.C. Morley's connections were retaining their 'senior' club status. The last report I found on Barnes was that they were playing in the Surrey Senior Cup in 1905. Maybe they made it to the start of the First World War.

A clue as to the date of Barnes' formation came with the death of leading F.A. Committee man E.C. Morley at his Barnes home of 26 The Terrace, reported in papers across the country on Saturday 22nd November 1924. Aged 94, it was said that he had been associated with the Barnes club 'since 1858'. As it is likely that the rowing club pre-dates this, then this probably means the football team, since other clubs such as Forest (Epping) were also extant at that time.

Map showing field by The White Hart Inn used as Barnes' ground is on the left of centre, next to the railway line of the London & South West Railway Company, walkable from Barnes station, although visiting teams are likely to have taken cabs or a brake.

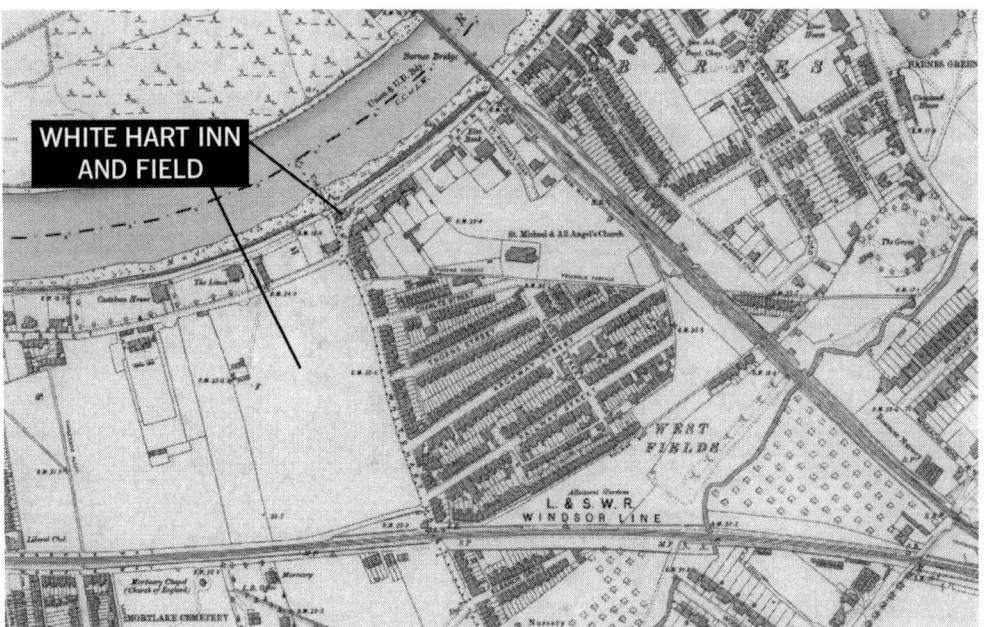

BEDMINSTER FC

Founded   -   1887 (as Southville)
Folded   -   1900 (merged with Bristol City)
Ground   -   1. Greenway Bush Lane
                     2. Ashton Gate, Bristol
Colours   -   Amber and Gold stripes, black
Headquarters -   Bedminster Hotel

Formed as a winter offshoot of Bedminster cricket club (f.1850), Wikipedia has 1887 as Bedminster's founding year, but the *Western Daily Express* of 1932, looking back fifty years on sport in the Bristol area said that there was a Bedminster FC before 1872, as 'in 1872, some Bedminster players moved over to the newly formed Clifton FC, and the older Bedminster club died out, but it was playing to rugby rules with twenty a side I believe, and based behind the Hen & Chickens inn'. Earliest players remembered include R.A and J.A."Frizzy" Bush, E.G. Murdoch, Dr. James Williamson Wallace, and W.H. Brown, and from an early nickname of Pirates, may have played in all black. In their early rugby playing days, a certain William G. Grace briefly turned out for them, but a bad injury changed his mind about the mauling game and he concentrated on cricket. Other players from the early 1870s were H. Harvey,G. Harvey, A. H. Hornsby, A. Hornsby, T. Lane, T. Skidmore, F. Bishop, T. Kerry, G. Lane, E. Williams, Jenkins, G. Lillington and Herapath. Bedminster won 12 of their 16 matches in 1872-3.

Football was slow to take a hold in Gloucestershire, and the area's newspapers did not take football seriously until a club was founded at Bristol. With only six clubs holding membership of the county association in 1888, the Gloucestershire Cup that year did not include Bedminster. The final that year being between Warmley and Clifton played on the St. George ground. Rugby and cricket being more popular in the county at that time (and still is). In 1892, Bedminster joined the newly created Bristol & District League, which, in 1895, became known as the Western League.

In 1892, this side opened the season with a match against Swindon St. Marks :-

		C.E. Giles		
	G.F. Jones		Reverend A.B. McFarland	
H.A. Marshall		C.E. Rich		F. Skeats
J. McCarthy	W. Griffiths	F. Milne	F.G. Batten	H.G. Miles

During the mid-1890s meetings were held at the Hope & Anchor inn at Redcliff Hill, when officials included president Colonel Hill, honorary secretaries Dr. Wallace and W.H. Burland and treasurer A. Smith. J. Wallace was first team captain and E. Harris the second eleven. As early as April 1894, there was discontent at the club, when players continued to fail to turn up for league matches, resulting in reserves being drafted in, and the subsequent home defeats prompted calls for the football and cricket clubs to separate and form their own committees.

One of their players, George Hemmens, died aged but 24 in 1899.

An old fixture card from Bedminster for season 1895-6 turned up in of all places, Australia, and it states that the team captain was S. Milne, with H.E. Smith as vice-captain; E.H. Cook was treasurer and C.M. Tallach was secretary. Matches were arranged against Swindon, Mangotsfield, Staple Hill, Bristol South End, and Eastville Rovers. At the end of that season, a tragedy occurred when the team were playing against Eastville Rovers in the semi-final of the Gloucestershire Senior Cup. A Bedminster player, H.E. Smith died following a severe injury. Greater still was the fact that on the day he was buried, he was due to be married! Tributes and a huge turnout from every club in the region, including his employers, J.S. Fry Co., did little to ease the grief of both his family and bride to be.

A trophy finally came along at the end of the 1896-7 season when, after a 2-2 drawn game, Trowbridge were beaten 1-0 to hand the Bristol Cup to Bedminster, in a match played on Ashton Gate on Wednesday 17th March. From the report in the *Western Daily Express*, it does not seem to have been the best of matches. In season 1899-1900, Bedminster finished a creditable 6th in Division One of the powerful Southern League, behind Tottenham, Portsmouth, Southampton, Reading and Swindon. New signings W.H and R.H. Davies from Bolton Wanderers, Saxton from Sunderland, Draycott from Newton Heath and forwards Boucher and Toone from Notts County improved the playing squad. Tim Boucher, born 1873, played centre forward, had scored 32 goals in 79 games for Notts County, and with 24 appearances and scoring 9 goals, he finished as leading scorer for Bedminster that season. When Bedminster amalgamated with Bristol City, Boucher left and joined Bristol Rovers, and later, City, ending his career with New Brompton (Gilingham) in 1903-5. Goalkeeper Alex Toone had spent a decade with Notts County, playing in 262 games for them, and also gaining two England caps in 1892. Another goalkeeper was Jimmy Whitehouse, once of Aston Villa and Grimsby. He too played only for the 1898-9 season before returning to Grimsby Town. At this time the club's secretary-manager was S.W. Hollis, and the treasurer was F.W. Burland.

Future Walsall Town Swifts forward David Copeland played one season -1888-89 - with Bedminster before later moving on to Tottenham and Chelsea. Much - travelled six foot full back Bob Crone joined from Notts County in 1897 where he ended his career which included four caps for his native Ireland. Robert Davies (b.1876) gained Football League experience with Bolton Wanderers before coming to Bedminster in 1899 for one season, then moved on to Bristol City. Another one season player was Billy Draycott who came from Manchester City, having also played for Newton Heath, Stoke and Port Vale. Another experienced player who ended his career with Bedminster was Albert Flewitt (1872-1943) who played for Lincoln, Everton and West Bromwich Albion as an inside-forward. A tall and distinguished looking man, Flewitt was the proud owner of a large RAF-style moustache. Alf 'Jasper' Geddes (1871-1927), was a much travelled and greatly experienced forward who had two spells at both Millwall and West Bromwich. Bob Kelso (1865-1942) was a very experienced defender who ended his career with Bedminster, having played for most of the big northern clubs, including Preston, Everton, and Renton at a time when they were proclaimed 'champions of the world'. He gained 7 caps for Scotland and also played for the Scottish League XI in 1898, just as he was leaving Dundee for Bristol. Another Scotsman was James Lamont, who played out his last four seasons in Bristol, after coming down from Partick Thistle. Another ex-Thistle man was winger George McVean, who made his name at Liverpool and Burnley. He did in 1907 aged only 36.

Still as a Southern league club, the Amateur Cup was entered from 1895, without success, as they never got past the qualifying rounds, often going out to clubs like Bristol St. George or Clifton. With clubs like Queens Park Rangers, Bristol City and Bristol Rovers below them, and a second division containing Watford, Fulham, Chesham, Brentford and Wycombe, the Southern League was then the strongest league outside of the Football League. Southern League sides Southampton were beaten F.A. Cup finalists that year, losing heavily to Derby County, and Tottenham would go on to win the F.A. Cup a year later, and become the only club to win the cup from outside the Football League, a record surely never to be equalled. At the end of the season, Bedminster amalgamated with Bristol City, although many saw it as an absorption, although it was Bedminster's Ashton Gate ground which was developed, and not City's St. John's Lane ground. During 1900 - 1904, the club played home games alternately at the two grounds. With both clubs only two miles apart, it was inevitable that they would either merge or fold. Bristol Rovers soon came to an agreement with the new City not to both play at home on the same Saturday. Manager Robert Campbell had a wealth of talent at his disposal when Bedminster and Bristol City merged, although the new first team was mostly Bedminster players, and only John MacLean, Billy Jones, Paddy O'Brien and David Robson from City made the cut.

Bristol City themselves had been formed on Thursday 12th April 1894, as Bristol South End, from a meeting called by Fred Keenan and John Durnat, who used to be Bedminster players, so it could be said that those two men created Bedminster's demise. Playing in red shirts and navy shorts, they became known as the 'Garibaldis'. Unable to join the Western League until 1896, Bristol arranged a series of prestigious friendlies against teams like Tottenham, Preston, and Swindon, who were the region's top club. A meeting held at the Hope & Anchor inn on Redcliff Hill in the same month saw the players entertained and fed by the club, with guests coming from the Bristol League committee. Club secretaries Dr. Wallace and WH Burland agreeing with treasurer A. Smith that they had a healthy future. It appears that the doctor's son, James Williamson Wallace was the team captain. He too became a doctor, living until aged 76, where he died in 1948 in Southville. Things were not all harmonious though, as letters to the Bristol press at the end of the 1893-4 season complained of a lack of solidarity from the players themselves, the end of the season coming with a series of defeats mainly brought about by games when only three or four first team men turned up. It was urged that the cricket (f. circa 1854) and football teams go their separate ways and concentrate on their own sports, and that a new committee comprised of the town's businessmen would better serve the football club.

Bristol South End quickly entered both the F.A and Amateur Cups, but soon discovered that long established clubs like Old Carthusians could beat them 10-0, although they did beat Slough 5-1 in their debut F.A. Cup qualifier on 5th October 1895. Finishing runners up in the Western League at the first attempt, South End applied to join the Southern League. Sam Hollis was employed as their first ever manager (from Arsenal) and they voted to turn professional in May 1897. The Southern League campaign was a great success, and soon they were applying to get into the Football League, but polled only a single vote. Soon, however, in 1901, they got into the Second Division, and the rest, as they say, is history.

Tracking down the old Green Bush Lane ground, this turned out to be an enclosed 5 acre cricket ground behind the local school at the junction with North Street. That ground is now an Aldi store and its car park.

BEDMINSTER.

Photo by T. Burchill, Redcliff Hill.

MOUNTFORD (Trainer). CRONE. TOONE. R. H. DAVIS. S. W. HOLLIS (Sec. and Manager).
BRAMLEY. W. H. DAVIS. DRAYCOTT WILSON. CHAMBERS. AYRE.
W. H. BURLAND (Fin. Sec.) WHEELAN. FLEWITT. BOUCHER. BECTON. GEDDES. SAXTON.

BOURNEMOUTH GASWORKS ATHLETIC

Founded   - 1899
Folded   - 1973
Colours   - Red and white stripes, white
Ground   - 1. Eastlake, Upper Parkstone, Poole
               2. Alder Road, Branksome (from about 1929)
Nickname   - The Gasmen, the Lights
Secretaries - C.S. Dominie (1910s) J.F. Boyce (1920s)

Very few works teams achieved the status of this south coast utilities football club, especially in the 1920s when they reached the final of the Amateur Cup. Founded in 1899 as a works side, they entered the Hampshire League's West Division in 1904. By 1906 they had added the suffix Athletic, and local opposition came from the Poole, Blandford, Weymouth Whiteheads, Boscombe Athletic, Bournemouth and Bournemouth Wanderers clubs. Their first trophy success came when they beat Radipole 5-2 in April 1906 to lift the Dorset Junior Cup. The Gasworks ground would be used for many of the county junior and minor finals.

Entering the FA Cup almost as soon as they were founded, they never managed to battle through all the preliminary and qualifying rounds to reach the 1st round proper. Their reserve team played in the Bournemouth & District League. In January 1909, two BGW men were chosen to play for Dorset against Hampshire - forwards Galton and Greenhalm. Five years later, G. Brown, Ingram, Andrews, Stout, T. Dempsey, and Beaumont were similarly favoured. By 1930, W.H. Phillips and H.J. Conibeer had aggregated nearly 100 county caps between them. In 1911, still known as Branksome Gasworks, the club applied to the Dorset FA to run two equal strength sides, one in the Hampshire League and the other in the Dorset League, which was denied even though the club had 40 players, and they were instructed to join only the Dorset League. In 1913, an unusual event happened on the Gaswork's East Lake ground when it was the venue for the final of the Dorset Senior Cup. Having won it for the previous four years, the Gasworks themselves did not feature in match. The Royal Welch Fusiliers FC had beaten them 6-0 in the semi-final, and went on to beat Longfleet St. Marys in the final. The Eastlake Ground lay in Poole itself, just off the Ashley Road, and was hemmed in with three cul-de-sacs, namely Belmont, Weymouth and Pearson Roads, but the ground was built over circa 1930 and now the extended Pearson Avenue and a row of shops on Ashley Road occupy the spot. Development was confined to one grandstand erected in 1919 on the western side of the 2.82 acre ground, behind which lay several large houses in extensive wooded grounds.

In April 1919, the gasworks company got into trouble for discharging oil and polluted water into the sea near Poole much to the annoyance of the port authorities and the Harbour Master. Their sports ground on Alder Road was adjacent to the gasworks, and had a pavilion and a grandstand which was added in 1919. In 1920 the Dorset Cup was resumed after a long break due to the War, and this caused the Dorchester recreation ground to be "swarmed with people coming into the town in cavalcades of motor cars and quite 5,000 people were present". The finalists were Gasworks and Weymouth, who had just finished their league programme and has finished 1st and 3rd respectively. However, a goal after just five minutes was enough to give Weymouth a surprise win and after the cup was being presented to them by the mayor A.L. Tilley, the league trophy was presented to the Gasworks captain Dempsey. The sports facilities at Alder Road included two bowling green and tennis courts on Yarmouth Road. Accustomed to sweeping away all local opposition, it was a rare and unexpectedly heavy defeat which met them when they travelled to the ground of Yeovil & Petters United on Saturday 14th September 1921, they were outplayed to the tune of 7-2, the match played in a torrential downpour. After winning the Dorset League in 1920, in 1922 they moved up into the 1st Division of the Hampshire League and won that title in 1922, which began a very successful era for the club. Team captain at this time was W.H. Phillips, who was selected several times for the county team. Locally, their main rivals were the Portland and Weymouth clubs.

Bournemouth Gas Works were known as "the Lights".

In 1929-30 the 'Lights' reached the Amateur Cup final, meeting Ilford on West Ham United's Upton Park Stadium, when a 1-1 half-time score resulted in Ilford scoring a further four times to win the trophy. En route, a shock 2-1 home win over Ithsmian League side Wycombe Wanderers was thanks to second half goals by Lovell and Cornibeer. Welton Rovers were dispatched 4-0 in round 2, and then another big name was taken when Barnet were sent packing 3-1. In round 4, mining side Percy Main Amateurs were overcome 2-0 and in the semi final played at Portsmouth, Wimbledon were beaten 2-0 in front of a bumper crowd of 6,000. The game had really been a steal, as Wimbledon had seen the best of it, but two quick goals in succession near the end from Lavell put BGW into the final. Ilford needed two games to get past stubborn Northern Nomads in their semi-final, but experience told as holders Ilford kept the Amateur Cup in east London for the 4th year running with a 5-2 win in front of a crowd of 21,800 at Upton Park on April 12th. A great shock awaited BGW in the opening round of the following year, when Barnet gained ample revenge by thrashing them 9-3 ! Regaining their composure, BGW returned strongly in 1934 to reach the semi-finals before bowing out 1-2 to the strong Stockton club. In the following season, BGW found the famous Casuals too strong in round 3 and were beaten 5-1 at home. Although round 3 was sometimes reached, they never again made the same impact on the Amateur Cup.

The Dorset Cup was always a happy hunting ground for BGW, and they went on to win it no less than 10 times between 1909 and 1939. Their frequent opposition in Dorset Cup finals were Weymouth who by 1925 had appeared 12 times compared to Gasworks' 8. I was surprised to find that the Dorsetshire Cup was first played for as far back as 1877 when Weymouth College beat Dorchester. This Gasworks side defeated Weymouth 2-1 in the 1925 final watched by a crowd of 4,000 -

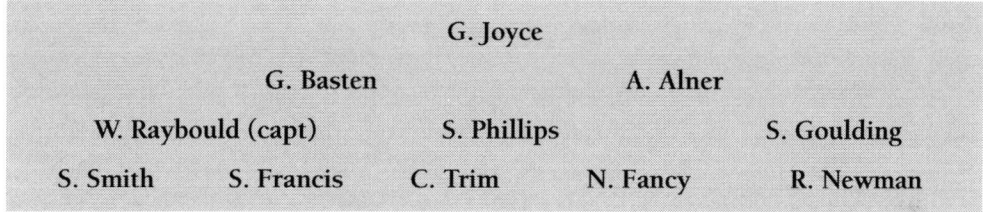

G. Joyce

G. Basten   A. Alner

W. Raybould (capt)   S. Phillips   S. Goulding

S. Smith   S. Francis   C. Trim   N. Fancy   R. Newman

During 1929-30, BGW played nearly 100 games and took just over £1,000 in revenue. The 1930s saw BGW continue to be one of Hampshire's best sides, and were county champions a further four times, in 1932, 1935, 1936 and 1938. For some reason, they waited until October 1934 to obtain associate membership of the Football Association (*Western Gazette*). A record 8 trophies were won in season 1935-6, their most successful yet. When Shaftsbury were the Dorset League visitors in March 1937, they left having been blitzed 11-0 with Scott, Ware, and Rathbone all netting hat-tricks. Attendances at this time were typically around 600-800 and more for Amateur Cup games. BGW were no slouches at cricket either. In July 1942, they defeated the Army XI by 94 runs to 72 on their sports ground. Petrol rationing during the War restricted the scope of sports teams to travel very far, and BGW remained in the Dorset League throughout the decade, apart from their away ties in the Amateur Cup. April 1948 must have been a hot month, for heath and woodland fires were breaking out in the district, and at one point, there was a fire on the embankment directly adjoining the Gasworks ground on Alder Road.

More success followed in the 1950s, as they won the Hampshire county cup in 1953 and 1954. A best effort of reaching the 3rd qualifying round of the F.A Cup also sealed another rewarding season. After 1957 the club's fortunes took a nosedive, and following relegation to Hampshire Division 2 where they only finished mid-table, they left and rejoined the Dorset League, and dropped down a level They then went on to dominate Dorset and secured nine Dorset League titles. Derek Reeves (b.1935-1990) who briefly played for BGW in the mid-1950s, signed as centre forward for Southampton in 1954, where he scored 145 goals in 273 games until he moved on to Bournemouth in 1962 for £8,000. His career ended with Worcester City. His 39 goals in the old Third Division in season 1959-60 remains the record to this day.

The loss of their ground on Alder Road in 1972 directly led to the closure of the club after 73 successful seasons, and the site is now built over with the houses of Dereham Way.

Their old players, now in their eighties, still meet to to talk about old times.

CHESHAM GENERALS

Founded   -   1887
Folded   -   1912 (amalgamated with Chesham Town)
Colours   -   White shirts and black shorts
Grounds   -   1. Top Park   1887-8
                    2. Portobello Farm   1888-90
                    3. Co-op ground, Bellingdon Road 1891-2
                    4. New Town ground, Brockhurst Road 1892-1912
Headquarters -   Chess Vale school

Chesham is a town nestling in the Chiltern Hills in south Buckinghamshire, with nearby neighbours Aylesbury, Amersham and Marlow. Known as the town of the four 'B's in the 18th and 19th centuries - beer, boots, brushes and Baptists - the population in the 1890s was only about 9,000 and is still only 21,000 today. Despite a weak history in terms of achievements, I could not resist having a peep into the brief history of the only club outside of the U.S.A which had the name Generals in its title, and I wondered if it came from a military connection. A team simply called Chesham FC entered the F.A. Cup of 1885, and when Chesham Generals came into being, this prompted the earlier club to add the title 'Town' to their name in 1899, in a gesture to assert their chronological superiority. Chesham sprang from the Christ Church chapel at Waterside, initiated in 1879 by the Reverend Reade, at first calling themselves Chesham & Waterside FC, using the cricket ground off Amy Lane, and the Temperance Hotel as headquarters. They played on a meadow rented for £4 annum from Benjamin Fuller on Missenden Road. After two years, they were evicted due to "spectator damage to hedges and fences", and they folded in January 1883. Overlapping their demise by around two years was a second Chesham FC which continued on with more success, and after single season stints on meadows known as The Pigs Trough off Pendall Lane and Frogmore, they played on the cricket ground which they developed with a small stand. Ground-sharing with the cricket club would lead to years of disputes, as the football pitch overlapped the cricket oval, until finally in 1930, the footballers moved into the adjacent meadow.

A rival church team from the General Baptist chapel was formed in 1887 and, under the guidance of Sunday school superintendent Stephen Dodd, played on a part of the town park known as the Top Park Ground, as it was the only part of the park which was flat.

They soon moved to a 3 acre field which they rented from Portobello Farm where they stayed for two seasons. It was bereft of spectator facilities and they probably got changed in a farm outbuilding. In 1891-2 they moved again to another field off Bellingdon Road, when gate money started to be taken. This ground seems to have been fenced, with a small pavilion, and was owned by the Co-op and later became home for the Chesham Cup final for local teams. I believe that Lownden Avenue was built through it circa 1893-5. In 1893, Generals moved to what became called the New Town Ground, a narrow meadow off what is now Brockhurst Road. The two clubs' grounds were now a mile apart, with Chesham's being in the town centre, and the Generals' being next to the chapel.

The original Chesham saw themselves as the senior team, and joined the newly created Southern League in 1894, but they dropped down into the Athenian League by 1912.

Chesham FC were the bigger outfit, with an impressive array of backers, including Lord Chesham as club president, and a numerous committee which included Colonel Trueman and Captain Fuller, with G.J. Stone being the financial and administrative cornerstone of the club.

Both teams continued in friendly rivalry throughout the late Victorian and early Edwardian era, with the Generals seemingly pulling up to 'level pegging' with their town rivals. Competitions regularly entered included the Berks & Bucks, the Amateur, and the F.A. Cups.

Entering the F.A. Cup for the 1892-3 season, the Generals were trounced 6-2 at home by Maidenhead in the 1st Qualifying Round, and Chesham Town also went out immediately, but by only 1-2 away to Bristol St. George. At their AGM of 1893, held at the Institute, it was revealed by secretary & treasurer W. Hawes that an income of £59 had left them five guineas in the red on the season, but were able to assure gatekeeper Walter Glasgow that they had retained their meadow for the next season (*Berks & Bucks Herald*). In 1898, the Generals reached quarter-finals of the Amateur Cup after beating the 3rd Grenadier Guards and Marlow, only to fall 2-4 to the Old Malvernians. The following year, Marlow certainly got their revenge when they thrashed them 8-1 following two drawn games. Earlier, in 1895, when drawn against the fast rising Tottenham Hotspurs, it was the name of the Generals who went through, as it coincided with the week that Spurs announced that they had voted to turn professional. The Generals' team during 1899 was -

		Jones		
	Rance		Birch	
Dean		Reynolds		Harris
Pollock	Reading	Baldwin	Dweight	Woods

The side was not at all stable during this period, with not a single player remaining from their regular side of 1895 in the above line-up. The Generals kept on plugging away in the F.A. Cup, but almost always got knocked out in the first match. It was not until 1900-01 that they reached the 'dizzy heights' of the 4th Qualifying Round, after beating rivals Town (0-0, 3-0) Aylesbury United (1-0), Marlow (5-3 away) before being humiliated 0-11 at Reading on November 17th. Remarkably, the same three clubs were their opponents two seasons later, when Shepherds Bush knocked the Generals out 2-0 in the 4th Qualifying Round once more. In summing up the 1902-03 season, it was said that "the Town had a reasonable year, but the Generals had a better one still", alluding to them winning the small Berks & Bucks League. The Generals continued their forlorn hopes in the F.A. Cup, only for Town to put them out 3-0 in round Q2. At their AGM of 1904, with once again, almost an unchanged committee and leading men, such as F. Mayo and A. Reynolds, a small balance of £7 was declared. Their 1904-05 season was also described as 'poor' at their AGM, the Generals having finished bottom of the SEL behind teams such as War Office, St. Albans Amateurs, Aylesbury United, Hitchin, and the reserve sides of Brighton, Luton, Spurs, Queens Park Rangers and Woolwich Arsenal. At this time, six clubs formed the Bucks & Berks League, comprising both the Cheshams, Aylesbury, Slough, and two sides from Maidenhead, Town and Norfolkians.

In 1905, both Chesham clubs were in the South-Eastern League (Div.2), along with clubs such as Tunbridge Wells Rangers, Southend United reserves, West Hampstead, Royal Engineers, Ashford, Hastings and Clapton Orient. Chesham Town were also competing in the early round of the F.A. Cup, but they too rarely got past Q3, and although competing side by side, Town were generally a nose in front of their younger rivals. A continuing problem for Chesham Town was the fact that the cricket club had first call on their ground, and did not vacate it until the end of September, thus forcing Town to arrange to play all games away from home for the opening month of the season.

At their 1907 AGM, it was revealed that the Generals were £7-16s-10d in the red, a sizeable sum then for a village team, although they had donated seven guineas to the Chesham Hospital Fund. Officers returned were: secretary Mr. Mayo, A.T. Stephenson as treasurer, and Mr A. Lazenby-Liberty as club president, with a committee of a further twelve. Competitions entered for the year included the Berks & Bucks cup, the Eastbourne Charity, the Bucks Charity, and the South-Eastern League. Their ground became the venue for the annual fete and village sports events. The *Bucks Herald* reported in February 1907 that a powerful gale had ripped through the town, and had blown down the stand at 'their New Town football ground'. Much of this ground description comes from Dave Twydell's *'Gone But Not Forgotten'* series, as at no time does a football ground appear on any Chesham map, except that of the Chesham cricket club. The Berkhamstead Road side was fenced in, likewise the Essex and Britannia Road sides, and facilities included a pavilion, a small stand for about 100 people, and a club house or changing room in the south-east corner. There was little however, to stop passers-by gaining a free view of the match from the surrounding houses and streets. The stand on Brockhurst Road was later removed to the Cricket Ground after their amalgamation. The New Town ground was requisitioned for the troops during the war, and built over in the 1920s. This Generals eleven played away to Redhill in September 1908, losing 1-2 :-

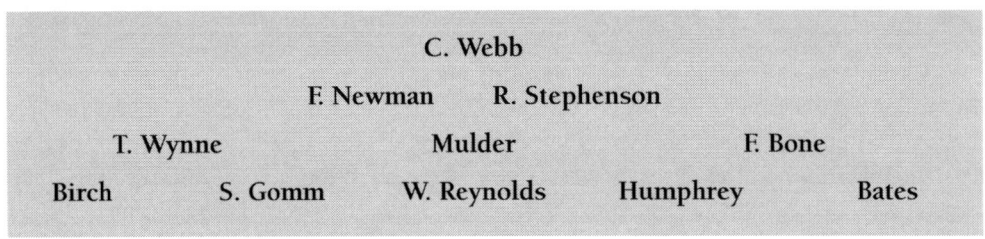

C. Webb

F. Newman   R. Stephenson

T. Wynne   Mulder   F. Bone

Birch   S. Gomm   W. Reynolds   Humphrey   Bates

I had searched high and low for any reference to the Generals' colours to no avail, but got a hint when they travelled to play a team called Clarence from Luton in December 1908, when the home side had to change into cherry and white stripes instead of their normal black and white stripes. This intimates that Generals wore black and white stripes. However, rare photos in Peter Gibbins' book about the history of Chesham United show the Generals in a white shirt and black trousers, although live action photos from 1910 show a team in white playing one in black & white stripes, and so remains inconclusive.

By the time the Generals paid their entry money for the F.A. Cup of 1907-08, they had fallen down the (already low) rankings, and were forced to take part in the Preliminary Rounds for small fry teams, and still needed a replay to get past Watford works team Victoria. Their reward was a 0-5 home drubbing by powerful London Caledonians who probably only sent their reserve eleven anyway. Large defeats did not seem to deter the

two Chesham clubs from continuing to enter the national competition, but defeats by Wood Green Town (9-3 over Generals on 19th October 1910 and 5-0 over Town on 2nd October 1909) demonstrated that they were going nowhere unless they amalgamated, which the clubs did in 1917, midway through the Great War. Season 1909-10 saw the Generals compete in the Spartan League, carrying forward a balance of £15 according to the *Luton Advertiser*. For the General's reserve team, League opposition at this time came from Chesham Town, Amersham, Wendover, Aylesbury United reserves and Aylesbury Church House – a very limited range of the six clubs which made up the Aylesbury League's South Division.

As elsewhere, both Chesham clubs lost many good men in the war, and neither team had enough players left to function as a club without pooling resources. An isolated success came in 1911 when the Generals won the Berks & Bucks Charity Cup. I found another small amateur team who also picked up the name of Generals at this time (1910) when I came across a picture of the Wycombe Generals who won the Berks & Bucks minor cup that season.

An announcement in the *Bucks Advertiser* that "Chesham Generals are to merge with Chesham Town and that the ground is sold" appears to have been slightly premature, as the Generals carried on for a couple of more seasons. When the Generals met rivals Town in November 1912 in the Amateur Cup, a crowd of 800 witnessed a good game which saw an opener by Richardson for the Generals, levelled out by a Stillman equaliser. Both clubs were now back in the South-Eastern League, with their reserve sides both playing in the Aylesbury League. With the outbreak of war in Europe, football began to wind down, but in season 1913-14, Generals won both the Spartan League (after a close tussle with Aylesbury United) and the Berks & Bucks Charity Cup again, beating Wycombe Wanderers in the final. At the end of the same season, Chesham Town finished bottom of the Athenian League. Midway through the war period, it was decided to amalgamate the town's two clubs as being the best way forward. The newly combined club spent two years at Frogmore meadow before settling into, and sharing the cricket ground. Despite spending £1000 on a new stand and making ground improvements, this arrangement eventually led to wrangles, as the cricket and football seasons overlapped, and the United moved into the adjacent field in 1931 when Slough Town were the visitors.

With Barnes, Keen, Vine and Carter scoring the goals for the new combined United club, their first season (1919-20) started off well enough with six wins out of eight in the opening two months, but most of those were in the Berks & Bucks and Amateur cups, and ended the Spartan League with 12 wins and 6 defeats, whilst the reserves played in the Great Western Suburban League. Result of the season was probably when they beat Uxbridge (Amateur Cup finalists of 1898) by 8-0 on 4th October, with a glut of goals from Keen (3), Carter (2), Barnes (2) and Stillman. Although the new club - Chesham United- sometimes reached Q4, it was not until 1966 that they reached the 1st round proper of the F.A. Cup, only to be trounced 6-0 by Enfield. Two years later, as Amateur Cup finalists, they were given passage through to the 1st round proper once more. From a population of only 18,000 it was said that over 20,000 followed them to Wembley for that 1968 Amateur Cup Final. Said to have been 1000-1 outsiders at the start of the competition, Chesham United were outclassed in the final against Leytonstone, and Gray tucked home a fumbled Tilley cross for Leytonstone's third amateur Cup success. En route, United had played 17 cup ties, and had put out such top names as Oxford City, Dulwich Hamlet and Corinthian-Casuals. In existence today, I am reliably told that their ground still contains the original stand from that 1880s cricket pitch which they rebuilt plank by plank on their Meadow Ground.

Above photo shows Chesham Generals (white shirts) in action. Photo courtesy Dave Twydell.

CLAPHAM ROVERS

Founded - 10th August 1869
Folded - Circa 1911
Grounds - 1. Clapham Common 1869-71
2. Bedford Hill, Balham 1871-76
3. Streatham Common 1877
4. Wandsworth Common 1876-95 at least, with Hope Tavern as HQ
Colours - Cerise and french grey hoops (later halves), navy or white flannels

If Clapham Rovers were to read this today, the first thing they would point out is that they were a general sports club, albeit one of London's most successful and best known, but its members were just as adept at athletics and rugby as they were at the association game. They were formed by Robert Seymour Whalley, and William E. Rawlinson, who was elected their first honorary secretary. They played their first two seasons on any available space on Clapham Common; at over 200 acres of common land for the parishes of Clapham and Battersea, it became a park under the Metropolitan Commons Act of 1878. Containing three ponds and a bandstand, Rovers were not only at the mercy of the wintry weather and the sudden falling of darkness before matches were concluded, but also restricted by being unable to charge spectators to watch on public land. There was neither any means to secure the chosen area for their exclusive use. Their large middle class membership self-funded the club so that acquiring revenue from spectators was not a priority.

The club would later play home matches on the newly created sports field on a section of Wandsworth Common, and used the Hope Tavern (just outside Wandsworth Common station) as headquarters. The exact playing location of which part of the Common used is uncertain, although years later, the Casuals played on a field by the Surrey Tavern, which was also their headquarters, although I deem this too far from descriptions given later. The members' first decision on August 10th 1869 was that the club would play rugby games one week, and association football the next! Remarkably, in their first two years, they only lost two matches, one at each code. Their first ever recorded game was on 1st September that year, when they beat the Westminster school XI by 1-0. The return game was also won on November 22nd, when they won 2-1 that year. They also defeated the famous Wanderers by 1-0 in their first month of existence. Rovers were still learning their trade when they went to play Charterhouse school on Wednesday 20th October 1869, and were well beaten 5-1 by the already well practiced boys there. That early Clapham team was -

R.H. Birkett, P. Birkett, J.E. Tayloe, C.C. Huggins, A. Nash, A.J. Nash,
A. Thompson, A.T. Beachcroft, E.C. Leggat, J.R. Newcombe, J. Urlwin.

Clapham Rovers' fixture list for 1869-70 season was fairly large, for a club's first full season. Home and 'return' fixtures were announced against Wanderers, Hampstead Heathens, Walthamstow, Hitchin, Marlborough Nomads, Brentwood, Forest, and Upton Park. At that time, there was still some cross-over of soccer and rugby, with Nomads and possibly Brentwood playing both codes. By January 1870, Clapham had enough members to put out two teams each Saturday, one playing rugby rules, the other Association rules.

Reginald Halsey Birkett, (1849-1898) was a London-born renowned all-round Victorian sportsmen. A furrier and hide dealer by occupation, his father was a noted surgeon in Hackney. When the Rugby Union Association was founded in January 1871, Reginald Birkett was a leading founder member, with Clapham Rovers at the forefront of early organised rugby, along with Richmond and Wasps. Clapham were also founder members when the Surrey Football Association was founded in 1877. Birkett is also in the record books as the scorer of England's first ever rugby try. At least three Birketts played with Clapham Rovers, and another with Grey Friars, although websites only mention Reggie, brother Louis, and son John, from the Edwardian era. Reggie and Louis attended Lancing College in 1866-67, where the passing game is claimed to have been invented, and played for Lancing Old Boys before joining Clapham Rovers. His son John would later captain the England rugby side. A family man, Reggie died before his 50th birthday when diptheria took hold of his mental health and in a state of delusion, jumped out of a bedroom window and fell to his death on the last day of June 1898 (*Mid-Sussex Times*).

Many teams used public spaces such as Clapham Common as their 'free' base, and one of these was the C.C.C. club, or the Clapham Common Club to give the full title. They were active across the 1860s and 1870s, and their fixtures are sometimes hard to distinguish from Clapham Rovers. The (London) Rangers FC, who existed only from 1876 to 1882, and notable for little other than having the later famous Sir Frederick Wall as a player, also played on Clapham Common, using the Invitation public house on Auckland Road, Wandsworth as a base. In 1869-70, Clapham's fixture card included return matches against Wanderers, Forest, No-Names, Brentwood, Barnes and Gitanos football clubs, suggesting that these were well established clubs by the time Clapham Rovers were formed. Indeed, we know that some went back to at least 1862-3 season. Boys versus men did not seem to matter, and when the C.C.C team went over to Brentwood cricket ground to play the boys of the grammar school in November 1867, the boys won comfortably by 3-0. There is perhaps some small logic to this; weekend football teams for leisured gentlemen possibly never had time to practice, whereas the schoolboys were likely to be out on the field every day, developing their team play and individual dribbling skills. Another ground-sharing neighbour of Rovers was the Alexandra FC. Clapham's rugby skills must have proved useful when they went to play Charterhouse school XI on Wednesday 26th January 1870. Winning 2-1 after agreeing to play extra time, the match had to be played on the 'Under Green' due to the main field being relayed with new turf for the cricket season. The surface had no grass, and was hard and gravelly. It must have resembled the parade ground used as a football ground by the Surrey Rifles FC. Unusually, Reginald Birkett did not guard the 'sticks' as he often did; instead C.E. Neapan took on the role, as they swapped positions for the day.

At the end of 1871, Clapham Rovers left Clapham Common and found a field at Balham where there remained until 1876. At that time, there were two cricket grounds within half a mile of Balham station: one by the county lunatic asylum, which ground is now occupied by Pavilion Square on Beechcroft Road, and one on Bedford Hill, which now forms the lower part of Tooting Bec, a park we know they also played in. The park off the top of Balham Park Road has to be ruled out because it was heavy woodland at that time, and Pavilion Square is almost a mile from Balham station, in Tooting. Until the house

Sir John Forbes, once a Clapham Rovers player. Right, a Baines football card, usually given away inside packets of cigarettes, often gave fanciful depictions of the teams they were intended to portray, often with completely the wrong colours, although Clapham's cerise and french grey seem to be correct here.

building boom of the 1880s, Balham was a village based around the junction of Bedford Hill and the A24 High Street. Less than a mile in any direction from this point, and you would be either in Clapham or Upper Tooting. If one of those cricket grounds was not home to Clapham Rovers, then any one of the many fields around Sarsfeld Road could fit the bill. Their sports day of April 1874 was held 'in a field belonging to Sir Charles Forbes at Broomwood (House)'. Broomwood Road was later built in the vicinity of an old cricket ground which lay at the end of Lambourne Road until the 1880s.

Clapham Rovers were both instrumental and participants in the first ever F.A. Cup competition, then known as the English Cup. Clapham Rovers can hold on to one record that can never be taken away; when Jervis Kenrick scored the opening goal against Upton Park on 11th November 1871, it was the first ever goal scored in the world-famous competition. Upton Park were beaten 3-0 away in round 1, but mighty Wanderers beat them 3-1 at the next stage, and famously went on to become the first winners. Oddly, Rovers did not enter in 1872-3, possibly because their entry did not arrive on time for the deadline. In the following season, Rovers were given a walkover when drawn against the Amateur Athletics club. Cambridge University's ad-hoc team were problematical opponents, and it took three games to split them. A replay on Saturday 29th November on Parker's Piece, after the first game had been drawn at Balham on the 15th, saw the teams locked at 1-1 in front of "very numerous spectators". The constant rain made the field very slippery, and several players came a cropper. On the previous weekend, a crowd of 700 saw the Cambridge- Oxford match. The third game in London saw Rovers go through by 4-1 thanks to goals from Field(2), Kenrick and Howard, the game finishing in darkness at the Oval. The 'Cantabs' had been favourites, but several of their best men were unavailable for the third game. On the same day in Sheffield, the Royal Engineers had played there, and won convincingly 4-0 at Bramall Lane in a game played one half Sheffield rules, the other London rules. The first 'taste' of provincial football came when the Sheffield FC then came to London to meet Clapham in the 3rd round, but were beaten 2-1. Clapham were now in the semi-finals, and were drawn against Oxford University, whilst the best team in the country - Royal Engineers- met the Swifts. Both matches were played at the Oval, the 'Sappers' going through 2-0, and the team from the 'dreaming spires' progressing with a single goal against Rovers. This meant that both finalists had returned as beaten finalists of the previous two years. Favourites, Engineers had a disappointing final where they didn't perform to their best, and Oxford won 2-0, the second goal coming when a speedy counter-attack by the whole Oxonian forward line ended with Patton putting the game beyond doubt.

Clapham Rovers held their annual sports day on Saturday April 19th 1873, on a "delightful paddock at the front of his Broomwood mansion house, lent for the day by Sir Charles Forbes, Bart, when the elite of the neighbourhood, including a great many ladies, graced the occasion by their presence". Rovers' player Reginald Birkett won the high jump with a leap of 5 feet 6 inches, and other footballers present included R. Matthews of the Crystal Palace club. Buried at Brompton cemetery, Baronet Forbes (1803-1877) of Newey, Aberdeen was succeeded by his son, also Charles as 5th baronet in 1877. Broomwood House, designed by J.T. Groves, became the residence of William Wilberforce, the well-known anti-slavery campaigner. After its surrounding gardens and lands were built over, the house found itself sitting between Hillier and Wroughton Roads by 1890. Sadly, the house fell into disrepair and was demolished around 1922. The five acre tree-lined field used by Clapham Rovers for sports days (and I suspect at other times too) was built over at around 1905 by Broomwood School (now Thomas's London Day School) and Wisley Road.

When England played Scotland in March 1875, Clapham Rovers' Richard Lyon Geaves became the first Mexican-born man to play for England, having been educated at Harrow and Caius College, Cambridge. He joined the Prince of Wales' Yorkshire Regiment and lived to the ripe old age of eighty.

In January 1877, Clapham were forced to play their home rugby matches at Streatham Common - over two miles away - as "their Balham ground was required for building on". Comparing maps from 1875 with one for 1890, the area which became mostly built over were the fields either side of Rossiter Road, which fits in with the desirability of having a ground within a few minutes walk from a railway station. It also appears that upon the death of Sir Charles Forbes that year, Broomwood Park grounds were no longer available to them, and they found a new ground near Wandsworth Common station "and 20 minutes walk from Clapham Junction" (*South London Press*).This, for any average person on foot, gives a limit of one mile, which by the most direct route, brings us just past the top end of Wanstead Common. When Rovers held their 1881 sports day, reference was made to the slow mile race times due to the roughness of the ground beyond the 100 yard marks, and a high wind meeting athletes going up the hill". The Surrey Tavern cricket ground (almost 2 miles from Clapham Junction) is quite flat and level, so too Wandsworth and Wanstead Commons.

In 1879, Clapham Rovers battled through to the final of the F.A. Cup (then called the English Cup) for the first time, but were up against an Old Etonian side which was bent on revenge from having lost the finals of 1875 and 1876. The Etonians had chosen their best men available such as Arthur Kinnaird, Edgar Lubbock, John Chevalier, Harry Goodhart, Lindsay Bury, Edward Christian and John Hawtrey in goal. Despite the pale blues having much of the play on a blustery day, Clapham remained calm, and knew that in goalie Reggie Birkett and forwards Cecil Keith-Falconer and Edward Growse, they had fine players of their own. The winning goal came on the hour, when Etonian Goodhart ran the ball down the right wing and 'middled' the ball. Rushing in, Charles Clerke sent the ball high but under the crossbar to score, which event was greeted by "loud and prolonged cheers from all parts of the Oval ground". Clapham rallied, but failed to score, and Eton had finally won the cup.

At the end of the following season -1879-80-, Clapham Rovers achieved their greatest triumph when they returned to defeat Oxford University to lift the F.A. Cup with a much changed team led by star player Francis J. Sparks. Only Reginald Birkett, Norman Bailey, Robert Ogilvie and Edgar Field remained from the 1878 team, which made up their defence. Beating Romford 7-0 in round 1, they also kept a clean sheet against South Norwood in round two, winning 4-0. The high scoring continued with another seven goal battering, this time to the Pilgrims FC. The 4th round saw unknown quantity Hendon play up well, but were overcome by 2-0. In the year (1880) of the sudden demise of the Wanderers, the quarter-finals saw the best four teams in the country face each other; there was no easy opponent. Oxford University edged past the Royal Engineers by the only goal of the game, and in a repeat of the 1879 final, Clapham also squeezed past the Old Etonians by the same score. For reasons which Charles Alcock must have kept to himself, there remained five teams at this stage; provincial danger side Nottingham Forest drew a bye into the last four. Why on earth intelligent men like Alcock and Morley couldn't organise a pure 32-16-8-4-2-1 knockout competition remains a mystery. Ok, so there were 54 entrants in round 1; so why not have (54-32) 22 matches in round 1 to eliminate 22 teams, leaving (54-22) 32 teams in round 2? Ten clubs would draw a bye in the first round, but better to have 'favours' early on than at the semi-final stage which is ridiculous. And so, with three clubs in the semi-final, one would draw a bye, and that chance fell to Clapham Rovers. Favourites Forest played well against Oxford University, a previous winner, but another game decided by a single goal put the academics through. With three previous final appearances behind them, Oxford had the advantage of experience, but as last year's beaten finalists, Rovers had the hunger of revenge. Oxford, in navy and white halved shirts, had the better of the first period, with a Phillips' free kick whistling just over the tape. Clapham, now playing in cerise and french grey halves, came back and mounted clever attacking passing movements of their own, with Lloyd-Jones and Ram both going close. Oxford came out strongly in the second half and got two quick corners. For much of the second half, play was evenly balanced, but with ten minutes to go, Sparks centred the ball, King made a mess of his clearance, and Lloyd-Jones rushed up and shot the ball between the posts. The *Field Magazine* said that "this feat quite brought down the house, with vociferous cheering, throwing up (into the air) of hats, and other demonstrations of delight from their supporters". A last gasp effort from Oxford saw a Childs shot saved by Reg Birkett, and the cup was in Rovers' hands at last. Their victorious team was -

		Reg Birkett			
	Robert Ogilvie		**Edgar Field**		
Vincent Weston		**Norman Bailey**		**Arthur Stanley**	
Harold Brougham	**Felix Barry**	**Francis Sparks**	**Edward Ram**	**Clopton Lloyd-Jones**	

The Clapham side that day were an eclectic mix of characters. Arthur Stanley was a noted tennis player who competed at Wimbledon between 1881 and 1885; Norman

Bailey was a lawyer, Edward Herbert Ram, a small and nippy inside forward was a noted architect and water-colourist noted for always wearing a straw boater hat, Clopton Lloyd-Jones was a Shropshire cricketer, and Francis Sparks was the England football captain. The curiously-named Clopton Lloyd-Jones, described by a team-mate as " a very neat dribbler and a dangerous shot at goal " was Shropshire born in 1858 and lived at the family home of Hanwood House near Shrewsbury. He also played for Shrewsbury Castle Blues, a notorious team who were disbanded in 1886 due to consistent violent play, and played cricket for both Salop and Herefordshire. Like many middle class Victorian gentlemen, he also excelled at athletics, rugby and tennis. Sadly (as usual) Hanwood House was sold to the developers and demolished in 1972. His Cup Final medal was sold in 2008 for £2,400. Edward Ram was also involved with the short lived (1877-1881) London club Hawks FC. Ram became a noted architect involved with many key buildings in Hong Kong, including the library, hotels and golf courses and the racecourse grandstand. Returning to Kensington in 1919, he died of emphysema in 1946. His grandson John Miskin wrote in 2003 that he recalled Ram as five feet five inches, immaculately dressed and always with straw boater and walking cane, reminding one of a smaller version of Maurice Chevallier.

In the following season, Clapham started their cup defence in resounding fashion, annihilating Finchley by 15-0 on November 13th 1880. Old Etonians also got double figures, putting ten past Brentwood without reply. Clapham drew a bye in round 2, but, ominously, so did Nottingham Forest. The third round saw the Swifts put up a good performance, but were beaten 2-1 on 8th January, whilst Aston Villa suddenly threw the spotlight on themselves by beating the Forest 3-1. The Darwen club beat Sheffield Wednesday by the surprising margin of 5-1, and Wolverhampton railway team Stafford Road caused an upset by putting the Villa out, 3-2. Upton Park proved stubborn opposition in round four, but Clapham edged home by 5-4 on 12th February, but the shock of the round saw Aston Villa beaten at home by Wolverhampton team Stafford Road. Sheffield Wednesday and the Royal Engineers also became 4th round casualties. Once again, in round 5, six teams remained! Stafford Road were beaten at home on their Foxes Lane field 2-1 by Old Etonians in front of 8,000 people, but Clapham met their match when eventual winners Old Carthusians put them out 4-1. In the third match, Darwen drew the attention with a 15-0 thrashing of Romford, but it was a false hope, for Charterhouse dealt with them in the semi-final.

Season 1881-2 marked the point in which the balance of play begun to move away from the southern amateurs, and clubs from Lancashire, Yorkshire and Staffordshire were starting to take control of the competition, many of whom were already secretly paying their imported star players two or three pounds a week. If there was one side which Clapham could have chosen to avoid in the 1st round, it was Old Etonians, but that is what happened, and it was the scholars who edged through by 1-0. Eton went through to the final for the next two years, which marked the end of the old amateur era, and the start of the new, when Blackburn Rovers were beaten to win the Cup in 1882, but sister club Blackburn Olympic got revenge in 1883 to become the first provincial winners. Saturday 1st February 1881 must have sent a shock wave through not just Clapham but to all London clubs, because on an Oval ground which was battered by driving snow and sleet, ᵇlackburn Rovers visited, and thrashed Clapham the Cup-holders by no less than 7-1 in ⸱ where the *Sheffield Telegraph* said that 'the northerners had an easy time of it' and ⸱r just seven minutes, followed by a Bambridge header into his own goal. If the

1883 Cup Final was the 'end of the amateur dominance' then this 1881 match was an early warning of times to come.

Clapham Rovers never again made it to the last stages in the F.A. Cup, although in 1883-4 they got to the 3rd round, losing again 1-2 to Swifts, after promisingly crushing Rochester 7-0. Again in 1885-6, they got to round 3. A 12-0 thrashing of faded officer's club Surrey Rifles in round 1 saw them draw a bye into round 3. Surprisingly, here, they withdrew when drawn away to South Reading FC, and in the following year, they went out 0-6 to Old Brightonians at the first hurdle, this proving to be their last appearance in the competition. Older opposition was met head on in January 1888, when Rovers drew 4-4 with the Old Westminsters on Vincent Square in front of several hundred spectators. In the early years, Rovers' matches had been played on the 220 acre Clapham Common, which was half in Wandsworth and half in Lambeth boroughs. Quickly, public open spaces such as this were soon over-run with a plethora of football and rugby teams, as well as other forms of sport popular in the day. Clapham Rovers soon joined the old boys' circuit, and this was their team which lost 1-2 away to Charterhouse school on 23rd November 1870-

Reggie Birkett, A.C. Rover, W.R. Dent, G.F. Hamar, J. Dimsdale, R. Luck,

Louis Birkett, J. Walwyn, C.C. Leggett, C.P. French, J. Holden.

The Hope Tavern was used as headquarters by the sportsmen of Clapham Rovers.

Clapham Rovers must have met the Wanderers on top form on Saturday 3rd October 1874, for they were well beaten 5-0 on the Kennington Oval with goals from H.S. Otter (2), Charles Woollaston (2) and Hubert Heron. Revenge was sweet five years later, when Clapham thrashed Wanderers by 8-2 on the opening day of the 1879-80 season, with goals from Barry (4), Stanley, Sparks, Taylor and Rumball, with Woollaston getting the Wanderers' goals. A year before, in October 1878, Rovers again trounced the Wanderers by 5-1 with goals from Sparks, Bevington, Jarrett, Bailey and Princep. In 1876, the Leyton FC were thrashed 7-0 on October 28th, with goals from Curwen (2), Wild (2), Bastard, and Bouch. This may have been the first match played on their new ground at Wandsworth, although the exact location is not known. However, I found an advert in the *Sporting Life* for 1st May 1880, placed by the secretary F.W.F. Collier of Burlington Lane, Chiswick,which stated that *"their field is near to Wandsworth Common station, on the L.B.S.C. Railway"*. I rushed to my old map and also Google Earth on-line mapping tool, and determined that although there were rough fields on both on the sides of the railway station, in view of their status as a general sports club and probably needing more than one pitch, I eliminated the Wandsworth Common side of Belle Vue Road, since it was a public open space. Maps were notoriously out of date, the Wandsworth Common station created in 1869 wasn't even shown on an 1874 map, yet by 1890, all the surrounding rough land and fields had been built on. With Balham station (later renamed Wandsworth) only 800 yards away, the search must fall within a radius of 400 yards, otherwise they would say that their ground was close to Balham station. With the Hope Tavern right by Wandsworth Common station, I might have expected this to have received a mention. A three acre triangular piece of land adjacent to Wandsworth Common station, shown as rough ground in 1890, yet today is a playing field, remains one possibility. A cricket ground in front of the Surrey Tavern, 350 yards along the Belle Vue Road, and later used by several clubs, including the Casuals also falls within the parameters. The 8 acre Surrey Tavern site is currently known as the Sir Walter St. John sports ground. Following through to read an account of the sports day advertised on May Day 1880, mention was both given to a groundsman, Harry Andrews, and that one race finished by the cricket pavilion, the ground being "at Wandsworth Common in close proximity to the station".

Another high scoring match took place in 1879 when Clapham won 4-3 away at the Mosquitoes 'ground' which was merely another section of Clapham Common. Clapham Rovers' status continued to grow, and as an indication of this, the Glasgow club Queens Park were playing them in an annual fixture by the early 1880s. In 1881, when Clapham played the Swifts in a high profile friendly at the Oval before a large crowd in January, I noticed that helping Rovers to win a hard fought game by 2-1, were two Wanderers players, Wace and Woollaston; additionally, two Wanderers men acted as umpires: Charles Alcock and A.H. Stratford, the referee being Major Marindin of the Royal Engineers FC.

Many of Clapham Rovers' men were capped for England in both the official Internationals, and the unofficial ones of the early 1870s, when 'Scotland' was drawn merely from Caledonians residing in London. Norman Coles Bailey by far led the list with 19 caps, although he was also a regular for Old Westminsters and the Swifts. Edgar Field and Francis Sparks each were capped twice, with all the following gaining one cap:- Reginald Halsey Birkett (plus rugby cap, along with his brother Louis Birkett), the Rovers' best dribbler, Walter Buchanan, Richard Greaves, Robert Ogilvie, James Princep, T.S. Baker, Jarvis Kenrick, Alexander Nash, R.S. Walker (3 'caps' and 4 goals).

Norman Coles Bailey (1857-1923) was probably the greatest full back of the age; following an education at Westminster school, he became a solicitor. He gained 19 England caps, and became a committee member of the FA, rising to its vice-president during 1887-1890. A keen footballer, his other clubs included the Old Westminsters, Wanderers, Swifts and Corinthians.

Clapham Rovers generally played on the Common.

James Frederick McLeod Princep (1861-1895) owed his 'handsome dark looks' to being born in India. Schooled at Charterhouse during 1874-78, and trained at Sandhurst Royal Military Academy, he came the youngest ever player to appear in a Cup Final, until I believe Wayne Rooney took his crown over a century later. Alcock said of Princep - known as the prince of dribblers- "he seldom makes mistakes, and possesses a cool and sound judgement". Others said he was "a fine half back, always cool, strong on his legs, combining plenty of strength with great accuracy and kicks splendidly with good judgement". A professional soldier with the Essex Regiment, he saw active service in the Egypt campaigns around Khartoum, attaining the rank of major. He died from influenza caught while playing golf in Scotland in the rain, before he had opportunity to return home to his London address of 46 Thurloe Square. Edgar Field (1854-1934) was educated at Lancing College where he played for the school team, but his first club was Reading FC, whom he joined around 1874. He qualified as a chartered accountant, although the 1891 census describes him as a wine merchant. It is likely that he was spotted as a Clapham Rovers play when selected to play full back for England in March 1876, although availability as much as expertise, was the key point in those days, and you were much more likely to be capped if you played for one of the London clubs, as no doubt the selectors merely went on recommendations. He moved to Derby in 1913 where he died in 1934. The Right Honourable John Frederick Peel Rawson (1860-1926), to give his full title, was a Cambridge Etonian who in professional life was a barrister, and entered politics in the Edwardian era, becoming the M.P. representing Cambridge University, and later, in the 1920s, held many posts including Justice of the Peace and Privy Councillor. As a goalkeeper, he was described as cool, sometimes too cool, and gave cause for alarm on occasion! A committee member of the Corinthians, he served on the FA committee during 1885-6, he played in three cup finals for the Old Etonians. His brother Frederick Rawson also played for Clapham at outside-right, although he lacked weight and could be knocked off the ball at times *(K.Warsop, Early FA Cup finals & the Southern Amateurs).*

In 1886, Clapham Rovers rugby team ran out to a huge crowd numbering 10,000 when they travelled north to play Hull in December. Clapham suffered an embarrassing defeat at the hands of The Swifts when they went to their Dolphin Ground at Slough on Saturday 10th 1888. Lyndhurst scored six as Swifts won 10-0. Travelling with only ten men, Rovers had to borrow Grant as stand-in goalkeeper in 1892, when this eleven lost 0-6 away to Maidstone -

	F. Grant	
H. Duncan		R. Ingram
P. Rathbone	C. Forester	E. Rathbone
A. Keeley H. Dixon	A. Cronin	H. Dunsmuir H. Rathbone

In 1889, the *Hartlepool Mail* ran an amusing story when, in April, Clapham Rovers finished their rugby tour of Yorkshire, having played at Leeds, Halifax and York, finishing against Hartlepool Rovers. The Clapham footballers were followed back to the railway station by a group of ladies. The footballers addressed the crowd, saying that Hartlepool ladies were the prettiest they had ever seen, and that should any of them be seeking a husband, then a letter to their club would do the trick! In 1890, when playing at home to Hull, the Clapham ground was described as 'west Kensington'. However, they held their annual sports day at the Stamford Bridge athletic grounds on Saturday 3rd May in the presence 'of a fashionable gathering' (*Lloyds Weekly News*).

By 1893, crowds exceeding 1,000 were watching their home games at Wandsworth Common, partly due to the fact that it was public land and you could watch for free. Figuring out where they played presents a puzzle as it was a big area, much larger than what is left today, as nearly all of what was Wandsworth Common has long since been built over. In the 1870s it stretched from St. Anne's church to beyond Spencer Park on the other side of the A214. Much of the southern portion was marshy scrub land, and there was a big lake, known as the 'Black Sea' occupying much of the area next to Spencer Park. Emanuel school had a cricket ground with a pavilion, as it still does, but I don't think this qualifies as public land. Another possibility for their ground lay behind the vicarage on Lyford Road, where there was a playing field with its own pavilion. Long since built over, it would have stood between Burcote and Loxley Roads today. The main problem with playing in public parks is that you could turn up and find some other team playing there, and you would have no right to make them move somewhere else. The area that Clapham Rovers is likely to have used would have been between St. Anne's Crescent (then St. Anne's Hill) and Geraldine Road by Wandsworth church, a later construction.

Clapham briefly entered the Amateur Cup, in 1893-4 season, where they got past Crouch End 2-0 in the 2nd qualifying round to meet Tottenham Hotspur, who, having just announced they had turned professional, were thrown out of the competition. In round 1 proper, it was Clapham's turn to scratch when they were drawn away to Bishop Auckland, a team who would go on to become an Edwardian legend. A combination of the thought of a 500 mile round trip and the likelihood of being thrashed anyway, produced the combination which led to that decision.

It was not all gloom, as I found in 1902, the Surrey Mirror praising Clapham Rovers in the way which they had put Reigate Priory out of the Surrey Charity Shield. By winning 3-1, the reporter praised the good combination play of Clapham. This suggests that, although no longer a leading club, Clapham were still alive and well in Surrey. One match in 1910 saw them well beaten 7-0 by Old Malvernians in round 1, but what caught my eye was the raft of 'famous' surnames from a bygone era, such as Vidal, Bambridge, Lindsay and Day. Played on the Reigate Priory ground, here is the last Rovers side I could find :-

A. E. Begg

E. Morris   **E. T. Bolton**

H. Robinson   **H. Ost**   **E. G. Millar**

R. Laughton   **M. Hammill**   **R. C. Bambridge**   **F. J. Hall**   **A. L. Gray**

R.C. Bambridge was the son of the famous Charlie 'Bam' Bambridge, of the Swifts and Corinthians from the 1880-1890 era, and was described as 'a chip off the old block' by the *Nottingham Evening Post*.

When the newly formed Amateur Foootball Association held its first meeting in July 1907, the Clapham Rovers official B.A. Glanville presided over it. Rovers were still running a reserve team in 1910-11, as they were found losing 1-3 to Oxon in the Surrey Junior Cup, and the first team had been competing in the Surrey Senior Cup, but I could not find them playing in any league. Clapham Rovers were still in existence in 1912, although matches against Brentwood school and Goldington were indicative of the level to which they had receded. Rovers, like many other clubs, responded to the call to arms at the outbreak of war in 1914, when thousands of footballers led the way and enlisted. In this way, hundreds of football teams never made it to the other side of the war in 1918. Clapham Rovers were one of the casualties.

CROYDON COMMON

Founded - 1897
Folded - 1917
Ground - 1. Whitehorse Road Rec. (extant)
          2. The Crescent
          3. The Nest
Colours - Claret shirts, nickname 'the Robins'

Croydon Common FC began life as a church club in 1897 after a local benefactor Ralph Cole decided that the area would benefit from having a football club to provide the local youths with something to do. Following a meeting held at St. Lukes Mission church, in Boulogne Road, they chose the name because the area used to be part of the rapidly disappearing Croydon Common.

Their first ground was waste ground on Whitehorse Road, known as 'the Dust Bowl', and is still there today. Early colours of blue and gold gave way to claret shirts, white shorts, and these colours were retained for the remainder of its existence. Early rivalry came from the West Croydon FC, Croydon Wanderers, and the Croydon rugby club, who counted first class sides such as Blackheath, Rosslyn Park and Guy's amongst their opposition. Their second home was The Crescent, now the site of the Crescent Junior School. Early directors were John Fuller and Richard Whiting.

After a few years of friendlies, the 'Robins' joined the Surrey County F.A., and soon won its first competition, beating South Norwood 4-0 to win the Croydon Charity Cup, the match played in a snow blizzard. Season 1905-06 saw a haul of trophies despite only average league form: the Surrey Junior Cup, the Surrey Junior League Cup, the Croydon Cup, the Sutton Hospital Cup, and the Surrey Herald Cup soon filling the trophy cupboard. By 1907, the manager John Bartlett thought the town was ready for a professional club . Despite a weak public response, he forged ahead and floated 20,000 ten shilling (50p) shares which he hoped would finance a new ground and a new club. Optimistically, Bartlett had managed to get 'Croydon Town' accepted into the Southern League, but the shares weren't taken up, and suddenly he had a situation where he had a non-existent club without a ground, and Southern League fixtures to fulfil. So he turned to the amateur Croydon Common and converted them wholesale into his professional team. He bought a group of experienced players at the end of their careers from clubs such as West Ham, Southampton and Tottenham, including half back George Hunter. Unfortunately, Hunter was spotted by Aston Villa and he signed for them in 1909. Another Croydon player who went on to better things was George 'Lady' Woodger, who signed for Crystal Palace before moving north to Oldham Athletic before returning after four years to sign for Tottenham Hotspur in May 1914. Jack Harrow (1888-1958), a strong tackling full back, left for professional terms with Chelsea in 1911 after three seasons with the Robins, where he racked up over 300 appearances. Bert Hodgkinson (1884-1939) was a journeyman left winger who came from Southampton in 1909 and left three seasons later for Southend. John Lewis (1881-1954) was another who came from Southampton. His one season stay produced 14 goals in just 10 appearances, but he ended his career by returning to his previous club, Burton United (now defunct). Jack Little left Croydon when they were wound up and played over 240 games for Crystal Palace in the 1920s. Alex MacDonald (1878-1949) was a tall Scot who started with Everton before ending his career with Croydon in 1907. Bob Spottiswood may have only played 11 times for the Robins in 1908-9, but he then went on to manage no less than Internazionale Milan between 1922-24.

Messina Wilson Allman (1883-1943), known as 'Dick', was a journeyman forward who had been at ten clubs before his spell with Croydon during 1912-15. He scored 21 goals before moving on to Crystal Palace. Percy Barnfather (1879-1951) was a diminutive winger who had three spells with Croydon. Arthur Box, a tall goalkeeper, came from the Potteries but stayed only for 1910-11. The previous goalie, Bob Evans, had come from Blackburn Rovers, via his native Wrexham. David Gardner (1873-1931), a Scottish left back, came via West Ham and Newcastle. Harry Hadley (1877-1942) had played for most of the top Midland clubs before he came to Croydon in 1908 from Southampton. Bob Thompson started out with Croydon before signing for Chelsea in 1911where he scored 23 goals in 83 appearances over 12 seasons despite having *only one eye*. Despite being a left back, Arthur Hutchins scored 10 goals in 38 games in season 1914-15. Philip 'Billie' Yenson made over 200 appearances for the Robins during 1909-1915, a club record. Whilst at Bolton, he had played in the 1904 Cup Final against Manchester City.

In 1908-09, Croydon also competed in the Western League, meaning that they played over 80 matches that season, but success came when they won the Second Division of the Southern League and finished mid table in the Western, United and South-Eastern Leagues. Better yet was their fine F.A. Cup run that year. Battling through all the qualifying rounds, they achieved their finest result yet when winning 2-1 away at League club Bradford, which got them through to round 1 proper. As today, when the 'minnows' eagerly await to see if they have drawn one of the big boys and thus reap a financial reward, Croydon drew First Division Woolwich Arsenal. Rubbing their hands with glee in anticipation of a big crowd to swell the coffers, they switched home venue from their undeveloped field to the cavernous Crystal Palace ground. Twenty thousand turned up to see Croydon take a deserved 1-1 draw. In the replay, Arsenal were two up after ten minutes, but Croydon matched them for the remainder. There would have been a connection between the two clubs at this point, as Henry Norris owned both Arsenal and Croydon Common clubs.

It was at this point that Croydon moved from their Crescent Field to Selhurst, and rented a ground from the London & Brighton South Coast Railway Co., and it became known as the Nest. All three Croydon grounds were within 800 yards of each other. They weren't there long before a fire broke out at the end of November 1908 and seriously damaged the long stand, which was of wood and corrugated iron construction. Now having to play in the higher First Division of the Southern League, players came and went, but their detriment. Losses included Bob Evans their Welsh international goalie, and former internationals Sam Wolstenholme and Percy Barnfather, and although some good men were signed, such as new goalie William Balmer and Bill Yenson, the side never gelled, and results suffered. A 10-0 defeat at Northampton was the low point in a relegation season, which saw Barlett ousted and Nat Whittaker brought in as new manager. Whittaker too, was soon on his way, and replaced by Sandy Tait, and slowly the team improved back to mid-table status.

For season 1910-11, the directors, worried at the club's financial position, thought that returning to an 80-game season would be a good idea. It was not, and soon, the Robins had to sell chief asset Jack Harrow to Chelsea for the bargain price of £50. Chelsea thought they had found a bargain bin, and came back to buy fifty goals-a-season forward Bobby Thompson. After a couple of seasons of average league positions, their only bright point was in reaching the 1st round proper again of the F.A. Cup, going out after replays against Leicester Fosse and Woolwich Arsenal. On Monday 12th March 1912, the club called a public meeting to appeal for help. The ground rent of £150 could not be met but one gentleman offered £50 if the other £100 was raised. (*Lichfield Mercury*)

New manager John Bowman from Norwich brought an upturn in fortunes and in 1912-13, Croydon won the Southern Football Alliance title, to which they added the championship of Division Two of the Southern League in the following season. Sadly, this upturn in fortunes coincided with the outbreak of the war, and twelve players signed up for the call to arms. This of course had an effect on the team, who ended 1914-15 bottom but one. In June 1914, the *Daily Herald* reported that Croydon Common had signed inside left George Ryder, whose previous clubs had been Bolton, QPR, and Arsenal. Aged 28, he stood 5'8" and weighed 11 stone 10 pounds. It was remarked that players Upex and Rayner had been retained. At the end of May 1912, Croydon Common went on a tour to Sweden, playing six games in eight days, remaining unbeaten.

The list of now well-known clubs which populated the Southern League in the Edwardian era, would raise eyebrows today: West Ham United, Southampton, Millwall, Swindon Town, Norwich, Plymouth, Watford, Tottenham and Crystal Palace. But these were the days of only two divisions of the Football League which did not expand until after the end of the Second World War. Football carried on hesitantly after 1914, but many leading clubs went into voluntary suspension. There was an uneasy feeling about playing football when tens of thousands were fighting in the trenches. It was not exactly popular to go and watch football games either, and attendances were well down. Clubs in each region

Edwardian era photo of a Croydon Common versus Norwich City game in progress. Note the tiny stands and the poor quality playing surface.

of the country played each other without pay in leagues such as the Lancashire or Midland League. Twelve London clubs formed a London League or Combination, and Croydon Common for a short while had weekly games against Arsenal, Chelsea, Spurs, QPR, Brentford, Fulham, West Ham, Crystal Palace, Millwall, Fulham, and Clapton Orient. Their 0-0 away with Orient drew a 5,000 crowd, the same number which watched Blackpool v Bolton in the Lancashire League. Wartime teams, however, were almost assembled randomly from whoever was available, with locally-based footballer soldiers being asked to guest for any nearby club. When Croydon Common played away to Brentford on Saturday 15th April 1916, the entire Brentford team were 'from the military', and

several of the Croydon men too. Corporal Hunter led their attack, with Kirby, Williamson and Price in defence, and Chester on the right wing, all drew praise for their efforts. On the following weekend, Croydon registered their biggest win for some years when they beat Reading 10-2 in the London Combination. The Sunday Mirror reported in August 1916, when previewing the forthcoming season, said that the London Combination would once again go ahead, with all of last year's clubs, excepting Croydon Common, who have been replaced by Southampton.

Under public criticism for continuing when other leagues had been suspended, the Southern League now came to a halt until 1919-20. However, Croydon Common, like many other clubs, did not resurface on the other side of the war. Their directors had been the ones who had brought most of the 5000 shares sold, and had reached the point when it was pointless to carry on with annual losses. The railway company obtained a court winding-up order on the Robins for failing to pay ground rents, and in March 1917, the club was wound up. The Nest was later used by Crystal Palace FC from 1918 to 1924, before Selhurst Park was built, and when they left, a local team called Tramways played on it. The ground record is thought to have been when 25,000 saw Palace play rivals Millwall in 1922. The Nest was later bulldozed, and now sits underneath the British Rail Selhurst railway depot. The 5.24 acre ground was only lightly developed; there was a stand down the Norbury brook side. Access to the hemmed-in ground was from the Selhurst Road, and the ground lay facing the Selhurst railway station and the Seventh Day Adventist church. Railway sidings and the modern low level Selhurst railway maintenance depot now occupies the ground.

Many thanks to Alan Futter's comprehensive book *Who Killed The Cock Robin*, 1990 from which a great part of the above was extracted.

The Croydon Common team circa 1907.

CRUSADERS FC

Founded - 1862 (if not earlier)
Folded   - Before 1877 and again circa 1905
Ground   - 1. Brentwood
             2. Essex county ground, Leyton (see text notes)
Colours - Unknown

When the first meeting of interested parties met in the Freemasons Tavern in Fleet Street, London in 1863 to formulate the Football Association, the Crusaders FC sent along Herbert Thomas Steward as their representative. Steward's main interests lay in rowing, and was president of the Leander R.C. Born in Westminster in 1838, he became a surveyor and architect. At the historic F.A. committee meeting on 26th January 1870, where all clubs agreed to outlaw any form of handling, which defined the split between association and rugby teams, Crusader William J. Dixon was elected onto the committee. That meeting was attended by representatives of the following clubs - Wanderers, Clapham Rovers, Brixton, Pilgrims, Hampstead Heathens, No-Names of Kilburn, Upton Park, the Amateur Athletics Club, Lincoln, Nottingham, and Newark.

In 1864, Crusaders went to the Vincent Square ground of the Westminsters on Wednesday February 12th, and drew 1-1 thanks to an equaliser by Cleasby. The Crusaders team that day was -

> E.O. Berens, F.D. Cleasby, H.C. Malkin, R.W. Munroe, T. Morton, Paley, Severn, A. Thomas, J.L. Wharton, R. Wharton, E.W. Wylde

Despite his unusual name, I found nothing for E.O. Berens, a surname popular in Prussia and Germany. Played in continuous rain, the game was called off as a tie, soon after the Crusader's goal. In the strange language of the day, each goal was called a 'game'. To a modern onlooker, the style of play would have resembled something like an Aussie Rules game, with the ball being patted down to feet, caught and a mark made, mauls and rucks, and no forward passing. The two sides had met in 1863, with Crusaders departing from Vincent Square as 2-1 victors thanks to goals from Thomas and Malkin, suggesting that Westminsters were a regular opponent in the 1860s.

Charterhouse school were on the Crusaders' fixture list for 1869-70 season, and they first met on 20th November 1869, no goals resulting. A match away to Westminster School on Vincent Square also in November saw an embarrassing 0-7 reverse to the more organised boys, who no doubt practised daily, not helped by the fact that only seven Crusader men turned out. Having future stars like R.W.S. Vidal, who got four goals, on the pitch, made the Westminster boys a hard nut to crack on their own ground.

In early December that year, Crusaders met the Wanderers on the ground of the Old Westminsters, namely Vincent Square. On a wet and slippery ground, goals from Alcock and Kennedy gave Wanderers the win. Crusaders were praised for plucky play, but in front of ' a good number of spectators' the Wanderers 'were too strong for them'. The Crusaders team in that game was -

W.J. Dixon (captain), J.M. Yates, J.P. Nichols, J.E. Tayloe, G.H. Lee, C. Stephenson, R. Baker, E. Lubbock, E. Hall, J.E. Smith.

Captain Dixon, Baker, Lubbock, and Stephenson, all being well-known members of other clubs, principally the Wanderers. Wanderer and Old Etonian Arthur Kinnaird was also a Crusaders player in 1869-70 season. The return match was played on the Oval on Saturday 11th December 1869 when goals from Arthur Baker and J.C. Smith gave them a famous 2-1 win over Wanderers. Baker was one of two borrowed men, as Crusaders turned up with only 7 men.

Crusaders played the Old Etonians on the Queens Club ground, West Kensington in February 1888, when the *London Standard* said they had a lucky win of 3-1. In March 1890, Crusaders were one of only a few clubs to beat the Old Westminsters on their own ground that year when a single goal gave them victory in Vincent Square. The name 'Crusaders' like other similar appellations - Swifts, Wanderers, Ramblers - was soon copied around the country, and before long there were teams of the same name operating in Colchester, Northampton, Bristol, Birmingham and even Belfast, which certainly did not assist in the research!

Puzzlingly, at the start of the 1887 season, in November, the London Standard said that "the 'Crusaders' had up to now been known as Brentwood FC; a revival of the club was underway, and they were planning to move to Leyton". There were indeed match reports for 'Brentwood' in the previous decade, such as when they thrashed Chelmsford 13-0 in October 1882, but there were also match reports for 'Crusaders' too! This meant that there was some unravelling to do! The new committee, led by Mr. Britten, decided that if they called themselves 'Crusaders FC' from the moment of the move to the new location (as was suggested), then they said that this would at first cause confusion to the public. They agreed to call themselves the Brentwood Crusaders for one season, and then adopt the new name once the public had got used to them playing in Leyton. Shades of Wimbledon turning into Milton Keynes a century later! One of the reasons why the club officials wanted to move from Brentwood to Leyton was that public interest was greater there; it must also have meant they got to hear about a vacant ground.

What this means is that if Brentwood became Crusaders in 1888/9, then the team known as Crusaders throughout the 1860s and 1870s must have been a different club. Either that, or the original Crusaders altered their name to Brentwood and switched back to it; but that does not tie in with the worry which the club had about the public getting confused with the name change and move to another district. As Brentwood, this second Crusaders club entered the F.A. Cup in season 1879-80 but were knocked out at the first hurdle by South Norwood. Returning in 1880, they were thrashed 10-0 by the Old Etonians, who went on to reach the final. Undeterred, they tried again in 1881, but lost 1-3 away to Marlow. A 4-2 win over Barnes saw them through to round 2 for the first time in 1882, only to face the Etonians again, but this time, they only lost by 2-1. Hanover were walloped 6-1 in 1883 to again make the 2nd round, where they were lucky enough to draw a bye. Romford proved no threat in the 3rd round as they were beaten 4-1, and Brentwood were in the dizzy heights of the last 16. Sadly, the journey ended when Cheshire side Northwich Victoria put them out by 3-1. Encouraged by this, Brentwood paid their guinea in 1884 and overcame Barnes by 2-0 in round 1 again. Yet again, the name of Old Etonians proved to be their undoing, when they ran out 6-1 winners. Steady improvement saw Brentwood ease past Maidenhead by 3-0 in the autumn of 1885 to meet Lancing College Old Boys in round 2, who they duly beat 6-1. Once more, lady luck was with them as they drew a bye in round 3. Every expectation was eclipsed when they beat South Reading by 3-0 to reach round 5 for the first time. Avoiding such big names as West Bromwich Albion, Bolton, Swifts and Blackburn, Brentwood were drawn first out of the hat to play north Staffordshire side Burslem Port Vale, who, probably on the basis of travelling difficulties, gave them a walkover. This put Brentwood into the head-spinning echelons of round 6, where they drew the dreaded name of Blackburn Rovers. Rovers, at their peak, and professional to a man, had won the cup for the past two years, and were almost unbeatable. A valiant effort from Brentwood saw them keep the score down to 1-3 and they were 'out' with the final tantalizingly in sight. 1887 was the last time the name of Brentwood appeared in the cup until recent times when the new Brentwood Town was founded in 1954. Let us now return to the London of the 1890s.

On Saturday 7th February 1891, Brentwood, now called Crusaders, travelled to Oxford to play the University on the Parks, but were well beaten by 5-1 thanks to goals from Wood, Wilson, Rhodes and Palaires, with the Crusaders point scored by Evelyn. When Crusaders drew the Old Etonians out of the hat in the 1892 London Charity Cup, there was almost nothing to chose between the teams. Indeed, it took four matches before there was a decision. For their first replay in February, at Leyton, was a 4-4 draw, and the attendance was 2,500. Crusaders goals were scored by Sykes, Connel and Wilson (2). Remarkably, Etonians were 4-1 ahead at the break. Star forward Hogarth was missing from the team, for he was busy playing for Wolverhampton Wanderers against Everton in a First Division match ! Eton was vanquished, and Crusaders went on to the final where they defeated the strong Old Foresters by 3-2 to lift the London Charity Cup, a trophy donated by the Right Honourable Reginald Harrison.

At the club's AGM of 1893, team captain F. Horsman thanked the large gathering at the George Hotel, summing up a good season in which of 19 matches played, they had won 14, drawn 3 and lost only 2. Secretary Bailey reporting a small balance in hand of about two pounds. Whilst some teams were fading away by the 1890s, others were on the ascendancy, and so it was when Crusaders went to the Manor Ground in Plumstead of the Royal Arsenal on Boxing Day 1893, and were trounced 7-0 with the Crusaders' defence described as very weak by *Lloyds Weekly*.

Crusaders' Leyton county ground was somewhat overcrowded for the 1894-5 season, as not only were the Casuals also playing there, but the Corinthians had also arranged to play all of their best matches there, involving visitors such as Aston Villa, Queens Park, Preston North End, Bolton Wanderers and Sheffield United. To open their 1895-6 season, Crusaders went over to play London Caledonians at their ground next to Tuffnel Park. The *Pall-Mall Gazette* commenting that the grandly-named Caledonian Park, was in fact, a dump! Five-all was the result, with forwards Compton and Mercer, and defender Simpson attracting merit for Crusaders.

By 1899, most teams belonged to one of the hundreds of leagues which had mushroomed around the country, copying the resounding successes of both the Football League and the Alliance, and the Combination in the north. Thus, it was very hard to find any Crusaders' results at this time, but buried amongst hundreds of small-fry games in Lloyds Weekly, I found that the Crusaders had played Ashburnham, but the venue was Battersea Park. Even regional newspapers, by the end of the century, had changed their football focus to the national scene, with most of the page turned over to the best First Division games of the day, with Second Division, Southern League and other leagues pushing the old amateur teams well down into the small print. Even the annual University match at Queens Club of 1900 was criticized for a standard well below earlier years, and only regional cup finals would give the amateur teams anything other than a single line mention. The demise of the 'first' Crusaders therefore seems to have been just after 1900.

Main pavilion at the Essex County ground at Leyton.

THE CRYSTAL PALACE FC

Founded - 1861
Folded - 1877
Colours - Thin blue and white hoops, navy
Ground - The Crystal Palace sports ground, Sydenham

By the time the workers and groundsmen at the Crystal Palace Pleasure Grounds decided to call it a day for their football team after fifteen years, the famous Lancashire club Accrington hadn't even kicked a ball yet, and Aston Villa were just youths messing about in Aston Park. Thus, very little at all is known or recorded about this very early club which not only were founder members of the Football Association in 1863, but were one of the original fifteen clubs who played in the first ever English F.A. Cup in 1871. Frederick Urwick, Lawrence Vivian Desbrough, George Twizzel Wawn, George Marriette, Hawker and Gray were the club representatives at the historic 1863 F.A foundation meetings. Wawn (1840-1914) was born in county Durham, became stationed with the army in Sierra Leone where at retirement, had attained the rank of honorary Colonel. I found him on the 1901 census living at 102 Foster Hill Road, Bedford, with his wife, two sons and a servant. Wawn passed away in Newquay, Cornwall. His son John later was stationed in the British Consulate in Japan.

Playing football on the east side of the Crystal Palace grounds near Penge, the groundsmen also strengthened their side with a few professionals from nearby villages of Sydenham and Penge. Sadly, contrary to what I had previously thought, this original Crystal Palace did not, unlike its later namesakes, actually play on what became the Cup Final pitch. When landscaped, designed and built, having been moved in its entirety from the original location of Hyde Park, much of the site was dedicated to water. Lakes, fountains and man-made waterways ran everywhere. The grand central walkway approach from Penge up to the magnificent glass exhibition hall had massive water fountains on the scale of Versailles Palace on either side; these became the athletics ground (east side) and the football stadium. The football ground had basically been built on a drained lake, and so it had the appearance of a large oval bowl, the ends of which were formed into huge terraced banks, and an existing pavilion in the centre was enlarged in 1894 with a pair of 5,000 seater stands built on either side by John Aird & Sons. The stand roofs had a distinctive A line shape and sat back from the touch-lines in an unusual V shape. For the first few years there, Cup Final crowds were about 50,000 but as we come into the 1910s, they went well past 100,000, and unlike Wembley Stadium, built to supersede the Crystal Palace, there was room for more. Thus, back in the 1860s and 1870s, our original Crystal Palace FC would have played their games on the cricket field over by the Crystal Palace Park Road, still in use today as a general public recreation area. Cricket had been played on 'Penge Common' since 1857, and both the footballers of Crystal Palace and the London County Cricket Club (founded by W.G. Grace in 1896 but folded in 1904) played on it.

As one of the founder-members of the F.A., Palace continued to hold an interest in the early regulations, and indeed one of their men James Turner was elected F.A. treasurer from 1864-68. Indeed, Palace's D. Allport was one of the three men entrusted to secure the purchase of the original F.A. Cup in 1870. Crystal Palace games were being reported in *Bells Life* in 1864; on Saturday 27th February, they went over to play the Barnes Club, losing 1-2. One of the goals, occurred when a Barnes player caught a high bouncing ball and brought it to the ground with his hand. Making a 'mark' (as in rugby today when taking a place kick at goal), he sent his 'free' kick over the heads of the Palace men into the goal. The Palace captain Turner drew praise for plucky play. This patting down of high balls was one of several features of the 1860s game outlawed by the time of the inaugural English Cup.

The Crystal Palace cricket team may well have been the same group of men who played football in the winter months, as was commonplace around the country. During July 14th-16th 1864, the Crystal Palace C.C. played the Gentlemen of Kent, with both sides fielding 22 men, possibly using 11 men for the 1st innings, and a different 11 in the 2nd, to give all club members a match. Playing only about six or eight times a season, and with few being reported, I was pleased to find this brief report of when Palace played Clapham Rovers at the end of October 1865 'at Penge'. The *Sportsman* praising the efforts of the 'heavier Crystal Palace side' who won 2-1, mainly thanks to the exertions of R. Abraham and J. Turner (goalscorers) and Rhode and J. Cockerill. Both London and provincial newspapers were peppered with adverts proclaiming the multitude of forthcoming attractions at the Palace, and thus, buried within adverts for hot air balloonists, military bands, floral displays, dog shows and sailing events, there would often be a single line entry for the next Crystal Palace football match.

On Saturday 30th November 1867, a match was played to start the season between 'the eleven' and 'the club' who won 1-0 with a goal in the second half by Scott *'during the absence of the goalkeeper'*. Torrential rain made some of the less hardy players leave the pitch for the last half hour, but reserves Chamberlain, James Cutbill and Ralph Cutbill, all drew praise for their efforts.

The first eleven that day was - Walter Cutbill, A. Cutbill, C. Huggins, J. Cockerill, D. Allport, W. Allport, Henry Lloyd, A .Lloyd, J. Sharland, Butterfield, and Parr.

On Saturday 14th December that year, Crystal Palace went to play the boys of the Forest School at Snaresbrook. Now you might think that men v boys was no fair match, but Forest School, under the training and captaincy of master H. Tubb, were the equal of any at the time, and had won all but one of their matches thus far; and so, when the game ended 0-0, the future of the next edition of the 'old Foresters' could be assured. Three sets of brothers made up most of the Palace side: W, A, and R. Cutbills (all Forest old boys), D and R. Allport, and H and A. Lloyd, the others being J. Sharland, J. Ellis, T .Chidley, J.A. Kolle, and C. Farquhar. Forest School probably played in the school colours of royal and navy blue. The Cutbills also turned out for the Old Foresters FC. It would be a remarkable coincidence if the three Cutbills were not the same trio who later popularised the game of shinney on the frozen Cambridgeshire fens.

Crystal Palace announced their fixture list for the 1868-69 season in *The Sporting Life* with home games arranged against Bedouins, Wanderers, Oakfield, Barnes, West Kent and C.C.C. Away fixtures arranged were against Forest School (1-1), Reigate, Civil Service and the C.C.C. the short season running from 5th November to 20th February. The home game against Wanderers on 28th December, was played in a gloomy drizzle, and on a slippery surface, Wanderers' forward Baker scored the winning goal with a shot which went dead centre between the posts. However, both teams were censured for their continual use of the hands, especially Palace, who 'knocked on, handling the ball whenever a chance was offered'. This suggests it was a feature of the home side's play, despite all use of 'hands' having been struck out of the F.A. rules long since.

On the afternoon of Wednesday 23rd November 1870, the footballers of Crystal Palace played the 'celebrated' Wanderers FC on the Kennington Oval, no score resulting, these being the Palace players ;-

D. Allport, Charles J. Chenery, F. Soden, F. Abell, F. Luscombe, A. Lloyd, James Turner, Alexander Morton, E. Spreckley, J. Fletcher, A. Bouche.

The return game, also at the Oval, was played on Wednesday 17th January 1871, when Crystal Palace and Wanderers could muster only 15 men between them. Almost a different 'team' of eight men lost by 3-0 to a Wanderers 'seven'. The Palace eight included W. Allport, F. Alpe, F. Soden, C.F. Maurice, C. Farquhar, C.J. Smith.

Reporting the fixtures for the leading London clubs for season 1866-67, the *Sportsman* paper listed regular weekly games for teams such as Wanderers, Westminster, Forest, but only a handful of games for the Crystal Palace club, and almost all were at home. Indeed, apart from an opening match between club members on Saturday 24th October, only home and away matches against Barnes, Reigate and the Wanderers were on their fixture card for the whole season, with no more than two matches a month arranged.

The representatives of the Crystal Palace club sent in a proposal for an amendment to the F.A. regulations 3 and 4 on 1st February 1868, which was duly passed, and related to lowering the membership fees. An annual fee of one Guinea (£1/1/0d) had existed from 1863, and this in itself was too costly for many provincial clubs; Palace suggested five shillings or half a crown for associate membership. Additionally, they proposed that the F.A. committee number twenty, with five forming a quorum, again passed.

Playing around 1860, the following men were leading players who also played a part in formulating the laws of the game when attending early F.A meetings. Francis Day, born Westerham, Kent in 1838 (the same village where Alice Liddell, Lewis Carroll's muse died) and was the owner of the Black Eagle brewery in Bermondsey. He then took over his fathers business with footballing partner Wickham Noakes. James Turner, a wine merchant, became the first president of the Royal College Of Veterinary Surgeons, and was treasurer of the Football Association during 1864-68. Shipping insurer Henry Lloyd lived only to be 28 and was brother-in-law to James Turner. Two other brothers including stockbroker Theodore all played for Crystal Palace, with Theo refereeing the 1873 England-Scotland match. Fred Urwick was a local wine merchant, indigo-merchant John Louis Siordet was of Swiss origin, although born in Clapham, and accountant Lawrence Vivian Desborough lived and worked all over the world, including New Zealand, Bombay and Egypt, where he died in 1892 *(Andy Mitchell, scottishsporthistory.com)*.

Suggesting that they were a competent side, they entered the inaugural English Cup competition, and immediately made a name for themselves (well, with historians, anyway) by reaching the semi-finals. A goal-less draw with Hitchin (f.1865) saw both teams go through under the unusual rules of the competition at the time. A clear win by 3-0 over Maidenhead in round 2 saw them matched against the Wanderers in the 3rd round. Yet again, another stalemate enabled both clubs to progress in the next round, where, finally, the Royal Engineers proved too strong for them, and by 3-0. The Morning Post had little to say about the match, played on the Kennington Oval on the afternoon of Tuesday 12th March 1872, save that "the Engineers had the best of it". Remarkably, it was announced that Engineers would meet the Wanderers at the same venue in 3 day's time to contest the final ! So much for cup final preparation week. The Palace team that day was -

A. Martin

D. Allport (captain)

W.M. Allport   **D.M.Armitage**

A.Bouch W.Bouch F.Chappell E.J.Chenery E.J.Lloyd P.S.Rougnet F.Spreckley

The result was somewhat predictable as Palace had lost 1-3 to Engineers in the previous month when they met on the 14th February in a friendly, when T. Allport scored their goal.

In November 1872, England arranged to play Scotland at the West of Scotland cricket ground, and Palace men Charles Chenery and 40 year-old goalkeeper Alexander Morton were selected to play, although Morton had to withdraw being injured. Morten's debut was not long in coming, and he captained his country at the second International the following season, along with Robert Kingsford, who also played for Wanderers. Two more Palace men were called up in 1876, again to face Scotland, when keeper Arthur Savage and centre forward Charles Smith made their debut, and even the match was umpired by Palace man James Turner, a slightly built man. Arthur Savage by comparison being a tall, well built bewhiskered fellow. On the eve of the Scotland v England game of March 5th 1876 he was described as "a very good goalkeeper with a strong kick" by the *Athletic News*.

By the mid-1870s, almost every type of sporting and leisure activity could be found at the Crystal Palace ground, including curling, ice skating, lacrosse, pigeon racing, hockey, sailing and ball sports. It was home to many organisations including the Surrey Bicycle Club, the Crystal Palace Cricket Club, the Imperial Bicycle Club, several bands and orchestras and horticultural, athletic, choral and operatic and aquatic societies. In short, it was the main amusement zone for most Londoners, and day-trippers from elsewhere.

The following season, 1872-3, Palace again looked forward to the English Cup, but had the misfortune to meet possibly the best team in the country that year - Oxford University, who edged past them by 3-2. Oxford, with wonderful men such as Walpole Vidal, Ottoway, Birley, and Chappell-Maddison, went all the way and were unlucky to lose the final to Wanderers by 2-0. Whether Oxford would have beaten Queens Park in the semi-final (the Scotsmen scratched, unable to travel down on the appointed day), remains a moot point, but in the following year, they came back to win it.

More bad luck followed in 1873, when they pulled the Swifts out of the hat. Swifts would (in the 1880s) become one of the best amateur teams in the country, but still had the edge in 1873, and won by 1-0, and went on to reach the semi-finals. 1874 saw another 1st round exit, this time by 1-2 to Cambridge University on Parker's Piece, after the first match had been goal-less. Crystal Palace finally emerged through to the 2nd round in the winter of 1875 when they defeated the footballers of the 105th Regiment by 3-0 in a replay, on November 20th at the Oval thanks to goals by Neame, Smith and Barlow. The first match had been a goal-less draw on 6th November at the Crystal Palace ground, the Regiment having only recently moved to Aldershot from Sheffield (*The Morning Post*). Their reward was to once again meet the Wanderers, who had little difficulty in winning 3-0, and indeed, they went on to beat Old Etonians 3-0 (after a 0-0) and win the Cup. A silver plated glass bottom pint tankard recently came up for auction and raised £550 at a London auction house. Inscribed " to captains Allport and Neame, season 1873-4, 'big-side matches". This phrase, used at the leading public schools, usually alluded to the rugby game, when 15 or more a side would be used. This suggests that Crystal Palace tried their hand at both codes. Crystal Palace continued to play ordinary friendly fixtures during the second half of the 1870s. On Saturday 23rd October 1875, *The Graphic* simply stated that Clapham Rovers had defeated them by 4-1 at Balham, giving no further details.

When two Crystal Palace men were selected for the 1876 England-Scotland game in March, the *Athletic News* said of forward C.E. Smith "he is the best forward from his team". Goalkeeper Maynard was relied upon for safe hands and a good strong clearance kick.

Crystal Palace FC played on the cricket ground area which was very flat.

For their annual general meeting held in September 1876, the footballers of Crystal Palace assembled at the Crystal Palace Inn, where the following officers were elected :-

president - J.S. Noakes, vice president - A. Moorhouse, treasurer - J. Lockwood, team captain and honorary secretary - John Marsh, match secretary - H. Coldwell. In addition, a committee of eleven was voted in. The club was looking forward to a good season, and so we know they lasted until perhaps 1877, although no more of their matches were reported in the papers after their 0-3 defeat to Wanderers on December 11th 1876. When player Charles Eastlake Smith was chosen to play for England against Scotland in March 1876, his name became added to the many single-capped footballers. It is thought that the footballers were told that they could no longer use the ground for football, possibly because of new owners taking over the sporting side. Strange then, that in the 1890s, the Crystal Palace grounds became the new home for the F.A. Cup Finals, with both the Corinthians (1897-1905 & 1922-1937) and the Casuals (1922-1925) also making it their home ground.

The famous Crystal Palace football ground took on greater importance after 1893, as the cricket authorities of the Kennington Oval refused to allow football there after the summer of that year, and clubs like the Corinthians switched to the Queens Club in West Kensington, and the Cup Final was played for twenty years at the Palace, which itself was only superseded by the building of the national stadium at Wembley in 1923. Another displaced club which had to find a new home was the well-known side the Old Westminsters, long-since dismissed from Vincent Square. Unable to play at the Oval, they moved to a new ground at 'Wembley-park, where Edward Watkins new tower is to be built'. The move seemed to suit them well, for they thrashed no less a team than the Swifts by 13-2 in their ground debut game in October 1893.

Curiously, on Saturday 30th November 1895, a 'new' Crystal Palace amateur club was founded, and to the delight of the suffering south Londoners, who since the closure of the Oval, had not been able to witness a top-class game. A match against Aston Villa (!) was arranged to kick-start the club, with a team chosen by N.L. Jackson (of the Corinthians) . The amateurs did very well to be holding Villa to 3-3 until the last fifteen minutes, when they collapsed and conceded four to lose by 3-7. Now if you check with today's Crystal Palace FC, they say they were formed in 1905 by J.H. Cozens, general manager of the Crystal Palace Company with the help of legendary sportsman Charles Burgess Fry. So my discovery of an 1895 'Crystal Palace' throws a spanner into the works! The Crystal Palace Company went bankrupt in 1909, and there was talk of the State taking over it as a national park, as there was an annual turnover of two million visitors. Further prestigious matches were arranged for this new Crystal Palace FC of 1895-6; on 3rd September 1896, a Germany XI came over, and Sheffield Wednesday, Dundee, Derby, Wolves, Bolton, Nottingham Forest and several leading Old Boys clubs were lined up to attract the crowds for the new football team. Clearly something happened which caused this unreported venture to be swiftly brought to an end, but I could find no reports of it in the London papers.

The magnificent Crystal Palace buildings were famously burned to the ground in 1936, in London's biggest fire. Today, the Crystal Palace National Sports Centre occupies the location of the old Cup Final football ground, although the current pitch in the middle of the athletics track is off-centre and to the right of the original one, and is only about two thirds of the old massive ground which was bigger than the Wembley Stadium, built in 1923 to replace it. Edwardian images of Crystal Palace with 120,000 spectators show acres of space for tens of thousands more, and in my opinion, it would have been better to have spent the money building new stands and facilities at Crystal Palace, and we would not have had the White Horse fiasco final! The Crystal Palace ground, with its vast natural ampitheatre, high banked ends and strange 'V' formation stands always had more 'romance' about it than the purpose-built and less capacious Wembley Stadium. The backdrop of the tall switchback fun-fair, and the breathtaking splendour of Paxton's glass palace, made Crystal Palace my favourite football ground above any other. In a strange twist of fate, today's Crystal Palace (a Premiership team as I write) have submitted plans to redevelop the not-so-old National Athletics stadium (built in 1960 on the old cup final ground) and move into a 40,000 capacity all purpose stadium there.

The Crystal Palace grounds, showing the two vast arenas, each capable of holding around 150,000 spectators. Football was played to the left, athletics events on the right side. The Crystal Palace Athletic Stadium sits almost exactly on the left of the picture, where the old Cup Finals used to be played before the days of Wembley Stadium.

A rare presentation tankard from the original club.
(With kind permission from Bonham's)

FOREST FC

Founded - 1859, reformed 1868
Folded - 1864, again about 1875
Grounds - Forest School :Georges Lane, Leytonstone and the Green in front of
Forest School;
Forest FC 1. Field at rear of the Merchant Seaman Orphans Asylum,
E11.
2. Public open space on Leyton Flats after 1868
3. George Lane, Woodford 1869-1870 (school grounds?)
Colours - 1860s Red with white pinstripe
- 1870s Scarlet fronts, black at the rear (including trousers and caps!)

A letter to the *Sportsman* paper in January 1867 from a man named Peter Pangloss tells of how he used to travel on the Great Eastern Railway to Leytonstone, where he used to watch the 'manly efforts of the alas! now defunct Forest club'. Where does he now go, he asks, to watch good football? Should he stand by the Thames and watch the Barnes club, the Wanderers in Battersea Park, the Crystal Palace or the Richmond clubs, all of whom he says 'have afforded me much pleasure'. Instead, he went to watch Blackheath play the Richmond club, and was aghast to see that for more than half the game, 'the ball was in the arms of the players'. At one point, the ball never touched the ground for ten minutes during which time, players indulged in kicking each others' legs and shins repeatedly. He concluded that such 'football' should be re-named 'hand-ball' and thus he invited a public discussion through the media of the press to take place. Directly underneath the missive, the editor had inserted a letter from the F.A., reminding member clubs that any proposal alteration of the rules were to be sent by letter before February 1st to the secretary R.W. Willis at his address of 7 Billiter Street, E.C.1. The F.A. then took the opportunity to list the current set of playing rules, and reminded clubs that their one guinea fee entitled them to send two representatives to monthly meetings. Goals were fixed at eight feet by eight yards, with a tape across the top; throw-ins were to be returned at right angles to the field (soon to be altered to any direction and using both hands). Interestingly, four years after the founding of the F.A., the 'touch-down' was still part of the rules, wherein a ball sent wide of the goal, if touched down first by an attacking player, will be called a touch-down, but only count in the event of no goals being scored in the match. This today would simply be a goal-kick.

Even though Alcock was writing for the *Sportsman* newspaper, no reports of any Forest matches could be found between 1859 and 1862, suggesting that they played matches between their own members for pleasure and exercise (even though Forest School had begun to play other clubs in 1861). I believe this would have been on the recently cleared part of southern Epping Forest which is today called Leyton Flats. Forest's first game against outside opposition seems to be when they met the Crystal Palace club at home on 15th March 1862, winning 1-0. During 1863, Forest won all of their 9 matches, scoring an impressive 30 goals, conceding only once all season. By playing matches for their own enjoyment on public land, Forest no doubt attracted the curious interest of perhaps between twenty and a hundred spectators, as later matches alluded to 'a fair number of spectators'; indeed when Forest went to Charterhouse school, they took about twenty followers with them - the advent of the first 'away fans?'.

On Saturday 21st March, Forest brought their 1862-63 season to a close, when they again entertained the Crystal Palace club at Leytonstone. In a two-hour long match, Forest went a goal behind after ninety minutes, but Charles Alcock came through with two individual goals in the last half hour to win the game 2-1 'amid great applause', and put a happy seal on Forest's unbeaten season. This suggests a home following perhaps in the low hundreds. At this time, it has been suggested that their shirts closely resembled that of Harrow school, a peculiar pin-striped loose shirt and knickerbocker outfit which brings to mind a certain Andy Pandy. For anyone under forty, ask your mum!

Even *Bells Life* carried no reports of the earliest Forest games, although they did run adverts from club secretary Alfred William Mackenzie appealing for opponents to come forward, as by 1863, only Forest, Barnes and Crystal Palace were playing to strict F.A. rules.

Although two demonstration matches had been organised between the top 22 players from the London area in the new year of 1864, Forest and Barnes beat them to it, by playing each other to the new universal 1863 rules at Christmas. Despite frequent stops to refer to the rulebook (!) the game was played amicably, with Forest winning 1-0.

Below, a remarkably early football report on the match between Barnes and the Forest clubs, when "only thirteen men" turned out for the oarsmen. Forest, winning 1-0, managed with only twelve men, and afterwards avowed to use the new Football Association rules henceforth, having played to Harrow rules previously.

FOOTBALL.

FOREST CLUB v BARNES.

The return match between these clubs came off on Saturday, Dec 12, at Leytonstone, the ground of the Forest Club. Fifteen on a side were to have played, but owing to accidental circumstances the Barnes collected only thirteen, while but twelve met for the Forest. Play commenced at about a quarter to three, the Forest Club winning the toss for goals. The game was a very spirited one, and after about an hour's hard play the Forest Club obtained a goal. This was the only one got during the game, and thus victory rested with the Forest Football Club. The Barnes men played a good game, and strove hard to obtain a goal, but without success. There was some talk about the rules upon one or two occasions, and we regret to say some little temper displayed. This shows the good of the new rules drawn up by the Football Association, for when they have come into universal use, games can be played without dispute. We have much pleasure in stating that the Forest Club have resolved "That the rules of the Football Association be the rules of this club, and be used on all occasions with the exception of such matches as are already arranged."

Founded for season 1858-59 season, by the Alcock and Thompson sets of brothers, they probably spent the first two or three seasons playing among themselves or against Forest school. A 1-0 win against the Crystal Pace club on 15th March 1862 was Forest's first match against a team from outside Leytonstone. By the end of the 1862-83 'season', Forest FC had played 9, won 9, with 30 goals scored and just one conceded. Forest defended a claim that they had never yet been defeated (although they didn't exactly tour the metropolis) until their offspring the Wanderers defeated them in late 1864.

Forest FC were busy, by their standards, when they played three matches in the first few weeks of 1864. *Bells Life* reported that they had met Kings College fifteen on the club grounds at Leytonstone, where goals by Tebbut (variously spelt with and without two 't's) and Absolom gave them a 2-0 win "played before a large muster of spectators". This probably means around two hundred since the population of Leytonstone and nearby hamlets was 2,200 in 1861. On January 6th, they went over to play Harrow and even took some followers with them. The ground could hardly have been in a worse condition, resulting in the usual 0-0 result, with players soon splattered in thick mud. Referring again to the difference in the way the game was played regionally, the report said that despite a bad and new ground, and strange rules, a hard fought game ended once more, goal-less, with Alcock for Forest urging that 'every man do his duty' despite boots heavy with mud, which made running impossible. The third game was when 'Thompson's XI' came to Leytonstone and played out a 2-2 draw, "on Leyton flats", an improvement on last year's defeat there. For Forest, Charles Alcock and Pardoe got the goals, with replies by Thompson and Greaves for the visitors, played in a downpour. Forest, captained by J.F. Alcock, included the Tebbut brothers, Pardoe, Cutbill, Cotton, Edwards, Finlay, Gillespie, Burnett, Jackson and Gardiner. At the time of the creation of the Football Association in London (1863) , Forest's representative at those meetings was Cowper Donne Jackson. The life and times of FA Cup creator Charles William Alcock is well known enough as to be celebrated, but his older brother John (b. 1841 Sunderland) seemed to have a life in two parts. Founder and secretary of the Forest FC, I have it that he married a prostitute, and later had her committed as insane. He fell back from public life, and brother Charles took his place on the FA committee in 1869. He died in Hertfordshire in 1910 aged 69.

As early as 1866, there were books on football. *Beeton's Standard Book Of Games & Sports*, was intended to give an account of how to play the game, and what equipment and skills were necessary; additionally it described the rules played by each college or public school. It said that the difference in rules between, say, Rugby and Winchester are 'so irreconcilably diverse from each other that no compromise can ever be possible'. Indeed, compromise between the rugby and association game was not possible, and the two codes remain apart to this day.

It is generally accepted that 'from the Forest club sprang the Wanderers' and most people say that the Forest simply changed their name to the Wanderers sometime in 1863, the foundation year for Wanderers. If so, how then did the Wanderers played Forest on 26th February 1870 at the Kennington Oval, winning by 7-0 ? This was the game when the match report commented on Forest's remarkable outfit of 'scarlet at the front, and black at the rear, from their caps to their stockings they looked a grotesque outfit'. At 7-0, and following an Alcock hat-trick, he switched sides and played for the Forest team! Forest had to borrow H.C. Poundle from the Civil Service club to make up an eleven (*Morning Post*).

This could not have been the Forest school XI, because the school colours are dark blue and light blue; indeed later that same year, on 10th December, Forest school played the Forest club on their Georges Lane ground. So clearly not only were Forest a separate club pre-dating the Wanderers, they also continued on after key players left and formed that club. It seems that Forest were playing in the late 1850s, folded at the end of 1863, but were active again for the start of the 1868-9 season. Perhaps that letter from Peter Pangloss was the catalyst for Forest to re-form?

Founded in 1834, some form of school football was played during the 1840s but cricket and hockey prevailed during the 1850s. Forest school played an important role in the development of both football and rugby in England in the 1860s, mainly due to the new headmaster, Frederick Barlow Guy, appointed in 1857, promoting the healthy virtues of football, resulting in the school team becoming difficult to beat, due to daily practices. The school had its own rules until 1867, and expected any visiting teams to play to them. The earliest recorded game against outside opposition was on 16th November 1861 when they lost 0-3 to a Westminster School eleven calling themselves the 'Bouncing Bricks'. Two Foresters, Henry Tubb and W. Cutbill were on the committee which formulated the first rules issued by the Football Association in 1863. When they competed in the F.A. Cup in 1875, the school were beaten for the only time that season by Oxford University, and had otherwise only conceded two goals in their fourteen matches. Whilst still at school (!) Forest player Percy Fairclough played for Essex against Berkshire in 1877 in a match played on the Upton Park ground in West Ham park. The school continued to compete in the cup until the 1878-9 season, and to this day, remain the only school to have played in the F.A. Cup.

Forest school themselves were actually quite a formidable outfit, especially at home, where they were rarely beaten, even by teams of men. The school team played its matches on the rough Common in front of the school, and thus is a very important location in the cradle of early football .Using an unlimited amount of players in the 1850s, although with cricket and hockey the favoured sports, 'soccer' did not rise to the ascendancy until about 1858. Old oak trees lined the common, and an old iron railing fence marked the northern 'goal'. The roughness of the field matched the roughness of the boy's exuberance and legendary battles between individuals were played out over the years, one such being Charles Alcock's mauls with school captain F.J. Poole, where the object seemed to be 'to hell with the ball and hoist the antagonist over the railings'! Forest School were playing other nearby outfits as early as 1861, although their own school rules, used for home matches, were later described as 'a mix of Harrow, Rugby and Charterhouse rules'. Sounding progressive, dribbling was encouraged, whilst the rougher elements of tripping and shinning were outlawed.

In April 1867, Forest school trounced Upton Park 6-0, although the school, as did other public schools, used their own peculiar version of the rules, and this was commented upon in several of their home games, where visiting sides had lost 'because they were not acquainted with the Forest school code'. When Forest school drew 0-0 with the Crystal Palace club on the school grounds in December 1867, no reference was made to the rules, but the Sportsman remarked that the school team had won all but three of their games that year, and that the team captain, Henry Tubb had been training the team for success. Considering that in the 1860s, the general idea in football was simply to enjoy oneself, and to demonstrate fancy kicking and clever dribbling runs, then this concept of co-ordinated team play and daily training seems revolutionary. It was no wonder then, that when the boys left school and formed teams such as the Forest and Old Foresters, that they became successful outfits. It was a remarkable achievement that virtually all of Forest School's fixtures were against teams of older men, and that they were rarely defeated.

Returning to the 0-7 defeat at the hands (or feet) of the Wanderers, this was said to be the first game played 'according to the new no-handling rules'. A hat-trick from Alfred Baker had propelled Wanderers into a five goal lead, and so Charles Alcock switched sides, and played the last quarter of an hour on the Forest team! Baker, the leading Wanderers goalscorer, also played for the No-Names club from Kilburn, alongside his two brothers, H.J. and W.F. , and No-Names also included Arthur and George Pember, and C.M. Tebbut, a Wanderers regular.

With no such thing yet as player contracts, or any rules which restricted a man to one particular team, players were free to turn out for as many teams as his enthusiasm and limbs would allow, and sometimes, a team would consist of half the men from another. The short lived 'Flying Dutchmen' club, when playing against Westminster school in February 1868 contained names such as R.W.S. Vidal (Westminster, Oxford University, Wanderers), Charles Alcock (Old Harrovians, Harrow Chequers, Wanderers), Charles Tebbut (Forest, Wanderers) and H. Stephenson (Westminsters, Wanderers) and Harold B. Dixon (Wanderers). It was almost as if, when a team such as Wanderers couldn't raise a full team, then those who were willing to play, would contact another group of men, and create a new team, to which they gave frivolous names. A Forest player who continued on to play for the Wanderers was Alfred Westwood Mackenzie. A local man, born in 1840, he became an insurance manager with the Guardian Insurance Company. With his brother Sir Morrell Mackenzie, he was a co-founder of the London Throat Hospital. Alfred was invited to the F.A Jubilee dinner in 1913, where he was presented with a silver casket.

As late as 1887, when the Swifts of Slough were one of the top amateur teams in the country, the Forest School held them to a 1-1 draw, Stevens for the boys equalising Dr. Smith's earlier goal. In March 1868, Forest school played 'the Old Foresters' on the 28th at Walthamstow. Whether this was a properly set up old boys club, or just a tag to give to the returning ex-pupils is uncertain. Even the Wanderers couldn't beat the school team, when both of their fixtures were draws, 1-1 and 0-0 that season. In October 1868, the *Sportsman* reported that 'the Forest Club, a few years ago being one of the most prominent of the dribbling club, has been revived under the management of P.G. Rouquette* (captain) and R. Piper (treasurer and secretary). I traced a Philip Gracchus Rouquette, born June 1846 in Clapham, and listed as a Walthamstow banker in 1881, who fits the profile, and he had five brothers, one of whom was Henry Seymour (see below), and thus, aged 22, I feel this is our man. Philip died in Henley in 1924. Players for the revival included J. Conquest, A. Frost, A. Lloyd, Charles M. Tebbut, J.M. Townsend, W. Man jnr. *"The old field in front of Forest Place at Snaresbrook would continue to be used"*. This probably means that Forest disappeared (by changing their name to Wanderers) after the autumn 1864 and reformed in September 1868. I spotted that unusual surname* once more in 1878, when one H.S. Rouquette was a judge at the sports day of the Walthamstow football and cricket club. In 1870, Forest opened the season with a trip to play Woodford Wells, who were a fifteen-a-side rugby team, Forest taking only ten men, were ran somewhat ragged, but managed a draw, both sides 'touching down once but failing to convert the kick at goal'. In completed contradiction to the modern rugby game, where the try is all-important, and the converted place kick merely add an extra couple of points, it was the reverse in early rugby. Touching the ball down over the opposition goal-line permitted a free-kick at goal from a point fifteen yards back on the field. The ten-man Forest team that day bore no resemblance to its early days -

	H. Masterman	
L. Phillips		J. Gibson
W. Bouche		Piper

| H. Fowler | H. King | J. Kolle | T. Spreckley | F. Walters |

"The Forest club met the Wanderers club *for the first time*" so said the *Sporting Life* newspaper on Wednesday 27th January 1869, referring to the previous Saturday. Beaten 3-1 at Woodford by a rather weak Wanderers eleven (only Alcock, Yates, Hooman and Vero were recognisable names), this Forest side scored through a scrimmage - L. Philips, B. Walters, L. Walters, W. Bouche, A. Bouch, J. Townsend, H. Shelton, H. Fry, J. Conquest, C. Pearson and R. Piper. William and Alfred Bouch, brothers to John, also played for the Crystal Palace club. Born in Dulwich in 1844, John Bouch (or Bouche) was a clothing wholesaler in Surbiton. He took over his father's business but it went bankrupt in 1902. His sister Jayne married Morton Peto Betts, the well-known old Harrovian Wanderer. John, along with David John Morgan, were the Forest School's representatives at the early F.A. meetings. The Danish surname of Kolle was more difficult to pin down. A Johannes Christiansen Kolle born in September 1851 and a James Kolle, born December 1853, both in Denmark, fit the age profile, but neither came to England.

Other games in 1869-70 were played against Hampstead Heathens, Upton Park, No-Names, and Clapham Rovers (lost 1-4 at George Lane), although they only seemed to play about once a month. Wanderers were again met on 5th November 1870, but since Wanderers also sent two elevens to play the Harrow School on the same day, winning the 1st team match 2-1 but losing the 2nd teams match 0-5, then it is hard to say whether the eleven which won 2-0 was a Wanderers' 3rd team. A curious snippet of information regarding the Forest ground said that "the goal with the least mountainous country was chosen which was fortified by a large bed of rushes". If this referred to the Leyton Flats site, then rushes suggest a pitch marked out near either of the two lakes; however, the venue was described as 'Woodford' which is a mile north of Snaresbrook, but there are no lakes or ponds at that place. The Forest School ground at George Lane, was described as being in Woodford in a match against Clapham Rovers, and it seems that at least three different district names were given to the same place.

Adding further confusion to the 'Snaresbrook scene' was the formation in October 1876 of the Old Foresters football club, membership being exclusive to former pupils of Forest school. Their first secretary was A. W. Letts. Their inaugural match was at Walthamstow against the Ramblers FC, winning 2-0. Foresters could possibly have been either a re-formed Forest Club, or that they simply changed their name to the Old Foresters, since after 1876 Forest were no longer heard of. The Old Foresters quickly became the premier team in Essex, and after winning the Essex Senior Cup in 1884, 1885, and 1886, they withdrew to 'give somebody else a chance'. They disbanded in 1894 but reformed and play to this day in the Arthurian League in the school colours. For more on the Old Foresters, P.C. Adams wrote a small centenary book in 1976 entitled *From Little Acorns*, ISBN 978-0950553108. The last match I could find for Forest in the 1871-2 season, was when they played Wanderers at the Oval on Wednesday 22nd March. Ambling on to the field at 4pm, they lost 1-2 to a Wanderers team which had just finished playing Upton Park immediately beforehand! This was the Forest side that day -

P.J. Rouquette, J. Kirkpatrick, W. Bouche, E.D. Chave, W.R .Dent, E .Fry, M. Jutsum, H. Masterman, B. Piper, F. Poole, H. Shelton, T. Spreckley.

The unusual surname of Masterman seemed exclusive to the county of Dorset, but having searched the records, I found no one born between 1845 and 1855 with that initial who even left Dorsetshire. Millner Jutsum also played for the Upton Park club during 1877-79, and became a solicitor. In January 1872, Forest went over and played the Upton Park club, but owing to heavy rain through the night, saw just six of their men turn out by the kick-off, and Forest had all the play but at the call of time had capitulated to a 0-0 draw. The Forest eleven was much different to the above match, with William Bouch now as captain, and the rest of the side being A. Bouch, A. Lloyd, H. Skelton, H. Masterman, G. Fleet, C. Armitage, B. Ridgway, C. Kolle, Morton Betts.

The Green in front of Forest School was a favourite place for young footballers like Arthur Kinnaird and Morton Betts to learn the game of football at a time when it still resembled a rugby match with few rules!

So where *exactly* did the Forest football club play their matches? Well it seem to me that no-one has actually bothered to find out, and that is my particular interest. Most books will tell you 'near the Merchant Seaman's Orphanage Asylum' and that today, that building is Snaresbrook Crown Court. Therein lies the first red herring; there were, remarkably, *two Orphanages* in Snaresbrook in the Victorian era, and two often get mixed up. Snaresbrook, little more than a hamlet of Leytonstone 150 years ago, grew around the staging post of the Spread Eagle hotel. The railways came through in 1856, by which time, the Wanstead Infant Orphans Asylum had been built in 1843 near the Eagle at a huge cost with railway benefactor's money. Later, in 1862, on the other side of the main road to Norwood, the aforementioned Merchant Seaman's Orphans Asylum was built along with its own chapel, both building are extant, as the Orphanage became a Convent in 1921, and in 1937 the buildings became Wanstead Hospital. Due to rising maintenance costs, the Orphanage was transferred to a new site at Wokingham in Kent. The Wanstead Orphanage became the Royal Wanstead School, and in modern times, the Snaresbrook Crown Court, the largest such in England. So there we have our first distinction: there were two different orphanages. Maps of the 1860s show a five acre field right below the Seaman's Orphanage, by Nightingale Farm, and this ticks two of the boxes of site descriptions we have, namely ' a field next to the Seamans Orphanage' and as it sat exactly north-south, also allows for a match description which said 'the visitors kicked off with the sun full in their eyes' (i.e goalpost facing due east-west). Orchard Close today occupies part of that field, a hundred yards to the right of the old Wanstead Hospital.

Well that seemed to be that, until I found the actual advert placed by honorary secretary Alfred Mackenzie in the *Sportsman* on Thursday 29th October 1868, when he informed the reader that the Forest FC were reforming, and crucially that they would *use the old ground in front of Forest Place, Leytonstone*. Well, here was a spanner in the works, for sure, but I thought that with the name of a road to go on, I would find this location without any trouble. I was so wrong - it took me a week to discover that 'Forest Place' was not a street, but the name given to a group of properties built circa 1860 at the bottom of Whipps Cross Road (the A114, then known as Assembly Road, after the Assembly House). Luckily, those gothic properties are still there today, near the Sir Alfred Hitchcock hotel, and the parish church of St. Andrew. 'Opposite Forest Place' therefore, gives us the land at the bottom of what's left of Epping Forest, known today as Leyton Flats; a recreational area criss-crossed with many old paths, yellow gorse bushes and old trees. Checking back to maps of 1850 and 1881, there were only two main paths extant at the time, and thus the Forest FC probably played on the area between those two paths. This places this location halfway between the A114 and the Wanstead Orphanage, on common grazing land. The odd thing

With much of Leyton Flats covered in scrub land and ancient trees, only the flat section facing a group of houses known as Forest Place would have been suitable for Forest FC to play their football.

is; at the rears of the Forest Place dwellings, there were two large fields, both tree-lined, totalling 13 acres. Now why would a football team chose to play on rough and sandy-marshy common land when they could have better rented on one of the fields behind the houses instead? Adjacent to the fields was a large country house, Wallwood House, which probably owned the land, and stood until the 1930s where are now Chadbrook and Ashbridge Roads. Those two fields are now Maple and Dyson Roads by St. Andrews church. The Leyton Flats are today heavily criss-crossed with several time-worn pathway, but maps of 1865 show only two distinct paths, but wherever you position a rectangle of say 100 yards x 70 yards, a path runs through the middle of it. Both Leytonstone and Snaresbrook stations (1856) are within half a mile.

Epping Forest, once a 6,000 acre royal hunting ground, had suffered heavily during the early 19th century, as land had been illicitly seized and fenced in, with homes being built on the land, which by 1870 was down to 600 acres. Eventually, something was done about it, and in 1878, the Epping Forest Act handed control from the manor to the Crown. Despite first hand information, this Forest Place 'ground' does not fit the Merchant Orphanage description, whose goals faced east to west, and thus I believe that Forest had two separate grounds, as described. Frequent match descriptions talk about the heavy mud of the ground, and as Leyton Flats were sandy and boggy, with nearby lakes formed soon after the football years, this second site meets post 1868 descriptions. Finally, the only known photo of the Forest FC shows them in a field which has some sort of cultivated shrubbery or bush as a backdrop. This is not the natural fauna of Epping forest, which features gorse bushes and sandy scrub land, and thus I think that the 1863 photo is from their Merchant Orphanage field. The phrase 'use the old ground' also suggests to me that Alf Mackenzie didn't mean the 1863 field, or might have said 'the usual ground', or the 'same ground'; and his meaning was that they were reverting back to playing on public open spaces once more.

The only known picture of the Forest football team.

Note the structures in the background, the pathway, the seemingly well trimmed grass, and the use of chairs, unlikely if the above was taken on Leyton Flats, and I believe this location was the field adjacent to the Merchant Seaman's Asylum, erected in the year before this photo was taken in 1863. The young Alcock brothers, John and Charles, stand to the left of centre, John in dark trousers. Most of them are wearing a turban-style cap with a tassel, whilst Arthur Cutbill on the right appears to be in a bowler hat. At least three men appear to be wearing the unique pyjama-style striped outfit of Harrow school, depicted as a pink-red colour in *Historical Kits* website.

In the 1890s, a new and possibly connected team, Forest Swifts began to play matches on Grove Green, Leytonstone.

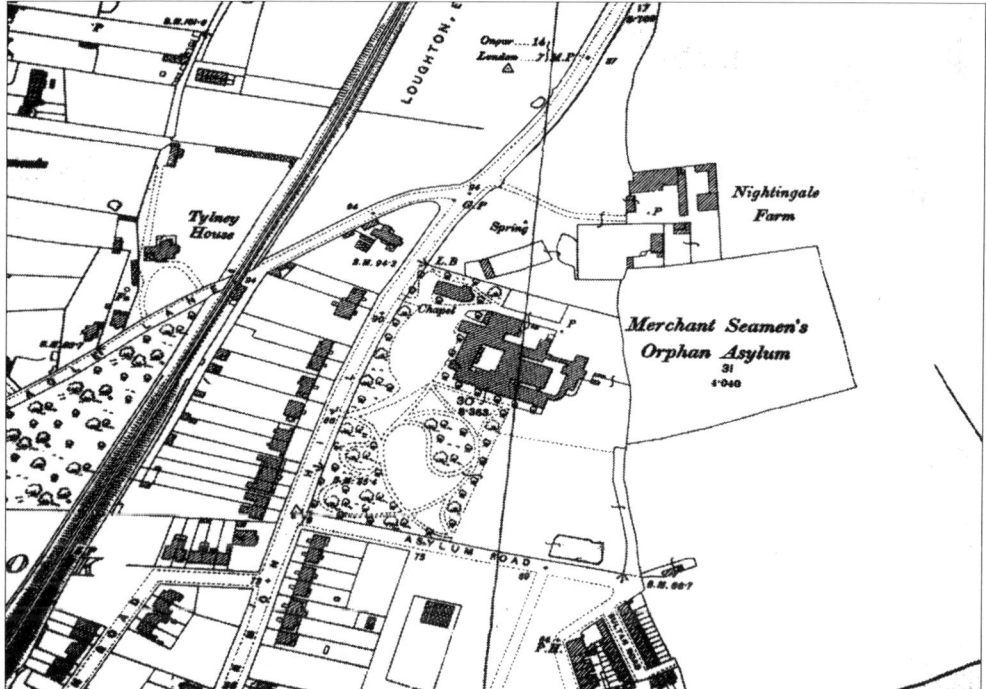

One of two probable sites where the Forest FC, and possibly the Wanderers in their first season under the new name.

GITANOS FC

Founded - Circa 1866
Folded - Circa 1881
Colours - Hoops of white, mauve and red
Ground - Nomadic, see text

Little, if anything is known about the Gitanos club, other than the name is the Spanish word for Gypsy, and you will probably read about them here for the first time. Likely to have played in any one of several London public parks in the early 1870s, Gitanos were recorded as playing at the 'Princes Cricket Ground, Hans-place, Sloane Street in 1875' with the additional information that Gitanos were formed by members of the Civil Service in London. Imposing properties began to be erected around the private square between 1877 and 1888.

You can already guess that the 'Princes Ground' in Knightsbridge has long since been built over; not that Gitanos owned it (merely played in it), but if they did, they would be trillionaires by now as it was gradually built over with exclusive five storey terraced properties being Cadogan Square, Clabon Mews and Lennox Garden Mews, with what little remained being left as Lennox Gardens, as a private park. I believe that Lord Cadogan still owns this prime location, where apartment prices are typically £6 million, and that his family have owned the land for several hundred years. If you want the whole building, then expect to lay out over £25 million. *Murray's Handbook to London, 1867* says that ' the Princes Cricket Ground was a fashionable resort during the season, where tennis is also played. Membership is one shilling, and one lady guest may be admitted'. Its perimeter was about 650 yards, and the ground was quite level and flat. The associated building, once the Princes Club, appears to still be there as No.16 Cadogan Square. This use of a private park in the heart of London, suggests a club of wealthy individuals who played purely for their own enjoyment, not particularly encouraging spectators, although the well-heeled promenaders who were walking their ladies in the park, would surely have paused to watch with some amusement. The cricket ground, in its day, was one side of the park, and stretched from the back of Stanley Street (now called Ovington Street) eastwards to St. Simon's church (extant on the corner of Moore and Milner Streets), and thus the wooded Lennox Park marks the western edge of the old cricket ground. Reconstructing Princes cricket ground using modern mapping tools, I estimate the area to have been 5.36 acres.

The earliest game I found for Gitanos was in December 1867 when they met a team called Yverdun House at Blackheath. Containing elements not yet divorced from the rugby game, goals by Thornton and Stephens secured the 2-0 win. The players' names were as follows – Lord Naas, H. Stephens, H. Manners, Lord Lewisham, A.C. Marriot, O. Daly, C. Whitmore, D. Gibbons, L. Henry, A. Thornton, and T. Duckett. As you can observe, these were no ordinary working class footballers! If I have the correct Lord Naas, his father, the 6th Earl of Mayo (Ireland) was Governor-General of India, but was assassinated on the Andaman Islands in 1872, where contemporary sketches illustrate a man in middle age. In 1867, our Lord Naas, Dermot Robert Wyndham Bourke, born 1851, would have been still only sixteen.

Again, if I have the right Lord Lewisham, William Heneage Legge, Viscount Lewisham, also born May 1851 in Westminster, became the 6th Earl of Dartmouth in 1891. Arthur (later Lord) Kinnaird was born 1847, was a little older, but again, all fit the age range of young men between 14-20.

Amongst earliest matches I could find were two games in a week against 'Bedouins' and Clapham Grammar School just before Christmas 1868, when not only did Gitanos include Lord Naas and the later Lord Kinnaird, but also H.P. Stephens and C.E. Neapan (Oxford University). Additionally, the 'Bedouins' team included E.E. Bowen and W.F. Baker (both of the Wanderers), demonstrating that teams were being created almost ad-hoc by players who couldn't get enough football without playing for different teams almost every day of the week. At the end of the 1860s Gitanos were playing Wanderers, Charterhouse School, Barnes, Harrow Pilgrims, Westminster School, whilst the cricket eleven travelled far and wide over the south-west and played matches in Dorsetshire, Hampshire, and Essex. At the end of October 1869, Gitanos suffered the inevitable 4-1 defeat when only seven of their men turn up on the ground of Upton Park FC – C.E. Neapan, H.P. Stephens, A.J. Fine, W.G. Swan, H.V. Smith, R.P. Gill, A.C. Harper and four borrowed men, suggesting that the common problem of men failing to turn up was making a mockery of what might have been. I found the answer to the problem, when I discovered that Gitanos also played the Westminster School on the same day, when a full strength eleven including Reginald Birkett and J.H. Giffard, were beaten 2-1 on Vincent Square, with yet to be famous R.W.S. Vidal scoring for the boys. In Christmas week, Gitanos lost 2-0 away to Charterhouse, when goals by Matthews and Inglis gave them the win, although it was remarked that Gitanos ran out of puff after about an hour's play *(The Sportsman)*. In March 1870, Gitanos, containing Charles Alcock, J.H. Field and captained by C.P. Stephens, were no match for Charterhouse School on their own ground, who beat them by by 3-0. Gitanos played the Wanderers at the end of November 1870 at the Oval but fielding only these eight players, they were soundly beaten by 5-0:-

> **C.E. Farmer (captain), E. Lubbock, F. Miller, E. Jones, J.S. Daley,**
> **S.A. Dasent, C. Fairfield, and D. Round.**

In the previous week, also at the Oval, they had lost 1-2 to the Civil Service FC, when both sides could only field nine men. As some players are likely to have been members of both clubs, it is likely that when 18 men turned out, they divided an equal share between them, much as is done in school playground football. Gitanos players who drew merit were captain J. Daley, J. Dasent, and the Hon. T. Pelham. Thomas Pelham (1846-1916) was the son of the Earl of Chichester, a great philanthropist and a close friend to both Arthur Kinnaird and Quintin Hogg, with whom he devoted himself to the poor youths of London, resulting in the formation of both the London Ragged School, Polytechnic, and the Boys Club Movement. Educated at Eton and Cambridge, Pelham also became the Head of the Harbours & Fisheries Board.

It appears that Gitanos also shared players with the Wanderers, although it would have been their 'lesser' men, although this Gitanos team which drew 1-1 (scorer Field) with Wanderers on Monday 17th January 1870 has a whole defence comprised of Wanderers* men :-

Quintin Hogg*

Edgar Lubbock*   **James Kirkpatrick***

J.F. Giffard* C.H. Daley Charles E. Farmer* J. Beattie J.F. Gordon   S. Field

The Morning Post also place the words Civil Service in brackets after the Gitanos name, alluding to the team comprising several men from that organisation. In the above match, the return fixture from the previous month where they had already drawn 1-1, Quintin Hogg went in goal to replace Kirkpatrick who sustained a shoulder injury. Later that same year, Gitanos played the Charterhouse School XI on the 'under-green' (as the 'high Green' was being re-turfed for the cricket season), but were beaten 3-0 with goals from Inglis, and a brace from H.V. Smith. Known more so as a Wanderers and Old Etonians player (he played in the 1872 for Wanderers and the 1875, 76 and 79 FA Cup finals for Etonians), Edgar Lubbock (1847-1907) was a tall and spindly man of high society status, who certainly played the game purely for his own enjoyment. He became a director of Whitbread Breweries, a deputy governor of the Bank of England, and a lawyer to boot. Even those achievement paled behind his father, Sir John Lubbbock, *who had his own bank.* Alcock thought highly of him as a footballer, and when used as a defender "had no rival as a back, with a useful and accurate kick". Wing-half Tom Giffard was a civil service man who worked at Somerset House in the city as an assistant to Alfred Stair (1845-1914), the head of Inland Revenue. Stair refereed three Cup Finals, and turned out for Upton Park between 1867 and 1874. Played in front of 'a great many spectators including the headmaster' this Gitanos team were described as 'the the well-know Gitanos club' :-

C.R. Daley

C.W. Alcock

H.P. Stephens (captain)   **T.H. Giffard**

T.R. Lumley E. Taylor C. Wheatley H. LeCoq E. Field G. Morgan F.R. Byng

Notice the already outdated 1-2-7 formation. One un-named player (probably Alcock) was constantly rebuked by the crowd for the outmoded habit of 'hacking' i.e. persistent kicking of opponents shins. Gitanos played the Civil Service FC on the afternoon of Wednesday 16th November 1870, when in a game described as fast and evenly matched, these nine men turned out at the Oval, losing 1-2 :-

F.R. Newcombe, J. Daly (captain), J. Dasent, the Honourable T. Pelham,
G. Holden, W.H. Turner, H. Marratt, H. Thompson, G. Hamar.

When Gitanos played Eton College in December 1870, the match was described as being 'the now annual fixture'. The *Sportsman* said of Gitanos that they 'represent to Eton what the Wanderers are to Harrow'. This gem indicates that Gitanos were a precursor to the

Old Etonians FC, who were randomly reformed until 1878, when the college followed the example by the cricketers, and made all Etonians automatic members of the football team. The Gitanos team for that match has several familiar names in it from the Wanderers :-

Stapylton, Courthope, Bonsor, Cuthell, Dasent, Farmer, Furguson, Kinnaird, Lubbock, A. Harcourt and the Honorable T. Pelham. On Saturday 1st February 1871, Gitanos played the redoubtable Royal Engineers FC on the Princes ground. In a closely contested match, where Gitanos seemed to have given as much as they got, the Sappers opened the scoring just before the break, and repeated the trick just before the call of time. Small clues about the Princes ground included 'Gitanos kicked off against the wind at the club-house end' and that goals had tapes for crossbars *(The Morning Post)*. Captained by A.P. Barlow, and with the Honourable H. Montgomery in attack, the team comprised : full back M. Farrer, half backs A.C. Thompson and W. Lindsay, and forwards J. Strong, J. Sturgess, A. Trower, J. Giffard, F. Wilson, St. J. Mildmay, and Griffith.

The Princes Ground was the cricket field of the Princes Club, a private club for London gentlemen of a certain social standing, mainly officers and civil servants, which was originally set up in Chelsea by brothers George and James in 1853, primarily as a real tennis and racquets club. A park was created in 1871 where is now Cadogan Square, when lawn tennis and croquet were added, and later cricket, when the M.C.C began to play there. The grounds became fenced in as roads were built around it after 1876, and by 1887, only a small section remained, and the club closed down. Reverting back to racquet games, a new club was opened in 1886 in Knightsbridge, which existed until the end of the Second World War.

On Saturday January 6th, 1872, Gitanos played the Civil Service at the Oval. If I said 'it was a game of two halves' you would take the wrong meaning: each side fielded just five players. On a mud-splattered pitch, the players soon became indistinguishable, as is often the case in a rugby game. It was no surprise that the game ended a 2-2 draw, with the wonderfully-named the Honourable N. de C. Dalrymple retiring hurt before the end.

Gitanos briefly played in the English (F.A.) Cup, with no success. Beaten 3-0 at the first hurdle by Uxbridge in the winter of 1873, they were never heard from again, although they did carry on for a few more years. A sometime player Edgar Field (1854-1934), an old boy of Lancing College, went on to play more famously for Clapham Rovers at the end of the 1870s, and featured in their Cup Final appearances of 1879 and 1880 in the full back position.

On 26th January 1876, Gitanos met the Civil Service club on the Kennington Oval and goals by Griffith, Birley and Charles Meysey gave them a clear 3-0 win, suggesting a certain level of competence. Saturday 23rd November 1878 saw Minerva playing in West Ham park, against the Dreadnought FC, who were just one of several teams who used that venue as a home. A year later, this Gitanos side lost 1-3 to the energetic boys of Westminster School in November 1879 when "the superior training of the boys' asserted itself" in the last half -

	W. Tayloe					
	S. Harry Goodhart			Radcliffe		
W. Carr				Hon. Alfred Lyttleton		
C. Cratchley	J. Brand	A. Catley	J. Chance	G. Nugeee	F. Govett

A match played at Eton College on 18th October 1879 saw Gitanos defeat the Etonians by 'one goal to two tries'. This sounds as though it was a match played under rugby rules, when at the time, a goal counted superior to a try (touchdown), unlike the modern rugby game where it is the other way around. Gitanos were still active going into the 1879-80 season, as they were beaten 3-1 by Westminster school on November 8th on Vincent Square.

On Saturday 17th October 1879, Gitanos "were clearly over-matched" on their visit to play the Old Etonians, and were beaten 7-1, with neither eleven containing any well-known names. I could find no trace of Gitanos as we move into the 1880s, and a footnote at the end of a Gitanos match reported in the *Morning Post* of October 28th 1878 probably provides the answer. On the previous Saturday Gitanos had played the boys of Westminster School on Vincent Square, losing 2-3, with this side -

R.W. Shepard

A.G. Churchill **Ernest Bambridge**

E.Charles Bambridge **C.W. Daley**

S.H. Goodhart H.B. Sedgwick W. Carr G.M. Nugee F.L. Govatt H. Poland

At the end of the match report, it stated that the Gitanos had '*recently amalgamated with the Old Runneymede Club*'. At the end of October 1878, Gitanos played one of their last matches when they were defeated by the boys of Eton College.

The original Princes Club Grounds occupied most of the area shown below Pont Street. It gradually lost more and more land until only the private Cadogan Square Garden is left. The area where Gitanos played football is Lennox Gardens.

One time player for Gitanos, Arthur G. Guillemard (also of West Kent FC)

GREY FRIARS FC

Founded	-	1875-6
Folded	-	Circa 1882
Ground	-	1. Greyhound Ground, Dulwich (circa 1876-8)
		2. Forest Gate, Leytonstone E.7
Colours	-	French grey and pink halves
Headquarters	-	Greyhound Inn, Dulwich (rebuilt facing as the Crown & Greyhound today)

Again, I was intrigued merely by the name, although this small and short-lived London club did take part in the F.A. Cup for a while. Thanks to research done by *Robin Horton* who ploughed through all the Charles Alcock annuals in London, we now know that Grey Friars played in exactly the same colours as did the Clapham Rovers who were around at the same time. One wonders if there was a connection between the two clubs, although I never found any players who crossed between the two. Despite existing for less than a decade, Grey Friars were in action almost every month.

Based at Forest-Gate, an area of open space which was formerly the tip of the great Epping Forest known as Wanstead Flats, Greyfriars were another gentleman amateur team who possibly started out using the old Greyhound ground which they shared with the Pilgrims among others. Forest-gate as it was shown on old maps, was merely a hamlet at the crossroads of the old Romford to London Road and the A114 which led to Leytonstone, although it was served by two small railway stations. By about 1880, Forest Gate also meant a larger area which included the Spotted Dog ground on Upton Lane, and this may have been used. Once a countryside coaching inn, surrounded by oaks and other old trees and ivy-covered, its flat and level field at the rear had been a cricket ground in the 1860s. Sadly today, the Spotted Dog pub lies boarded up and neglected, its once whiteboard coverings now peeling off, the tram-lines which served it long since torn up, and its former tranquillity now of a bygone age, surrounded as it is on all sides by tenements, shops, and the Floron rest home.

In terms of trying to identify the source of their name, I found an old church school in Reading called Greyfriars, so possibly they were old boys of that place? In the 1880s the 'Greyfriars football & cricket club' annual gatherings were held at that school. There was also an ancient small Franciscan theological college in Oxford of the same name which was disbanded as recently as 2008, which again sounds a possible source candidate.

In January 1878, Greyfriars met the St. Albans club at Forest Gate, easily winning by 5-0, *Lloyds Weekly* giving no further details. This 1878 side won handsomely by 4-0 on the Flodden Road ground of the Surrey Rifles FC on March 2nd - T.G. Stafford (captain), F. Thompson, R.G. Ellis, J. Frost, J.W. Sharpe, A. D. Stafford, R.D. Green, R.B. Sinclair, R. Cane, E.H. Bubb. Later that year, in the autumn, the Greyfriars entered the F.A. Cup where they were drawn against Great Marlow of Bucks. Marlow were already a competent team, so Greyfriars did well to win 2-1 on 9th November and enter the 2nd round, where the were drawn against London side Minerva. Played on neutral ground at the Upton park on 7th December, Greyfriars were beaten 3-0. Greyfriars looked the more likely to open the scoring, but after 25 minutes Bain broke away and scored for the home side. Turner headed in a corner kick after about an hour, and Minerva continued to repel all efforts by Greyfriars to reduce the deficit. Near the end, Frank Hearn added a third. The team was similar to that listed for the Surrey Rifles game, except that Bennett and Strensham were on the left wing, instead of Cane and Bubb, and Williams was in goal. Small changes to the 1878-9 side included Gifford in goal, Strensham and Thompson on the wing, and E.D. Ellis was now captain.

Greyfriars returned a year later and were drawn against another small London side, Hanover Athletic, whom they beat by 2-1 on November 8th 1879. Featuring Quintin Hogg and Arthur Kinnaird, those two philanthropic wealthy footballers were pioneers in the salvation of the poor and needy, and promoted the education of the working man. Hanover team played purely for exercise and enjoyment, later being renamed the Polytechnic FC, who I believe played in red and black hoops, and later halves. In round 2, Greyfriars crushed unknown side Gresham by 9-0 on December 20th to enter round 3 for the first time. Compared to 1878, entries had increased such that a 5th round had been added to the competition, and thus there were still 15 teams left at that stage. Because the fledgling F.A. still hadn't worked out how to put the byes in the early rounds thus giving a perfect 16, only eight clubs had to play off, and Greyfriars were one of the fortunate ones who got a bye. Round 4 still had the silly situation of having ten teams in it, which ultimately left the more ridiculous one of Clapham Rovers getting a semi-final bye into the Oval final. Still left in the 'hat' were the 'big four' of late 1870s football - Etonians, Engineers, Clapham and Oxford. Greyfriars were drawn against the Royal Engineers on February 18th 1880, and after a plucky performance were only beaten by one goal to nil.

Meeting Marlow on 19th January 1880, and having previously beaten each other once, interest was great to see who would win what was at the time seen as a decisive third contest. Played at the Greyhound, Dulwich, the two sides were evenly matched, and it wasn't until right winger D. Stransham scored midway through the second period, that the two sides could be separated. The team evolved into that shown below, except that W. Gifford stood in goal, Rutherford was replaced by Young, and Sharp and Kirkpatrick were replaced up front by Cane and Turner. E. D. Ellis was captain at this time.

Encouraged by this, Greyfriars entered the FA Cup again for the 1880-1 season, and were drawn against the Windsor Home Park club, whom they beat 3-1 on the Dulwich ground behind the Greyhound Inn, a week following a goal-less draw on November 13th, a game ruined by high winds and much ball chasing *(Sporting Life)*. This 1880 eleven is almost entirely different to the one listed below only two seasons later -

			J. Davies				
	A.E. Young				A.J. Frost		
	C. Broadhurst		T. Stafford			M. Turner	
E. D. Ellis	S. Thompson		E. Cane		R.D. Green	G.P. Matchett	

Round 2 saw a close game with Maidenhead, but the Forest- Gate club again emerged victorious on December 11th, scoring the only goal of the game, as their better defence held firm. Round 3 beckoned once more, and for the second time, Greyfriars drew a bye.

On the eve of their next round match, Grey Friars (as they were billed) went up and played the powerful Oxford University side at The Parks on Saturday 5th February, and the 0-3 defeat was a respectable result considering. On the 11th, Greyfriars seemed to be getting into shape for their impending cup tie with the Etonians, by playing the Old Foresters on the Forest School ground. Played on a quagmire of a field, Greyfriars were commended for managing to string some passes together, but the more experienced Foresters scraped home by 3-2. Greyfriars seemed to have a settled first eleven at this time since the only changes they made for the Foresters game was replacing Frost with P. Lockhart, Turner with Ellis at left half, Birkett for Matchett, with Fisher taking Ellis's right wing position. Stafford and Cane drew praise for 'putting in a good shift'. A Reggie Birkett had played in the first ever England international rugby match, when a game against Scotland took place on 27th March 1871, so here then, is a tenuous link between Grey Friar and Clapham Rovers. Many other clubs handed on their old kits to other clubs, and I wonder if Grey Friars didn't end up with an old Clapham kit, perhaps when they switched from hoops to halves?

The 4th round ended their run on 19th February 1881, when the eventual cup finalists the Old Etonians comfortably defeated them by 3-0 (Lloyds gives 4-0) in a tie played on the Dulwich ground (Derby Telegraph). Greyfriars, who fielded the same eleven as given above, never again competed in the national competition. There was still always the popular London Cup, and Greyfriars competed in that in their final years. At the end of Febuary 1881, when there was a general meeting of the Football Association at the Freemasons Tavern, Queen Street, London, the Grey Friars did attend and I also found them playing matches against South Norwood and Mosquitoes in March. J.H. Birkitt competed as an athlete representing the Grey Friars FC in May, June, July and August in several athletics meetings across London in the summer of 1881. However, none of the London papers had the name of Grey Friars at the start of the 1881-82 season in October.

The old coaching inn The Greyhound in Dulwich Village had a football ground at the rear which was used by several clubs until it was demolished when the owner of its rival, the Crown which faced it, bought the Greyhound then demolished both pubs in 1900 and built and new one in their stead

The last games I could find for a Greyfriars (again reinforcing the connection with the town of Reading) was when a Greyfriars 2nd team played out a 0-0 draw with Reading Minsters 3rd team at home on 28th January 1882, reported in the *Reading Mercury*. I don't think this was the original club. The two elevens had met a week before on the Minsters' Prospect Park ground, when this Greyfriars reserve team were beaten 2-0 :-

			Grumwood			
	Russell				Peters	
	Goodey				Burton	
Staveley	East	Blake	Hawes (capt)	Earley	Thorne

A map of Forest Gate at 1870 shows any number of fields available for recreational use around West Ham Hall, although the likeliest looking field is the one by Forest House. The Spotted Dog ground of Clapton and West Ham Park both lay half a mile due south, but postcards from around 1900 describe the well-used Spotted Dog ground as being on 'Upton Road, Forest Gate'. Set in a rural location with old oak trees and covered in ivy, the Spotted Dog was an old coaching inn, which, by 1905 was well served by the electric trams which allowed good access to the ground which lay behind the original inn. Used for cricket since the 1860s, the field was flat and level, and by 1900 had a white wicket perimeter fence, with a low level stand down one side of the pitch added in Edwardian times.

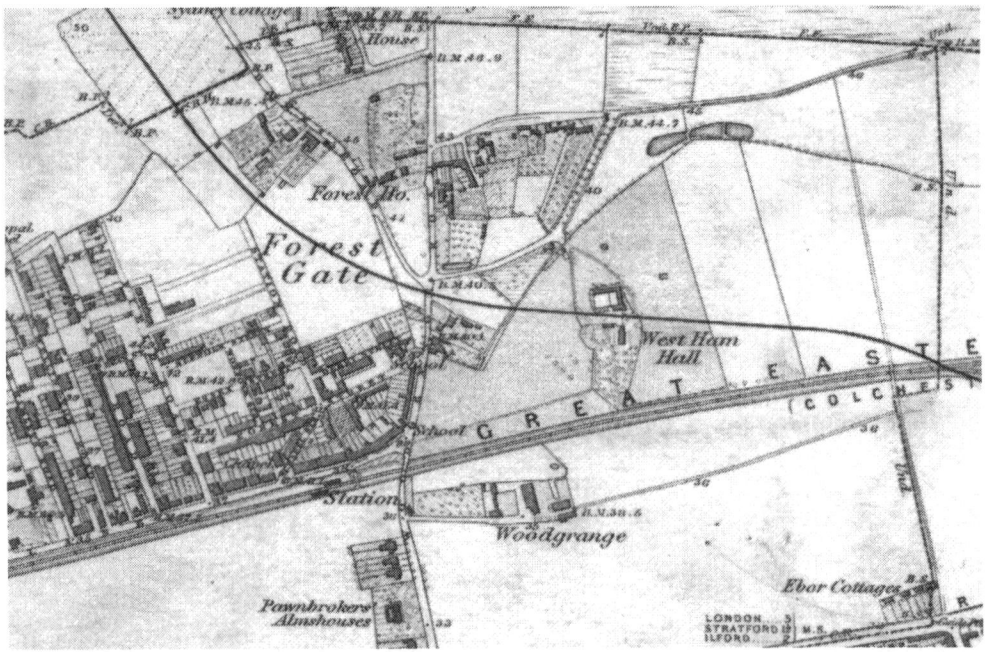

Reported in the *Berkshire Chronicle*, a Greyfriars Church team eleven from November 1881 contained none of the above names. When the Hotspur v Hendon cup tie was played in October 1883, the referee was our "Mr. E. Cane *(late of the Grey Friars FC)*". I don't know whether this implied Grey Friars had folded, or that he had simply left the club.

The Greyfriars FC name surfaced again in October 1886 in the *Berkshire Chronicle* but I cannot say if it was the same club reformed, since none of these 1886 players resonated from 1882 in their 2-0 win over Garfield FC on the Recreation ground -

		W. Lloyd		
	H. Earle		E. Stocks	
	W. Cox	C. Bargent	W. Jerome	
R. Malpass	C. Warner	A. Exall	W. Durman	J. Borden

This Greyfriars were competing in the Reading Junior Cup in the late 1880s, but by 1888 contained only four of their 1886 side, in Cox, Warner, Earle and Exall. Playing matches variously on Reading Rec and on the South Reading ground, I would guess that they originally folded in Dulwich, and a new club from their *Alma Mater* started up, probably by younger men in Reading.

A concert on behalf of "Greyfriars football and cricket club" was held on the evening of Tuesday 6th March 1888 at Greyfriars school room in Reading, Berks. The names of several ladies who provided the singing entertainments, and three or four gentlemen, were given, prominent of whom was a Fred Burton. As he appears to have been a player of Greyfriars, I must assume that the connection was that the team was formed for old boys of that school who found professional life in London.

HAMPSTEAD HEATHENS

Founded   - 1867
Folded   - Circa 1873
Ground   - Hampstead Heath common
Headquarters - Ayre Arms, St. Johns Wood. London
Colours   - All white, with black stockings (unconfirmed)

The Hampstead Heathens' secretary announced in the press in September 1868 that they would commence their second season on the 10th October, and any club desirous of organising a match with them should write to W.E. Titchener at 10 Downshire-hill, Hampstead. This allows me to report anew that their foundation date was a year earlier than currently thought. A match away to the seven man No-Names of Kilburn played 5th December 1868 was lost to a fluke goal when Arthur Baker drove a shot at the Heathens' keeper, who opened his legs and let the ball go through the posts. Despite being " notably faster and better organised" they were unable to score an equaliser.

The Heathens must have been struggling to make up a seasonal fixture-card for 1868-69 since the Sportsman newspaper had listed all the fixtures already arranged by the London area clubs, and no Heathens fixtures were on it. Additionally, there was also another club called simply 'Hampstead'and these were regularly listed as playing at Finchley Road, and yet another called 'Hampstead Club' (probably one and the same) to add confusion to things. With both rugby and association football fixtures listed mixed together at the time, it's impossible to be certain the last two were rugby or football clubs, even by looking at their opponents' names. Interestingly, Heathens' football captain, T.E. Tichener, also played rugby with the 'Hampstead' team at Finchley Road. As the Heathens' meetings were held at the Ayre Arms on Finchley Road, a hostelry next to the famous Lords cricket ground, this hints at the Hampstead (rugby?) club playing *at Lord's*.

We all know the name of the famous Wasps rugby club today, of course, but on Saturday 19th December 1868, the Wasps played Hampstead Heathens under 'association' rules. This Heathens team won by 1-0 :-

> H. Sharpe (captain), Evans, Lawford, Pitchford, J. Bouvey, Bond, Bowman, Chamberlain, P. Tatham, S. Tatham, A. Sharpe.

Infuriatingly, we do not know the Heathens' colours (although I thought I read somewhere that they were all white with black stockings), yet when the Wasps were founded, they declared colours of black and yellow hoops. As with many other early clubs, they would have relied on wearing their own coloured caps to identify them from the opposition. As was often the case, it is reasonable to assume that the club was founded by their captain, Henry Sharpe. Whichever section of Hampstead Common they played on, the land was subject to poor drainage, comprised as it was typically of a ten foot depth of fine yellow and red sand over a bed of waterproof London clay, causing large areas of marshy ground to form. A nearby club, No-Names of Kilburn, would have also been operating less than a mile away due west. The opening of the Hampstead Heath railway station in 1860 would have helped visiting teams travelling to play them.

Lending visitors the Old Wykehamists five men who were members of both clubs, Hampstead Heathens were defeated 1-0 at home on 16th January 1869 when a goal by Lindsay decided the issue. All four Latham brothers turned out for the home side, who were captained by W. Banting, with Sharpe absent. The same thing had happened the previous Saturday, when the No Names turned up with only 6 men, Heathens lending them two of their own players until half time when the missing visitors turned up. This time, Heathens won 2-0 to do the 'double' over them and *The Sportsman* took delight in naming and shaming the absent Baker brothers for the No-Names club.

Played on Hampstead Heath on Saturday 30th January 1869, the Heathens inflicted one of Wanderers' heaviest defeats when they trounced them by 5-0. Wanderers, with over fifty men to find an available eleven, took a weak team of nine men, one which the Sportsman said "they did not appear to know their game, and at least two goals were down to having the wrong man in goal, wasted time chasing their adversaries about the field, who were too quick for them". In praising the efforts of the Hampstead side, they remarked that "it was their first season" although that was not quite correct. The Heathens were quite shocked at having trounced such a notable club as the Wanderers by such a margin at their first ever meeting. Wanderers that day were comprised many men unfamiliar to me, apart from Wade, Jutsum and deWelch. On the same day the Hampstead RFC met the City of London at the rugby code, whilst the Mars AFC mistakenly played the Wasps RFC and played ninety minutes completely bemused as to the rules of the handling game. The Hampstead ten-man side for that Wanderers match was -

H. Sharpe, Bovey, Crawford, Chamberlain, Evans, Pitchford, Lake, Riley, P. Tatham, S. Tatham.

At their annual general meeting of 1869, held at the Eyre Arms in St. Johns Wood, the following officers were elected : Elice (Ellis?) Clark, honorary secretary; C.E. Atkins, treasurer; W.E. Tichener, team captain, and a committee quorum made up by Parnell and Mathias. The Ayre Arms, a substantial Georgian building which stood next to Lords cricket ground, on Finchley Road, was named after the Ayre family who were the local landowners at the start of the 19th century. Heathens played the Forest Club on Saturday November 20th 1869, and the return game a fortnight later. The Heathens' fixture list for 1869-70 was a very limited card; No-Names home (2-0) & away, Wanderers home & away, Forest home & away, and Clapham Rovers home & away. By comparison the 'Hampstead Club' announced a large fixture list of 18 matches, although all their opponents did seem to be of the rugby variety.

A trip to Kilburn to face the No-Names on 6th November 1869 saw the fitter and better organised Heathens comfortably win by 3-0 with goals from S. Tatham, R. Brown and P. Tatham. Still captained by H. Sharpe, credit was given for all the goals "which were got by taking the ball to the posts and not by place kicks from distance".

This Heathens side were beaten 1-0 at home by the Wanderers in December 1869 -

J. Crawley-Bouvey

H. Sharpe (captain)   H. Brown

H.R .Leach   G. Riley

P. Lawford   H. Chamberlain   J.P. Tatham   W.H. Pitchford   H.K .Evans

Interested parties were instructed 'to catch the 2.15 train from Broad Street to Hampstead Heath station on the North London Railway line'. The formation, of three centres, a pair of wide men, was atypical, but the use of two full backs (as opposed to a full back and a three quarter back) was rather unusual at the time. The return game, in the following March, saw much the same line-up, excepting that Brown was replaced by C.B. Dimmond, and A. Baker replaced P. Lawford. The word 'substitute' was used in Victorian football reports, but this does not mean that a player was replaced during the game if injured. Rather, it meant that a team was not able, on the day, to field the side which it had previously announced it would put on the field. You may think this does not matter, but very often, the promise of the visiting side bringing its 'star' players would boost the attendance, and if at the kick-off, those stars were not seen on the field of play, then many people would find it a let-down and leave the ground. Playing only once a fortnight, other teams met during 1869-1870 included Forest (Snaresbrook), Charterhouse, Wanderers, Herts Rangers, Non-Names, London Athletic, Wasps, and Crystal Palace (*The Sportsman*).

When No-Names were the visitors (from less than a mile away) in January 1870, both sides were poorly represented, and play was described as not 'A1' and a goal by Henry Lake was enough to win the match for the home side. The Heathens' lack of facilities meant that, on Saturday 17th December, when the Wanderers were the visiting team, they had to get changed in the Railway Hotel next to the station, having caught the 2.10pm from Broad Street to Hampstead. This suggests a ground within walking distance from the station. By 1870, the Heathens' defence was usually the pairing of the Tatham brothers, with H. Sharpe being captain for the 1870-71 season. Wanderer Alfred Baker, a Charterhouse friend of Kinnaird, was introduced into the Heathens' team for his debut on Saturday 19th March 1870. This 9-man Heathens side played against Wanderers on 18th February 1871 at the Oval, the match immediately being followed by the match between Royal Engineers and Crystal Palace, who took their places on the field after watching Wanderers win 2-0.

G. Crawley-Bouvey

S.E. Tatham (captain)   H. Mitchell

H. Lake   W .Pilchford   G. Leach   F. Barker   C.B. Diamond   F. Lyall

When England played Scotland in November 1871, Heathens' H.J. Lake was selected to represent his country, in a team selected almost entirely from London players. Other Heathens selected for representative duty included captain Tatham, and R.B. Mitchell. In ordinary matches, one of the last reports I could find was when the Heathens lost 2-0 away to Wanderers at the Oval in early December 1871, although a return with Wanderers was played in the following along with a match at home to the Lausanne club. As they played on Hampstead Heath, they could not expect to place on the same location at every home match, but probably tried to make a particular section their 'home'. Mention was given in a match against the Putney club to their being an 'uphill and a downhill' feature to the pitch.

Hampstead Heathens were one of the original entrants when the F.A. Cup was created in 1871-2 season, but this may well have been their swansong as their matches were no longer reported upon after this season. Drawing a bye in round 1, they defeated the oarsmen of the Barnes FC 2-0 (Dunage, Weston) after a replay, in round 2 to reach the 3rd round, where only five teams remained in the competition. The first Barnes tie was played on December 23rd at Barnes, when the sides drew 1-1 (Barker), which at least tells us that they were extant into 1872. On the previous Saturday, FA

The Eyre Arms was an old coaching inn, and was used by the footballers of the Hampstead Heathens as headquarters.

Cup finalists Royal Engineers beat them 2-0 (Wikipedia says 3-0) on 16th December 1871 to not only end their fine cup run, but to put a closing mark on the life of the Hampstead Heathens club. J.P. Tatham was club captain going into 1872. The last games I could find were Forest on the 20th January 1872, a week after the Barnes FA Cup replay, and home to Clapham Rovers on the 27th, lost when Vansittart and Kenrick scored for the visitors in what appears to be *their last ever match* before folding at the end of their season. I knew I had seen that unusual surname somewhere, and when I next watched the popular TV show Heartbeat, Rupert Vansittart was the actor who played the lord of the manor.

Ownership of the land occupied by the various sections of Hampstead Heath and the old common passed into public ownership following the Hampstead Heath Act 1871, and the area was taken over by the Metropolitan Board of Works. This, coupled with the Bank Holidays Act that year, led to an explosion of recreationalists pouring into the Heath, which had already seen popular use in the 1860s. This may have directly led to the folding of the club, who may have found it increasingly difficult to secure a 'safe' area on the common on which to play football. With most players also members of other clubs, such as Wykehamists, they simply began to turn out for those instead.

A present day club of no connection, but using the same name, competes in the Southern Amateur League.

HANOVER UNITED

Founded - Probably 1879
Folded - Circa 1890 (became Polytechnic FC)
Grounds - 1. The Limes, Barnes (1879-84)
          2. Merton Hall Farm, Wimbledon (from 1885)
Colours - Blue and white halves

Hanover United appear to be a contemporary of Barnes FC, in that they were fundamentally a Thames-side rowing club whose members were general athletes. Thanks to research done by Robin Horton, we know that Hanover played in light blue and white halves, colours popularised by Blackburn Rovers and the Old Etonians.

Membership numbered in the hundreds by the 1880s, and were drawn chiefly from the London Polytechnic which had been founded by Quintin Hogg. Swimming, cricket, rowing and football were their principal interests. The earliest football match I could find was 25th October 1879 when Hanover drew away to Upton Rangers in West Ham Park. Hanover entered the FA Cup in 1879 but lost 1-2 (0-2 according to *Bell's Life*) to Greyfriars in November 1879, fielding this eleven -

A. Sargeant	
L. Deas	G. Scabble
H. Nottingham	H. J . Nottingham *
H. Apted F. Dodd T. Farharquason	E. Raveni C.H. Tile

A fairly unique name, a T. Farquharson was also a leading member of the Dorsetshire club, Panthers FC. I also found Hanover active at rugby, rowing and cricket during the late 1870s. An annual regatta was held on the Thames , and an annual sports day held at the Polytechnic ground at Merton.

They briefly continued in the FA Cup but were defeated 1-0 by West End FC the following season. Played at Shepherds Bush on 6th November 1880 before a 1,000 crowd, the fast and closely fought game was won when Harkness scored after 40 minutes, with the play of Ravani and Smith drawing much praise *(The Referee)*. West End – who played in navy & white halves - must have been a competent side for they eliminated the Remnants 3-2 in the following year. Hanover United luckily drew a bye in 1881, where they met the strong and well established Upton Park club, and were defeated 3-1 at the Limes, Barnes, with the Honourable Kinnaird officiating alongside N.L. Jackson, later founder of the Corinthians FC. Played under miserable weather, few hardy souls watched the cup-tie, with another famous referee, S.R. Bastard playing on the wing for Upton Park. The Hanover team that day was -

		H.T. Nottingham (captain)			
	Quintin Hogg		H. G. Giffard		
	J. Nottingham			J. Arnold	
C. Irvine	J. Deas	E. Stanning	F. Farmer	E. Dodd	F. Ravim

In July 1882, the cricket club of Hanover United got into trouble when a letter was published in the *Sporting Life* from the secretary of a visiting team who claimed that Hanover were operating some kind of a scam. Invited to the Limes ground of Barnes FC, they arrived on the field to play only to be confronted by Hanover's 2nd team. Showing Hogg the letters of arrangement clearly stating that it was a 1st team fixture, half their eleven returned in disappointment to the Barnes railway station, where they came across the Hanover 1st eleven en rout to play elsewhere. A robust conversation ensued, ending with the Hanover 1st team captain saying that should the visitors wish to return, they would play them. However, the visiting team secretary later found out that such a thing had happened to at least three other visiting teams, and that it was a rouse just to get better quality games for the Hanover seconds. A similarly named team called Hanover Athletic were also active around 1881, and played in orange and blue on Primrose Hill.

Hanover seemed to have a poor 1882-83 season, as they were losing most matches. After squeezing past the rugby-playing Mosquitoes FC 1-0 in October, Acton FC trounced them by 6-3 on 25th November in a 2nd round FA Cup tie, and a fortnight later a full strength Clapham Rovers beat them by 7-1 at Wandsworth. With most of the Clapham forwards scoring, including a Ram hat-trick, the Hanover eleven once more seemed to follow the pattern of rounding up any eleven players available on the day -

		Clifford			
	Scoble		Quintin Hogg		
	Nottingham			Harris	
Ravine	Horsfield	Totman	Irvine	Whittington	Stanning

Hanover United met the Dalston FC on New Years Day 1883. Played at the Limes, Barnes, Dalton retired as 1-0 winners against this Hanover eleven still playing the outmoded 2-2-6 formation -

		J. Crick (captain)			
	W.G. Adams		G. Clifford		
	J. Arnold			J. Bangerter	
Raynor	Coulson	Council	Bird	Settle	Godwin

Less than twelve months later, an almost entirely different eleven met Old Arlington Rovers in a friendly, although since they used to put several elevens out each Saturday, was probably not their first eleven -

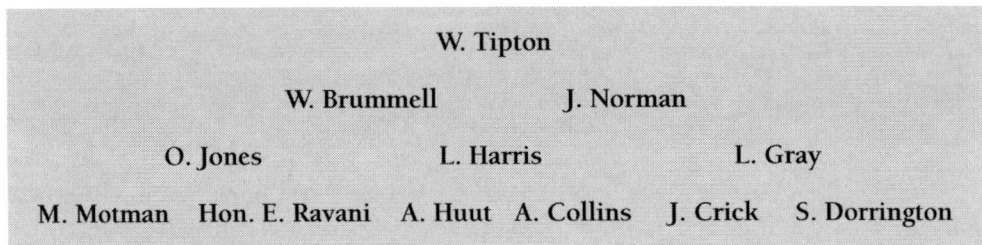

Note the outmoded six forwards arrangement, made possible as they appear to have fielded twelve men! Tipton seems to have been their best man as goalkeeper, for he was still in that position in 1887 when they played Windsor on Boxing Day in Home Park. Quintin Hogg by then seems to have retired from the team.

Hanover United persisted with competing in the FA Cup, although they usually went out at the first hurdle, and 1883 was no different, being trounced 6-1 at home to a more organised Brentwood FC. Refereed by Morton Peto Betts, the Nottingham brothers were back in the side at goalie and half back, alongside Quintin Hogg (*Sporting Life*).

Lambeth Palace grounds, of all places, was the odd venue when Hanover played the Alexandra FC on 3rd November 1883. It was clearly not the Hanover 1st team, as reference was made to "the usual wrangling so well known to all the Hanover junior teams" when Alexander sent in a shot which was saved, but the goalie then stepped back behind the line clutching the ball. Alexandra claimed a goal, but the referee was too far away, and dodged the issue by stating he hadn't noticed it. A second and third goal soon put the issue beyond doubt.

In October 1884, Hanover squeezed past Reading Minster by 1-0 (one of their best results) to meet the Old Forester in the 2nd round of the FA Cup. Here, all money was on the old boys team, but Hanover edged through by 2-1 to enter the 3rd round for the first time ever. There were by then, some seriously powerful teams left in the last 32, such as Aston Villa, Queens Park, Blackburn Rovers and Nottingham Forest. However, all those sides were in the Northern & Midlands half of the draw, but Hanover were still up against the Swifts and Old Carthusians in their half. As it was, they drew Kent side Chatham away out of the hat, and after a spirited effort, were beaten 0-2. The London *Pall Mall Gazette* merely reporting the scoreline. Season 1884-85 had been their best season yet, to which they added a semi final appearance in the London Cup, going out to Old Foresters, and having eliminated Dulwich Hamlet in the 4th round. In probably their most important game to date, the Honourable E.C. Ravani selected Hunt in goal, Rennie and Scoble at backs, Harris and Adams at half backs and Kraneaslach, Totman, Stanning, Crick and Dakin, and himself in the forward line. Played at The Oval on 7th February before an attendance in excess of a thousand, the Foresters, featuring the three Guy brothers, proved too strong on the day, and ran away with it to win 6-0. At least they had the pleasure of being refereed by Charles Alcock, the Secretary of the Football Association.

No doubt buoyant from the previous season's exploits, Hanover United once more paid their entry guinea into the FA Cup. Drawn against Romford, they were held 1-1 at home on 31st October, but knocked out by 3-0 (*Sporting Life*) in the replay a week later, Hunt, in goal, having plenty to do. Romford themselves were then eliminated 3-1 by the Old Foresters in the 3rd round.

At their grand and sumptuous annual dinner, held at the Holborn Restaurant in the city centre in November 1885, many references were made to the colour blue, the "Blue Devils" regiment, and by naming the captains of their various sports clubs, Hanover United had sections devoted to football, cricket, lawn tennis, rowing, running, cycling, and that the toasts were to "Quintin Hogg and the Royal London Polytechnic". When Hanover played their annual match at Home Park against Windsor on Boxing Day 1885, I was surprised to see that the Right Honourable Arthur Kinnaird played for them at half back, with the oddly named (and frequently mis-spelt) F. Krausslach scoring both winning goals for Hanover. Hanover also played a goal-less morning match against the Windsor reserve team, the Phoenix Athletic.

The football team remained active throughout the 1880s, as I found them competing in the London Challenge Cup for much of the decade, although up against teams like Upton Park, Clapham Rovers, Old Etonians, Old Foresters, they were never going to win it. There were still no leagues to compete in and matches were either friendlies or local or national cup ties. Friendly 1886 opposition came from Upton Excelsior, Olympians and Clapham. Memories of 3rd round heady heights were consigned to memory when Hanover United once more failed to get past the opening round of the FA Cup in October, when the Old Wykehamists beat them 3-0. October 1887 was no different, with a heavy 0-5 Cup exit at the hands of the Old Carthusians, probably the best amateur side in the country at that time. The Carthusians went out in the 6th round, giving a good account before losing 2-4 to eventual winners West Bromwich Albion. After the introduction of Qualifying Rounds in 1888, Hanover United were not one of the 92 clubs who submitted an entry form and did not again compete in the competition. This eleven were drawn against Hendon in the London Challenge Cup of 1887 -

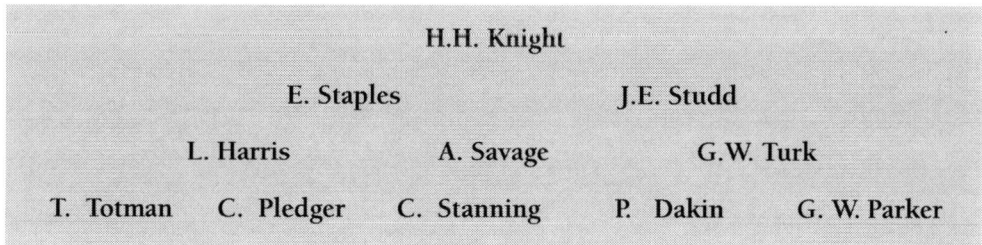

		H.H. Knight			
	E. Staples		J.E. Studd		
	L. Harris	A. Savage		G.W. Turk	
T. Totman	C. Pledger	C. Stanning	P. Dakin		G. W. Parker

Players were instructed to catch the 2.17pm out of Waterloo station to Hendon.

As Hanover United Athletic Club, they were still very much alive going into the 1890s, as several meetings and gatherings at the exclusive Holborn Restaurant in central London revealed that they now expanded their interests to swimming (baths at Regent Street), lawn tennis, quoits, rowing (the Thames at Chiswick), and other athletic forms of exercise. E.C. Ravani was in charge of the 'boys football team' who now wore 'the best bib and tucker' and not the old dirty shirts of yesteryear. Much reference was made to the phrase "Blue Devils" so I assume that was their colours. Their membership seems to have been from students at the Royal Polytechnic Institute which the philanthropist Quintin Hogg was the founder.

Other famous old footballers who were members, included Lord Arthur Kinnaird and H.G. Morley, and Hogg of course. Hogg set out to provide facilities and means for the social, educational, athletic and even spiritual needs of young people of London, he devoted a great deal of his time and wealth into realising its creation, even paying for new swimming baths and other projects out of his own pocket, including a gymnasium, a 37 acre sports field, and a boat-house. By 1886, the Polytechnic Harriers became a leading London athletics organisation, and the Polytechnic and Hanover clubs began to put on annual jointly hosted events. The Sportsman described Hanover United Athletic as a powerful and wealthy organisation, and with Barnes, one of London's leading rowing clubs. I could find no results beyond 1890 for Hanover, only those for the Polytechnic FC, still playing at Merton Hall.

In 1905 'Hanover United Cricket & Football Club' held their 10th annual dinner at the Horns Hotel, Kennington Park, although without the word 'Athletic' attached. A team called Hanover Athletic (founded 1889) found playing the Polytechnic, Footscray, and Brunswick Athletic clubs at football in 1906 could be a revival of the same club, now with a ground at Stuart Road, Newlands.

Studying old maps from the 1880s, for the Merton Hall ground, nearly all the area from the A238 Kingston Road down to where the old railway used to curve (now a walk-path on the edge of Abbey Recreation grounds) was open fields belonging to Merton Farm. If Hanover played on the cricket ground down by the curve of the railway line, then sadly the small industrial estate off The Pathway now occupies the 3.5 acre field which housed a pavilion in the corner by the railway. However, that field is shown as an orchard on some maps of 1895, but as a cricket ground in 1896! More probable is a large 8 acre field which had the Merton Park station right next to it, which had a path running directly to the cricket pavilion, just 400 yards away. By 1900, most of the farmland had been built on with Bournemouth Road and its adjoining streets, and the cricket & hockey ground was moved lower down to in between the two railway lines. These ground today are known as the Nursery Road Recreation grounds.

Hanover United evolved into the Polytechnic FC, who, judging by the myriad of different shirts, hadn't yet decided on their own outfit.

Founded - 1864
Folded - Circa 1876, when re-branded as Old Harrovians FC.
Ground - None, sometimes Harrow school Field, also Kennington Oval
Colours - Blue quartered shirts* (probably white flannels)

Harrow Chequers were a short lived club for old boys of Harrow school. My old football notes, written over a thirty year period from a multitude of sources says that the team was founded on 14th December 1864 although I cannot say by which individuals. The football field at Harrow, at 150 x 110 yards, was closer to what became the standard size, as compared with Winchester's 80 x 27. Their limited fixture card included only teams with which they had an association, such as Harrow school, Wanderers, Civil Service, No-Names, (Epping) Forest, Oxford University. They were an important club in the very early years, as they helped to take the game around the greater London area. A trip to Oxford in November 1866 saw them beat the Christ Church team by 'two bases to nil'; as they were 'kicked' by Robinson, is seems clear that these were goals scored in the modern sense through upright posts. Though not listed below, later Wanderer Charles John Morice (1850-1932) joined Chequers as his first club after leaving school in 1865, before joining the Barnes club. An Old Harrovian and outside left, he was chosen to play in England's first ever international in November 1872. He worked on the London Stock Exchange, and is the great-grand-father to actor Edward Fox.

One of the Chequers' first opponents were the Civil Service Club, with whom an annual pair of fixtures was arranged. This team played a score-less draw with them on December 19th 1866, thus failing to get revenge for their two bases to nil defeat of 1865 -

			W.B. Money (goal defence)			
			Edward Bowen (back)			
A. Crompton	F. Broughton		H. Montgomery		S. Pelham	J. Martin
W. Haddow	S .Gore				J. Gibson	C. Archer

Well known players Charles Alcock and James Kirkpatrick were on the Civil Service team, along with Rob Broughton who drew notice as a future promising player of note. *The Sportsman* remarked that (the ladies) spent some time admiring the wonderful physiques of both sets of players with 'wide shoulders, handsome faces, and muscle' on display. This twelve-man team played at the Harrow school football field on Boxing Day 1866, winning 1-0 against a team chosen by R.M. Thornton :-

Tupper, Money, Thornton, Smith, Kennedy, Burch, Baxendale, de Morgan, Prior, Archer, Ponsonby, Baker.

The Sportsman had little to say about the actual game, instead criticizing the waterlogged and muddy state of the field, ticking off the masters of the wealthy public school for failing to maintain decent paths to the football area. The 'goal' as registered by C.J.Smith, appeared to be a punt which sailed high between the sticks, with none of the popular and confusing (to modern readers) rouges being scored. Four days later, Chequers went to Kilburn and played the No-Names club on a wet and windy day. Winning 2-0, the N.N opening goal was described by *Bells Life:* Chequers' goalkeeper Fred Barlow took what we would call today a goal kick, but sent the ball short, and Baker ran up to it and returned it through the unguarded posts. A second from Charlie Alcock put the game out of reach, despite the exertions of Rhodes and Scovell for the visitors. Interestingly, having inferred that Fred Barlow was the Harrow goalie, R.D. Elphinstone's defence of his goal was commended, suggesting a sort of 'rush-back' goalie principle. Once more, on the following Thursday 4th January 1867, Chequers went to Reigate to play the Priory club there. 'Harrow rules' were agreed to be used, which meant that some handling and hacking was allowed, with the exception that the Harrvovians, should they catch a high ball, could not give it to another player of their side, as it was stated that Reigate did not use 'hands' at all. Advantage or not, Chequers won 3-0 with goals by Balser, Scovel and Mylne. An opening 'goal' which was not allowed would have made it 4-0, but was wiped out merely because it bounced in off Bence-Jones' shoulders ! In that game, Reigate Priory would have been in blue and white hoops, but they later played in halves of chocolate and blue.

Harrow Chequers travelled north to met Oxford's Christ Church College on November 15th 1866, winning there by 'two bases to nil'. One fancies whether one Reverend Charles Dodgson (Lewis Carroll) watched the game as it was the year following the publication of 'Alice's Adventures In Wonderland'. Dodgson would have been 34 at the time, and spent most of his life at Christ Church, and was fond of taking the Miss Alice Liddell and her sisters on walking trips around Oxford, although by 1866, Alice was beginning to drift away from Dodgson. Other fixtures that year were against Civil Service, Harrow school, Reigate Priory, Westminster Vacation, Wanderers, and No-Names. *The Sportsman* remarked at Christmas 1866, that Harrow Chequers' two games against the Civil Service club were 'an annual fixture'. Crompton, Money and Montgomery were singled out for their play which was described as 'a treat to witness' but the game ended on the Civil Service 'ground' in Battersea Park without a goal being registered. Many teams used Battersea, but it seems that Civil Service had secured an area all of their own, and drew crowds in the low hundreds. Interestingly, the game, played only a week before the Harrow game described earlier, saw only Money of the Chequers team play in both matches. This once again, indicates a play-for-fun team who wish to give their many members an equal opportunity to turn out for the side. The Civil Service side included two men who would become Wanderers' stars - Charles Alcock and James Kirkpatrick. Coincidentally, Chequers scratched when drawn against Civil Service in the F.A. Cup of 1874.

When Chequers played the Radley College team on St. Andrew's day (30th Nov) 1867, there was little of interest in the match itself, as wind and rain, plus a poor display by Harrow, left the game a lottery. However, two items assisted with the mental picture of the game of 1867; the Radley goalkeeper Evans was in the habit of dribbling the ball into attack after having made the save, and when Chequers had an early shot at goal, *the ball went over the post*, as opposed to the tape which had been made law in February 1866. Chequers were said to be 'brilliant one minute and hopeless the next'.

Harrow Chequers football club seems to have disbanded around 1868, but following a meeting open to all old Harrovians at the Pall Mall Restaurant in London on Wednesday 25th October 1869 at 6pm, the club was resurrected once more. A match played on Boxing Day 1872 against the Wanderers ended remarkably as 4-4, vindicating their decision to get back together again. In 1869, one wag commented that the Wanderers and Harrow Chequers "were virtually the same team". This was probably the reason why Chequers scratched, when the two clubs were drawn against each other in the 1st round of the inaugural English Cup on 11th November 1871.

> **Featuring three Kingsford brothers, the Harrow Chequers eleven that day was – M.P. Betts (captain), R.C. de Welch (back), K.K. Kingsland, J. Kingsland, F. Kingsland, E.E. Bowen, C. Colbeck, C. Metcalf, A. Heath, W. Patton, G. Carnegie.**

When England played Scotland in November 1871, three Chequers men were in the squad; Morton Peto Betts was chosen to play, with Fitzgerald H. Crawford and E. Ellice as reserves. In 1872, on Saturday 27th January, as a precursor to the England v Scotland game at the Oval, 'London' played 'Sheffield' and two Chequers' men were in the home side, namely Morton Peto Betts and W.P. Crake. William Parry Crake (1852-1921), played for Chequers during 1871, and often played for the Wanderers and Barnes, and his Harrow education allowed him membership of the Old Harrovians. Morton Betts, of course, being well-know to football historians as the man who won the first F.A. Cup final for Wanderers, whilst playing under a pseudonym of 'A.H. Chequer'. Educated at Harrow and Cambridge, Betts played in goal or full back positions. His other teams were Old Harrovians and Wanderers. A fine cricketer, he batted for Middlesex and Kent, and died in France in 1914. On Saturday 24th February 1872, no less than four Harrow Chequers were involved in the England - Scotland game at the Oval. Morton Betts was a late injury withdrawal for England, and Robert F and Fitzgerald H. Crawford and Edward H. Elliot played for 'Scotland' who were comprised of Scots resident in London! Even more bizarre was the name of another withdrawal: one William Gladstone, M.P., son of Prime Minister to Queen Victoria. At a meeting of the Football Association in the same month, it was the Harrow Chequers club which proposed that rule that there should be a regulated and fixed size for a ball used in association matches. It was clear at this time that the corner kick as we know it had not yet fully developed into one taken from the far corner of the field, since Harrow Chequers and Sheffield FC proposed a 'short' corner (as in hockey) where the ball is returned into play from a point six yards either side of the goalposts, at the same point in the modern game where the goal area line meets the touchline. Even in 1875, at further FA meetings, rules were still being ironed out, with many points put to the vote in an effort to get London and Sheffield rules together. It was only in that year that it was made clear that scoring direct from the kick off and even corner kicks was not to be permitted.

In the 1874 fixture, Chequers man Reginald Courtnay de Welch (1851-1939) was also in the London team. Welch, educated at Harrow, also played in goal or as back for Old Harrovians and Wanderers. The son of a barrister, he went on to become principal of Farnham College, where he worked for 44 years. he also held a unique record of being the only man to appear in both the first FA Cup Final and the first International match. Another football-cricketer, deWelch served on the FA committee during 1872-74, and gained two caps. On New Years Day 1874, Chequers played Wanderers at the Oval, but only nine men turned up for them. Losing only by 1-2, the *Morning Post* remarked that Harrow played with remarkable energy (perhaps they didn't celebrate the new year so much then), with W.Welch for Chequers being conspicuous, and Colback for scoring their goal.

The Chequers went over to the Uxbridge cricket ground on 10th October 1874 and played the home club, winning by 1-0 with this, possibly the strongest eleven they ever fielded – W. H. Hadow, A.A. Hadow, R. Barker, de Welch, H.S. Otter, J.G. Black, A.H. Stratford, Alec Morton, Bevington, A. Greig. Playing for Uxbridge FC were all three Heron brothers – Hubert, Henry and Frank. (*Windsor & Eton Express*). Interestingly, there is a Chequers Hotel in Uxbridge.

This entirely different Harrow Chequers side utlilizing eight forwards drew 2-2 with Westminster school on Vincent Square three weeks later, on the last day of October 1874:

		Burn (goal)		
	E.E. Bowen (captain)		W.L. Haddow	
O.C. Bowlby	G.B. Walker	H.H. Bowyer		C. Colbeck
C.J. Longman	T. Fowler	A.A. Hadow		J.J. Black

With a remarkable *eight forwards* this was already behind the thinking of the times, when most teams were using a pair of backs behind a three-quarter back, but this was an upper-class gentlemen's team playing for their own amusement. Bowlby and Walker were the scorers. E.E. Bowen was also a Wanderer. I could not find any consistency of venue which led me to believe that Chequers had a home ground; their home game with Herts Rangers in November 1874 being played at the Oval.

Sometime player Charles Morice, born in London in 1850, was Harrow educated which in turn permitted him to turn out for any one of the Harrow-based teams. By profession, he was a London stockbroker, and was the great-grandfather of the well known actors Edward Fox and his son James Fox (Lewis TV programme). Morice also played for the Barnes club. He was capped at outside left for England's first ever official match against Scotland in November 1872.

The Chequers played the Wanderers on Saturday 9th January 1875 at the usual Oval, with the fame of Wanderers being such that even the *York Herald* some 200 miles away reporting on the one-sided game, won 9-1 by the home side. The following month, Harrow Chequers representatives attended the meeting of the F.A. and made a suggestion about altering the playing rules. Along with Sheffield FC and Royal Engineers, they got acceptance that at a throw-in, the ball should be returned to play by a players of the team opposite to that which put it out. Which is a long way round to say 'we put it out, so it's your throw-in'. Cleverly, but somewhat manipulatively, Harrow requested the new law be passed only on the proviso that the Sheffield F.A. adopts current and future F.A. laws. In November 1875, C.F. Nayes of the Chequers, was in the London team which played its annual Sheffield fixture.

When Chequers played Herts Rangers in March 1876, and drew 2-2 at Watford, the *Herts Mercury* said of the Chequers that "they all worked well, but lack as a team that playing together necessary to ensure victory". This however, was the last football match containing the Harrow Chequers that I could find, suggesting that the team folded suddenly in the summer of 1876. Waiting until the winter of 1875 before entering the F.A. Cup, Chequers scratched when drawn away to Leyton, and thus never actually played a game in the competition. Using the same player-base, the club was started up again in late 1876 under the name of the Old Harrovians, when James Herbert Falmer took over from de Welch as secretary in 1886 until 1891. Today, the Old Harrovians still play in all-blue at Sudbury Hill, Harrow, in the Arthurian League, alongside many other famous names including Old Etonians, Old Carthusians, Old Westminsters, Old Foresters and the Old Wykehamists clubs.

* Based on a cap worn by a Harrow Chequers player when Wanderers played Queens Park in Partick in 1875.

In January of 1903, one C.L. Tupper was awarded the K.C.L.E in the New Year's honours list. It was explained that whilst now the Financial Commissioner for the Punjab (India), he was in fact the founder of the Harrow Chequers football club "for old Harrovians, which club subsequently merged with and into the Old Harrovians FC". Tupper had also previously been a Wanderers player before he went out to India.

Harrow Chequers often played their games at the Surrey Oval, courtesy of Charles Alcock. In the 1870s, it was little more than a tree lined flat field, with a six foot planked fence and a pavilion, but no spectator facilities at all.

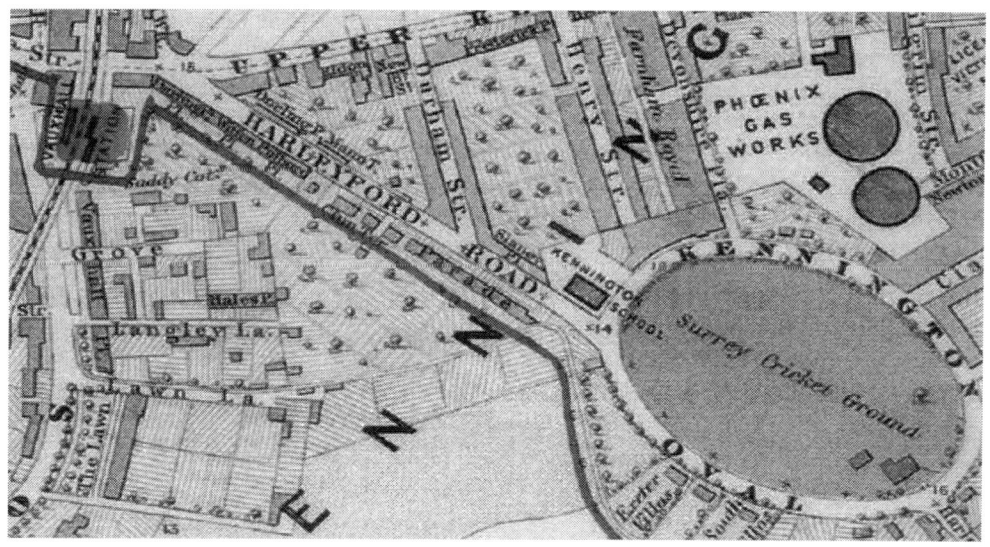

HENDON FC

Founded - 1875 Revived 1893, 1896
Folded - 1893 and again in 1934/5 (as Hendon Mk 2 out of Hendon Rovers)
Grounds - 1. Hendon cricket ground, Brent Street 1875-84
          2. Finchley 1884-
          3. Welsh Harp ground from 1902
          4. Station Road 1900 and 1903
Colours - 1. White shirts, blue nicks, red stockings (1876)
          2. Red, white and blue (1879)
          3. Scarlet and white halves (1881)
          4. Blue shirts, later green shirts, and green and white halves (20th C.)

With the current Hendon a well known name in semi-professional circles since the 1940s, I had assumed that they were the same team which played in the F.A Cup throughout the 1870s and 1880s, but today's Hendon was not named as such until 1946, having spent life founded as Hampstead Christ Church in 1908. They were at least four different teams called Hendon FC over the years. Trying to unravel the threads of football in Hendon, the different teams who used the name, folded, changed their name many times, with seemingly parallel teams operating simultaneously all stemming as a club once called 'Hendon' will have your head spinning as it did mine. The story is relatively straightforward until the team moved out of town and renamed themselves as Hampstead in 1909, when this left the door open for anyone else to start calling themselves Hendon. To put into modern terms, when MK Dons left their home base of Wimbledon, to relocate at Milton Keynes, and the supporters club started up their own AFC Wimbledon, which is the real Wimbledon? Although I feel it won't be long before MK drop the 'Dons' tag, and shed like a lizard's tail, any links to Wimbledon, at least a future historian should be able to tell the two teams apart, unlike the one you are about to read.

During the 1870s and 1880s, Hendon was a hotbed for sport, especially at the Welsh Harp inn by the lake, with sculling, pigeon shooting (!), polo, cricket and ice skating on the lake, and racing being the most popular activities. Football was lucky to get a look in. The Hendon Cricket Club turned their hand to football in the winter of 1875, according to the Hendon & Finchley Times, incorporating football into their title, and thereafter holding annual sports days on the cricket field at Brent Street. The earliest mention I found on Hendon FC was when a useful Leyton team were beaten 2-1 at home on October 10th 1877, and J.H. Powell and S. A. Ince were named as the scorers. The return friendly, played on December 8th was drawn. Hendon were beaten 3-2 at home on 10th November by the Pilgrims club, but Hendon's scorers were not named. In December 1877, Hendon played the Minerva club at Ladywell and won handsomely 6-0 according to *Lloyds Newspaper,* who had the unfortunate trait of the naming the away side first, and unless you knew whose home ground it was, you would get the result the wrong way around. With the concept of league football over a decade away, all of Hendon's matches during the 1880s were either friendlies or cup ties.

Hendon competed in the F.A Cup from 1877 until 1888, when the qualifying stages were introduced, but after that date never again appeared in the competition proper. In

1877, they went out at the first hurdle to Marlow, who were then Buckinghamshire's top team.

Played on Saturday 9th November, Marlow won 2-0 on the Hendon ground (*London Daily News*). In the following season, Reading put them out when a single goal determined the tie.

Hendon met Upton Park on their West Ham park ground on 16th November 1878, the game ending 1-1. Several other matches were being simultaneously played in the park, involving teams such as Dreadnought, Buxton College and Gresham. Season 1879-80 saw Hendon's most successful yet, when they reached the dizzy height of round 4 of the F.A. Cup. The Old Foresters, Essex's premier side, proved a stubborn obstacle in round 1. A 1-1 draw was followed by a 2-2 draw but in the third game, Hendon won through by 3-1. The second round saw an easy game when rugby-playing Mosquitoes were trounced 6-1, *The Graphic* calling it 'a stinging defeat'. For some reason, the game was played on Kennington Oval, which must have been the Mosquitoes choice of venue as per the early rules, when first out of the hat didn't mean you were at home, merely could nominate the venue. Then a bit of luck, as Hendon drew a bye in the third round. In round four, Hendon had the misfortune to be drawn against cup-holders Clapham Rovers, and despite a spirited display, were knocked out 0-2. The two sides also met at Wandsworth on 19th January 1880 with Clapham well on top, winning 6-1. The following season saw Hendon sail through the first round with a 7-1 win over St. Peters FC, but quality opposition was met in the next round, when the famous Old Etonians put them out by 2-0. The Hendon 1st eleven in 1880 was -

H. Redford					
W. Howard				A.B. Coutts	
W. Redford				J.G. Coutts	
R.F. Mayhew	J.E. Colt	Hart Buck	H.O. Ince	J.H. Ince	J.A. Powell

Season 1880-81 saw an ignominious FA Cup exit when Reading trounced them 5-0 at the first hurdle, but Hendon returned the following season by producing their longest ever F.A. Cup run, amazingly getting to the fifth round. West End (London) were beaten 3-1 in round one and then Chatham were edged past by 2-1. The name of Reading popped up again in the draw for round three, but there were several clubs in that town, and it was the weaker South Reading who were steamrollered by 11-1. Round four saw revenge gained over Marlow from back in 1876, as they were beaten 3-0 to put Hendon into the last 8 for the first time. Once more they had to face the redoubtable Etonians (*who were cup-holders*), but there was no disgrace in the 2-4 defeat which followed. Further quality opposition was played on Saturday 19th November 1881 when Hendon went to the Dolphin Ground of the Swifts, and although beaten 3-1, we find the name of another Hendon player when Raven scored for them.

In the following season, the auld enemy the Etonians were again pulled out of the hat in round one, and this time, watched by 1,000 people and captained by R. Redford, Hendon pulled off a famous result when they beat them by 3-2 on Hendon cricket ground

(Hendon & Finchley Times). Sadly, another one of London's strongest amateur sides awaited them in the next round, and it was only to form when the Old Westminsters beat Hendon by the narrow margin of 2-1. *The Graphic* said that ' in Vincent Square amidst the cheers of a sympathetic neighbourhood, the Westminsters have beaten Hendon, a team who recently lowered the colours of the Etonians'. That phrase ' to lower the colours' was in popular use in the day, and was yet another reference to comparing a game of football to a battle. Goalposts were often referred to as 'citadels' and 'defences would be breached' when goals were scored, as if Rourkes Drift was being re-enacted on grass. When Hendon cricket and football club held its annual sports day at the end of September of 1883, the two leading officials were none other than N.L. Jackson, founder of the Corinthians FC, and Morton Betts, legendary scorer of the first ever FA Cup final goal in 1872 for Wanderers. A.O. Redford, now of 19 Lanark Villas, Maida Vale, was the Hendon football secretary at this time.

November 1883 saw a squabble with the rising Hotspur club (not Tottenham Hotspurs-see Hotspur FC) when Hendon put in a grievance after losing to them in a London Cup tie. The match, replayed at Wimbledon was once again won by Hotspur - this time 3-1 - but we pick up another Hendon name when Coutts was named as scorer. Christmas 1884 saw Hendon invited up north to play the newly formed Derby County club on the Racecourse ground. Infuriatingly, the *Derby Mercury* named all the Rams men, but not the Hendon eleven, but from reading the match report we find the names of Coutts (defence) and in attack, Kelly and E.B. Perry. Perry became a regular choice in the South v North annual match. Oddly Hendon had to borrow two Derby men, goalie Farquharson and full back Weston. After an even first half, Hendon faded showing weaker stamina and Derby went on to win 3-1.

January 1884 provided small honour for the Hendon club when the Wilson brothers were chosen to play for The South v The North (4-2) played on the Oval ground, with K.P. Wilson scoring one of the South's goals. He was partnered at centre forward by Upton Park's Mitchell, with Arthur Dunn, Cobbold and the Bambridge brothers making up a somewhat legendary forward line. Season 1884-5 saw Hendon move to a new ground at Finchley, with players getting dressed at the Railway Hotel, Church End. An impressive curved corner building, the Charles Mackness family were the licensed victuallers in the 1880s and 1890s. The building stood on the corner of Ballards Lane until 1962 when it was demolished and replaced with The Minstrel, now the central Restaurant. Maps of the 1880s show no obvious football fields within walking distance from the Railway Hotel, but a likely candidate is the Christ's College athletic grounds between Lyndhurst gardens and Dollis brook (still there next to St. Mary's Junior school) which would have been a short cab journey away. Hendon were paired against another fading giant from the previous decade when Clapham Rovers were drawn out of the hat in the FA Cup. The first match ended 3-3, but in the replay, Hendon won by the surprising score of 6-0 to enter round two. Their cup run came to an end when Chatham gained revenge from a few years earlier by beating them 1-0. At Christmas, Hendon were invited up to Sheffield to play the old Sheffield club on Brightside Lane. The *Birmingham Post* said "played in very cold but bright weather, the home side proved invincible and although the Londoners competed well, Sheffield played with tremendous vigour and won 2-1 with goals in the second half after pressing the visitors severely". During 1884-5 season, player Charles Plumpton a wing-half, was selected to play for England, and in doing so became one of only three men to play for England at both soccer and rugby (a cap awarded in 1881). An education at Uppingham, Marlborough College and Trinity College Cambridge, where he gained blues at rugby and cricket, allowed him to take up the assistant headmasters post at Elstree School, Herts, from which base he was able to turn out for both Hendon and the Corinthians. His younger brother Geoffrey also played for England in 1900.

The next three season saw FA Cup exits at the first round stage. Going a goal down almost from the kick-off, Clapton beat them at home 4-0 in 1885-6, London Caledonians 2-1 in 1886-7, and in Hendon's final competition proper tie, the Old Harrovians put them out 4-2 in October 1887 at 'Hendon Gate' (*Birmingham Post*), after they had got past the Old Brightonians in the qualifying round. Hendon were also playing in the popular London Cup at this time, and a creditable performance on frozen ground against the Casuals in December 1887 saw them narrowly beaten. An amusing story arose from that match, when a local boy, Peddler, was arrested by the local policeman and charged with stealing a football from Hendon FC; sentenced to the workhouse, the boy boy twice escaped and was last seen hot-footing it carrying a stolen set of clothes. I noticed that with Hendon FC now playing at Finchley, the Hendon cricket club removed the word 'football' from their title.

Hendon played 18 matches in season 1888-89, winning 14 , drawing 1 and losing 3, scoring 59 against 30 goals. Impressive scalps taken included Clapham Rovers, Watford Rovers and the Casuals (3-0 & 6-0). Five players were ever-presents, including E.O. Kingdom, A. Henry, C.A. Evors, R.A. Redford and E.H. Kelly with defenders Merk, Hearne and Tidd all playing up well. Hendon FC began to hold their AGMs not in some impressive hotel or public house, but in the National School during the 1890s, and I wondered if this implied any lowering of their funds or status.

Hendon FC seem to have fallen off the radar in the 1890s, as the few matches reported about them were single-line friendlies against small fry London teams, and had fallen back into the Middlesex and London Junior Cups. Their chairman Mr. Cox said, when reviewing their 1893-94 season, asked why they had done well in the first half of the season, then faded badly in the last half. Captain Young thought it had much to do with the long term injury to talisman and goalkeeper Tom Drewell, after whose accident, heart was lost. I could not connect those names with the Hendon FC so far, and the reason became clear when, at the start of the 1893 season, the *Hendon & Finchley Times* stated that henceforth, a local team Hendon Rovers would be known as plain Hendon FC, and that "they have every justification for taking up this name". Clearly then, *the original Hendon FC (out of the cricket club) had folded.*

I thought I had unravelled this mystery until I read three years later, that the minor team Hendon (not Hampstead as per most sources) Christ Church, observing that the old Hendon FC would never be resuscitated, dropped the Christ Church tag, and declared themselves in a letter to the FA that they were now to be known as Hendon FC. This is the popular version you will find on Wikipedia and the Hendon FC website. On this single 1896 snippet alone, then, the present day Hendon have based their history, but there is much more to be done than find one single newspaper! Christ Church had only reached the level of the lower reaches of the London Junior and London North West Leagues thus far. Clearly there can only be one club called Hendon FC at any one time, so one version must have conceded. With 'Hendon' moving out to the Welsh Harp ground in 1902, there may well have been two Hendons for a short time! For about a year after, the local *Hendon & Finchley Times* still called them Hendon Christ Church.

Further snippets gleaned about "Hendon FC" from 1894-5 mentioned the name of Tom Drewell, so this must be the former Hendon Rovers version. *The Hendon & Finchley Times* provided some insight of the 1890s, when the new Hendon team was called "the Reds", and demolished the fading West Hampstead by 8-0 in October 1898. West Hampstead had recently failed to show when due to play the "chocolate & blues" of the YMFS Hendon team in a league match, and the commentator thought they should drop out of the league until they could keep an eleven together. In May 1897, the new Hendon held their AGM at the Mitre Inn, Chancery-Lane, where their pride and possession, the battered North West London Cup was being shown around to their supporters.

At an alarming disclosure of the London Football Association on 11th September 1900 at their offices at 61 Chancery Lane, London, it was stated that for the forthcoming season no less than 340 football clubs had been declared 'defunct, defaulting or resigned' although 196 new clubs had joined. The name of Hendon (the renamed Hendon Rovers) was now to be found in the qualifying rounds of the London Cup, where they were paired with Olympian FC. The opening years of the twentieth century found Hendon in the grandly named London League, although less than grand opposition included Novocastrians, Clapton Orient reserves, West Norwood, Barnet, Lower Clapton Imperial, and the evolving Tottenham Hotspurs who also played in the Southern League. Going into 1901, Hendon FC were in a fairly healthy position, with £30 in the bank from season receipts of £104. A 32 match season saw 21 wins, 3 draws and 7 defeats, although goals were only 97 to 53. The ground at "Holmbush" owned by Mr. Stephens, would be in danger of being lost, unless sureties and improvements such as a ladies enclosure was erected by the committee of Painter, Cunningham, Easter and Odell.

Hendon were looking for a new ground season by season at this point, and "returned to Mr. Batchelors grounds on Station Road for the forthcoming season of 1903-04". First visitors of the new ground were Alleyn in the London Cup on 5th October, having started the season on the Welsh Harp ground. With familiar names W. Painter, Maidlowe and Lowndes still in the side, Hendon lost the game 0-2. With crowds down to around 200, Hendon started to flounder financially, and several London League matches were not played.

The London League evolved into three divisions, whose lower tables were never published, and so I was unable to find much of Hendon in the Edwardian era in the newspapers. With almost nothing to report from the Edwardian era, I found an article about Rayleigh's fire chief who was celebrating his silver wedding anniversary in 1940. He was H.G. Thomas who 'played for Hendon before the old war'. His occupation however was in the world of cinemas, and served in the RAF in Italy as a mechanic. Looking at old maps of Hendon, the old cricket ground lay at the corner of Brent Road and Frances Terrace which became Brampton Grove, and there were several sports grounds down by the river on the south side, almost in Cricklewood. The town's sporting focal point, the Old Welsh Harp inn, sat on the edge of the river Brent by what is now the junction of the A5 flyover and the reservoir. Adjacent lay several football, cricket and shooting grounds between it and the sister pub, the Upper Welsh Harp at Cool Oak Bridge. There was also a cricket ground by the junction of Clitterhouse Farm Lane and the A5, which location is now part of Brent railway sidings. By the 1890s, Clitterhouse Farm had turned over a huge 12 acre field into a sports ground, between the recently created Midland Brent Terrace and Claremont Road. That field is now Clitheroe infant school. Later, the new Hendon would build a football ground in a large field on the other side of the road, which became known as Clitterhouse recreation ground. Other large fields near Childs Hill were also given over to athletics and tennis courts. With the villages of Cricklewood, Brondesbury and Hampstead nearby, the original Hendon footballers would have had several other clubs within a four mile radius to compete with. It is therefore difficult to say with certainty where Hendon played, but Brent Road cricket ground was gone on maps of 1896, and Institute Road was built through the middle. Institute Road was later renamed Brampton Grove should you wish to search for it.

The Hendon cricket club were at Brent Road from 1852 to 1892, and the original football team sprang from them. The British History Online website claims that 'Hampstead Town played on Cricklewood Lane from the 1880s' but this cannot be correct as there was no Hampstead Town until the 1910s, although this may mean that Hendon, having been ousted from Brent Road cricket ground, found a new home on Cricklewood Lane (then called Childs Hill Lane), which seems plausible. That cricket & football ground now has Hocroft Avenue and the A41 running through it. By 1906, Hendon mark 2 (who used to be Hendon Rovers) seemed to have gone, and several other small teams started up in town, notably Hendon Alexandra and Hendon Crescent. Hendon version 2 died out for lack of support and constantly moving about from ground to ground every couple of seasons. The name of Hendon was once more open to takers.

In 1908, the team which became the modern day Hendon (f.1946) and started life as Christ Church Hendon, won the Finchley League division 3 at the first attempt, and subsequent promotions took them through the divisions. Having twice tried to name themselves as Hendon, in 1909-10 they altered their name to Hampstead Town, won the Middlesex League, joined the Athenian League in 1913, dropped the Town tag in 1926, and in 1933, there came another name change to Golders Green FC which was altered again in 1946 back to Hendon! Once they had joined the Athenian League, it became easy to chart their progress, despite the three name changes. Season 1914-15 was a relative success, and they finished 4th with 10 wins, 6 draws and 6 losses but a goal difference of only 43-37. The Athenian League regrouped after the War with the same set of twelve teams, and Hampstead continued to do well at Cricklewood Lane, finishing 3rd and 4th in 1921 and 1922, although they were conceding two goals a game. Season 1922-23 saw a dip down to 8th, with only 9 wins but 13 defeats. For the following season, they added the Town tag to their name, and finished 5th for the next two years. In 1925, they went back to plain Hampstead, and 15 wins and 66 goals gave them 4th place. The defence fell to pieces the following year, and they conceded 78 goals, and ended down in 13th place. 1928 saw a slight improvement to 11th, but a big improvement in 1928 saw them climb to 2nd behind champions Leyton. Two doldrum years passed before they were runners-up again in 1933, this time to newcomers Walthamstow who won the title at their first attempt, and continued to dominate the Athenian League during the 1930s. In 1933, for some unfathomable reason, Hampstead became Golders Green, who, after two years finishing 3rd, became a mid-table side. The Athenian League was suspended for the War, and in season 1946-7, Golders Green returned to their origins and decided that they wanted to be known as Hendon FC again! Playing at first in blue, then green, then green & white halves, their grounds were at Record Lane and from 1926, Cricklewood Lane, a 3.5 acre field midway between Farm Avenue and Childs Hill church, now the intersection of Cricklewood Lane and the Hendon Way. A 1936 map shows the Cricklewood ground gone, and a new ground created a few hundred yards south where it still remains off Harman Drive, but is now called the Brondesbury sports club ground.

The team which started out as Hendon Rovers, and then called themselves Hendon when Christ Church Hendon left town to become Hampstead (I hope you can follow this) must have been started up again as Hendon Town, as I found Hendon Town playing in the second tier of the London League in the mid-1920s, which rarely made the news, but I then discovered that there was no Hendon club in 1929-30 as they had no ground. They were still playing in the London League in 1931-2, but now in the Premier Division, when the *Chelmsford Chronicle* mentioned that they had beaten Finchley 1-0 played on Christmas Day, and lost the return fixture 0-3 on Boxing Day. So much for footballers' Bank Holidays then ! The other teams they played that season were - Tilbury, Chelmsford, Carlshalton, Beckenham, Cray Wanderers, Tooting, Dagenham and Grays Athletic, so the standard was still pretty good then into their last few years. Sadly, Hendon Town were rock bottom with eleven defeats in twelve, and their reserves were bottom of the 2nd division with seven defeats in eight, so the writing was on the wall. Surprisingly, at the end of the 1931-2 season, having dropped the Town tag, and with Chelmsford and unbeaten Park Hall challenging for the title, bottom placed Hendon wrecked Chelmsford's chances by beating them 3-0. The *Chelmsford Chronicle* managed to do a long match report without so much as mentioning any of the Hendon team names. Hendon Town then set up a charity fundraising match in 1932, when the original Hendon FC (from the cricket club) raised a team and the two 'Hendons' played each other! Despite many memories of olden days being brought back up, the cricket club decided against continuing with their own Hendon. Thank goodness. Despite optimism for the 1932-33 season , which spoke of new players strengthening the 1st and 2nd teams, including ex-Arsenal and West Ham player Danny Burgess, having the pitch drained and lifted, Hendon were operating outside their means. At this point, the Hendon who had been playing in the London League folded for the last time. Their ground constantly flooded was the problem, and to end the season, had to play every night of the week at the start of May to finish their fixtures. They were thrown out of the London League on 16th June.

Hendon Town were said to have been " known as Golders Green after 1933 on losing their place in the London League after many years, and reverted back to being called Hendon in 1946". This is easily disprovable as yet another Wikipedia error, when I found the actual article in the July 7th 1933 edition of the local paper, which actually says that whilst Hendon have struggled to find a ground yet no-one helps them out, Hampstead FC (who used to be Hendon) were offered one in Hendon, as people thought they came from that place, so they changed their name to Golders Green. Hendon in fact folded again at this time, just as Finchley and Golders Green were in the ascendancy. This was the last Hendon eleven I could find, in May 1933 -

		Godding		
	Whistler		Eddis	
Steele		Cashmore		White
Wilson	Romain	Bramley	Burgess	Marsdon

Players dispersed to other clubs, White and Ellis to Golders Green, and Burgess to Finchley FC. During the 1920s and 1930s, Hampstead's leading goalscorer was Freddie Evans, with 176 goals in his time at the club, although this is listed under the history of Hendon FC on their website (which is technically correct since Hampstead reverted to being Hendon in 1946).

In March 1939, the Hendon & Finchley Times made the ridiculous claim that "the Hendon FC had been going since 1874" which as I have shown, is far removed from the truth, with at least four different unconnected clubs carrying the town name through the decades, with at least six occasions where they folded and reformed with different names. Referring to the Hendon which briefly was Golders Green, a fine season was reported on, with only four out of eighteen games lost, naming half back H. Mark as player of the season.

Reformed after the Second World War, Hampstead, as Hendon (!) once more played football in the Athenian League, still based at Claremont Road. In November 1949, the Italian football team, used their ground in preparation of their international against England, played at White Hart Lane. Despite my lengthy preamble thus far, which I feel needed doing in light of misleading histories elsewhere, I hope to have disentangled some of the Hendon spaghetti.

The modern Hendon really only got going in the 1950s, where they rose to become one of the country's top semi-professional sides. They played in the Athenian League from 1914 until it ceased in the 1960s, and were generally a top four side. Oddly, in the years when they were Golders Green, they fell back to mid-table. The 1950s proved to be the start of their successful era, with several Athenian titles and three Amateur Cups captured. Further successes came in the London Cup (5) and the Middlesex county cup (15 to date). The Middlesex Charity Cup was won in 1946-7-8 to add to earlier wins in 1934 and 1939. Titles and cups came thick and fast in the 1950s and 1960s. They were Isthmian League champions in 1965 and 1973, Athenian champions in 1953, 1956 and 1961, London Senior Cup winners in 1964 and 1969, but most importantly, Amateur Cup winners in 1960 (2-1 v Kingstonian), 1965 (3-1 v Whitby) and 1972 (5-1 v Dagenham). They nearly retained the Amateur Cup in 1966 but lost the final 1-3 to Wealdstone. In 1973 they reached the 3rd Round of the FA Cup. Leytonestone were overcome 3-0, followed by a 3-0 away result at Merthyr Tydfil, before putting up a terrific fight against mighty Newcastle United in January 1974, coming away from St. James' Park with a 1-1 draw, but were beaten at home 4-0 in the replay. Hendon mark 5 joined the Isthmian League in 1963 and have remained there since but have recently been turfed out of their 4.2 acre ground at Clitterhouse Farm, where they had resided for 81 years. They were forced to ground-share with Staines Town, then Harrow Borough and as I write, with Edgware Town at their Silver Jubilee Park ground.

HERTS RANGERS

Founded - 1865
Folded - 1882
Colours - 1. Dark Green and Orange (until 1873)
          2. Black & Grey hoops
Ground - 1. White Lion field
          2. Upper Nascot
          3. Meadow on Langley Road, Watford
          4. 'Near Watford Junction station'

Hertfordshire Rangers were known to the Football Association by 1866, so we can say that they were extant by the end of 1865 at least. At such times, association and rugby football were indistinguishable as both codes allowed handling, bringing the ball down with the hand to control it, hacking, tripping, mauling, and pack-like manoeuvres, and many clubs would adapt to whatever rules their opponents were used to on their home ground. Even when the English Cup was started in 1871 by the F.A., 'pure football' was not universally played across the land, with many local variants displayed across the regions, but it was the Cup, which, by compelling all entrants to use the London Rules of the F.A., which was the catalyst for national unity of the rules. No map from the 1870s would describe any field used for football as a 'football ground', until it was made permanent with stands and so on, and thus, studying maps around the late 1870s of north Watford, and Langley Road in particular, which stretched from the railway station at St. Albans Road and out through Nascot, no clues to their field became obvious. However, in 1871 they listed their ground as the White Lion field in Alcock's Annual. Listed as licensees in the census for that year were William and Rebecca Wood, and their 35 year old son William, and daughters Mary and Annie. The White Lion is not really on Langley Road, but before the start of it, on St. Albans Road. A large field faced it, and this is where they must have played until housing was erected at the St. John's Road end about 1876, and by 1880, Wellington and Canterbury Roads had been built over it. They would before then have had to move out along Langley Road to a new meadow, away from the built-up areas. I was drawn to a 5.6 acre square field which lay facing the junction of Langley Road and Park Road, at the rear of two large houses known as Highfields and Oaklands. Thus, Langwood Gardens and Pinewood Close as near as I can say, occupy the spot today. Whichever field they used on that unmade lane, there were no facilities available for changing, and they probably had to erect a tent in which to change. Various descriptions such as 'Upper Nascot' and 'Langley Road' are likely to have been one and the same place, as there were only two possible fields on that road before houses began to populate the area at about 1882. Whilst most old football grounds give way to the developer, some have a habit of staying around under continuous recreational use for over a century, and thus I was drawn to a field lying between Langley Road and the North Western Railway lines, at the rear of a large house called Colnhurst, which by the 1890s had become two 2.6 acre fields sharing a pavilion. Over the Edwardian era, this became a single field again surrounded by woods. By the 1930s, it had become a proper sports field with a new pavilion, and Colnhurst was now Shirley House prep school for boys. A new road, Shirley Road, was built to connect the sports field with Langley Road. By the 1970s, Shirley House had become Cassio College, and Nascot Wood Junior schools built alongside it. This century, Cassio College appears to have been transformed into Nascot Grange when it was sold for £30 million in 2007 and became a new neighbourhood.

Early meeting place for the players of the Hertfordshire Rangers football club.

Thanks once again to research done by Robin Horton, we know that Herts Rangers' odd colours were dark orange and dark green, probably hoops during the 1870s. This was certainly no off-the-shelf outfit, and they must have had them specially made. An even more sombre jersey of black and grey was worn after 1873-4 season. Drawing their players from students of Cambridge University, and the Elstree (f.1838 now a BUPA care centre) and Aldenham (f.1797) schools, the latter drawing up its own football rules as early as 1825, I found no clue in those schools' colours as to Herts Rangers' almost bizarre jerseys. Kennedys house at Aldenham had orange colours, and East house colours at Elstree were green, but unless the founders had been through those public school houses, I see no reason to combine such sombre colours.

In an age before the 'Cantabs' had their own association team, Herts Rangers were always in danger of drawing from too small a player base, and this is what led to their demise at the very end of 1882, at which point they had struggled to assemble a team of any capability. Their two best players over their 17 year existence were Old Westminster Robert Barker, and Francis John Sparks (1855-1934), both of whom gained an England cap in 1872 and 1879 respectively, and both of them were frequently called into the London representative side. Sparks was one of London's leading players, and turned out for several clubs; St. Albans Pilgrims (1873), Brondesbury (1873), Upton Park (1876-8), Herts Rangers (1878-9), Clapham Rovers (1880-3?). Born in Billericay, Essex in July 1855, he married in 1884 having been on the F.A. Committee from 1876-80. Thrice capped, he captained England in March 1880 in the away game with Wales when he scored two of

113

England's goals in a 3-2 win. Sparks was also regularly called up for representative games by Essex and London.

I was lucky enough to stumble across a report of the first match played by Hertfordshire Rangers against another club, when I found an account of when they received the Westminsters on Saturday 8th December 1866. Losing to a single goal, *The Sportsman* congratulated Rangers on putting up such a good performance in consideration of them agreeing to use Westminster school rules instead of association rules, which they played. Likely to have included the men who founded it, this was the Herts Rangers side that day -

> **A.W. Hammans (captain), R. Barker, W. Boyd, H. Finch, H. Mellor, M. Wagstaffe, C. Kidson, C.M. Tebbut, R. Warwick, A. Merry, W. Woolrych. Charles Tebbut was also a member of the Forest FC.**

Robert Barker, born June 1847 in Wouldham, Kent, was educated at Westminster school and Marlborough College where he excelled at both the rugby and association game. He joined Herts Rangers when he left college, thus by 1865, he would have been 18, suggesting he could have been a founder. He later played for Wanderers and the Old Westminsters. In professional life he was a civil engineer and rose to become Chief Assistant Engineer on the London, Dover, and Chatham and South Eastern Railways. On November 30th 1872, he was called up to play in goal for England against Scotland, but was replaced in the second half by Surrey Rifles' forward William Maynard, and Barker assumed his usual position in attack.

Apart from the Sheffield newspapers, very few football matches were reported upon until the early 1870s, and thus the next earliest match I could find involving Herts Rangers was when they met No-Names of Kilburn on their ground on Saturday 14th December 1867. A heavy home ground based on clay made the game a slow one, and with only seven players making themselves available to travel, Kilburn ran out 3-0 winners against this Herts side -

> **Robert Barker, F.N. Skaranke, S.C. Wise, M.M. Wagstaffe, P. Kier, F. McLean, C. Kitson.**

Herts met for the first time, the Wanderers on Saturday 29th December 1867. Waxing lyrical, *The Sportsman* opened the account of the game with " What troops are these that visit us from afar; whose gallant men bespeaks them trained to war". Clearly, football was being thought of as representing a battle, but using the ball as ammunition. Arriving with but seven men (again), Wanderers' weak performance in yet another 0-0 draw was put down to " the seductive allurements of the gay and festive season" which basically meant they could only find seven sober men. Encouraged by their numerical advantage, Rangers pressed the Wanderers ranks which were mainly concentrated around defending their 'citadel' (goal). Again turning to folklore mythology, the 'heroic' seven were likened to the group of Spartans who held out against the hordes of the Persians. Barker in goal, Hammons and Hartshorne were singled out for good play, the rest of the team being - Skaranke, Kidson, A. Day, B. Day, Copeland, Warwick, Hearne, Clutterbuck. On Saturday 7th March, Herts Rangers were beaten 1-0 at home by the No-Names Club, who began the match minus five latecomers who thought they had time to walk to the ground from the station and arrived half an hour after kick-off. Outclassed, the Rangers men adopted a bizarre strategy of forming a semi-circle around their goal for most of the game, making no attempt to even get into the visitors' half of the pitch.

The only other match I could find pre-1870 was when they lost 0-1 at home to an eleven selected by W.O. Hewlett on Saturday 19th December 1868, when Barker and Searanke played well to no avail, the visitor's goal remaining secure. Hardly anyone remained from their 1867 team with the Lake and Bird brothers now featuring in the side, alongside Kerr, Smith, Evans and Fowler. During the early 1870s, Herts Rangers held their AGMs at the Clarendon Hotel, Watford. For the 1871-72 season they announced fixtures against Hampstead Heathens (25/11), Clapham Pilgrims (2/12), Aldenham (9/12), Meteors (16/12), Lausanne (23/12), St. Albans Pilgrims (6/1) with return matches against the above during the remaining Saturdays in January and February 1872. Football was at a low key during 1872-75, with only two or three matches played by the club, and one of these was against Aldenham public school, and also Kings Langley, illustrating the dearth of opposition in the county. 1876 brought an increase in fixtures, with Cricklewood, Cambridge University, 1st Surrey Rifles,and several XIs chosen by local gentry. Season 1875-76 saw the following results – South Norwood 2-4, Surrey Rifles 2-2 and 2-1, Rochester 4-1 and 1-2, Upton Park 0-3 and 1-1, Kings Langley 3-0 and 3-0, Woodford Wells 3-1, Oxford University 2-8, Harrow Chequers 11-0 and 2-2, St. Albans Pilgrims 2-0, Barnes 2-0, Aldenham School 2-2 and 6-0, Cricklewood 0-2, Godolphin School 0-0, Cambridge University 1-0. One wonders what might have been the cricket score had Oxford University met Harrow Chequers! Leading scorers for the season were F.J. Sparks (24 !), with T.B. Day (4), Jervis, Barker and Greaves (on 3), and Haddow, Holland, Berry and Gilbert with 2 apiece. Many others scored once, totalling 51 goals as against 27. Eleven wins, four draws and five defeats constituted their 20 match season, most of which wasn't reported on. Herts Rangers were as much a one man team as you could get! Francis Sparks (frequently spelt with an added 'e') was much travelled, and his club career included St. Albans Pilgrims, Brondesbury, Upton Park, Clapham Rovers, the Wanderers and Windsor FC. Once they lost Sparks to Clapham Rovers, Herts Rangers went quickly downhill.

On Saturday 19th March 1876, Herts met that curious club, Harrow Chequers at Watford. On a bright sunny day, Rangers kicked off downhill with both the wind and the sun at their backs. At the end of ninety minutes, both sides were level at 2-2 thanks to goals from Barnard and a free-kick which was deflected under the tape by a Harrow defender, which clawed them back from 0-2 down. The *Hertford Mercury* said that 'as usual, Sparks, Holand and Barber did most of the work'.

Rangers made a draw with the Westminster school XI on Vincent Square on Saturday 28th October 1876, neither side able to score a goal (*Lloyds Paper*). When Herts Rangers travelled to Marlow to play them in the English Cup on Saturday 4th November 1876, the home side had never got past the 1st round previously. Successive eliminations by Maidenhead, Pilgrims, Royal Engineers and Swifts had given the home side an inferiority complex. Thus, Herts captain Robert Barker saw nothing but a victory for his side. In the most remarkable match description I have ever read in probably over 1,000 newspapers, the report in the *Bucks Herald* should be held up as a standard even today for match reports. The scene is laid out like a battle, with every home player straining every muscle and nerve, and eventually battle through from a goal down by (who else but) Sparks, to

win 2-1. Let me give you some small sections of that 1876 match description -
" - the ball goes like lightning and players and spectators alike tremble for the result, but "Well done Hewett!" is shouted out, and the goal is saved...... inch by inch the enemy are forced back, until the Rangers goal is reached and vigorously assailed; bye after bye is made but no fatal shot.......it is within three minutes of time when Cox takes the ball for the last time down the side in capital style; the enemy try in vain to essay him; he middles the ball and Shaw is in waiting; his shot is sharp and straight, and the umpires flag indicates the goal is carried. Then an immense cheer is heard all around the ground which indicating Marlow's well won victory".

After the match, both teams shared a supper at the Crown Hotel, laid on by landlady Mrs.West, and Rangers captain Barker declared that in Marlow, they had met the strongest country team they had yet played against. Such descriptions of a blood and thunder match, where the underdog gains a cup victory, then shares a supper at which the defeated captain bestows honour on his assailants, is surely the epitome of the golden age of amateur football.

This was the Herts Rangers side that day :-

H.E. Ellis

L. Evans ('long back')

C.B. Field   **W.G.Gervis**

R. Barker S.T. Holland R. Smith F.J. Sparks C. Geary F.W. Watkin E.G. St.John

The fashionable formation being 1-2-7, with two pairs of wing-men, and no less than three centre forwards. This was the classic formation until about 1883 when teams like Cambridge University pulled one of the centre forwards back to create the new position of centre-half, which then became the standard position to be occupied by the team captain as it gave him the best overall view of the field of play.

Nottingham Forest were the distinguished visitors on Saturday 22nd December 1877 when Rangers played them at Watford. Winning 1-0, the *Hertford Mercury & Reformer* said that 'the difference of playing style between the two teams was very marked'. This suggests that one side were showing the new style of passing to each other, and the other, the old fashioned public school way of heads down dribbling, backed up with rushes and scrimmages. My money is on the Forest for the passing game. After this date, the quality of Herts Rangers' opposition seems to have taken an upturn.

F.W. Hotham of Herts was chosen to play for London in the annual representative game against Sheffield in December 1877. Easily winning the away fixture 6-0, the London side, based around five Wanderers players, edged home 2-1 at the Oval. Played on a very dull day, the *Huddersfield Chronicle* reported that the Oval authorities had 'erected a marquee for the benefit of the ladies, who were conspicuously absent'. Old Harrovians were the visitors to Watford at the end of January 1878, when the two sides fought out a 2-2 draw, with the closing goal being scored by charging the goalkeeper, ball and all, over the line. It was the second time the two sides had been unable to decide superiority that season.

When Herts Rangers next played the Old Harrovians at home on Saturday 12th

November 1878, teams were assembled at 12-a-side. Goals from Sparks and Barnard secured a surprise 2-1 win with Barnby replying for Eton (*Bucks Herald*). A rare high scoring draw was the result on Saturday 26th October 1878 when Rangers went over to Vincent Square in the heart of London to meet the Old Westminsters, who were always strong on their home field. The 'pinks' increased their 2-1 half-time lead to 3-1, but Rangers came back to level the scores at 3-3. The Bucks Herald applauded the game, saying that the play "was fast and interesting throughout". This fixture seemed to have developed into an annual home and away game, as Rangers won 3-1 at Vincent Square in March of the following year, after the two sides had met at Watford earlier. Other fixtures for 1877-78 included Old Harrovians, 1st Surrey Rifles, and South Norwood.

During 1875-1881, Herts Rangers competed in the F.A. Cup, known then as the English Cup. Indeed, in the early 1870s, papers in the Sheffield region called it the 'London Cup'! There were only 32 entrants when Herts Rangers competed in the 1875-6 national cup. They secured a handsome 4-0 win over Rochester of Kent in round 1, but then met the might and skill of Oxford University in round 2, and were thrashed 8-2 by the 1874 Cup winners, who reached every semi-final during 1872-1877. The *Sheffield Daily Telegraph* said that the Rangers ground at Nascot, was "singularly unfit for football, being irregular and heavy". Remarkably, Herts scored first through Gilbert, but a steady onslaught by the Oxford men who were much bigger and faster, saw all six of their forwards overwhelm them and bring the score to eight. For Herts, Sparks, Barker and Longman drew praise in this side:-

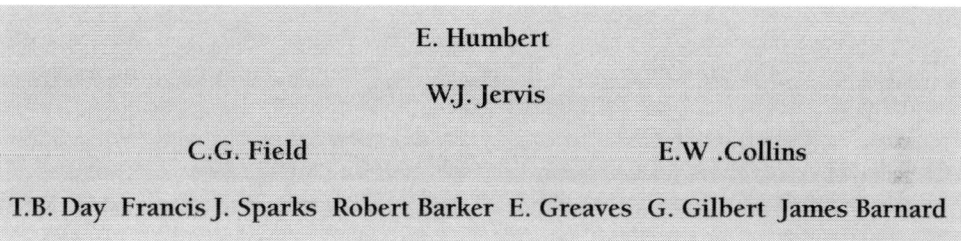

E. Humbert

W.J. Jervis

C.G. Field   **E.W .Collins**

T.B. Day Francis J. Sparks Robert Barker E. Greaves G. Gilbert James Barnard

Undeterred, Herts Rangers entered again the next year, but were narrowly beaten 2-1 by Marlow. With hopes of another chance to get past the first round in 1877, they were dismayed to be drawn against Oxford University again, who duly beat them by 5-2. There was an irony about their early exit from the Cup in the following year, for it was one of the sources of their own players which caused their demise-

Robert Barker   *Francis Sparks*

Cambridge University. Although football at Cambridge went back almost thirty years, they had never really kept a regular football team together, and it was not until 1874 that they began to play with any regularity. The teams met on Saturday 11th November at the Kennington Oval, which was an odd venue if you think about it. However, in those days, first out of the hat did not mean you played at home; merely that you had choice of venue; and thus, Cambridge chose the Oval, possibly as it suited some of their players who had returned home to London for the weekend. The other curiosity had you been a spectator there on the day, was that Cambridge's 2-0 win was played immediately after another cup-tie, but what a corker it was! The mighty Wanderers, cup holders, were humiliated 7-2 by the Old Etonians at the first stage, after three years of consecutive F.A. Cup victories against the best in the land. Wanderers, once the greatest name in world football, were starting to lose players who were instead chosing to play for their old colleges and universities, and so the balance of power got shifted just at the time when the rise of the provincial clubs was beginning to happen. Minerva were beaten 2-1 to commence the 1879-80 Cup campaign, only for Herts to withdraw when drawn against the Pilgrims FC in round 2. The London illustrated newspaper *The Graphic* in its Christmas edition offered no explanation, although as the club was to fold three years later, an inability to gather eleven capable players on the day, was the likeliest reason.

In April 1879, Herts Rangers star player and leading goalscorer Francis John Sparks (1855-1934) was selected to play for London against Sheffield in the annual representative fixture, having already turned out for Essex, but both of these were eclipsed when he got an England cap in the same month for the annual match against Scotland. During this period, Percy Fairclough, Kennedy, the Villiers brothers, Humbert in goal, and the Day brothers formed the nucleus of the side until they folded. The loss of star player Francis Sparks mid-1879 must have been a blow, as he joined and helped Clapham Rovers win the F.A. Cup, and in those days, there was no 'transfer money' generated to enable a top class replacement to be obtained. Many small clubs folded when their star players were enticed to the bigger clubs.

Herts Rangers returned to the national cup at the end of 1880, and cruised past a faded Barnes FC by 6-0. Barnes weren't the only fading name from the earliest days, as monumentally, the 'celebrated Wanderers' withdrew from their 1st round game against Frederick Wall's club Rangers FC, never to grace the competition again. Herts' traditional exit point of the 2nd round was neatly side-stepped when they drew a bye out of the hat, but the might of the Old Etonians awaited them in round 3. Once winners, and thrice finalists, Eton had little difficulty in overcoming them. This was the Herts team who were knocked out of the English Cup at the 4th round stage 3-0 by the Old Etonians on Saturday 4th November 1881, in a game played at the Kennington Oval -

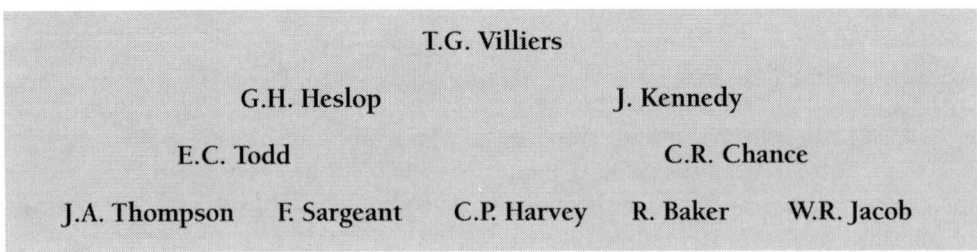

The Rangers played a strong Etonian side with only ten men, which may have made them sacrifice a forward into the midfield department, in a game refereed by F.A. Secretary Charles W. Alcock, and one of the umpires was Major Marindin! Eton's first goal came early on, when Herts thought that Chevallier was offside, and the defence stood still and watched him proceed to put the ball through the posts, only to find that no 'offside' was given; the ball was again in their goal when Clerke scored but was ruled out. A third Eton goal just after the restart sealed the game, when McCaulay prodded the ball home from a scrimmage. Novelli headed the ball under the tapes for Eton, but that was also ruled out for offside, before Anderson scored yet again for the 'home' side near the end to seal a comfortable Etonian cup success. Herts Rangers' final attempt in the Cup came at the end of 1881 when the Swifts proved too strong and ran out 4-0 winners at Slough.

Almost no match reports appeared in the Hertfordshire or London papers for 1880-2 seasons, and it would seem that the club was struggling to carry on. Rangers' only games for 1880 were against South Norwood, Highgate School, Aldenham School, Langley United, and the Barnes FA Cup tie. During 1881 they only played Aldenham, The Swifts, and Clapham Rovers in October, when they lost 2-0 on a drizzly day. Oddly, left winger W.A. Jacob was now tried in goal, with full backs Herrick and Flood, half backs Kennedy and Evans, and forwards Barker, Sergeant, Morton, Yates, Macintosh and Tooms. In December 1881, only 8 men turned out for them (a sure sign of imminent collapse) against Highgate School, and had to settle for a 0-0 draw. A week later, they met Upton Park but no report was found. The quality of opposition for 1882 took a nosedive; Nascot and Acton (3-1) in January, Hemel Hempstead away on 25th November, (won by 3-1 with 3 Sergeant brothers present), and the return scheduled for 3rd February 1883, but I don't think it was played. For a club whose name is non existent going into 1883, I was surprised to read in the 11th October 1882 edition of the Sporting Life, that of Hertfordshire Rangers " the headquarters of this powerful club is at the Malden Hotel, Watford Station, not far from their ground. Secretary and treasurer, E. G. Gordon of 3 Oswestry Villas, Queens Road, Watford offers the season's fixtures – Highgate, Aldenham School and Clapham Rovers in October, Swifts, Barnes, Old Harrovians and in November; Upton Park and Acton in December, Acton and Barnes (return) in January; Old Harrovians, Cambridge University and Hendon in February and Hendon and Aldenham returns in March of 1883. It seems odd that none of the 1883 fixtures were fulfilled. I checked the Old Harrovians' matches actually played for the 3rd, 10th, 17th and 24th of February, and none of them involved Herts Rangers. I could find no reason why they would fold without warning, unless their field was sold for housing.

The West Herts sports club grounds.

Hertfordshire Rangers seem to have finally called it a day at Christmas 1882. The football flag for Watford would be picked up by Watford Rovers, formed in 1881, giving a neat overlap, who renamed themselves as West Herts in 1893. The Earl of Essex gave a group of schoolboys with property owning fathers permission to play football in his Cassiobury Park, and led by Henry Grover and Charles Peacock, founded the Rovers team, who then moved to Vicarage Meadow in 1882.

In view of the number of Herts Rangers players I found now in the Watford Rovers team of 1883, I would say that they may have amalgamated with Watford Rovers. Fifteen years later, Rovers merged with local side Watford St. Mary's and the new club, after another name change to West Herts in 1893, became the Watford FC of today. Upton Park FC also lost players to the new Watford Rovers. Watford Rovers, playing on the Rose & Crown meadow ground, now contained the Sergeant brothers, Alec, Alfred and Frederick, Jack Villiers and the Reverend J. Kennedy in 1889, although I found no Herts Rangers men in the Watford side of 1885. Of 22 matches played that season, Rovers won 15, lost 5 and drew 2. During the 1890s, West Herts competed in the Southern League after 1896 and turned professional the year after. As Watford FC, it wasn't until 1900 that they had their first real success, when they won the League's Second Division. By 1898, the West Herts Club sports ground on Casio Road facing Upton Road was six acres in size, with a pavilion and a fenced off football pitch within the grounds. Apart from the introduction of tennis courts and the demolition of the old pavilion, the West Herts Sports ground remains today much as it was 130 years ago.

HIGH WYCOMBE FC

Founded - At the start of 1872/ December 1871
Folded   - 1886
Ground   - Wycombe Rye, London Road
Colours - 1. Black and yellow hoops
            2. Black and orange hoops

Not to be confused with Wycombe Wanderers who weren't founded until 1887, High Wycombe, just known as plain Wycombe in their early years, existed during the 1870s and 1880s, and for a few seasons played in the F.A Cup. There were already several clubs in the district, such as Marlow, three in Reading, Swifts, Remnants, Chesham, Aylesbury (Dec 1873) and Maidenhead, with inter-county matches between Bucks and its neighbouring counties already an annual event. Likely to have sprung from the much earlier cricket club, whose meeting place was the Coach & Horses inn, the football team was probably started in the winter of 1871, although only the Darvill brothers' names were found in earliest cricket and football matches. The cricket club still have their own ground at the far end of the Rye.

Described as "only lately having been formed", the Wycombe FC felt pleased only to have lost 0-2 away to the established Maidenhead FC on Saturday 3rd February 1872, placing their foundation at either January or December 1871. The football season must have been very short in that location, since the Maidenhead club had no use of their cricket ground after the end of January each year, and any later matches would have to be played on away grounds for the "red & blacks". (*Reading Mercury*). It was from this report that I obtained the fact that Wycombe's colours were "black and yellow" (probably hoops). Return games with Maidenhead and Marlow followed. This then, is Wycombe's earliest team – Lethbridge, Butler, Treacher, Rumball, Skull, Darvill, Lane, Weston, Kedge, Betchel, Wilmshurst and Jull. Lethbridge is probably the departed captain mentioned later on. Their second season opened with a 1-0 win over Maidenhead at the end of October of 1872 at the Rye, followed by a repeat result against Henley on 22nd November 1872 when they fielded this team – Baines, Bethel, Darvill, Kedge, Smales, Reeves, Redington, Littleton, Turner, Morisson and Treacher. (*Reading Mercury*). Either several men had departed, or they had the call of perhaps thirty or forty men to chose from.

Five days later, Wycombe FC went over and made a 0-0 draw with Windsor Home Park. At the end of December that year, a Mr. Disraeli consented to become a vice-president of the football club, along with Sir Charles Young, Bart., and Captain Carrington, MP. One must assume it was Benjamin Disraeli himself. By 1873, Maidenhead and Windsor Home Park clubs were added to the fixtures card. Playing in red shirts, a second club started up in 1873, called Wycombe Alexandra. I noticed some later surnames from the Alexandra team in their youthful ranks – Yoens, Bevington, Buckle and Howland. A third club, Wycombe Excelsior were added to the town before the decade was out.

As was their right as members of the Football Association, High Wycombe sent off their entry fee and competed in the F.A Cup of 1873-4 where they were drawn against Old Etonians. Eton scratched (probably as they couldn't assemble a decent eleven), putting Wycombe through to round 2 where they were narrowly beaten 1-0 by Maidenhead on

22nd of November. The Wycombe 'ground' as such was a large 800 x 300 yards open meadow on the south side of town by the river Wye where there stood the manor house, two paper mills and the remains of the old roman villa. The London Road ran alongside, and a waterway called The Dyke defined the other side. Having no ground of their own proved to be a factor in their stunted development, as no doubt, they could not charge spectators a fee on public open land.

On the evening of Monday 20th April 1874, held unusually at the Council Chambers, members of the High Wycombe FC held their annual meeting. Finances were healthy with seven pounds and two shillings in the kitty. Sadly, said secretary C.T. Baines, the season had been a poor one, with 3 wins and 9 defeats comprising their 12 game season, and this was put down to the loss of several of their best players, particularly their energetic captain (sadly not named but replaced in that role by Baines). Reference to 1872-3 was made, and the fact that the Wycombe Harriers club wanted to amalgamate with them (thrown out). The was also another team in town called the Alexandra, who were still active a decade later as a junior club. (*Bucks Herald*). Marlow FC became Wycombe's tradition first opponents of the season, and the Reading clubs followed.

Their second foray in the F.A. Cup saw Wycombe go out in the first round, 0-1 away to Woodford Wells on 31st October, watched by about 600 people. They could not have understood the gulf between themselves and the already formidable Royal Engineers team which faced them in the following November 10th. Witnessed by a crowd of about 2,500 people, Fifteen to nil was the final score, and you might have thought that would finish them off after that, but no, Wycombe came back the following season, only to scratch when drawn away to Cambridge University, no doubt due to travelling logistics.

In 1875, when Marlow came to play them in Christmas week the *Bucks Herald* said the event had made people wonder 'what had come to Wycombe, the game being so one-sided (to the advantage of Marlow) that it was 'not pleasant'. This was a reference to the fact that another big defeat had come only a fortnight after their humiliation by the Engineers. This Wycombe eleven, minus 1875 captain F. Dyer were beaten by 6-0 :

**A.J. Thurlow, J. Howland, E. Watkins, J. Newell, J. Youens, R. Hudson,
T. Thurlow, A. Thorne, F.W. Beasant, F. Stevens, F. Buckle.**

The redoubtable Wycombe men again entered the Cup for season 1877-8 and were rewarded when they defeated Wood Grange by 4-0 at home on October 27th. Sadly, they once more met one of the giants of football when they were drawn against The Wanderers in December, and were thrashed 9-0 on the Rye on December 15th. Trying to soften the blow, the *Bucks Herald* were quick to say that an overnight hard frost had made the ground hard and slippery. It was the full Wanderers 'cup final team' which dismantled Wycombe, with Wylie, Wace and Woollaston each bagging a brace, the others scored by Denton, Kinnaird, and an own goal (sliced into his own goal by Basett from a corner). The High Wycombe team which suffered that day was -

		A.G. Thurlow (captain)		
		W. Bassett (back)		
		J. Biggs (half-back)		
S.T. Brandram	S.T. Darvill	W. Grange	A.F. Graves	F. Hudson
R. Lunnon				A. Smith

The three Lunnon brothers went on to become stalwarts of the Marlow club, who played at Aldermeadow until 1898. Wanderers went on to retain the trophy in the final against the Royal Engineers, and understandably, High Wycombe never again entered the F.A. Cup. On Saturday 1st February 1878, Wycombe went over and played the (Vale of) Aylesbury club, recently founded. This was a different club to the one which became Aylesbury United, for they were formed by workers at the town printing press company. On a field lent by a James Crouch for the purpose, Wycombe's greater experience saw them comfortably win by 3-0. Lunnon and Milward's passing and dribbling was praised by the Herald, which added that with more practice, Vale of Aylesbury would come up to the visitor's standards. Compared with the above eleven, the side was much changed. J. Newell was now in goal, Graves fell to full-back, A. Lunnon and M. Chiltern were the half-back pairing, with the forwards being : R. Lunnon, W. Milward (left side), A. Thurlow, W. Grange (right side), T. Fisher, R. Chamberlain and G. Williams (centres). Sadly R.A. Lunnon departed and became long-standing captain of rivals Marlow FC who rose to the ascendancy. This 1-2-7 formation was a relic of 1860s football, and by the late 1870s, most

A Google Earth aerial view of The Rye at Wycombe, the general recreation ground bordered by the river and the London Road.

successful sides were either playing 2-2-6 or even experimenting with the 'modern' 2-3-5 system by the early 1880s. When the much needed Bucks & Berks Cup was introduced in 1878, it gave an outlet of excitement for a group of clubs who did not have to compete with the fear of meeting such giants as Wanderers or the Engineers, and it encouraged football clubs to be started up in villages as well as towns. A tie against Reading Minster was Wycombe's first ever draw. By this time, High Wycombe were joined in town by the Standard and Victoria clubs, and were generally known simply as Wycombe.

A county cup tie at Christmas 1879 against a newly formed side called Chesham & Waterside played at Wycombe Rye on the London Road ground drew local interest, since the visitors had borrowed some Aversham FC men. Level at half-time, Wycombe's stamina proved decisive on the frosty ground and they ran out 5-1 winners. In December 1880, another new club, the Mid-Bucks FC arose out of the ashes of the defunct Vale of Aylesbury club. The Vale must have reformed with a vengeance because in April 1884, they thrashed High Wycombe by 9-2 on their ground. By April 1886, Marlow were beating High Wycombe by 6-0 in the Bucks & Berks Cup on Wycombe Rye, and went on to retain the trophy again. Teams like Maidenhead, Marlow, Chesham and Reading had now left them behind. I could find no trace of High Wycombe after Christmas 1886, and indeed a match between Marlow and 'Wycombe' in April 1887 turned out to be a Wycombe eleven drawn from all the teams in the town, but were still completely outclassed, spending the whole match receiving shot after shot at goal, to the extent that Marlow sent in 44 shots which went wide, yet only one went where it mattered. All three Lunnon brothers, once of Wycombe, were now in the Marlow team, but in the summer of 1887, R.A. Lunnon continued to be the star of Wycombe cricket club, scoring 37 of their 85 runs when beating Viscount Curzons XI.

HITCHIN FC

Founded   - 1865
Folded   - 1915
Grounds   - 1. Dog Kennel Farm, Charlton
                2. Cricket ground, Butts Close, Bedford Road
                3. Top Field, Hitchin, Herts
Colours   - 1. Claret and Magenta (1869-71)
                2. Magenta and black (1870s)
                3. Magenta and white halves, navy (1880s)
Headquarters - The Cricketers Inn, Ickleford

A founding date of 1865 may sound improbable, but Hitchin were already an established club by the time they competed in the inaugural F.A. Cup in 1871. The local paper announced on 2nd December that year that 'a football club has been established in this town, Hubert Delme-Radcliffe is the president and the Reverend J. Pardoe the secretary. Members are admitted by ballot and pay 2/6d annual subscriptions...on Saturday last twenty players met for practice at Dog Kennel Farm despite unfavourable conditions'. Another man, A. Delme-Radcliffe was later mentioned in a Hitchin athletics day held on the Top Field. His son, also Arthur, (1870-1950) became a well-known cricketer for Hampshire. The Delme-Radcliffes are mentioned in Burkes Peerage, no less. Briefly, in 1559 the site of Hitchin Priory was bequeathed to Henry Delme-Radcliffe who passed it on to his son, the later Sir Ralph D-R, and it passed so on down through the family. Hubert, the local Justice of the Peace and landowner, died in 1878 and the Priory passed to his brother Francis Augustine. In 1860, Elizabeth Anne Lucas set up a charity which continues to this day, and Francis Radstock gave funds in 1869 for the building of almshouses and an orphanage. All this suggests a football team run by middle class people connected to the Priory and the Church. The Delme-Radcliffes had more than once held the office of High Sherriff of Hertfordshire. Their unusual colours of magenta (a pinkish purple) and black hoops certainly weren't sports shop standard stock, and so I imagine that the Delme-Radcliffes had them made up.

A match against 'Mr Elphinstone's eleven' was played in March 1866 again on the Dog Kennel ground. Confirming this, the *Hertfordshire Mercury* of 1866 gave report of a football match played at their ground at 'Dog Kennel Farm' on 1st December in which the visitors - the Wanderers no less - were victorious by 2-0. The Hitchin side was- Fred Lucas, Fred Shillitoe (captain), Reverend J.B. Parker, George Passington, Edward Longsdon, Lawson Thompson, George Lewin, Hill (goalie), Atkinson, and Mainwaring. In the strange terminology of the day, the local paper said that "the first goal lasted 44 minutes, when Alcock scored for the visitors". And again that "the second goal lasted half an hour (i.e the 75th minute), when the game was brought to an end with the familiar call of "no time". Fred Sillitoe was "swift, active and skilful" and it was remarked that the number of spectators would have been greater had the usual advertisements been put in place.

A further game, at home to Harrow Chequers was played on Boxing Day 1866. Inviting London clubs down implies a Harrow school connection. The farm was in the Charlton district of the town, about a mile due south of the present ground, and is still there off

Willow Road. The field they used was most likely the five acre field, then tree lined, which was opposite the cottages on Charlton Road by the junction with Brick Kiln Lane. That field is now part of the main 12 acre field surrounding the farm.

Founded as many were, as a winter diversion for the old cricket club, earliest secretary Pardoe was superseded by Edward B. Passingham. A new cricket club was reformed on February 1866 at a new field on Hitchin hill, with the Reverend Parker, William Lucas, James Neil, and Edward Passington at the helm, with members of the football club invited to become the nucleus of the new arrangement. Cambridge Old Harrovians were the visitors in April 1867, and were three goals too good for Atkinson, Elphinstone, Darton, Parker, Pardoe, Reed, Mellaindale, Shillitoe, F. Lucas, and J.J. Lucas, and Hill. Once more, a link between some of the Hitchin men and Harrow being likely. In the following November, Hitchin went over and played the Hatfield FC on Rectory Park. Despite being four players short of an eleven, Hatfield won the game 1-0. The AGM for the football club held on Wednesday 9th October 1867 at the Corn Exchange saw the same committee re-elected, with new fixtures added against Cambridge Etonians and the Wanderers. Funds were described as healthy. Captained by Fred Shillitoe, this nine man team met the Wanderers at home in November 1868 and lost to a single goal by Charles Alcock -

J. Reid, Reverend J. Parker, Hill (goal), Silver, Mallandaine, Wilkinson, Mainwaring, Bailey.

The suspected Harrovian connection seemed to be revealed in November when Edwin Lucas was called to the Bar at the Inner Temple in London as a qualified solicitor. *The Sportsman* commended Hitchin on their play and said it was 'much improved on recent years with the addition of some good new men to the ranks'. At their AGM held in October 1867 in the committee room of the Corn Exchange, officers elected were - Reverend J. Pardoe (secretary & treasurer), with Atkinson, Hill, Lucas, Parker and the Reverend Parker acting in committee. Matches arranged against the Cambridge Etonians (4th November) and the Wanderers (30th) were announced, along with a reminder that usual football practice would take place every Saturday afternoon, and the funds were in a flourishing state. In January 1869, the local newspaper stated that Hitchin FC had much improved of late, and were in a sound position, having beaten Welwyn away by 2-0 on Boxing Day, and two friendly matches since between the 1st eleven and the rest. On Saturday 13th February 1869, they were due to meet Clapham Rovers at the Dog Kennel Farm ground, but I believe they failed to show. Re-arranged for March 20th, and with new players James and George Ellard, Hitchin managed a creditable 0-0 draw off Clapham.

In the same edition of the *Hertfordshire Express*, one S. Perks, chemist, has "concocted the most delicious perfume which he calls the Wanderers Bouquet in honour of the famous football team of that name, and the label carries their colours of violet, black and orange". Having failed to discover in print the colours of the Wanderers FC in hundreds of match and after-dinner reports, it was gratifying to read this detail. After their 1869 AGM, the football club said that they were moving their matches to the cricket ground, and a claret and magenta cap was to be introduced as the club colours from that point. With matches generally played between sides drawn from their membership, the football and cricket teams drew 1-1 with each each other in November 1869, following a splendid 2-0 success over the Wanderers on Thursday 27th when goals by Sillitoe and Hill overcame the efforts of Emmanuel, Borwick and company.

With a dearth of clubs in Hertfordshire, Hitchin began to play the London clubs, and I found them on Clapham Rovers' fixture list for 1869-70. Beaten 4-0 at Clapham, the nine of above were augmented by J.W Lucas, C.T. Layten, H. V. Holgate, and J. Foster. Hitchin were rightly incensed when Clapham Rovers refused to play the return match in February 1870 "on account of the distances involved". Hitchin replied that not only was this the second time Clapham had pulled out , but the distance was the same for them when they went to "dark dreary London" (*Hertfordshire Express & General Advertiser*).

By 1873, the team was captained by E.G. Woodgate, and new players Hulme, Hazelrigge, Gilbert, Tuke, Gardiner and Loughborough now comprised the first team alongside Mainwaring, Bailey, Hill and Lucas. Nearby friendly opposition came from St. Albans Pilgrims, Hertford, and Hemel Hempstead.

Hitchin's main claim to fame is that of being original entrants of the F.A Cup from its inception in November 1871, when after a 0-0 draw at home to Crystal Palace, both teams were put through (as not being eliminated) where they were trounced 5-0 at home by the powerful Royal Engineers on the following January 10th. With darkness setting in, and wintry conditions prevailing, Hitchin conceded the game with fifteen minutes still to play out. In the following year, Hitchin scratched when drawn against Clapham Rovers, who had choice of ground (probably because of bad history between them). Played at the Lillie Bridge ground on 14th November, Hitchin were unlucky to be knocked out of the 1874-5 F.A. Cup when Maidenhead beat them by the only goal of the game, which saw E. Dawson in goal and the team still captained by Woodgate.

FOOTBALL.—HITCHIN v. MAIDENHEAD.—These clubs met at Lillie-bridge on Saturday to decide their first tie for the Association Challenge Cup. Vardy kicked off for Maidenhead against a slight wind, and for the first half the ball was mostly in the Hitchin part of the ground, several good shots at goal failing through the excellent play of Dawson, the goal keeper. During the last half of the match Maidenhead still held the advantage, and a goal was kicked for them by Nicholls. Maidenhead were thus the victors by a goal to nothing. Sides.—Maidenhead : C. A. Vardy (captain), W. Nicholson (goal keeper), W. Goulden, R. T. Denne, A. Brown, W. Bassett, O. Prior, G. H. Hebbs, F. Burnham, J. Baker, and W. Nicholls. Hitchin : E. Woodgate (captain), E. Dawson (goal keeper), J. Wilkinson, G. Jackson, W. Lucas, S. Tuke, A. Bailey, H. Bailey, J. Gardner, R. Bassett, and J. Taylor. Mr. Clark, of Lowood, was umpire for both sides.

1875 saw a repeat scenario when they again scratched to Clapham Rovers, and that was the last time they appeared in the cup competition proper, although they later played in the qualifying rounds.

In 1880, former players were on the committee; W.T. Lucas as president, R.H. Baker as secretary and treasurer, with S. Tuke as chairman. One wonders if Baker and Lucas were related to The Wanderers players of the same name, which if so, might explain their matches against each other in the late 1860s. It seems that they were only playing friendly matches at this point (1880), opposition coming from St. Neots, Huntingdon and Royston.

FOOTBALL.

WANDERERS 7. HITCHIN.

This match was played at Hitchin yesterday, and resulted in a victory for the Wanderers, who scored two goals to nothing. The toss was won by the Hitchin captain, who chose the upper goal with the wind. The superiority of the Wanderers soon became apparent, as the ball was flying about on all sides of the Hitchin posts, which, after about half an hour's play, surrendered to a kick by C. W. Alcock. With the wind and hill the Wanderers immediately commenced once more to pen their opponents, who shortly afterwards witnessed the second overthrow of their goal, a good side kick by H. Emanuel achieving this second score. For the Wanderers W. Rigden and L. Ogden were most conspicuous, and Shillitoe and Parker did good service for Hitchin.

The following were the players :— Wanderers.—C. W. Alcock, H. Elliot, H. Emanuel, H. Head, A. F. Kinnaird, L. Ogden, Hon. T. H. W. Pelham, W. Rigden, C. M. Tebbut. Hitchin Club.—F. Shillitoe (captain) Rev. J. B. Parker, W. Hill, W. O. Atkinson, G. Lewin, E. Logsdon, T. Mainwaring, F. Lucas, G. A. Passingham, L. Thompson.

Hitchin were overtaken by other clubs during the 1880s and their match reports were few and far between. Their playing record for season 1884-5 was played 18, won 10, drew 4, lost 4, scored 51 against 27. In the previous season, they played just 12, with only 2 wins and 10 defeats, scoring 10 and conceding 29. Their best players at this time were Payne, Hughes, Gilham, Bower and Woolf, as shown when they were the scorers against St. Albans at the end of October 1885. Having only played 30 games in two years is about a quarter of what many more successful teams who played both league and cup football were doing. It also didn't help that the Herts County F.A. wasn't formed until 1885, much later than many other areas where football had proved popular. The fact that the football field was now in constant use by all and sundry for fetes, marching bands, jamborees, cycling clubs, athletics sports days et al, probably meant that the footballers couldn't always secure the use of the ground. Season 1886-7 was opened with a good 4-1 away win at the St. Neots club, with the Amos brothers scoring for Hitchin. By this time, the local paper seems to have lost interest with football, and Hitchin in particular as their games were now reduced to a single line 'report'. By 1888, the standard of opponents seems to have dropped somewhat as they opened the season with a match against the Three Counties Asylum FC! However 'sanity' was restored when they defeated Luton by 4-0 a fortnight later on 13th October. A Kettering Cup tie against the same club a year later ended acrimoniously before the time was up when the referee disallowed a Luton goal on account of it being offside, and players left the pitch amidst ill feeling. 1889 saw the Asylum fixture repeated, with a 2-1 win gaining only a single line entry in the Herts Mercury whilst below the article a half column was given over to the doings of the Hatfield FC who were a very busy lot playing every week. In the 1890s, the Hertfordshire Cup was providing the cup-tie excitement for Hitchin, with opposition coming from clubs like West Herts, Cheshunt, St. Albans, Hertford, Apsley and Berks Grammar school. The creation of the much needed Herts County League in 1898-9 had already come too late for Hitchin who seem to have spent too much time filling their fixture card with friendlies and an annually brief excursion into the F.A. Cup. A new team in town sprang up out of the Blue Cross Brigade and basically superseded Hitchin, going on to win the Herts Cup in 1923 having earlier lost the 1907 and 1921 finals. By 1899, Hitchin were being left behind by other teams in the county, as demonstrated when Watford, having dropped the Rovers tag, beat them 7-1 to open the 1899-1900 season.

Hitchin's decision to turn professional around 1900 proved to be overly ambitious and led to the club's demise. A spell in the Spartan League (started in 1907) in the Edwardian era brought league football too late to Hitchin to save the club from poverty. Higher grade opposition now came from Chesham Generals, Marlow, Aylesbury United and Tufnell Park.

Trying to go too far, too fast, I call this the 'Icarus Syndrome'. To make matters worse, their grandstand burned down shortly thereafter in 1911, and with debts mounting up and no successes to speak of, the club slowly died, helped by the start of War in 1915 when many football clubs were put into mothballs. Oddly enough, maps across 1900-1920 show no football ground marked, either facing the Cricketers pub or where is now the Hitchin Town ground, until 1930. Thirteen years after Hitchin folded, a new club, Hitchin Town started up in 1928. This is surely a big enough gap in time to say that they were not the same club. New colours of yellow and blue, then more recently yellow and green (as per Norwich City) were taken up. Their 'Top Field' ground on the A505 Fishponds Road at the junction with Bedford Road does not quite match the description of the site of the original Top Field ground; 'Butts Close' is the large recreational field which was directly opposite the Cricketers pub where they changed, so I am not convinced that the current Hitchin Town are playing on the original 'Top Field'. The Cricketers is no more, converted to a large private house.

HOTSPUR FC

Founded - 1878
Folded - 1890
Grounds - 1. Forest Gate E.7 (nomadic)
            2. Field off Uxbridge Road, Ealing (1881)
            3. Battersea Park
            4. Victoria Park, Wimbledon (1887)
Colours - Navy shirts with Maltese cross on breast, white nicks

This London club had nothing to do with the famous Tottenham Hotspurs apart from sharing an almost unique name. Not only did it make research very difficult as most avenues lead me to the Tottenham club, but it also made life difficult for Sam Casey the secretary of Tottenham, who was fed up of getting letters intended for the 'other' Hotspur FC who had claimed the name first. Eventually in 1885, Sam Casey's Hotspurs added the prefix Tottenham, which signally the start of diametrically opposing futures. Remarkably there was also another club called Hotspur, up in Alnwick (Northumberland), plus both a famous ship and a racehorse of the same name, which all made for exasperating research! Founded in 1882, Tottenham Hotspur were very small fry until almost 1891 when they joined the short-lived Southern Alliance League. The description 'Forest Gate', a venue shared by several other clubs in this book, is rather vague, since until around 1880, it was no more than where the old A114 Romford Road intersected the Woodgrange Road (A118) by Wanstead Flats, a large area of open space used for general recreation. This description is only a mile from West Ham park and the well-known Spotted Dog ground, Upton Lane. Back in 1880, there were few buildings at Forest Gate, but today it has become lost in the general conurbation, and Forest Gate is now a larger area which would include the Spotted Dog ground, better known as the home of Clapton FC. Dating back to around 1530, the former hunting lodge to Henry VIII became a small group of buildings by the 19th century, and cricket has been played on the flat and level field behind it since the 1850s. Many

The much-used Spotted Dog ground, may have been the elusive 'Forest Gate' location as given by several teams in the 1870s.

football teams have used the ground, but today, the Grade 2 listed pub sits neglected and looking rather sad, once isolated in a rural tree-lined setting, now overlooked on all sides by tenements and shops. Originally a house, it became a pub around 1810 (*Clayton's 1820 maps*), and across 1839 to 1917 was run by William Vauss and family who enlarged it several times. A painting on the wall of the main room depicts the London coat of arms and dated 1603. Although the sports field remains, the 'delightful gardens' were sold off some time ago, and only one of the old oak trees still stands. Several other clubs had their bases within a two mile radius: Forest, the Old Foresters and the Wanderers at Leytonstone, Thames Ironworks, Upton Park, and the Essex county ground, used by at least four clubs at the turn of the century.

With League football still a decade away, our Hotspur's fixture list was made up with friendlies and entry into the London and English cup competitions, plus other hospital and minor cups. When our Hotspur met the unknown Kildare club in St. Peters Park in London on Saturday 18th October 1879, the *Lloyds News* simply said that Hotspur had won by 2-1, having been beaten 4-2 by the Finchley club the previous Saturday. That old London paper served the city's myriad of small clubs well in terms of always reporting on their games, but sadly usually only gave a single line statement limited to the score and the venue. Hotspur began to enter the F.A. Cup in the autumn of 1879, at a time when any club could do so simply on payment of the entry fee. Early rounds were always regionalized, to such an extent that you were likely to meet the same opponent year on year. On November 8th, Hotspur met the Argonauts at Forest Gate to decide their F.A. Cup tie, but after a 1-1 draw, a replay was needed, in which Hotspur went through by 1-0. In the second round, played on December 13th, Hotspur went out beaten 1-3 at home to the West End club, who strangely had been given a 1st round walkover against The Swifts FC (although they were yet to make their name). Friendly matches against Rangers (1-4) played at Clapton in January 1880 and London Cup ties against Westminsters at Fulham in 1882 and at Wandsworth in 1887 did little to help establish Hotspur's home ground, if indeed they had one. They never seemed to play at the same venue twice!

This was the Hotspur FC team at the end of 1879 -

			Parsons			
			Normandale			
	Ibbotson			Kaye (captain)		
Carr	Cherry	Cox	McIver	Maugham	Rees	Winter

Returning to the F.A. Cup, in the following season, Hotspur met their match at the first hurdle when the Reading FC beat them 5-1 on 13th November 1880. This eleven is different to that above suggesting team selection based on availability -

		W. Winter			
	John Kaye (captain)			G. Dowie	
	W. Robertson		Forster		Ibbotson
S. Carr	G. Randall	H. Maugham		G. Rees	G. McGivor

On 5th November 1881, Hotspur's single goal was enough to get past Highbury Union, but better was to come when they won 4-1 away to the Reading Abbey club in the 2nd Round three weeks later. The team was mostly as that given above, except that George Muir was in goal, the delightfully named Henry Christmas replaced Ibbotson, and W. Winter and J. Sutton replaced McGivor and Maugham in attack. Hotspur's ground on the Uxbridge Road, Ealing may have been one of two five acre tree-lined fields which lay within a few hundred yards of the Coach & Horses public house, one of which became Denmark Road..

Round 3 saw them return to Reading when following a 0-0 draw on December 17th against the Minster club, played in appalling conditions at Uxbridge Road, won the replay 2-0 on the following Saturday. The dizzy heights of Round 4 awaited. Sadly, the last 16 (14 teams actually) was full of the country's top sides, and when they went to the ground of the Upton Park club, they were well beaten 5-0. 1882 saw them enter again, no doubt full of optimism, but they fell 0-2 at the first hurdle to the Rochester club in Kent. Hotspur did not enter the FA Cup again until 1884 when they got past Uxbridge by 3-1 on November 8th. They met one of the country's top amateur sides however in the next round, when the Old Wykehamists beat them 2-1 at home on 6th December. The Wykhamists were comprised of the old boys from Winchester public school where the playing field was an exhausting 200 x 60 yards, and famous players included Claude Ashton, and William Lindsay of the Wanderers FC. Played on the Kennington Oval on Saturday 31st October, Hotspur were knocked out of the 1885-6 FA Cup in round 1 by the Old Westminsters to the tune of 3-1, who had their best ever cup run in reaching the 6th round before being outclassed by West Bromwich Albion 6-0. 1886 saw a name from the modern era as Luton Town were dispatched 3-1 on 23rd October, as the FA. Cup entrants now grew to 124. A trip to Chatham on November 20th proved a disappointment when a single goal put them out. 1887-8 saw lady luck give Hotspur a bye into round two of the FA Cup, where another away trip saw them narrowly lose 1-2 at Dulwich Hamlet on the afternoon of Bonfire Night. This seems to be Hotspur's last efforts in the national competition. Amazingly, in the following season, when Qualifying Rounds were introduced due to the burgeoning entries, Dulwich were annihilated 13-0 at home by London Caledonians!

On Saturday March 8th 1884, the combined Universities team played the London XI, and Hotspur's left winger C. Sutton was in the London team which sadly was trounced 9-0.

The London Challenge Cup seems to have been Hotspurs favourite hunting ground, and generally they did very well, reaching at least one final. When they won a London Cup replay in November 1882 against Hendon by 3-1, the venue of Wimbledon still didn't tell us which club was at home (or was it a neutral venue), but finally we get to discover a Hotspur scorer's name - Carr, who netted all three. In November 1884, *The Graphic* tells us that Hotspur defeated the Old Foresters 2-1 in the London Cup, which tells us that Hotspur were clearly a very competent side. When the Casuals crushed the Tottenham Hotspur by 8-0 in November 1885, our Hotspur drew 3-3 with Clapton, both matches being in the London Cup, confirming that both Hotspurs were concurrently active. The final of the London Challenge Cup was reached in March 1886 but was won by Ashburnham Rovers who beat Hotspur by 2-1, which shows that in 1886 at least the original Hotspur were better than their later famous namesakes! In the semi-finals, Ashburnham had defeated Pilgrims and Hotspur beat the Vulcans 5-0 at the Oval. The Birmingham Post gives a pretty description when it said that the game 'was favoured with charming weather, although the play was poor owing to Vulcans having an incompetent goalkeeper' ! Wagstaffe and C. Sutton were the main scorers, which allows us to slowly build up their players names.

There is no mention in Phil Soar's *Tottenham Hotspur-The Official Illustrated History (Hamlyn Publishing)* of Tottenham Hotspur playing against any Derby sides in 1886-7 (or indeed outside London at all), so the report of two matches in the new year of 1887 when 'Hotspur' played Derby County (1-2) and Derby Midland (1-3) both reported in the Derby Mercury, must refer to our Hotspur FC, implying that they had both the time, money and inclination to venture to the Midlands. Derby County had arranged to play Leeds, who failed to show, and so played 'London Hotspur' instead. This implies that the two clubs had links, possibly railway or cricket, which enabled County to speedily contact Hotspur. Played on December 29th, Sutton got the Hotspur goal, with Plackett's brace for Derby replying. In January 1887, old foes the Old Westminsters put them out of the London Cup when *two own goals* by Hardisley and Jeeves gave the 'Pinks' a 2-0 victory at Wandsworth Common.

These two elevens representing Hotspur played different opposition on the same day on 20th November 1887 -

		Balderson		
	Rocket		Johnson (captain)	
	Lattimer	Gaymer	Simpson	
Walters	Cattell	Jeeeves	Buckley	Elsmore
		•		
		Summerhayes		
	Green		Smithard	
	Keen	Griffiths	Harding	
C. Brunton	Hills	Stoat	Newham	J. Brunton

Victoria Park, opened in 1845 in Bow, London may have been their only 'home' ground, but by the end of the 1880s, it had become a very popular and populous park. A bathing lake (turned over to angling after 1930) offered everyday man the chance to have a free swim when public swim baths were still unaffordable for the lower classes; the park became a popular 'soap-box corner' for people like William Morris and Annie Beasant to vent their socialist views, and large crowds would gather to hear them. By 1888, it was said that every type and variety of religion would be found there, with reformists, agitators and socialists taking over grassed area where once, football and cricket were quietly played without interruption. Of particular interest to the present-day reader will be to discover two footbridge alcoves within the 200 acre park from the original 600 year-old London Bridge, installed at the Hackney Wick war memorial in 1860. Tower Hamlets FC and Victoria Park United currently play their home games in 'Vicky' park.

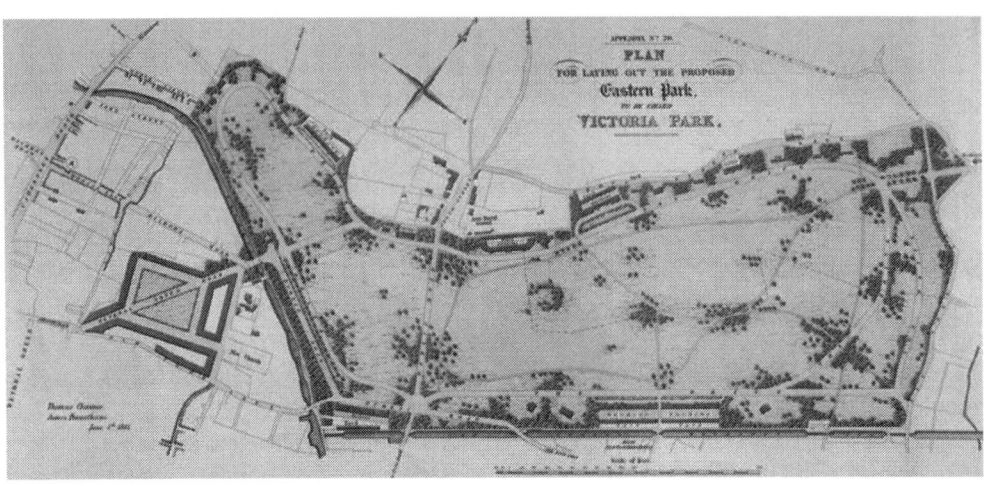

On Saturday 12th October 1889, whilst the Hotspur were playing away to Crouch End Vampires, a thief broke into the Old China Cup coffee rooms which had been used by the players as a changing room, and stole money and other articles. In January 1889, the *Pall Mall Gazette* reported that in the semi-finals of the London Cup, Casuals had edged past Hotspur 4-3 and that Clapton had beaten Royal Arsenal 2-0. I assumed that this 'Hotspur' was the Tottenham version that had finally started to make a name for themselves, but lo ! I see that Tottenham Hotspur were put out 8-2 by Old Etonians in the 1st round, and thus our little Hotspurs were still steaming ahead in the leading group of amateur clubs in the capital. Three times Hotspur had drawn level in that game with Casuals, only for Nixon to grab a late winner for the chocolate and pinks.

Once 1891-2 season arrived however, any searches for 'Hotspur' brought up only the Tottenham variety, and it seems that the original Hotspur had disappeared without trace. Their name was not listed amongst the entries for the newly created Amateur Cup or the qualifying rounds of the F.A or London Cups. I wonder if they had changed their name or disbanded when perhaps their best player C. Sutton left for another club, perhaps taking one or two others with him, a common event? I do hope it wasn't for the Tottenham Hotspurs.

ILFORD FC

Founded - 1881
Folded - 1979 (amalgamated with Leytonstone FC)
Ground - 1. Unknown to 1889
           2. Ilford cricket ground / Ilford sports ground (1894-1904)
           3. Newbury Park, Lynn Road, London (since 1904)
Colours - Blue and white hoops, navy

Football had been played in the Ilford district of London since the late 1860s when a club called South Park briefly existed. Formed in 1881, Ilford became one of London's most successful amateur clubs in the first half of the twentieth century. In what I believe is breaking news, Ilford were started by Alfred Wood and his two brothers, and Alf played in the first team for twenty years, and went on to serve on the Essex F.A. council for many years after (*Obituary of A. Wood 1941, Chelmsford Chronicle*). Another stalwart of the club, Edgar Charles Porter, player and secretary for 25 years, tragically fell to his death from a train in August 1934.

Early near success came in 1892 when they were narrowly beaten 2-1 by the Old Westminsters in the final of the London Cup, a story repeated in 1898 when Brentwood beat them 5-1 in the final of the same competition. The *Chelmsford Chronicle* reported in March 1891 that 'Mr Charles Stenning, formerly secretary to Ilford FC has been made a life governor of the West Ham hospital', rewarding his 'heart and soul' efforts to promote the Ilford club. Other early officers from the late 1880s included president W. Lusby, Reverend H. Barnes, Dr. Shimeld and J.W. Mumford, who remarked that they hoped to get use of the cricket ground at the end of Balfour Road (next to Valentine Park) for 1889. This had been obtained in November 1886 on the Ilford Park estate when 'an area of fifty yards square was re-turved to give a better wicket' (*Chelmsford Chronicle*). Inconclusively, there was also an 8 acre cricket ground less than a mile to the west, at the back of the London Cemetery by the river Rodding (both extant in 1950).

In season 1887-88, Ilford won 14, drew 9 and lost only 4, winning both the West Ham Hospital Cup and the Essex Cup. In the following season, an even better set of figures under the captaincy of Harry Porter saw 20 wins, 6 draws and just 2 defeats and a goal tally of 62-23. Annual general meetings in the 1890s were held in the Angel Hotel or the Reading Room. They had their sight set on bigger things though, in the shape of the London Cup. Their usual first team of 1891-2, and playing in blue stripes, dark shorts at this time, was -

A.J. Davies

J.A. Read   P. Drummond

Herbert Porter   F. King   Harry Watts

E.C. Porter   W. King   A. Porter   J.D. Hutchins   A.G. Milton

H. Gilby was club treasurer with W.J. Mays as financial secretary, with W. Taylor and Charles Stenning comprising their committee.

After competing in the Southern League 1st Division from 1894 to 1896, Ilford then dropped down and had two seasons in the London League, before reverting to the South Essex League. Their 1895-6 season was a catastrophe - losing all 18 games - to obviously finish bottom with a goal tally of scored 10 conceded 80. In 1901-02, Ilford entered the Amateur Cup for the first time and were surprise semi-finalists, but were beaten 4-6 in a thrilling match with the Old Malvernians at Tottenham's ground. At this time, their secretary Thomas Randle of 101 St. Marys Road, appealed for any good local players to come forward and have a trial on the ground. In July 1903, Councillor Griggs announced he was helping fund the purchase of Ilford sports ground, and that the club were going to move into it. Whether this came off is debatable, since another report stated that "in September 1904, Ilford lost the use of the town sports ground, which had been sold to developers. A new ground 'close to the station and with trams running past it' for the football club would be acquired on the Newbury Park Estate with a 21 year lease." This would become the Lynn Road ground. "A high fence surround denied any free viewing, and dressing room and spectator facilities would be provided to cater for athletics, fairs and carnivals". (*Essex Newsman*). The opening football match would see Ilford versus Clapton. By the 1950s, Lynn Road was hemmed in by houses on all four sides.

In common with most other amateur clubs, finances always remained perilous in the first decades, and it was no surprise when they announced a deficit of £27.8s.4d by president Councillor Ben Bailey. Club captain Walter Markham presented J. D. Hutchens a gold watch for thirteen years' service to the club as their 1905 AGM, where Councillor Griggs donated three guineas to the funds. A similar presentation had been made to Herbert Porter back n 1893. In 1905, Ilford were founder members of the Isthmian League and in 1907 they won the title undefeated, but as there were then only six clubs, this was no great feat. Nonetheless, at their 1907 AGM, treasurer George Clarke announced that receipts had gone up from £ 569 to £ 713 for the season. By 1907, Griggs was club president, at a time when a heavy winter had called off six home matches causing the club to lose valuable income.

During the Edwardian era, Ilford began to play abroad in matches designed to stimulate the growth of football in nearby countries. In 1909 Ilford were invited to go on a tour of Brussels at Whitsuntide, the first of several tours. At the outbreak of war, Ilford – as did many other teams - reportedly had 28 players posted with various regiments, many of whom would never return. After the loss of many of their players in the Great War, Ilford football club made annual pilgrimages to the battle fronts and placed wreaths for their former players. Second place in the Isthmian League followed in 1912, and as the years went on, more teams came than went, until by the mid 1920s, a season was over 26 games. Regular opposition at this time came from Leytonstone, Dulwich, Clapton, Charlton, St. Albans and Nunhead. Further titles came in 1921 and 1922, and thereafter Ilford were usually in the top five until 1939. After the war, they fell back into mid-table obscurity until 1958, after when they began a period of struggling near the bottom, apart from 1963 (4th), 1971 (5th), 1976 (5th) and 1978 (4th).

In 1914, Ilford thrashed Portsmouth Amateurs 8-0 in the 3rd round of the Amateur Cup, one of the biggest scores of their history. The quarter and semi-finals were frequently reached until finally in 1929, they beat Leyton 3-1 in the final on the old Arsenal ground. En route, they had beaten top sides Northern Nomads, Stockton and Dulwich Hamlet.

The cup was retained the following year when they beat the not so delightfully named Bournemouth Gasworks FC 5-1 in the final played on the West Ham ground. Once more, Dulwich and Nomads were beaten en route, confirming Ilford now as a top London amateur side.

Ilford had entered the F.A. Cup since 1895, but were dispatched 5-1 at the first attempt by a small club who had yet to make their name - Tottenham Hotspur ! Compelled to participate in the numerous qualifying rounds, Ilford rarely made it through to the 1st round proper, although in 1926-7, after beating London Caledonians 2-1, were eliminated 0-1 by Clapton in the 2nd round proper. In the 1930s, they reached round 1 proper for several consecutive seasons, but it was not until 1974-5 that they emulated the feat, beating Romford 2-0 in round 1 proper before bowing out 0-2 to Southend United.

A great many competitions were won in the first half of the twentieth century, including 13 Essex Senior Cups, the first three of which were won during 1888-90. In a parallel story to the FA Cup in 1897, Ilford won and lost the Essex Senior Cup in May 1924 when the silver trophy was stolen from a shop window which had it on display. Weighing 218 ounces, and being three feet high, thieves drove off at speed in a motor car, leaving the lid, weighing three pounds behind. Its replacement would cost £200, more like £7,000 in today's money. Ilford continued on the ascendancy and a steady stream of trophy successes came their way. The London Charity Cup was won five times, beginning in 1922, and ending in 1963 when they were joint holders. The prestigious London Senior Cup was won seven times, starting in 1901, and again in 1905, 1914, 1922, 1929, 1930 and 1954. A massive attendance (for two amateur teams) of 18,000 saw Ilford defeat Walthamstow Avenue thanks to goals from Potter, Dellow, Drane and Welsh to retain the London Senior Cup of 1930. Only defunct Upton Park FC, Old Westminsters and Old Carthusians had up to then retained the London Cup in fifty years. Matches on the continent continued on, and some results which look surprising today were achieved, such as a 5-3 win away to Cologne (Koln FC) in 1926.

In 1929, Ilford achieved national success when they won the Amateur Cup, and then retained it in 1930. In the 1929 final, played at Arsenal's Highbury Stadium, goals from Drane, Peplow and Potter saw them defeat holders Leyton 3-1, making their 3rd consecutive appearance. Drawing 3-3 away at Wealdstone in the opening round, few would have expected the replay to produce an 8-0 home win. Round 2 saw a 3-0 win at Gorleston, and Northern Nomads were defeated 4-2 on their own ground in the 3rd. Stockton put up a fight in the 4th round, but they too were defeated by 4-2. Dulwich Hamlet were overcome in the semi final played at Stamford Bridge by 4-1, whilst on Ilford's own ground, Leyton were beating Clapton. Defending the trophy, double figures were reached in the opening round of the following season when Eastbourne were hammered 13-1. A good 3-1 win away to London Caledonians in the next round saw the best sides avoided, when a comfortable 3-0 win over unknown Evenwood Town, put Ilford in the 4th round. Top side Dulwich Hamlet provided stiff opposition, but Ilford edged through by 2-1 to meet Northern Nomads for the second year running. Played at the Leyton ground, Northern Nomads held Ilford to a goal-less draw, but in the replay on the Dulwich ground, there was a repeat of last year's 4-2 scoreline, as Ilford reached the final again. Faced with rising Bournemouth Gasworks FC, the faster Ilford had no difficulty in running up a 5-1 scoreline at West Ham's Upton Park ground on April 12th, watched by almost 22,000 spectators. Ilford's attempt to become the first team to win the Amateur Cup three years running came to an end in the 3rd round of 1931, when four goals by Proud saw them beaten 6-2 at Bishops Auckland, who themselves lost in the semi final to Hayes FC. The usual Ilford team at this time was -

	Watson	
Triesman		Winterburn
Shappard	Craymer	Webb
Potter	Welsh	Dellow	Drane	Peplow

In January 1930, the death was reported of F.J. May, of The Whym, Southbourne Grove, Westcliffe, the managing director of May's Dairies. It was stated that he had been a founder-member of the Ilford FC. The club was rocked back in 1934 when their secretary Edgar Charles Porter fell to his death from a train just outside Forest Gate halt on the night of Saturday 13th August. It seems that he had been for a day-trip to Southend with friends for his son's wedding, fallen asleep on the train and attempted to exit the train as it pulled away from his destination. Porter had been "Mr. Ilford FC" having been a player with them for 25 years, secretary for 14 years, and chairman for the past 8 years. His loss reverberated throughout the club.

Season 1935-36 saw another appearance in the Amateur Cup final, but there was disappointment as The Casuals took the trophy after a 2-0 win in a replay at the West Ham ground after the two sides were locked at 1-1 on the Crystal Palace ground of Selhurst

FOOTBALL TEAMS. No. 44.—THE ILFORD (ASSOCIATION).

Park. A similar fate awaited them in 1958 and 1974 against Woking (0-3) and Bishops Stortford (1-4) respectively. In 1941, Alfred Charles Porter, their founder-member passed away in South Bendfleet, where at his funeral it was explained that he had been a lifelong player and committee man for both Ilford and the Essex County FA.

In the 1970s, their see-saw performances saw them finish 4th, 22nd, 5th, and 17th in the final four years leading up to the 1979 merger. Ilford were never big scorers in the league and rarely average two goals per game, except in 1926 (81 from 26 games), 1930 (84/26), 1937 (86/26), and 1975 (98/42). In modern times, the Essex Floodlit Cup was taken in 1971, 1973 and 1974, and the Essex Thameside Trophy in 1950, 1955, 1960 and 1971. However, after gracing the Isthmian League since its foundation, Ilford were relegated to its second division in 1977 and thus were in a weak position all round at the time of their 1979 merger with Leytonstone. In 1987, even the name was lost when the joint club was absorbed into a new side, Redbridge Forest, which in turn amalgamated with Dagenham to form Dagenham & Redbridge, and although a 'new' Ilford was started up in 1987 at a much lower level, the history and name of the old club had been consigned to history.

LAUSANNE

Founded - 1866
Folded - 1881 as a rugby club
Colours - Mauve with amber sleeve stripe
Grounds - 1. Rosemary Branch Quoits and Cricket Ground, Peckham
(1866-72)
2. Bennetts Field, Peckham 1873
3. New Cross Gate 1874
4. Dulwich 1875-81
Headquarters - 1. Rosemary Branch public house, Southampton-street,
Camberwell
2. Greyhound Inn, Dulwich 1875-81
Secretary - Frederick Noone, 17 Wilson Road, Camberwell

Historians of the rugby union game would know this club and be surprised to read that they also briefly played the association game. Indeed, they were one of the earliest of London clubs in an age when general sports clubs played several sports including lacrosse, tennis and athletics as well as both football codes. Clapham Rovers were a contemporary. A large membership of sixty enjoyed twenty a side rugby and fourteen a side association football in the 1860s and 1870s, and club colours were violet shirts with an amber stripe down the arm (*Dick Tyson- London's oldest rugby clubs*). On 26th January 1871, Lausanne sent a representative to the meeting of London's 21 rugby clubs at the Pall Mall Restaurant which resulted a few years later in the founding of the Rugby Football Union. I restricted my research however only to their adventures in the non-handling game, even though I found them playing cricket in the summer of 1866. Unfortunately I found only a handful of their football games in the London papers, and one of the first sent me down the wrong path. A match reported in *Bells Life* in December 1866, said 'Lausanne played the (equally oddly named) Geneva FC on a ground kindly lent by the Government' at Geneva for the purpose. The Lausanne's heavier men won 1-0 with this eleven - L. Howell, E. Leggett, F. Barlow, J. Ponsonby, R. Allfrey, R. Tideswell, G. Johnson, P. Hobson, W. Lamb, F. Lyon.' At first I thought it was a London venue, but the more I thought about it, both teams and venue were names from Switzerland, and as research went on, I hoped that the mists of time would clear. It took a while for the penny to drop inasmuch as I was reading about the first football match ever played in Switzerland, yet it was reported in the London papers! The first evidence of the Peckham Lausanne club came in July 1867 when they met a cricket team called Caroun on Clapham Common. Further cricket matches took place in 1868 against Clarendon and Granville at Blackheath. Matches against St. Georges Hospital in July 1869 contained the names of those who would also comprise the football team. Further cricket matches took place against Alliance, Clapham and Rye Hill in the summer of 1869. This eleven lost 0-2 at football to Brixton in December 1869, played on the Duke of Edinburgh ground, having played them away on 27th November -

George W. Marsden (captain), McLeod, Cohen, C. Keeler, F. Noone, Dummler, A. Walker, J. Walker, S. Walker, Foord, Davenport.

The eleven which met Leyton two years later contained only Noone from the above side, with new men captain Foster, the Reverend Willis, Hastie, Stevens, Maynard, Kelham, Moore, Edmonston now making up the team. Interestingly *The Sportsman* called Lausanne the 'Association of Merry Swiss Boys'. I was starting to think that these were civil servants or military who had been stationed out in Switzerland, and on return home, continued to play as a sports club. I then found Lausanne's somewhat limited fixture list for the 1869-70 season, which only included home and return matches against Penge, Brixton and City of London, starting in December and ending in February. Matches reported after 1870 tended to be the rugby variety, with opposition coming from Clapham Rovers, Flamingos, Penge Park and Mohicans. A match played at home to Clapham Rovers in January 1870 was probably under association rules, since there were nine-a-side, and the score was one goal apiece. Another game, played in the same month, away to Penge, was clearly of the rugby variety, as there were goals and five touch-downs recorded, although many of the above listed participated.

In March 1870, one Charles Dunt felt obliged to correct reports about incidents which caused unpleasantness in a recent match between his Streatham club and Lausanne, presumably on the Streatham ground. It appears that trees encroached the field of play, and a high ball went into the branches and out of play, but when the ball fell to ground, was taken up by a Lausanne player Kolle, centred, and Peckam scored a goal from it. Lausanne held their end of 1869-70 season annual dinner at Crosby Hall in Bishopsgate Street, London. Whilst trying to ignore Lausannes' cricket fixtures, I was intrigued to see a match arranged for July 22nd 1871 against the Royal Arsenal club! Rugby opponents included Clapham Rovers, Harlequins, Mohicans, Richmond and the Flamingoes, so they must have been ranked as a first-class rugby team.

In December 1871 the Brixton FC threw in their lot with 'the Merry Swiss Boys' (as Lausanne were nicknamed) and a stronger than usual eleven walked out onto the Rosemary Branch field to play the 1st Surrey Rifles team. Despite a 0-2 home reverse, their play was deemed to be improved, and the dribbling display of forward G.R. Fleet was remarked upon. Captained now by R.L. Dawson, *The Sportsman* made a comment that the 'Helvetians' i.e. Lausanne 'abandoned their previous tactics and endeavoured to shine individually rather than collectively'. This is quite strange since most other teams strived to exchange the dribbling game with the combination play by the late 1870s. A match just before Christmas that year revealed that on the day the Lausanne rugby team were at home to Oakfield, the association eleven travelled to play the Leyton club. The ground, said

The Sportsman was covered in a low-lying mist, and was "very small and spoiled by numerous small pools and gorse bushes". This sounds to me like the Leyton Flats at Leytonstone, where the old Forest FC used to play.

Playing home games on the Rosemary Branch Grounds (east of Blakes Road, part of the sprawling

THE OLD ROSEMARY BRANCH.

North Peckham Estate), they used the pub of the same name as headquarters on the corner of Commercial Way and Southampton Road, Camberwell. I could not find out who Rosemary Branch was, but her extensive quoits and cricket grounds lay to the east of now Southampton Road (now Way), and I would say that North Peckham Baptist Church sits near the centre of it. There is today, a Rosemary Branch theatre cum pub in Islington, which used to be an old music hall of the same name, where Marie Lloyd and a young Charlie Chaplin once performed. I then contacted the theatre pub on Shepperton Road, and discovered to my mirth that 'Rosemary Branch' wasn't a woman at all, but was the name given to a group of 17th century political extremists who used to meet and identified themselves by wearing sprigs of rosemary herb in their hatbands ! The grounds occupied a large area, with present-day Commercial Way (then North Street) being the southern limit and Gloucester Junior School on Daniel Way being its northern limit, in all some 400 x 400 yards. The nearest football club, the 1st Surrey Rifles had their Flodden Road ground a mile due west. The ground had gone by 1890, built over by several streets, which themselves have been rebuilt in the 20th century. Once unique, there are now several pubs of the same name in London and Cambridge.

Early secretary was Frederick Noone of 17 Wilson Road, Camberwell, a surname familiar to readers of a certain age who remember the Sixties pop group Hermans Hermits. A match at home with the Brixton club in January 1870 was clearly of the dribbling code, as goal-keepers were mentioned. The amusing item was that Lausanne's captain, Marsden, *kept on placing the ball just over the crossbar thinking they were playing rugby rules! (The Sportsman).* The rest of the team - Cohen, Dawson, Figg, Kelham, Hammond, Rummell, J. Walker, A. Walker, S. Walker, Noon, proceeded to secure a 2-1 win with goals from Figg and Hammond. Unusually, when time was up at 4.30pm, there was still plenty of daylight so they agreed to play on for another 15 minutes just for the fun of it!

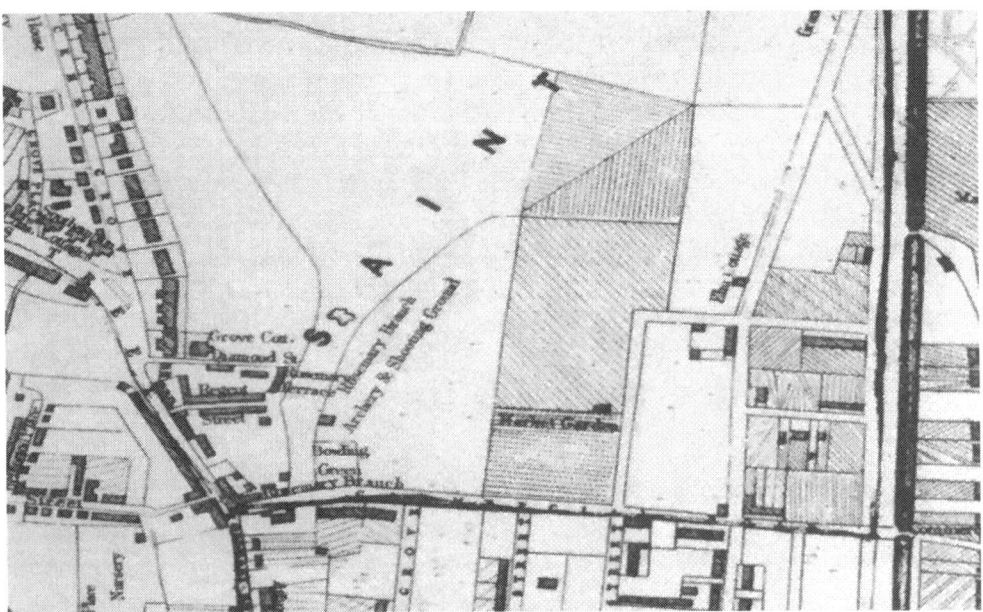

The extensive grounds behind the Rosemary Branch inn had room for bowling, archery, shooting, athletics and ball games. It is better known today as Peckham estate.

Lausanne went over and played the Hampstead Heathens on Saturday 3rd December 1870 and this was clearly an association match. Kicking off at 3.45pm, Percy Tatham scored within a minute, when he returned with a punt, a clearance from the Lausanne defence, which sailed between the posts. Further goals from Barker and Evans, where it was remarked that the Lausanne goal was weakly defended, saw the home side 3-0 up at the break. Captained by F.W. Marsden, with brothers J.W. and B. Nott-Bower in defence, they were augmented by Dawson, Drummler, Cohen, Rummell, Watson, Fred Noone, Stewart, and the Kelham brothers, George and Charles. On the same day, the rugby fifteen, using "mainly new blood" met the Red, White & Blue club at Hampstead Heath (*Bell's Life*).

Lausanne met the 1st Surrey Rifles FC three times in the spring of 1872, resulting in two draws, and a 2-0 win for the soldiers. Their team for 1872 ran – Dawson (captain), Holloway, Drummler, Cohen, W. Forster, Moore, Dearle, Davenport, F. Maynard, Newman, Parker, and Thompson. Their third meeting, held on the Rosemary Branch ground on 2nd March, was described by the *Morning Advertiser* as if they were having a military battle, with fortresses being assailed, posts heroically defended and so on! The most remarkable feature however, was the fact that the two sets of goals were no less than 200 yards apart! It was little wonder that, after running with the ball, players from both sides ran out of puff somewhere around the halfway line, and the game ended somewhat predictably, goal-less.

Lausanne held its annual sports day at Bennett's Fields, Peckham on 21st September 1871, instead of at Rosemary Branch. A fixture list for 1871-72 in *The Sportsman* giving details of about 25 matches, made no distinction between association and rugby matches, although only home and away fixtures against Herts Rangers, Surrey Rifles and Hampstead Heathens were at association.

After 1873 I could find almost no reports on Lausanne football matches, only cricket and rugby, and I wonder if they discontinued the dribbling game at this stage? In 1874 Lausanne relocated half a mile north to the district of New Cross, from where only rugger games were reported. In 1875 Lausanne once more relocated to Dulwich Village, and based themselves at the Greyhound Inn and its football ground at the rear, a venue much used by several later clubs. In February 1879, Lausanne went to the ground of the Harlequins RFC and won there by one goal and two tries, to two tries. This reinforces my conclusion that they were no longer playing the association game. Reported matches of any kind became scare after 1880.

Lausanne disbanded in 1881 according to Wikipedia, but I found a cricket match played by them in the summer of 1882, but nothing at all after that. It was at this point that I found out the origin of their name. There was a street in Peckham called Lausanne Road!

Having discovered the Lausanne colours of mauve with amber trim, I was intrigued when a clothing company, Black & Blue, of Pall Mall, London, were selling quality replica vintage rugby shirts, and listed Lausanne (1871) as being hoops of red, white and blue. This made me wonder if Lausanne merged (or became) with the rugby club of the same name? If that clothing company's research into defunct rugby clubs is to be believed, then Flamingoes played in light blue, and not pink as one would expect, that Gipsies (Gitanos?) were in green, red and white hoops, that Mohicans played in hoops of red, black and gold, and that West Kent played in plain dark green (contrary to my research, see page for West Kent FC).

LEYTON FC

Founded - 1868
Folded - 1. Before 1877
           2. 1911
           3. 1928
           4. 1975 amalgamated with Wingate
Grounds - 1. Hainault Road
           2. Leyton cricket ground
           3. Hare & Hounds ground, Lea Bridge Road E.10
           4. Shared Walthamstowe's Green Pond Road ground after 1937
Colours - 1. All white with blue hooped stockings and caps (1870s and 1880s)
           2. Blue and white stripes 1895
           3. White shirt, black shorts (20th century)

According to the *History of the Amateur Cup* by Bob Barton, Leyton were founded under the name of Matlock Swifts in 1889, and they changed their name to Leyton in 1893. This will be quickly be dismissed, as match reports from 1876-77 backs up the 1868 formation date. This puts them just behind Cray Wanderers as the 2nd oldest club from London who carried their name into recent times. Leyton should not be confused with Leyton Orient or Leytonstone.

Another early small club, the Trojans FC, founded 1869, used the Cowley Arms public house as their base in Leyton, and may have shared the Leyton county ground.

Leyton were one of the most active and certainly successful amateur clubs in London throughout much of the first half of the twentieth century, winning many cups and leagues in the London area, culminating in their two Amateur Cup successes of 1927 and 1928. The problem is, there have been so many amalgamations, and clubs calling themselves 'Leyton' over the past near 150 years, that the story is almost impossible to unravel. I tried

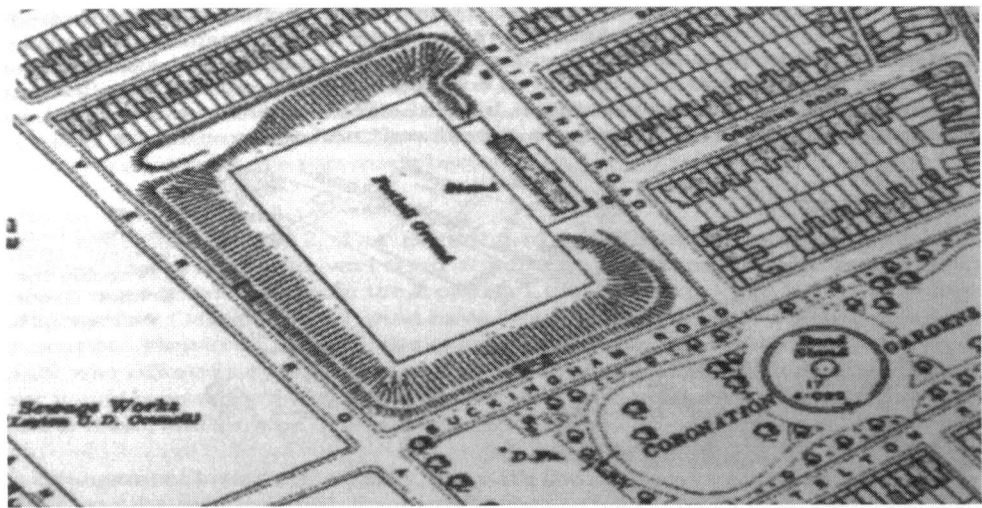

The Osbourne Road Ground in 1915. Large grass embankments and just one stand (east side). Image courtesy of Dave Twydell.

to follow the puzzle by reading through newspapers from the 1870 to the present day, but it's hard to join up the links. Having completed my research, Dave Twydell then sent me his Gone But Not Forgotten number 43, which includes Leyton, I was even more confused! The first incarnation of Leyton folded in 1880.

The *Chelmsford Chronicle* reported on one of Leyton's earliest games when on Saturday 17th April 1877, the last match of the season between Romford and Leyton, played on Romford's Great Mawneyes ground, saw the visitors gain a 2-0 win thanks to the efforts of G. Matchett, H.J. Bowen and J. Rawson. In the early years, Dave Twydell's Gone But Not Forgotten #43 tells us that they played 'on Cashford's Field at the end of Mayers Lane'. Leyton then moved to Coopers Lane, north of Leyton cricket ground, and again to James Lane, a location which is probably now called Abbots Park. Few records exist of Leyton's trophy successes prior to season 1891-92 when they won the Walthamstow Charity Cup, but suffice to say that every single year after that, the north-east Londoners appeared in at least one cup final every season until 1911. The Essex Senior Cup was captured 11 times, and the Junior Cup once, with many other successes including the London Senior Cup, the London Charity Cup and several Athenian League titles. In 1894,' Matlock Swifts' beat Whytham 4-1 to win the inaugural Essex Junior Cup; several sources claim that this team became Leyton, but as we can see, Leyton were already in existence at that time. It may well have been that Matlock Swifts folded and threw in their lot with Leyton to strengthen the team. Dave Twydell thinks that Leyton folded in 1880, reformed as Matlock Swifts in 1889, and reverted back to 'Leyton' in 1893. This is possible, but the only reference to Matlock in north-east London is a Matlock Road in the Leyton district. This does seem the most likely solution.

The *Chelmsford Chronicle* reported on Leyton's presentation night of Wednesday 20th May 1897 at the Lanthorne Rooms, Stratford, when Alderman Kidd presented the team captain Pugh with medals and the trophy which had been donated by Alderman Hay. In the following year, the club held its presentation dinner at the 'new dining hall' of the Essex county ground, where officials C.R. Higgins, and C.R. Ward of the Essex cricket club, congratulated the team on another fine season, adding that they hoped the team would

Lea Bridge Stadium in 1933. Image courtesy of Dave Twydell.

remain on the Essex county ground for years to come. Joining the inaugural South Essex League in 1895, they were champions for the first two seasons, and again in 1900, when their reserve team won the division two title. In 1897, Leyton took the bold step of joining the London League, but they weren't ready for it, and left two seasons later, having faced teams such as Fulham, QPR, and the reserves of Spurs and West Ham. In 1898-9, Leyton's 'A' team won the Essex Junior Cup trouncing Coggeshall 6-0 in the final. After returning to the London League in 1900, they slowly improved and finished 5th in 1905, by which time all the Football League names had left. In 1901, Leyton not for the first time, moved into the Hare & Hounds ground on Lea Bridge Road, E.10.

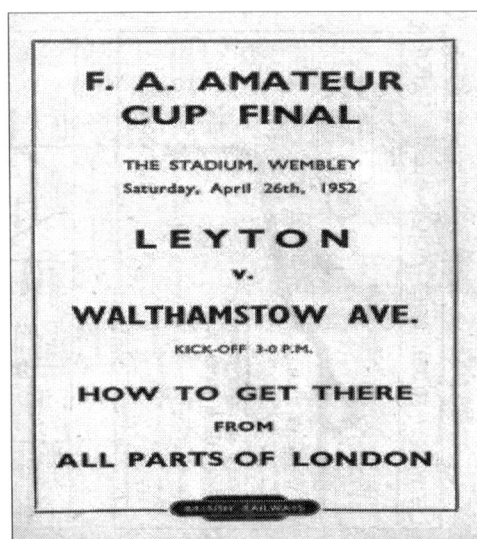

In common with other clubs who signed players on a one year contract, the *Dundee Telegraph* reported at the start of the 1905-6 season, that several Scottish players had gone south to join the Leyton club, making to fourteen the number of new players signed to Leyton in addition to retaining most of their first eleven. Such panic signings were commonplace and typified the antics of poorly-run clubs who wrongly believed that transfer activity would bring new faces through the turnstiles. At this time, Leyton moved again into a ground at Osborne Road which they developed into a good stadium capable of holding 20,000.

In 1906 they turned professional and joined the Southern League where they struggled until 1912. Strangely, the *Chelmsford Chronicle* when reporting on the club's AGM of June 1906, and its debts of almost £300, said that it was ' the first annual meeting of the club'. Whether this implies that Leyton had folded and reformed (for the 3rd time) at the end of the 1905-6 season, or whether it had been the clubs' first AGM (highly improbable after thirty or more years extant) suggests that despite Leyton's successes on the field, it was being badly administered off it. After a scare that Leyton were to fold in 1911, (denied and counter-denied) they then reverted back to amateur status and returned to the South Sussex League.

Leyton in 1912 now moved out of Osborne Road, which became the Bryant & May works team private ground, but in 1929, Leyton returned there. Between 1908 and 1928, Leyton reached the final of the London Charity Cup six times, but won only once, 3-0 v Millwall in 1912. Their final defeats were against Millwall (0-2 1908), 0-1 v Crystal Palace in 1928, 1-2 v West Ham in 1922, v 1-2 Chelsea 1927, and 3-6 v Millwall in 1928.

The *Portsmouth News* reported on 4th January 1912 that a new company, charged with administering the affairs of the Leyton FC, has lodged its registration with the Registrar of Joint Stock Companies (i.e. Company House, London). The club seems to have have folded and reformed at this point as in June 1914, the Western Mail reported that 'the new Leyton FC have applied to rejoin the Southern League's Division Two.'

Leyton hit a low point on September 16th 1914 when they were embarrassed to the tune of 0-9 by Swansea in the Southern League played on a waterlogged pitch in front

Leyton's regular home, the Essex County Ground, still exists today.

of 5000 spectators. At this point, several Councillors made a concerted effort to improve the fortunes of the club, with seven new professional players being signed up, including Collins, Horn and Cousins from Chelsea, and several promising amateurs including W. Hughes and J. Hughes, both being brothers to the noted West Ham goalkeeper.

After the war, the 4th (?) version of Leyton joined the Middlesex League for 1920-21 and then they joined the by then, weaker London League in 1921-22, winning the championship three times before joining the Athenian League in 1927 as Amateur Cup holders. They became a strong Athenian side, never outside the top six. Crushing Oxford City 8-0 en route to the final, Leyton needed a replay to get past Southall in the semi-final, which was watched by over 20,000 fans. In the final, watched by almost 13,000 fans who stood in a downpour, it was mostly Barking who held the upper hand, attacking the Leyton goal for much of the game. However, goals on the counter-attack by Cable (2) and Salmons gave Leyton a 3-1 victory on the Millwall ground on April 9th. The 1920s would see Leyton rise again as a leading London team.

The 1927 Amateur Cup was retained in the following year when they defeated surprise finalist Cockfield 3-2 played on Middlesborough's ground. Twelve thousand saw plucky Cockfield - a team comprised of unemployed miners - take a 2-1 lead by half-time, but Leyton, with 7 of last year's men in the side, came back to win. Cambridge Town had been despatched 5-2 in the semi-final, and Leytonstone 3-0 in round 4, in a competition which saw a mini-revival from Sheffield side Hallam, and Crook Town disqualified as amateurs because they had paid their men above and beyond their travelling and hotel expenses. Further success came in 1928-29 when they were crowned Athenian League champions, with 19 wins, 5 draws and just 2 defeats, scoring 78 goals in their 24 matches.

Leyton themselves were brought before the F.A., when in 1928 they were fined £50 and suspended for a fortnight when they broke regulations, although reporting newspapers did not reveal the details. On 4th October that year, the club was on the rocks, and was re-constituted with a new committee, presumably to distance itself from those officials responsible for the censures. This may have been Leyton FC # 5. Third place was achieved four times in the 1930s, with rivals of the time being Walthamstow, Hampstead, Southall, and Wealdstone.

In 1935, the club made headline for the wrong reasons, when their chairman Lionel James Smith was convicted of dangerous driving leading to the death of one of his passengers. He appealed, but lost that too, and was sent down in May, which was reported as far abroad as Hull and Gloucester. In 1937, Leyton were evicted from Osborne Road, and League club Leyton Orient moved into it, and renamed the ground Brisbane Road. A short stay at the Leyton speedway stadium followed. Success continued on until the Second World War, during which time (1937), they had to ground-share with Walthamstowe. They re-formed after the War, now back at the Hare & Hounds, to reach the Amateur Cup final again in 1952, by which time, they had got used to losing cup finals, as they had variously been beaten in the finals of the London Senior, East Anglian, Essex and London Charity cups during 1937-1952, a total of 8 finals ! The Hare & Hounds ground, quite compact at 2.64 acres, had a well drained level pitch, but only a small central stand with a pavilion behind it.

As with other leagues, the Athenian reformed in 1945, but following a season where they came runners-up, slumped badly, and were wooden-spoonists for four of the next five seasons. Only a 5th place in 1953 and 1957 brought any respite from the dangers of the club folding. In January 1950, Leyton were in the news again, when Leyton Council put forward plans to build a new community sports ground for the club on land which had lain unused for some time, but which was common land to the people. Leyton remained in the Athenian League throughout the 1950s and 1960s, with roller coaster seasons, winning the title in 1966 and 1967 followed by relegation in 1975. A key official was lost in July 1964 when chairman Ted Jones severed his connections with them.

Their 1965-66 championship season saw them take the title from Finchley on the slenderest of margin – a superior goal average of 76-28 against 83-39, with Finchley most unlucky as they won one more game than Leyton. Opposition at this time included Leatherhead, Dagenham, Maidenhead, Slough Town, Hounslow, Grays, Hayes and Edgeware. This trick was repeated the following season when their 73-32 goal average was superior to Bishop Stortford's 56-33, after both ending on 43 points, just above Finchley. Something akin to an exodus of players must have happened in 1967 for Leyton to go from top to bottom, and they kept on falling. Leyton fell straight through the Second Division too, with only 5 wins in 30 games in 1968-69 and were again relegated to the bottom rung, were they managed to finish 9th, playing teams such as Uxbridge, Marlow, Harrow Borough and Horsham. In 1970-71 Leyton finished at the bottom of the 3rd tier of the Athenian, with only Wingate and Epsom for company. A slight improvement to 9th, with Wingate 14th, seemed to give hope, especially as 12 were won and 11 lost. The amalgamation with Wingate must have been very brief, for Wingate continued under their own name at this time. Leyton finished 4th in Athenian Division 2 (3rd tier) in 1973, when the Athenian League underwent a considerable change, resulting in mass migration and restructure. Leyton now finished 3rd in the Second division and got promoted back up the the First, leaving Wingate in the Second, where they came a much improved 3rd. For season 1975-76, Leyton amalgamated with groundless Jewish club Wingate FC, but the combination could only finish 14th out of 16. They also found Tilbury FC different class when they lost by a record 1-11 in an FA Cup Qualifier tie. At this time, a whole host of legal wrangles and court cases ensue about who owns what name, and as far as I can see, the real Leyton ended here.

Remarkably, Leyton-Wingate won the Athenian championship in 1976-77, a point clear of Letchworth Garden City. The Athenian drastically shrank the following season when 17 clubs departed, and Leyton-Wingate finished runners-up. The title was again won in 1982, with a staggering unbeaten record which saw 28 wins and 8 draws, with a goal difference of 87-19. To celebrate, Leyton-Wingate said goodbye to the Athenian League, and joined the Isthmian League's Division Two. They eventually won promotion in 1985, but apart from runners-up spot in 1987, struggled. A couple of years later, Leyton-Wingate split up, and the 'Leyton' half now amalgamated with Walthamstowe Pennant FC and became Leyton Pennant. A Greek businessman (later jailed for massive VAT fraud) bought the Hare & Hounds pub and ground, and started his own 'Leyton FC' (version #6); meanwhile they took the Leyton Pennant club to court over rights of use of the Leyton name, and won their case. Not only that, but the judge decreed that the history of the team bearing the Leyton name be transferred to them! And so, Leyton version 6 continued on until 2011 when due to no support, they too folded. Meanwhile (are you keeping up with this?) Leyton Pennant changed their name to Wathamstow Forest. If anyone starts up version 7 of 'Leyton FC' - please don't tell me.

Leyton winners 1926-27. Included in the photograph are Graves, Preston, Grainger, Terris, Goldsmith, Salmon, Bowyer, Cable, Smith, Hawkinge and Hall who all played in the Final.

LEYTONSTONE FC

Founded - 1886
Folded - 1979 amalgamated with Ilford, and again absorbed into Redbridge FC
Ground - Granleigh Road, London E.11
Colours - Red and white stripes (1920s)
Red and white hoops, black (1940s)
All red (1960s)

Founded in 1886 as Cedars football club, they renamed themselves as Leytonstone in 1892, by which time, the many early football clubs in the area – Forest, Wanderers, Greyfriars – had all died out. After competing in the South Essex and Metropolitan Amateur Leagues, Leytonstone became founder-members of the Spartan League in season 1907-08, but joined the new Isthmian League in the following year. They remained in the Isthmian for the rest of their existence until, following a relegation season in 1978-9, amalgamated with Ilford and got back up into the Premier Division as Leytonstone & Ilford. Well at least that kept the name alive, unlike their final amalgamation in 1978 with Redbridge Forest, which saw the end of a famous old amateur club.

Their first success came in winning the London Junior Cup in 1894, when they beat unknowns Bostal Rovers by 2-1. Leytonstone entered the Amateur Cup in the third year of its inception, but were brought to earth when Great Marlow beat them 6-2 at home in the 2nd round of 1896. There was a gap of two years before they appeared again, but were edged out 3-4 away to Maidenhead in the 1st round. In 1899, a slight improvement saw them reach round 3, but different class Lowestoft crushed them 9-0, to repeat their scoreline of the previous round when they did the same to Cheshunt. Leytonstone did not enter again until 1907. In 1908, they reached the quarter-finals, only to be thrashed 8-1 at home by Clapton, who went on to win it. Further local successes came before the Great War, winning the Essex Cup in 1905, 1914, and the London Charity Cup in 1910. The South Essex League title was won in 1897, 1901, 1902, and 1903. More success came their way after the war, winning the London Senior Cup in 1920.

After the Second World War came Leytonstone's finest era, and they swept the board to proclaim themselves the best amateur team in London, winning the Amateur Cup in 1947 (1-0 v Wimbledon) and 1948, (1-0 Barnet) and reaching Round 2 of the FA Cup proper for the first time in 1948-9. Walthamstow Avenue, Woking, Enfield and Barnet were eliminated en rout to meeting Wimbledon in the 1947 final played at Arsenal's Highbury Stadium, where Leytonstone came from behind to win, with a backs to the wall last quarter of an hour to hold out. The following season, Amateur Cup wins over Erith & Belvedere (1-0), Tooting & Mitcham (2-0), Wealdstone (1-0) and Hendon (1-0) were all achieved away from home. Their semi final against Bishop Auckland, played at Middlesborough's ground, drew a huge crowd, only to see the northern representatives crushed 5-0. Sixty thousand fans filled the Stamford Bridge ground at Chelsea for the final against Barnet, but saw a drab defensive game decided when Groves scored what proved to be the winner. This was the Leytonstone side that day -

		Jarvis		
	Nicholls		Childs	
	Wilson	Paviour	Kavanagh	
Smith	Noble	Groves	Bunce	Joseph

The London Cup was again won in 1948 as was the Isthmian League title in 1947, 1948, having previously won it in 1938 and 1939, as Leytonstone continued to strengthen their leading position among the country's amateur clubs.

Season 1949-50 saw Leytonstone reach the 1st Round proper of the FA Cup, only to lose 1-2 at home to Chelmsford. The 1950s saw continued success, with more Isthmian League titles coming in 1950, 1951, and 1952. Another strong FA Cup run saw them once more reach the 2nd Round proper in 1951. Defeating Shrewsbury by 2-0, they were put out after a replay against Newport County (2-2,0-3).

The Granleigh Road ground became hemmed in by houses as the years went by, and a curious feature was the railway station platform and railway viaduct which ran outside down the length of the pitch. Vacated in 1986, Trinity Close, Willow Court, and Lime Court now occupy the spot, and the old viaduct is beginning to disappear from view with conifer trees planted in front of it. The ground record was set in 1949 for the visit of Watford FC, when 9,740 fans crammed into the Granleigh Road ground for a 1st Round FA Cup tie, won 2-1. In the 2nd Round, Leytonstone were again eliminated at home by Newport County in a thrilling 3-4 defeat. As one of the country's top non-league sides, Leytonstone had its fair share of capped players, although Albert Barrett was also capped for the full England side too. Leytonstone's many other capped amateurs included Ken Gray (28), Alf Noble (18), Leon Joseph (12), Doug Jervis (12), B.G. Harvey (12), Les Tilley (11), B. Moffatt (9), Ernie Childs (6). Leytonstone were still one of the best known amateur sides in the 1960s, and their 1966 double of the London Senior Cup and Isthmian League title was topped by winning the Amateur Cup in 1968, beating Chesham United 1-0 at Wembley Stadium in front of 52,000 spectators with this team-

		Hadlow		
	Tilley		Hames	
	Andrews	Thompson	Walker	
Charles	Gray	Diwell	Minall	Harvey

Their route to winning the cup included a 1-0 win over Southall, a 7-2 demolition of Bishop Stortford, an epic tussle with Enfield, which took three very tight games (0-0,0-0,1-0) before overcoming Sutton United 3-1 in a replay in the semi-final at Brentford's

Griffin Park. In the following season, Sutton gained revenge when they put Leytonstone out in the 4th round by the same score. The Essex Senior Cup was also captured in 1966 and 1967. As Amateur champions of 1968, Leytonstone were invited to Italy to play in the Barassi Cup against Italian counterparts STFE Roma, when their 1-1 home draw, and 2-2 away draws were enough to give them the trophy on 'away goals rule'. The competition continued on only until 1976, when Soresinese FC won a penalty shoot-out to become the first winning Italian team.

When the council-owned Granleigh Road was sold under their feet for a housing development, Leytonstone & Ilford were forced to move into the Green Pond Road ground of Walthamstow Avenue, an equally famous London club. Within a couple of seasons, they had all become one club, and the names of both Leytonstone and Ilford were consigned to the history bin.

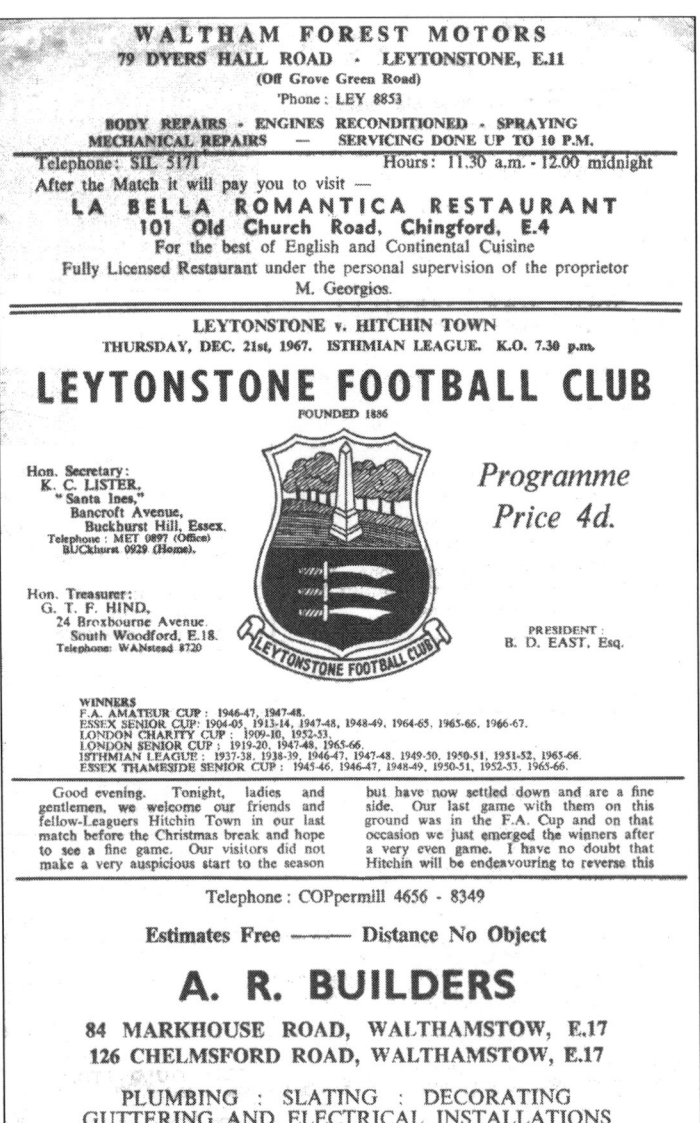

LEYTONSTONE v. HITCHIN TOWN
THURSDAY, DEC. 21st, 1967. ISTHMIAN LEAGUE. K.O. 7.30 p.m.

LEYTONSTONE FOOTBALL CLUB
FOUNDED 1886

Programme
Price 4d.

Hon. Secretary:
K. C. LISTER,
"Santa Ines,"
Bancroft Avenue,
Buckhurst Hill, Essex.
Telephone : MET 0897 (Office)
BUCkhurst 9929 (Home).

Hon. Treasurer:
G. T. F. HIND,
24 Broxbourne Avenue,
South Woodford, E.18.
Telephone: WANstead 8720

PRESIDENT :
B. D. EAST, Esq.

WINNERS
F.A. AMATEUR CUP : 1946-47, 1947-48.
ESSEX SENIOR CUP: 1904-05, 1913-14, 1947-48, 1948-49, 1964-65, 1965-66, 1966-67.
LONDON CHARITY CUP : 1909-10, 1952-53.
LONDON SENIOR CUP : 1919-20, 1947-48, 1965-66.
ISTHMIAN LEAGUE : 1937-38, 1938-39, 1946-47, 1947-48, 1949-50, 1950-51, 1951-52, 1965-66.
ESSEX THAMESIDE SENIOR CUP : 1945-46, 1946-47, 1948-49, 1950-51, 1952-53, 1965-66.

Good evening. Tonight, ladies and gentlemen, we welcome our friends and fellow-Leaguers Hitchin Town in our last match before the Christmas break and hope to see a fine game. Our visitors did not make a very auspicious start to the season but have now settled down and are a fine side. Our last game with them on this ground was in the F.A. Cup and on that occasion we just emerged the winners after a very even game. I have no doubt that Hitchin will be endeavouring to reverse this

LONDON CALEDONIANS

Founded - November 1885
Folded - 1939
Colours - Blue and white thin hoops, navy shorts
Grounds - 1. Elm Farm, Walthamstow 1886
          2. The Greyhound ground, Dulwich 1888
          3. Essex County Ground, Leyton 1889
          4. Tufnell Park 1890s
          5. Caledonian Park, Holloway 1893 (connected to the above)

London Caledonians were one of the most successful of all London clubs in the first quarter of the twentieth century. They were founded 'for the benefit of Scotsmen who lived in London'. Between 1889 and 1935, they amassed 5 London Senior Cups, 5 Middlesex County Cups, 6 Ithsmian League titles, an Amateur Cup and an appearance in round 3 of the F.A. Cup in 1927-28, long after the demise of other amateurs. The 'Callies' also won the London Charity Cup 5 times, in 1895, 1906, 1909, 1913, and 1925. They also shared the cup in 1907.

Along with the Corinthians, the Callies were one of the first of the pioneering clubs to cross the channel and after playing French champions Le Club Francais in 1898, went on to do annual continental tours to promote the game abroad. In the 1920s, they became known for playing "pretty football".

Formed in late 1885 by Hugh Scott-MacPherson, a proud-looking tall and slim man, at the Anderton Hotel in Fleet Street, they soon became a regular on the London amateur scene, and played friendly matches against established Old Boys teams, but almost immediately joined the Ithsmian League when it was formed, and duly became its first league champions. Their first match was not played until February 1886, which is why all books give that year as their foundation. They remained in the Isthmian League until the end of the 1930s, when they folded at the outbreak of World War 2. My best guess for their Elm Farm ground, was a field adjacent to the Elm House and lodge, at the junction of Forest Road and Palmerston Road, which is now Russell Road.

Entering the newly founded (1882) London Cup (later to have the word 'senior' added), the Callies were eliminated by the Old Harrovians 3-0 when they went to their ground on 17th December 1887. However, two years later, Caledonians more than got their revenge when they thrashed the Harrovians 10-1 in the London Charity Cup in November.

On Boxing Day 1887, Caledonians arranged to play the powerful Blackburn Rovers, and five days later, the Blackburn Olympic team were tempted down to London for the first time since 1883, to play the Callies on the Leyton cricket ground. In foggy and frosty conditions, it was Dewhurst who gave Olympic the lead on 23 minutes, as the Caledonian forwards squandered chance after chance. After the restart, conditions got worse, it now being impossible to see across the width of the pitch. At one point, a breakaway by Jimmy Costley for Olympic, saw him race down the wing and centre the ball - to no-one ! With players rapidly losing heart in the fog, two late goals by Burns turned the score around to give the Callies an unlikely 2-1 win against another famous name from the history books.

Such was the interest to see the Caledonians outside London, that when they toured around the country, large crowds assembled. At Easter 1888, the Callies travelled to Ireland where they played Belfast Cliftonville, and won 2-0 (although the *Morning Post* gives 2-1). They were also annual visitors to the Wellington Road ground of the Aston Villa club at this time (Villa Park not being built until 1897). However, their visit in September 1886, to open Aston Villa's season saw and embarrassing score of Villa 11-0 Caledonians. This, in mitigation, was one of the Callies' first ever matches. The Callies gave a better showing when the two sides met three years later at the Greyhound Ground, Dulwich. A large crowd saw Villa sneak home 4-3, with Burns and Lambie putting the Callies 2-0 ahead, only to see Villa draw level at half-time. Brown gave Villa a 3-2 lead, but Burns once again scored to level the scores. The winner came when Dickson got a 4th for Villa, as the Callies began to tire against their Football League opponents. Despite a decent attendance, the match was a financial disaster, as they had guaranteed the Villa a £15 purse, and the total receipts fell short of that sum by sixpence !

Another famous club from the roll call of English football was met when the Callies went over to the Kennington Oval to play the once-famous Old Etonians. On a heavy and sodden pitch, Cally won 2-0 at the start of November 1888. In the previous month, no less than the F.A. Cup holders, West Bromwich Albion were guests to the Queens Club, West Kensington, where following an evenly matched game, a pass from Bassett set up Wilson to score what proved to be the only goal of the game. It seems then, that once the Callies had got into their stride, they were a match for even the best professional sides at the time. In 1889, the Callies went to Anfield to play Everton, and a 15,000 crowd saw the visitors score a winner in the second half. Imagine today, an amateur team beating a Premiership side away from home! Later that year, Everton came down to play the 'return' match, and showed their class at the Oval, easily winning 6-1, being five up by half-time. The freedom of the amateur player was well illustrated in December 1889, when several Caledonians turned out for the Swifts FC in their match with the (Royal) Arsenal, played at Plumstead before 'several thousand' with Swifts winning by 5-0. In the same year, the Callies were strengthened when Hay, previously of Glasgow Rangers, moved down to London and offered his services to them.

In February 1891, Cambridge University won a thrilling match by 5-3 at Tufnell Park; however, the Callies got revenge on 'Oxbridge' when the Callies beat the famous Oxford University side by 6-2 at 'Tufnell Park' on October 30th that year. On Monday 3rd April 1893, the impressive fixture list of Caledonians grew even more so when they travelled to Glasgow to play the Celtic FC at Parkhead. Three goals down at half-time, the Callies responded in the second half, but neither side added to the score. On Saturday October 23rd 1895, the Callies shared a thrilling game with Oxford University, the game ending 4-4. In October 1891, the *Dundee Courier* carried a feature on William Stirling, described as Caledonian's burly goalkeeper'. At six feet and 170 pounds, and an astute mind, he was described in glowing terms, and it was said that the 28 year old had been with the Callies for five years, and he had no intention of leaving them. A huge crowd of 7,000 saw the Callies draw 1-1 against Millwall in October 1893 in a game which was described by Lloyds Weekly as ' a remarkably fast game'. The *London Illustrated Sporting & Dramatic News* remarked in late November 1893, that the Callies had only been beaten once by a London club in the previous two years, and that their recent defeat by Cambridge was the first home loss in two years.

The 1896 London Charity Cup final produced a shock result when Caledonians were humiliated 8-1 at Leyton cricket ground by the Old Carthusians, especially as the same two teams had contested the 1895 final, with Caledonians winning 3-1.

When Caledonians played their annual fixture against Oxford University in October 1895 a crowd of 6,000 saw a thrilling 4-4 draw. This was more than watched Nottingham Forest against Preston North End played on the same day! Again, when the Callies played the Casuals at Tufnell Park in October 1896, no less than 4,000 spectators turned out, but they were disappointed when neither side could score a goal. Similar attendances followed the Callies in their Amateur Cup exploits in the 1920s, suggesting a well-supported club. At this time (1890s), the Callies played on the Greyhound Ground at Dulwich, which had the Herne Hill sports ground only 200 yards away on the other side of the Turney Road. There were two rival pubs in the then village of Dulwich, the Crown, and the Greyhound, which had a large (250 x 200 yards) cricket ground behind it. Many teams, both football and cricket, used the ground over the years, but in 1898, the brewery reviewed the situation as their leases were up in 1907, and decided to demolish both pubs, but only rebuild the Crown at a cost of £4000 (which became the Crown & Greyhound) and by 1910, Pickwick Road and Aysgarth Road had been created where the pub and cricket ground used to be. A great shame to the end of a famous landmark.

Beaten by the Old Carthusians in the final of the 1899 London Cup, Cally bounced back to defeat the Old Westminsters in the final of the following year. Attendances were very rarely given unless large, but their home match against the Casuals, who shared their ground, drew 4,000 spectators on 14th October 1893 when the two sides drew 2-2. The Callies' varied fixture list was added to when they played the Royal Navy XI at Portsmouth in November 1907, when 800 people saw goals by Sutherland, Gibbons (2) and Rutherford give them a 4-1 win.

The rift between the Football Association and the newly-formed Amateur F.A. was coming to a head. The *Yorkshire Post* reporting in December 1908 that they had written to Caledonians, the Casuals and the Tufnell Park clubs, stating that they did not agree to those three clubs all sharing the same ground where some were members of the A.F.A and others members of the F.A. In 1908 Caledonians lost one of their players when R.C. Ralston signed terms with Aston Villa as an amateur, having said he had always wanted to play for them. Described as a 5'11" twelve stone full back (that was a big lad in those days) he had followed in the footsteps of William Fry who had previously played as a guest for the Villa from Caledonians.

In May 1909, the London Charity Cup was secured for the third time, with a 1-0 win over Nunhead, played on the Leytonstone ground. This came after their successful season of 1907-08, when they won both the Isthmian League and the London Senior Cup. As you can see from the opening paragraph, success was almost continuous for the Callies throughout the Edwardian era. After 1928, however, the club stalled a little, with only the Middlesex Senior Cup secured in 1934-35 to show from that decade. Their second great effort was in reaching the 3rd round of the F.A. Cup in 1927-28, when they won 1-0 at Northfleet in round 1, then beat Bath City by the same score at home. Although the 'big guns' were avoided in the 3rd round, Crewe Alexandra spoiled the party at Caledonia Park when they won 3-2 to end the amateur's run.

In 1908, Callie were again winners of the London Cup, when they defeated Dulwich Hamlet by the only goal of the game. They were back again in 1912, but this time Barking were too strong, and beat them by 3-0. Three years later, in 1915, with the First World War calling away thousands of footballers, Callie returned to beat Clapton 4-1 for another London Cup success. After a gap of a decade, Callies secured another London Cup success, when they beat Kingstonians 3-1 in the final of 1926. Defending their cup in the following season, they were defeated 4-2 by the side which had beaten them fifteen years before - Barking. A third consecutive London final appearance saw Callie overcome Dulwich Hamlet 2-0 to notch up their fifth London Senor Cup. This would prove to be the last appearance in the competition for Callie, but they had overtaken the achievements of the Old Carthusians and the Old Westminsters, who, being the dominant sides of the 1890s, had each won four London finals.

Entering the F.A. Cup in season 1912-13, the Callies got through the qualifying rounds only to be beaten by Wolverhampton Wanderers 3-1 at the Molineux. The Caledonian players travelled to Wolverhampton to find heavy snow had postponed their match until the following Saturday. They returned once more, some on Friday night, some on Saturday early afternoon, and they went straight on the pitch without preparation or training. In the following year, Callie's efforts were recognised when the F.A. gave them exemption to the first round proper, but they were beaten 3-0 at Huddersfield. Days of torrential rain had soaked the Huddersfield ground and gave the fast running Caledonian style no hope. The 1920s saw two wonderful efforts by the Callies. They won the Amateur Cup in 1923 when they defeated surprise team Evesham from Worcestershire by 2-1 in the final. Just failing to retain the cup, the Callies went out in the following year's semi final. Their previous best effort was in 1915 when they lost the semi-final replay against Clapton 0-1 after extra-time, after the first match ended goal-less.

The Amateur Cup by 1922-23 had qualifying rounds still leaving over sixty clubs in round 1 proper. Slough, the club formed by the demise of the Swifts, were thrashed 10-2 to sound out a warning, with Sloane scoring 6, with May, Barr, Stewart and McCrae making it double figures. One of the favourites, the Casuals had been eliminated in the 4th qualifying round by Wimbledon, who themselves were put out by Northampton Nomads, 0-2 at home. In round 2, there was a major upset when the famous Bishop Auckland, the holders, were put out by Stockton 2-0. The R.A.M.C. of Aldershot held the Callies to a 1-1 draw, but the Londoners won the replay 2-0 to move into the next round. Round 3 saw most of the remaining favourites fall; Stockton lost 1-2 to Eston United, Clapton lost 3-4 to Erith & Belvedere, Barking lost 4-1 at St.Albans, and Crook Town went down 1-0 to Evesham. Ilford scored seven past Southall in their replayed tie, and suddenly looked cup contenders. As luck would have it, the Callies were drawn against them in round 4, but a goal from May gave them a 1-0 win at Ilford, and the main threat had been eliminated. Evesham overcame Eston to meet Cockfield in their semi-final, whilst the Callies played St.Albans City. Played at Luton Town's ground, May again found the net, and an own goal sealed a 2-0 victory to put them in the final for the first time. Evesham became the first team from the West Midlands to reach the Amateur Cup final when they defeated Cockfield 4-2 at the Crystal Palace. With both teams making their final debut, nerves were on show, and it took Evesham twenty minutes to 'play up'. By then, however, Sloan had scored on 13 minutes for the Callies, with the 14,000 crowd cheering at the Palace grounds. Jones equalised for Evesham after 40 minutes, and the game was balanced for the second half. Play became scrappy in the second period, with no further goals scored, the game went into extra-time. Ten minutes after the restart, with Cally on the ascendancy, McGubben scored what proved to be the winner on April 23rd. The Callies' team that day was:-

			Dawson			
	B. Gates			E. Gates		
Blyth			Barr			Finn
McGubbin	Noble		Sloan	May		Hamilton

The Callies continued competing in the Amateur Cup throughout the 1920s and 1930s without further success, save a 4th round appearance in 1934. In 1936, the club celebrated its 50th Jubilee anniversary with a gala dinner evening where the founders of the club and the leading players were invited to go over old times. Club captain Bobby Noble remarked that now, (in 1936) they were struggling to find any new players with that Scottish ancestry which made their club exclusive. It was also revealed that when Mr. Courtney Clarke, landowner of the Tufnell Park ground died, the Callies lost a court case which meant they had to vacate, but immediately they secured a field right next door, and this became developed into their own ground, Caledonian Park, and the rising Tottenham Hotspurs were frequent visitors. One of the Callies all time greats was Andrew Ralston, a tall teenager who played for over twenty seasons, later becoming club honorary secretary. Ralston was held in memorium at the club for one particularly astonishing goal, scored in the Callies' 2-0 London Charity Cup final win over the Casuals in 1906. The Casuals goalie, a hefty fellow, hoofed a huge clearance from his hands which easily cleared the halfway line, when Ralston strode up and met the ball on full volley and returned the sphere with equal vigour, the ball sailing 60 yards into the Casuals' net before their goalie could get back into position ! One of the most remembered stories concerned Andrew Pringle, a player, who for a wager, went on the London to Brighton walk wearing day shoes, full morning top hat and tails, and astonished everyone by finishing in the leading group!

The death of Caledonian player and former captain Harry Melhuish was reported as far away as the *Dundee Courier* (although of course he was Scottish) in May 1936. "We are anxious to sign good players but find the dice loaded against us " said R. Noble, the Caledonians secretary in November 1937. "Scottish decent is a requirement, and we refuse to have any dealings with the 'sham-amateur' some of whom have signed for other clubs" he continued. One of their few captures in 1938 was Bob Cairs, from Dundee, a Scottish schoolboys internationalist. In December, Caledonians were humiliated 8-0 in the Isthmian League by Ilford. It was their heaviest defeat for thirty years. Only the loss of their full back McConachie, after five minutes, was their defence. It proved to be a bad year.

And so the Caledonians held out hope that they could continue to keep the traditions of the club alive with a dwindling source of Scotsmen - but they couldn't, and the club 'dried up' and finally had to resign themselves to the inevitable at the outbreak of war in 1939. Of the many fine players for the Callies over the years, I single out the following for mention :-

Ron G. Brebner   (1881-1914) was their goalkeeper in Edwardian times, who played in goal for the Great Britain amateur team in the 1908 and 1912 Olympics. He also, as an amateur, turned out for Huddersfield and Chelsea. Brebne joined from Northern Nomads in 1902 after leaving Edinburgh University.

John Lambie   (1868-1923) described as a teenage prodigy having played with Queens Park, he moved to London in 1888, also playing for Swifts and Corinthians.

Tom Fitchie   (1881-1941) moved on to play 63 games for The Arsenal, scoring 30 goals. He also played for Tottenham, Fulham and Queens Park, and was capped four times for Scotland.

Frank Scott-Walford (1866-1935) came from Birmingham and became Tottenham's first professional player in 1888 as a goalie. Sporting a startling moustache, he later became manager of Brighton, Leeds City, and Coventry.

W.A.'Willie' Porter   (b.1884) who had three spells with Caledonians.

Jackie Burns   (b. 1906) who won 16 England amateur caps, 9 as captain; a left half, he made a record 263 Football League appearances - 117 with Q.P.R. where he scored 29 goals, and 146 with Brentford where he scored a further 14 goals.

Bertie Fulton   (1906-1979) who also played for Belfast Celtic during 1925-1943; he gained 21 Northern Ireland caps and played for Great Britain in the 1936 Olympic Games.

Andy Sloan   Was a prolific goalscorer for the Callies, and was capped several times for Ireland in the 1920s.

The Callies' main ground, the 7 acre Tufnell Park, was also home to the Casuals, and today lies a mile due west of the new Emirates Stadium of Arsenal FC. Maps from the 1920s show the 7 acre site split into two halves. In the 1950s it became the North London Polytechnic sports ground, and is still a recreation ground at the junction of Tufnell Park Road and Campdale Road. Tennis courts were added along the Campdale Road side in the 1950s, and the top part of the ground, where once stood the railway cattle docks, became an industrial estate in the late 1960s.

LOVELLS ATHLETIC

Founded - 1918
Folded - 1969
Ground - Rexville, Alderney Street, Newport, Monmouth
Colours - Red shirts, white shorts

Lovells Athletic were actually the works team of Lovell's Sweet Factory who went on to become six-times Welsh League champions and Welsh Cup winners ! Founded by factory owner George Frederick Lovell in late 1918, the team soon became known as the Toffeemen.

Residing at Broughton, Clytha Park, Lovell was born in 1862 at Abergavenny, and opened up a shop at 125 Commercial Street. Before long, he employed 600 people at his Crindan works, and the same number at his Manchester factory. Soon, he had a range of cafe-shops in Pontypridd and Swansea, and depots in Liverpool and Wrexham.

Against a 1920s Newport backdrop of race riots, small pox epidemics, plagues of rats, and the infamous Dock Street battle between local and foreign sailors, the Lovells Athletic football club had improved from friendly matches to rival the Newport County team. Lovells joined the Western League in 1923 and won it at the first attempt with a record of played 20, won 16, drew 3, lost 1, goals for 43, against 10. Bizarrely, there was a huge slump the following season, with those figures reversed and they finished bottom ! They were relegated, but soon bounced back up. Along with Sheppey United, Lovells applied to join the Southern League in February 1927 but were unsuccessful. Opponents at this time included Yeovil, Weymouth, Bristol City reserves, Bath City, Minehead and Frome. In June 1928, Lovells resigned from the Western League ' on financial grounds' (*Western Daily Express*) and were elected to the Southern League West and took the place of Mid-Rhonda. Even so, Newport County lodged an appeal on the grounds of closeness of proximity, which was ignored. In December 1927, Lovells were brought before the Western League committee to explain why a certain G. Davies had played for them against Taunton, when he was not signed to them. They accepted the explanation that the club had four men called Davies on the books, and a mistake had occurred. They were fined two guineas. The team was still made up of local amateurs, with a sprinkling of paid part-timers such as player-manager Howarth and Morgan, two men signed from Bristol City in 1927. In the early 1930s, Lovell's leading goalscorer was star centre forward Gardiner. This side played Taunton in October 1932 -

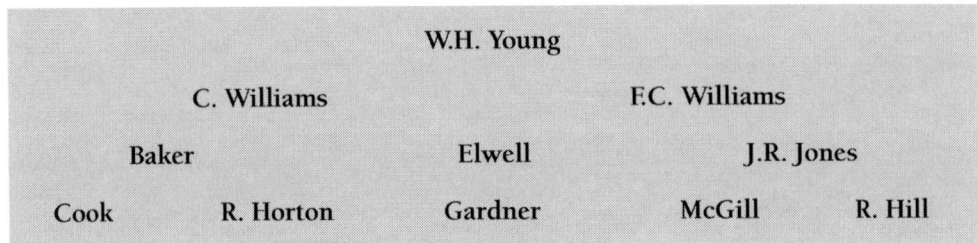

	W.H. Young	
C. Williams		F.C. Williams
Baker	Elwell	J.R. Jones
Cook R. Horton	Gardner	McGill R. Hill

Inside forward Horton would soon sign for Cardiff City in December that year. Most of the 1930s were spent in the Western League, but from 1947 to 1959 they were in the

Southern League. Generally a below average team, they twice finished 6th, in 1947-8 and 1956-7 in the 22 club league. 1939 and 1940 were championship seasons, when they won the Western League, and the Southern League (Western Division) respectively. At the outbreak of World War Two, the Football League was suspended, and clubs organised themselves on a regional basis, but wages were reduced to thirty shillings a week (£80 in 2015 money), but clubs were allowed to use guest players, often from footballers who had been billeted nearby, and thus small teams were sometimes boosted with a sprinkling a First Division men.

There were eyebrows raised in the Western League in August 1944, when goalkeeper Ferguson and international forward W.M. Owen were sold to Bristol City. The Lovell's ground was used when the Welsh F.A. staged a trial match in November 1947 between 'Anglo-Welsh' and 'South Wales' in an effort to discover new local talent. During the early 1950s, Lovells' regular league opposition included Kidderminster, Merthyr, Torquay United reserves, Weymouth, Exeter City, Gloucester, Chelmsford, Worcester, Yeovil, Hastings and Barry.

The Welsh League championships was won on no less than 6 occasions (*Football Club History Database*); 1932, 1938, 1939, 1946, 1947, (Wikipedia says also 1948) and in 1966, when they won 24, drew 5 and lost only 1 of their 30 games, scoring 80 goals against 23. In season 1959-60, despite only finishing 10th in the Welsh League, they scored 97 goals in their 38 matches, although 80 were conceded. In 1934, the record score of 12-0 was rattled up when luckless Llanelli were thrashed on Boxing Day.

Their ground was hemmed in a tight space between the winding river Crindau Pill and Albany Street, right by the factory. There were also tennis courts and a bowling green for the workers' recreation. Today, a small estate known as The Turnstiles occupies where the ground used to be. Two small stands, one behind the Albany Street goal, and one along the Alderney Street side were the only developments. The ground capacity was tested when Cardiff City were the visitors on March 31st 1945, when 10,000 people crammed into Rexville to watch the 'red toffees' play the 'blue birds'.

Lovells entered the English and Welsh F.A. Cups, with no success in the former, but having much success in their homeland. Lovells rarely made it through the qualifying rounds of the English F.A. Cup, often coming off second best to Llanelli or Barry Town.

They were unlucky against Bath City in November 1927, when the winners would have got through to the 1st round proper; Lovells' goalkeeper sliced a near-post corner kick into his own net to give Bath the victory. In 1930 the *Western Gazette* announced that Lovells and Taunton had joined the second division of the newly-formed London Combination, by which I presume they meant the Southern League. In February that year, two Lovell's players, E.Thomas and E. Jenkins were capped for the amateur international for Wales against Scotland.

Their best F.A. Cup effort came just after the War, in 1945-6. Beating Barry 5-1 in the 4th qualifying round, they then met Bournemouth, Wolves, and Bath City, each of whom were played home and away; this was the only time when instead of a straight knock-out, ties were played over two legs. Bournemouth were beaten 4-1 at home but the away game lost 2-3, Bath were beaten 2-1 at home and 5-2 away, but both games against Wolves in the 3rd round proper were heavy losses, 2-4 at home and 1-8 at Molineux. It was another decade before round 1 proper was reached, with wins over Cheltenham (2-1), Llanelli (3-0) and Barry (3-1) and Merthyr Tydfil in the qualifiers, only to lose badly 1-7 to Leyton Orient in 1956. In 1958-9 season, Llanelli took them to three games (1-1, 1-1, 3-2) only for Gloucester City to beat them 3-2 at home in the 2nd Qualifying round. In the 1960s, Gloucester and Cheltenham became familiar stumbling blocks, and Lovells never made it past Q2 stage.

It was a different story in the Welsh Cup. In 1947-8, they beat South Liverpool 1-0 on Shrewsbury's ground and then beat their hosts 3-0 in the final which was played at Wrexham. Hereford United put them out at the quarter-finals in 1958 by 2-1, but in the following season, they once more reached the final. Oswestry were beaten 1-0 in the quarter-finals, but it took a replay to get past Bangor City (0-0, 2-1) in the semis. Cardiff City proved too strong in the final, played at Newport County, who beat them by 2-0. There were two more quarter-final appearances, but Wrexham (0-2) in 1961, and Chester (1-5) 1969 ended their hopes.

Lovells were also successful in the Welsh Amateur Cup, winning it three consecutive years in 1926-7-8 and 1954, and were beaten finalists in 1923, 1924, and 1939. They also won the South Wales cup in 1931, 1937, 1941 and 1955. Despite various Welsh successes, it was probably wartime season 1942-3 when they achieved their best result - finishing above Manchester United, Aston Villa, Manchester City and Sheffield Wednesday to finish runners-up behind Liverpool in the wartime North Second Championship, with only four defeats in their 20 matches, scoring 63 against 22. They also became champions of the wartime Football League West in both 1942 and 1943, thrashing Swansea 9-0, Bristol City 6-0, and Cardiff City 8-4. In 1954, Lovells sold promising centre half Clarke to Tottenham for £1500, where he became a team regular and gained England 'B' caps. In April that year, the Lovells' ground was used for the Wales v England amateur international match. This side played Chelmsford in April 1950 -

			Williams			
	Fisher			Edmunds		
	Evans		Clerke		Bye	
Hodder	Noakes		Holland		Wood	Risdale

The demise of Lovells was swift, following the sale of the toffee factory in 1969. George Lovell's sweet empire was so well known around Great Britain that when he died in February 1949, it was reported as far away as Aberdeen. His great-granddaughter Lilian Handley was still alive in 2012, celebrating her 100th birthday in Newport. James Roblin (1927-2011) was working at Lovells in the late 1960s as a manager, when he entered a BBC competition to find a new football commentator; he ended up as a well-know pundit, but had been a top footballer in the 1950s, playing 13 times for the Welsh amateur team, once as a captain, and he also played for the Great Britain team in the 1952 Olympic Games.

Robling was a wing half in this charity match against Tottenham Hotspur in when Lovells played in red, white and blue hoops in September 1950 -

		Williams		
	Edmunds		Fisher	
Bye		Evans		Robling
Hodder	Wood	Lewis	Griffiths	Ridsdale

MERTHYR TOWN

Founded - 1908
Folded - 1934
Ground - Pen-y-darren Park
Colours - Green and red stripes, black shorts 1908-1910
Red shirt with green collar, white shorts, black socks 1911-1925
Green and red stripes, white shorts 1925-1929
Red shirt, green large V, white shorts 1930s

Founded at a time when rugby had already taken a hold of south Wales, and with unemployment and hardships around the corner, Merthyr Town FC were formed oddly out of an idea proposed by Merthyr rugby club and Merthyr Athletics Association, which led to the association game becoming so popular in the area that the rugby club died out by 1912. Along with Aberdare and Ton Pentre, they were accepted into the Southern Leagues Division 2 Section A, not so much because within a year of being founded, they had come on leaps and bounds, but simply because the Southern League wanted to expand its empire into Wales and the south-west. Outside players of experience were beginning to be signed such as Jack Jeffrey who'd played for Stourbridge and Aston Villa. By 1920, Merthyr had 20 professionals on their books. However by 1912, Merthyr had won the Second Division title and the South Wales Cup, but their First Division stay was brief, coming 12th in 1913 and relegated in 1914. Like so many other teams, they mothballed themselves in 1915 for the duration of the War. The club had some bad news on the night of Monday 3rd September 1917 when their treasurer Arthur Reynold suddenly died at home.

To give it its Welsh name, Pen-y-Darren parc was in the town centre, hemmed in between two converging roads, The Walk and Pen-y-darren Road, with the Taff Vale brewery and the Infirmary across the road, and strangely, several large trees inside the ground itself, which was only developed with banking behind the goals. It was approached by Park Terrace and there were churches of four different denominations within a hundred yards radius. The picturesque ground was still in use as of 2013 by Merthyr Tydfil AFC, but has lost its original oval shape.

Reappearing in 1919 when many didn't, the club were reformed by the generosity of Seymour Berry, who cleared the club debts and the club was restarted with a share issue of £2,400. The problem was, the demand for coal and steel dropped off in the early 1920s, and this contributed to shortages, strikes and unemployment all across the area, which in turn meant going to football matches was the last thing poor families could afford. Attendances dropped to the low thousands. One bright moment came when a full house of 15,000 turned out to see Merthyr's F.A. Cup qualifier replay against nearby Newport County on Wednesday 24th November 1925, but such times were too few and far between. Welsh clubs had been admitted into the F.A. Cup en bloc, but Bournemouth & Boscombe beat Merthyr 3-0 in the 1st round proper for 1925-6, and Bristol City beat them 2-0 at home in the following season's 1st round stage. Charlton Athletic needed two games (0-0, 0-2) to put Merthyr out in October 1927, but in autumn 1928, Merthyr finally got through to the 2nd round of the F.A. Cup. Dulwich Hamlet were beaten 4-2, only for Watford to put them out 2-0 in the next. Leyton put them out in 1929 at the first hurdle, and Bristol Rovers likewise in 1930.

Merthyr would have been relegated at the end of the 1919-20 season, had it not been for the fact that the entire First Division of the Southern League was used to create the new Football League Division Three, and Merthyr somehow found themselves in the Football League at a time they could least afford it. They were also running a reserve team in the Welsh League which added to running costs, and at one point, in the spring of 1925, the directors had to pay the players' wages out of their own pockets. In January of that year, Merthyr were warned about failing to control the crowd at a match involving them and visitors Luton Town. Repercussions included a ban on English clubs visiting their ground. On 23rd November 1923, Merthyr played at home to Swansea, who brought a huge following. Over 5,000 fans literally eat the town out of bread that day according to the *Portsmouth News*. Season 1924-5 was a terrible one, as they finished bottom of the Third Division. The top clubs that year were Plymouth, Bristol City, Swansea, Newport County, Swindon and Millwall, with Brentford and Queens Park Rangers at the bottom with Merthyr. You would have thought that opposition of that class would have brought in the crowds for Merthyr.

Already running out of funds, Merthyr sold Harry Foxall, a 27 year old centre back to Portsmouth in February 1924. Despite the money worries, the Portsmouth Evening News described Merthyr in March 1922 as 'a workmanlike team, and when they are in the humour, they can put up a great game'. In November 1925, Merthyr were riding high in the Third Division, and the *Derby Telegraph* thought this was mainly due to new centre forward Rumney, signed from Chesterfield at the start of the season. In May 1927 Merthyr bought Ewart Ford from Hinkley, having previously played with Scots side Queens Park. This was a curious move since they had just put ten players up for a free transfer on Monday 10th May (*Portmouth Evening News*).

The miners strike of 1921 had long-lasting effects, and this was compounded by the General Strike of 1926. Struggling both on and off the pitch, a reprieve came in 1928 when local grocer Sam Gibbon took over the club, but attendances continued

to fall whilst costs continued to rise. The directors took the unusual step in 1929 in announcing that they would select the team from now on, instead of a committee chaired by the captain. In December 1929, Merthyr put four players up for sale; J. Woodward, a goalie from Rangers and Queens Park; Walter Moyle, brought from Crystal Palace; T. Williams from Bristol City, and A. Gough, formerly of Walsall. Gate receipts had been barely half the weekly wage bill of £110 in the preceding weeks, and money was lost every time they turned out at home. In January 1930, the *Lancashire Evening Post* reported that

Merthyr had suspended their goalkeeper James Woodward 'for breaches of discipline'. His place was taken by reserve amateur goalie James for the next fortnight. Woodward's brother Tom had been the team captain that year. On Thursday 10th April 1930 came a great embarrassment; a 0-10 defeat away to Newport County in the Third Division South, almost equalling the rugby match the same day when Newport beat Bath 15-3. Finishing at the bottom once again, in 1930, the club went into liquidation. At the Football League AGM in June 1930, Merthyr were voted out, and they returned to the Southern League. Attendances were now pitifully low, sometimes barely 100 spectators, despite admission prices being reduced to just 2d. Sam Gibson announced that the club's deficit was now £1500 in 1930, but they would soldier on and apply for re-election. The 1930s was a continual selling off of any players which would raise funds, such as Sidney Nicholson and Emily Williams who went to Bournemouth & Boscombe FC; William Gannon, Clifford Williams and Ioriqueth Williams, all sold to Lincoln City. In September 1930, Harry Hadley was appointed new manager, replacing player-manager Albert Linden, who in turn superseded Albert Fisher, who left in 1913 to join Notts County.

The club slowly lingered on until Saturday 23rd June 1934, when the directors announced that Merthyr would be wound up, and that the £2,000 losses would be borne by the directors (*Hartlepool Mail*). In September 1939, Chelmsford City invited Arsenal over for a friendly match to raise funds from a full house crowd. Arsenal used 'the old Pennydarren Park ground as their headquarters for the visit' (*Chelmsford Chronicle*).

Merthyr Town FC circa 1913.

MINERVA FC

Founded - 1876
Folded - Unknown, circa 1913
Colours - Navy shirts, white shorts, monogrammed M badge, navy tassel caps.
Ground - 1. Tottenham 1876-7
          2. Ladywell, London 1878
          3. Lee, London 1893
          4. Crabble ground, Dover (if relocated)

Almost nothing is known about this club, and I believe that this is the only history of them you will find. Even their name eludes geographical researches. This was the case until I found the club featured in an 1891 edition of the *Illustrated Sporting & Dramatic News*. Confirming their founding date as being 1876, Minerva FC were comprised solely of employees of a London store, Copestake, Lindsay, Crampton & Co. Ltd of 5 Bow-churchyard, London. In their first season, they won all their matches.

On December 22nd 1877, Minerva were beaten 6-0 at home by the Hendon club at Ladywell. This was the first reported result for Minerva, who were already running a second team in 1877-78. 'Minerva' was, apparently the Roman goddess of wisdom, but this did not help to tell us from where they came, and indeed, all I could initially glean was that they were a club who played on the friendly London circuit from the late 1870s, and possibly moved back to the Dover area at the end of the 19th century. In terms of where they came from, until that magazine feature from 1891, the only connection to the name was a Minerva College at 75 Folkestone Road run by the Hart sisters, but this was a ladies college for London Jews, and that relocated to Leicester at the outbreak of World War One, so I has dismissed that idea. I later found a team called Minerva playing in the Dover area, a situation which reminded me of the school where the Remnants were based, which moved from Slough to Shropshire. I wasn't able to determine if Copestake, Linday, Crampton & Co moved from London to Dover.

Otherworldly opposition was entertained when Minerva played a team from Clapton called 'Mars' on Saturday 16th February 1878, and duly beat them 3-0 with Turner, Duthie, Anderson and Moyer gaining praise for Minerva. The two sides had played the previous week at Clapton with Mars winning by 3-1. Almost nothing is known about the Mars club, except I found them playing teams such as Richmond and Flamingoes too, so they clearly played both the handling and no-handling codes, like Clapham Rovers. By 1878, Minerva were running two teams. When Minerva played at Leyton, obtaining a 2-2 draw, Petty, Perkins and Turner drew the praise for the visitors.

In 1878, the Minerva FC were said to be playing at Ladywell, which is less than a mile due west of Lewisham in SE13. As a 'works' team from central London, they had no ground of their own, and rented what became available season by season. Studying Victorian maps across 1850-1900, I cannot draw a definite conclusion as to where in Ladywell they played. In a village, the first thing I look out for is the principal public house, as nearly all teams needed a meeting place and a headquarters, and virtually all of them chose the pub. However, of the two pubs on Ladywell Road in those days, no field behind them existed large enough. All the large fields were on the 'northern' side of the main road, one of them being an oblong field lying between the Lewisham and Deptford cemeteries on Brackley Lane (now Brockley Grove); the other possible field being at the junction of Ivy Road and Ladywell Road, now built over by Ladywell Close.

On 5th January 1878, Minerva drew 1-1 with the Hawks FC at Tottenham, in a game where Homer, Lloyd and Wilson drew praise, following a Minerva goal from Gladhill. The Lloyds Weekly however remarked *"that the Minerva defence was very weak"*. In October 1878, Minerva gained a good away win when they travelled to West Ham park to play the Dreadnought FC. Goals by Turner (2) and Alderson, gave them a 3-1 win. West Ham park was used by many teams, including Mosquitoes, Dark Blues, and Upton Park. When Minerva defeated Grey Friars FC 3-0 in the 2nd round of the FA Cup in December 1878, the match was played at Forest Gate, Leytonstone, although I believe Grey Friars were the home team.

Assuming that it was the same team and not one in Dover of the same name, I managed to locate Minerva's playing record for the year of 1878 in the *Kentish Mercury*; it read – played 21, won 12, drew 2, lost 7, but gave no goalscoring details.

When Minerva met the Old Etonians at the Oval on Saturday 11th January 1879 to play off their 3rd round English Cup tie, the rock hard ground was covered in several inches of snow. The *London Standard* said that the Etonians were expecting an easy game, but when Minerva kicked off, Eton were surprised how good they were. "Playing the Scotch game of skilful passing and heading cleverly", Minerva gave as good as they got in the first half, but they ran out of steam somewhat in the second period. However, a spirited effort saw Minerva fight back to draw level at 2-2 with full time only fifteen minutes away. They seem to have spent themselves out however, as they couldn't prevent Eton from scoring three more in the last few minutes to make it 5-2. *The Graphic* romancing that their 'Greek god has deserted them in their hour of need'. On Saturday 10th October 1879, Minerva, still at Ladywell, easily defeated Upton Rangers by 10-0. A fortnight later, Minerva thrashed Eagles FC by 9-0 at home. Originally employing a white band around each arm on their navy shirts, this was soon dropped.

The *Sheffield Telegraph* reported on a match between local side Millhouses and a 'Minerva' in January of 1880, who they beat 5-0. As all the other matches were of local teams, and no mention was given that 'Minerva' had come up from London, then I assume that this 'Minerva' were a Sheffield area team of the same name. There was no doubting that I had the right Minerva in October 1882, when they met and were overwhelmed by Upton Park in the London Challenge Cup, and slumped off the field at Dulwich having suffered the biggest defeat in their history – 18 goals to one.

In season 1889-90, Minerva ran three teams, whose aggregate results were- played 40, won 35, drew 2, lost 3, scored 191 goals, conceded 40. Their ground was described as being one of the best in the south of England' by the *Illustrated Sporting & Dramatic News*. By this time, they were based at Lee, in south-east London, in what is now Lewisham SE12. In 1872, the *Imperial Gazetteer of England* described the village of Lee as " a riverside pleasant, salubrious and picturesque place with a police station and a post office".

Minerva's place in the London football world received a severe reality check when they were humiliated 11-1 by the Old Westminsters in a London Senior cup tie on 23rd January 1892. From its inception in 1886, Minerva were also competing in the London Junior Cup, which was probably where they belonged. They were beaten in the 1887 final by Connaught FC (score unknown), but came back in 1890-1 to win it when they defeated Edmonton Albion by 2-0 on the Leyton county ground. Minerva were put out of the 1886-

7 Middlesex Cup by minor side City Ramblers, who won 1-0 at Stratford.

Minerva won the City of London Charity Shield for five years running from 1893 to 1898 until they were finally overcome by the London Olympic FC by 2-1 after a replay and extra-time on the Wood Green ground. I couldn't find out anything about this competition, but I suspect I was similar to the Mayor of Birmingham Charity Cup where just four or eight invited teams took part. Even the match report in *Lloyd's Weekly* failed to mention any players' names, save for Minerva's Pilbeam who retired hurt. Opponents London Olympic turned out to be another team exclusively comprised of workers from a City department store, also from St. Paul's district.

Reports of Minerva matches continued to be rare in the 1890s but one discovered in the *Bucks Herald* of 18th February 1893, said that Minerva had won 1-0 at Marlow, although the home team only contained four first team players. During the 1890s, Minerva's name would occasionally pop up in the Middlesex Cup results. I also found another Minerva FC playing in Glasgow, and a team called Edmonton Minerva

When Minerva went to play Chesham on Saturday 23rd September 1893, they came away with their tails between their legs after an 8-1 thrashing, despite Foulder opening the scoring for them after just two minutes. In February of that year, Minerva met one of the legendary teams of the 'first era' of football when they narrowly lost 1-2 to the Old Harrovians at Lee. When Fulham finally opened their Craven Cottage ground in 1896, after almost two years of developments, Minerva were the first ever visiting side, but Fulham won comfortably by 4-0. Other matches against Queens Park Rangers and Woodville confirms that Lee in county Kent was Minerva's base at around 1893-4. It seems that the Minerva cricket team which was active in the summers of the 1890s was the same club, as they played their matches at Lee Green too. Lee was a hamlet in Victorian London and has almost disappeared today into Lewisham, but back in the 1890s, there were two adjacent cricket grounds by the railway station, known as the Granville and Northbrook grounds, each with its own pavilion. However, at Lee Green itself, there were two cricket grounds - Ravenscourt and Gresham, and a separate cricket ground, all off the bend of the Weigall Road, and Minerva's ground would surely have been one of these. Surprisingly, all three grounds remain today.

Fulham were Minerva's main rivals in 1890s west London. Minerva were reported as playing in Wood Green at Christmas 1896, in Chiswick in 1898, and were still active as the new century approached, as I found they played the London Olympic club in January 1899, losing 5-1 at Shepherds Bush. They also drew 1-1 away to Folkestone in Christmas week of that year. Minerva were still active in Lee in 1900-01, as they were competing in the qualifying rounds of the London Cup. Little trace of Minerva could be found after 1901, as their minor level matches were no longer reported in the papers. Minerva visited the ground of Reigate Priory in early February 1907 (*Dorking & Leatherhead Advertiser*) and lost 1-2 in what was said to be a poor match, when fielding this side -

			Atkinson				
		McDiarmid			Robinson		
	Milne					Brocklebank	
Hay	Watson		McMath	Abbot	Hill		Munro

In the 1930s, a 'Minerva' competed in the Brompton & District League around Gillingham, but I doubt that this was the same club, although of the few Minerva matches reported upon, opponents were frequently from the Dover area of Kent. By 1900, the name 'Minerva' had become generic, and was also being used by teams in Tottenham, Edmonton, Brixton and elsewhere. In 1929, a Minerva met Dover Wednesday Juniors at Crabbe Court, but were beaten 5-3 on Saturday 7th March. I looked all through the various minor leagues in Kent at this time, but could not find where Minerva had been 'hiding' during the Edwardian era. They seem to have been a club without a base, playing low-key friendlies all over Kent, and indeed, they seem to have lost in almost every report I could find on them. Leading Division 2 of the New Brompton League in 1936 were Minerva Athletic, ahead of teams such as Old Bordenians, Lloyd Bank 3rd team, Whitstable Reserves, Faversham Invicta, Sheerness Garrison and Troy Town.

Crabbe Court (now Crabble Athletic ground) is still a sports ground in Dover, used by the town rugby club, but I would say it began life as a cricket ground. It is adjacent to both the River Recreation ground and Dover Athletic FC (since 1934). Interestingly, a nearby street is called Minerva Avenue.

A rare photo of the Minerva FC in 1891. Notice the cap and tassel and centre panel.
The players are, from back row, left to right - J.R. Tillett (right half back), L. McKenzie (left half back), T. Mole (centre forward), R. McGreggor (left back), J. Stamp (umpire). Middle row- W. Gill (right back), H.P. Strong (outside right), J. Gilchrist (inside left), W. Clee (goalie), H.S. Rowley (left wing). Front row - W.H. Wilson (inside left), T. H. Chicken (centre back). The splendid trophy is the London Junior Cup, first won by Connaught FC.

NEW CRUSADERS

Founded - 1905
Folded - 1914
Ground - The College Ground, 144 Longlands Road, Sidcup, Kent
Colours - White shirts, black shorts

The club was founded by Samuel Farnfield, headmaster of Sidcup's private Austral School, who had earlier founded the Cray Wanderers in 1860 in the village of St. Mary Cray, who at first played on Star Lane, now a cemetery. Samuel had eight sons, and six of them all played football for Cambridge University. The six sons formed the nucleus of the New Crusaders. Said to be "within five minutes walk from the railway station", the New Crusaders ground should have been easy to locate, especially with the clue word 'college' but tracking it down proved elusive as it seemed that Sidcup did not have any colleges in the 1905-1915 period; its current three colleges are all post-war creations. I could not find any ground which fitted the description 'college grounds, five minute's walk from the station'. Eventually, thanks to Mike Float and his book on football grounds of south London, we find that an un-marked private school on Longlands Road was their home, despite several large fields being adjacent (the later named King George's and Longlands Recreation grounds). Sadly, the almost triangular shaped school grounds were built over by Austral Close at around 1932, although the tree-line separating Bexley allotments from Longlands Road are the original trees which formed the boundary of the Austral school. This indicates that the football pitch must have used up 90% of the available space, leaving only about a five yard perimeter for spectators. The school became Austral's Club during the 1950s and demolished in the late 1960s, having hosted many of the leading pop groups of the day, as 'mods' gathered there on Lambrettas and Vespa scooters. Numbers 2-8 Austral Close were built where the school stood.

In what must have been one of their first ever games, this New Crusaders side played Tunbridge Wells on their Neville cricket ground to start the 1905 season -

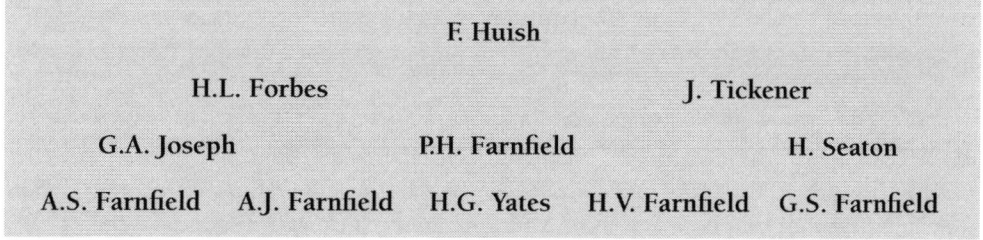

		F. Huish		
	H.L. Forbes		J. Tickener	
G.A. Joseph		P.H. Farnfield		H. Seaton
A.S. Farnfield	A.J. Farnfield	H.G. Yates	H.V. Farnfield	G.S. Farnfield

Clearly, the Farnfield family were the nucleus of the club. Played in sheets of rain and wind, the Crusaders ran up an 8-0 lead by halftime, and concluded at 13-2 ! 'Comparable to the great Corinthians' ran the summary from the *Kent & Sussex Courier* of 15th September 1905, as they continued to eulogise about the array of talent of the visitors. Their forward play was described as like 'a well oiled machine' with H.V. of the Farnfield brothers being the best player on the pitch, his play described as 'perfection in dribbling, passing and shooting'. I can offer no explanation as to why they were a wonderful combination from the outset, except that no doubt the Farnfield family must have all grown up developing a sixth sense about each other's play.

Entering the F.A. Cup from the off, they astonished with the score of 16-0 over Woking, the biggest ever debut score. After they got through the qualifying rounds and were drawn at home to Plymouth Argyle in the 1st round proper (last 64) but Plymouth offered to switch grounds, because the Crusaders' undeveloped ground only held 4,000 people but the offer was turned down. Plymouth won an exciting game by 6-3 in January 1906, but were themselves trounced 5-1 by Aston Villa in the next round. The ground record was broken at Romford in March 1906 when 3,303 people assembled to see their side make a draw with Crusaders. Possibly some kind of record was also broken in the fact that all six Farnfield brothers took the field, namely : Algernon, Archibald, Gilbert, Percy, Herbert and Bernard. Three of the brothers also played for Clapton circa 1905. It was said by some that the New Crusaders were the best amateur team ever, apart from the Corinthians. The only other time I can recall six brothers was in the Ruabon Druids team of the 1880s. Despite great anticipation of Crusaders adding to their incredible tally of 160 goals in the previous 25 games, the match ended 0-0, and a replay at Sidcup was also drawn 1-1. The season's tally reached an amazing 207 goals.

When Crusaders went to the Reigate Priory ground for a charity game in April 1906, the five Farnfield brothers comprised the entire forward line, winning 3-2, giving 'the finest display of football ever seen on the ground' with their long-range passing being most effective. In the same month, silverware was added to the trophy cabinet when Dulwich Hamlet were beaten 3-1 in the replayed final of the London Senior Cup played at Herne Hill cycle grounds. This was some achievement for a new club in its first year, as Dulwich were the leading amateur team of the London area in the Edwardian era, later monopolising the Amateur Cup, and often drawing huge attendances of up to 15,000. In May 1907 the Eastbourne Charity Cup was won, beating Richmond AFC 2-0 in the final. 'Only' 104 goals were scored that season, as the Southern Amateur League was won, scoring an average of 5 goals per game. Trophies continued to be amassed; the Kent AFA Cup, the AFA Senior Cup, and the Kent Charity Cup were also taken. In October 1908, New Crusaders, with 'only' three Farnfield brothers, thrashed Reigate Priory 9-0 in the league, without the services of the Buck brothers, who had departed from them to form a new team, Surrey Wanderers. In November 1908, England sent a team out to play Bohemia, and two New Crusaders - H.A. Milton and J.A. Joseph were in the team comprised of Corinthians and University men. 1909 saw New Crusaders champions of the Southern Amateur League for the 4th successive year, and Amateur AFA Cup winners in April, having beaten Casuals 5-1 in the final. Regular opponents at this time included Casuals, Ealing, Reigate Priory, Civil Service, Ipswich Town, Crouch End Vampires, Eastbourne and Richmond Association. The Amateur Cup was entered from 1905,and wins over Nottingham Jardines (2-1), Ealing (5-1 away) and a three game tussle with Romford (0-0,1-1,4-1) saw them meet Oxford City in the semi-finals at Reading, where they lost 2-4 to the eventual winners. Evans had put Crusaders 2-1 ahead but Hodges and Dickson for Oxford put the tie out of reach in front of a near 6,000 crowd. In the following season, the two sides met again, but in round 2, where Oxford again won, but only by 1-0. Crusaders never again made any impact in the Amateur Cup.

Annual fixtures were arranged with Cambridge University, with wildly differing results. The 1907 fixture at Sidcup, watched by 2000 people, saw Crisp score a first half hat-trick to put Crusaders out of sight, with the score extending to a remarkable 10-2 by full time. In the following year, the situation was reversed as the Cantabs ran out 5-1 winners at Sidcup. New Crusaders drew large crowds wherever they played, with 4,000 watching their away game at Ipswich against the Casuals in April 1909, which they won 5-1. December 1907 brought together two of the country's top amateur clubs to settle some debates, when New Crusaders met the Corinthians head-on at Queens Club, West Kensington. However, missing two of the Farnfield brothers, and their first choice goalie, Corinthians ran out 5-0 winners in front of 800 spectators.

Between 1908-1910, New Crusaders undertook annual trips on the continent, and beat several teams who today are world-famous; Barcelona (twice), Nice, Sporting Lisbon, Marseilles, and Benfica were all put to the sword. In 1909, the *Dorking& Leatherhead Advertiser* said that New Crusaders 'were still a force in the amateur football world, if not as strong as their sensational first season'. In January 1910, a side which Crusaders regularly gave a hammering to - Reigate Priory - finally beat them for the first time on the College Ground. On Saturday 9th April that year, Ealing were beaten 2-0, and the New Crusaders' goal tally for the season went passed the 100 mark.

On 7th December 1912, New Crusaders crushed Ipswich Town 7-0 with Eric Farnfield getting six goals himself (*Nottingham Evening Post*). In April 1913, the New Crusaders' application to join the Ithsmian League was considered by the league committee, and they were admitted, taking the place of Tunbridge Wells, who were far from happy about it. However, in May 1913, the decision by the club to resign from the Amateur Football Association was reported as far away as Dundee. It seemed to have something to do with the fact that they had failed to hand over their share of the A.F.A Cup Final gate against Ipswich Town. They then joined the Football Association, presumably as an admittance that they took money out of that Amateur Cup final match. *The Sportsman* of April 1913 said that New Crusaders had rising expenses to be met, and were caught between two rocks, too strong for almost all amateur clubs, but not professionally equipped to compete on terms with the League clubs, despite winning the Southern Amateur League four years running.

The last time I found a reference to New Crusaders was in July 1914 when John Malden, a player with the club throughout the previous season, and also of Ipswich FC, had been appointed headmaster of King Charles School in Tunbridge Wells. Most amateur football clubs sent around half of its players off to war in 1914, and this led to hundreds of them never reforming in 1919, and New Crusaders were one such casualty.

With the first team on tour in Spain, this hastily-assembled side represented the club in the 1914 Kent AFA Cup Final played at Dover at Easter - Reverend H.V. Farnfield, F.H. Wood, L.S. Daws, Payne, H. A. Hambledon, J.J. Westmoreland, L. Pirk, J.S. Davis, S. Davis, H.J. Hambleton, L. Pyrke (scorer). The 2nd Lancashire Fusiliers were the opposition, but New Crusdaders had a long-standing commitment to tour Spain and southern France, which they made when they were in the Amateur Football Association. Fusiliers had beaten Whitstable 2-0 at the Hall-by-sea ground at Margate on 1st March to gain revenge on their semi final exit of the previous year (*Dover Express*). Played at the Crabble Athletic ground, a crowd of 4,000 saw New Crusaders 'reserves' win 1-0, giving ' a display of accurate low passing and with a good understanding between the players'. It would have been 2-0 had not Fusiliers goalie J. Davis saved a penalty around the post. The senior cup was won by Maidstone, and the junior cup by Eccles. That Kent cup final was the last meaningful game, as the club was not resurrected after the war in 1919. A final appearance, where they scored seven goals, was at the Bickley Park school, where one of the Farnfields had become headmaster.

Out of 36 competition entered for over the years, they had won 19 of them, amassing 747 goals in 220 games. *(Statistics supplied by Ian Fordyce)*

The Google Earth aerial view below shows the site of the Astral School and its grounds. The football pitch must have virtually reached Longlands Road and even then could have been no more than 65 yards wide and barely 100 yards in length. A football field which lay due south, now part of the park, did not exists before 1950, as it was part of the allotments fields.

NO-NAMES (KILBURN)

Founded - Pre 1862
Folded - Circa 1872
Grounds - Kilburn and Walthamstow
Colours - Unknown

When captains and officers of the various interested parties met on Monday 26th October 1863 at the Freemason's Tavern in London, for the purpose of creating the Football Association, it was the captain of the No-Names club of Kilburn, Mr. Arthur Pember, who was elected permanent president. Other officials included F.M. Campbell (treasurer), Ebenezer Morley (secretary) and on the committee, John Alcock (Forest), H.T. Steward, H.T. Wawn (Crystal Palace) and James Turner. John's brother Charles would soon take over from R.W. Willis in 1868 who replaced solicitor Morley as first secretary. In an early and experimental Sheffield v London match played in 1866 to try and get the two organisations to play the same rules, Arthur Pember was the London captain, in an eleven comprised of four Barnes men, three Wanderers, and three No-Names players, Arthur Pember, Arthur Baker and Arthur Tebbut.

Little could they have realised at the time, just how monumental an organisation it would prove to become, that at first they only agreed to meet annually, in September! It would not be long before monthly meetings were needed, to sanction the ever growing applications for membership (annual fee being one guinea) and to make the various cup draws and hear appeals from clubs who felt they had a grievance, usually against another team which had beaten them. Appeals included many things, such as ineligible players on the opposing team (who were thought to be members of other clubs), wrong height or size of the goalposts, unkempt state of the home ground, too much snow, biased umpires and referees, and games abandoned before ninety minutes due to bad light, and so on. It is thought that their name (N.N.) is a thinly veiled reference to the backers of mercantile shipping insurance, who are known as "Names" on the London Stock Exchange, where Arthur Pember worked. Pember (1835-1886) was then better known as an author and investigative journalist in an age before such undercover activities were thought to have existed. He specialized in the expose of the truth behind the American and English society facades, and was acknowledged for his book "the Mystery and Miseries of the Great Metropolis". A highly educated man, he was well versed in finance, politics, education, literature, science and current affairs, and departed England in 1868 with his family to have a career in the U.S.A shortly after the American Civil War as a New York journalist. He died in America, in North Dakota on April 3rd 1886. Married to Elizabeth Houghton in 1860, he lived at 30 Carlton Road, Kilburn, moving from No.26 following his wife's tragic death in childbirth. He married Alice Grieve, daughter of a wealthy wine merchant two years later and they had four children. He joined his father as a stockbroker at the firm of Jones Lloyd & Co. According to *Dick Weindling & Marianne Colloms*, No-Names played "on a field opposite his house" which means (after studying several old maps) that it was where is now the Paddington recreation ground on Carlton Vale. Pember would fail to recognise his street today, for all the lovely detached house have gone and groups of blocks of flats - sorry 'apartments' - now fill the road. Only the spire of St. Augustines church would be recognisable to him today. Wondering if the facing Carlton Tavern was around in Pember's time, I was shocked to read the story of the 1920s Grade 2 listed pub, the only building in the street to survive the Blitz, was literally bulldozed to the ground one weekend without notice or permission by the new owner, a property developer (that's the polite version) from Tel-Aviv, Israel on April 8th 2015. Both publican Patsy Lord and Westminster Council were outraged, and Ori Calif & Co. were ordered to rebuild the pub as an exact replica within 18 months , 'brick by brick'. Public protest had saved a tiny part of London's heritage, but will it look the same when it is finished?

The grade II listed Carlton Tavern replaced the original pub which had been bombed in 1918 by early German airplanes. A pub on the same site on a 1860s map certainly means that the footballers of the No-Names FC used it as a base for home games, as the entrance to their field was through where the gates are shown above.

Without the research by *Weindling & Collins* for whom I remain grateful, I was struggling to say for certain which field No-Names used, and I was mistakenly focussing my search around West End Lane, Priory Road and Oaklands Hall. Pember's house lay on the side of the road which backed onto the church, and although in the 1860s there was a field between his back garden and the boundary wall of the church, it was only 50 yards wide, and so for their ground, we must be looking at the top end of what is now Paddington Rec. As to which exact field they would have played on, there were plenty to chose from, since it was nothing but fields all the way down to the Grand Union canal at Paddington, a mile due south. However, as football needs a field of at least two acres, and match descriptions talk about 'sun in their eyes, (meaning a field running east to west) I can rule out the tree-lined fields to favour the one which lay off Randolph Avenue, which for the most part is now the tennis courts and the gardens of Carlton Mansions, as a map for 1872 shows two small permanent structures which could have been pavilions. The Paddington cricket & football ground, once a fully developed stadium, but lower down and existing as such until about 1985, was not created until about 1890 as a running and athletics ground, by which time the pioneering No-Names had been gone for a decade. It is possible that it was built where football used to be played, and so I name it a second choice of exact spot. This was also 200 yards' walk from the Carlton Tavern, so why walk past two fields to use that one? Match reports mention a big dip in front of one of the goals, but the old cricket pitch is comparatively level, unlike the area by the cafe and tennis courts.

The Carlton Vale end of Paddington Rec has undulating east to west terrain.

Barnes were a regular on the No-Names fixture card, but the 'Oarsmen' beat them 4-0 at home and 2-0 away in season 1862-63. On January 30th 1864, No-Names once again received the Barnes club, one of only a handful of London clubs extant at that time. Described only as 'at Kilburn', the home side kicked off 'uphill and against the wind, with the sun in their eyes'. Well at least that confirms that the ground was running east to west. Goals from W. Baker (2) and A. dePothonier saw off 'the Oarsmen' with the Barnes goalkeeper coming under criticism for being slow to react to shots. This was the 14 player No-Names side that day :-

> W. Baker, Henry Baker, J. Baker, Alfred Baker, Renshaw, Daly, George
> Wawn, Mitchell, Collins, Alexander Morton, Lendrum, dePothonier, Giles,
> and Arthur Pember (captain).

The Bakers went on to play for Wanderers. Four brothers in the same team suggests that they, along with Pember, founded the club. Alfred Joseph Baker (1846-1900) was born in Willesden, where his father Henry was an auctioneer. By his early twenties, he had built up a reputation of one of the fastest sprinters in London, and indeed, won the AAA 100 yards race in 1870. Still later, by 1895, his low running style with the body bent forward was recalled by commentators who placed him as yet unsurpassed in the capital. He married Marion Sayers in 1871, and in classic Victorian fashion they had six surviving children. Baker followed his father in the family business of Baker & Baker Co., and was capped three times for England in 1870-71. Historian have traced his 58 appearances for both No-Names and Wanderers, where he scored 15 goals. Often playing for the Kent or Middlesex county teams, Alfred was elected a committee member on the F.A. in 1872. Ironically, he died while sprinting to catch a train on 3rd January 1900 at Willesden Junction. A lesser known player, George Lawson, Somerset born in 1838, rose to become Assistant Under Secretary of State in the War Office by 1895. An old Marlburian, he joined the Civil Service in 1855 as a mere clerk, and was knighted in 1897. Lawson also turned out for Civil Service and the Crusaders.

Returning to the Barnes game, the attendance, although not remarked upon, must have been at least moderate as the players were warmly applauded as they left the field of play. *(Bells Life)*. Their splendidly-named forward George Twizel Wawn also played for the Civil Service FC. Born in county Durham in 1841, he joined the War Office in London in 1859 having obtained an MA degree in Durham University. He married his first cousin Mary Ward Wawn and by 1870 was living in Eastbourne, Sussex with his two children. His football was curtailed in 1873 when he posted to the African Commissariat. He attended the earliest meetings at the Freemason Tavern in London and was instrumental in forming the early rules of the F.A. with Ebenezer Cobb Morley, he later rose to the rank of Major in the Army, living to the age of 74.

A fortnight later, simply billed as 'Kilburn', the No-Names went to play the very capable boys of Charterhouse School, the result being a goal-less draw. The greater weight and age of N.N being used to advantage for the first half hour, but the boys fought back well on a wet and slippery surface. Once again, it was Giles and Baker who caught the eye. This eleven played the formidable Royal Engineers on their ground at the Great Lines, Chatham on Saturday 9th March 1867, losing 3-0 :-

Arthur Pember (captain), George Pember, H.J. Baker, Alfred Baker, W.F. Baker, Charles M. Tebbut, J. Nicholas, H. Nicholas, S.T. Holland, H. Emmanuel, C.E. Picard.

Alexander Morton (1831-1900) is credited in some sources as being England's first captain- goalkeeper, when he played against Scotland in March 1873. He played with the No-Names during 1863-66 before joining the old Crystal Palace club where he remained until 1874, sometimes (24) turning out for the Wanderers club. Born in Paddington, London, he married Flora Hedger in 1855, and began his occupation as a stockbroker on the London Stock Exchange, where no doubt, he was not a "Name". In 1874, Alec Morton, now 42, was displaced as the Wanderers' goalkeeper by William Grieg, although Charles Alcock rated Morton as the finest goalkeeper in the world during the 1870s. Sometime No-Names player Giulio Tyler-Smith was born in Piccadilly in 1849, where his father was an eminent obstetrician. Often listed as J.C. Smith, he excelled at sprinting at Westminster school, when he played in the Middlesex county side, and later turned

Arthur Pember and his outstanding facial adornment.

out for Old Wesminsters, Crusaders, and the Flying Dutchmen clubs. In professional life, he became a tea and coffee merchant at Cassell & Co., and joined the Middlesex Rifle Volunteers. He died in Seaford, Sussex in 1900.

If you look at the Wanderers' section, you will see that several of the No-Names team also turned out for them. A year later, the same RE v NN fixture was played on 8th February. *The Sportsman* noting that No-Names assembled a full strength side which travelled from London to Chatham, Kent. Although the Engineers were 'much improved since last seen' the result was again 3-0. Unfortunately one of the Kilburn men had an accident on the greasy surface of the Outer Lines field, and Fleet sustained a broken collar-bone, which was attended to by the Engineers' medic, Dr. Cockburn. The first three named players in this side were singled out for plucky play :-

H. Emmanuel, C.M. Tebbut (captain), J. Fleet, A. Nicholas, A. Bird, C. Gordon, C.J. Schwabe, J. Bone, O. Jeinder, A. Clarke, C.M. Green.

Team captain Charles Mansfield Tebbut (1839-1898) was born in Wanstead, Essex, which ties in with his connections to the Forest club. He was also a renowned cricketer who turned out for Middlesex during 1866-70. He passed away in South Hampstead from apoplexy. He was a staunch supporter of cricket in those two counties, and donated large sums of money at a time when the Essex county club were about to fold. He remained on the Middlesex county committee for most of his adult life. When England played Scotland for the first time in what has since been de-classified as a proper international match on Saturday 25th February 1871, Charles Tebbut was the referee in that 1-1 drawn match. Why de-classified? Well there were seven Wanderers men in the England side, but the 'Scots' team were all public school chums residing in London, including Quintin Hogg and William Gladstone, son of the Prime Minister, three Oxford University men, two Old Etonians, and two Civil Service FC players. Even Queens Park's Robert Smith was a West Norwood player. 'Scots' men Frederick Inglis and William Lindsay were born in India, whilst James Kirkpatrick was born in Canada!

At this time, Captain Francis Marindin was not yet the inspiration for the Engineers, for he was out-ranked by Major Harrison, who was their early influential player. No-Names played the Victoria Rifles football team on Saturday 8th December 1866 but the pitch was described as even heavier than usual due to the rains. Goals from Pember and Baker (as usual) secured a 2-0 win, attributed mostly to 'the regular practice together of Kilburn'. From that match, their goal was said to have been defended heroically by 'N.N's finest'. This was in fact Arthur Pember. Other sides played that season by No-Names included Herts Rangers, C.C.C., and Victoria Rifles.

On Saturday 30th November 1867, No-Names played host to the Wanderers at Kilburn, *'over a heavy ground on clay soil, under constant rain'* (The Sportsman). In a fast game, where the ball was constantly going from one end to the other, and with falling sleet, N.N's A. Bird put the ball through the Wanderers' posts to secure victory as light fell away to dusk. The N.N team that day was -

Alfred Baker, S.T. Holland (captain), A. Fleet, Charles M. Tebbut, H. Emmanuel, V. Borradaile, H.N. Good, C.N. Green, Dr. Alex Morton, Charles J. Maurice.

When No-Names beat Wanderers 1-0 on Saturday 30th November 1867 thanks to a goal by Bird, another tiny snippet of their ground came to light. On a slight slope, and on heavy clay soil, there was also a bowl shaped dip near one of the goals. The annual home fixture against Herts Rangers was played on December 14th in 1867, and again, rain spoiled the game, but the heavy ground made the game difficult for dribbling. Changing ends at every goal, Kilburn won 3-0 with efforts from Alf Baker (2) and Fleet, and as usual, darkness drew the match to a close. I found further games for No-Names in 1870, when they met Forest, Barnes and Upton Park. When George Gordon was chosen to play for Scotland against England in March 5th 1870 (unofficial friendly), he was listed as a No-Names player, so too England's Alfred Baker. No more was heard from the N.N's after the end of 1871, coinciding with the rise of the Wanderers.

In November 1887, a grand ceremony was held to open the new Kilburn public park on the Kensal Green side of town, on land donated by the Ecclesiastical Commission. The Lord Mayor of London, Sir Reginald Hanson, read a letter to dignitaries present that Queen Victoria had given consent to name the park, the Queens Park.

Still active in later life, the three Tebbutt brothers, keystones of No-Names Forest, and the Wanderers clubs, as part of a winter ice-hockey team in Leytonstone circa 1900.

NUNHEAD FC

Founded - 1888
Folded   - 1948 (1941)
Grounds - Browns Field, St. Asalphs Road, Nunhead
Colours - Medium blue shirts, white shorts
             White shirts, navy shorts 1930s.

According to Wikipedia, Nunhead FC began life as Wingfield House FC playing on 'Brown's Field' in 1888. I found Wingfield House playing away to Penge in January 1899 where they lost 1-2, and against teams like Cray Wanderers, Old Askeyans, Dulwich reserves, Crown Athletic and Clapham a year earlier in the Southern Suburban League. Problem was, I found football match reports involving Wingfield House long after I found match reports about the Nunhead FC, such as when Wingfield House won 4-0 away to Dorking in April 1904. I then found a reference to a player named Archer whom Wingfield House had loaned to Tottenham Hotspurs in March 1904. Nunhead's early club secretary was H. Evans of 2 Lindo Street, S.E.

A fire broke out on Browns Field in May 1894 when 'two immense faggots (piles) of timber erected by the South London Rifle Club caught fire and an immense blaze took hold of nearby house fencing'. During the late 1890s, the footballers of the 3rd Grenadier Guards also shared the ground for their London League matches. Browns Field was also used for tennis and cricket, and many charity theatrical cricket games took place there. I also found Old St. Stephens FC playing there in 1893-4. The first match I traced by Nunhead wasn't until 1897 when they beat Belmont 2-0 'at Peckham'. All their matches seemed to have been friendlies against other local sides at this point.

Their earliest success came in 1908 when they won the Surrey county cup, which coincided with Nunhead making Browns Field their home ground. Defeating Guilford 2-0 before an attendance of 4,000, the *Surrey Mirror* said that 'Nunhead were a very smart workmanlike team'. Judging by the front cover of Mick Blakeman's excellent club history, Browns Field was never fully developed, despite a healthy following, save two small barrel-roofed stands along both halfway lines, a pavilion and paling fencing around the perimeter to keep the crowd at bay. Set in the middle of a large open space between Aspinall Road and Ivydale Road, there was a railway embankment of the Chatham Railway behind the Aspinall Road end. At this time, Nunhead signed E.J. Cotton, a prolific goalscorer from the Dublin Bohemians club

In the January of that year, a letter appeared in the Surrey Mirror suggesting that the district's strongest teams - Dorking, Guilford, Redhill, Nunhead, Woking and Dulwich Hamlet - could be brought together to make a strong league. The national Amateur Cup was also a good opportunity for clubs like Nunhead to make their mark, and in January 1908, Nunhead took a good name out when they defeated London Caledonians, although the Callies' time had yet to come. In the same month, Nunhead's H.R. Dolley was selected to play for the South v North game. March 1908 also saw them beaten in the final of the London Charity Cup against Shepherds Bush (later to become QPR) on the Herne Hill cycle ground. The two sides had only just met in an Athenian League game, with this eleven playing for Nunhead -

	C.H. Collis	
H. Clegg		F. Muncey
G. Clement	G. Symonns	S.J. Love
H. Stansfield	F. Kenyon	C. Stansfield	H. Marsh	F. Morris

In early 1910, Nunhead's S.C. Simmons was chosen as reserve for the trails for the England amateur international match in February, but did not make the final eleven. Stansfield however, signed for Bury that month at inside forward and made his debut against Oldham Athletic. It didn't seem to upset Nunhead, who trounced London Caledonians 8-0 away at Tufnell Park in the next game. At this point, Nunhead had joined the Isthmian League. Sadly for Nunhead, they were knocked out of the semi final of the London Amateur Cup 2-0 by Dorking in March. In May 1910, there was a very close finish to the end of the Isthmian League season, with Bromley as champions on 26pts, and Nunhead pushed into 3rd place on goal difference by Clapton after they had both finished on 24 points with an identical record of 10 wins, 4 draws and 4 defeats. Highlight of 1911-12 season was in reaching round 3 of the Amateur Cup before going out 2-1 after a replay against eventual winners Stockton.

In 1913, Nunhead's Sanders played for England in the amateur international against France in Paris on 27th February. 1914 saw Nunhead gain exemption from the qualifying rounds of the Amateur Cup, but it also coincided with the start of the War, and Nunhead found themselves mixing with the big boys when due to petrol rationing, London's Football League sides competed in the London Cup, and Nunhead must have been pleased to only lose by 1-2 away to Tottenham Hotspur on 21st September.

Their most successful period came in the 1920s and 1930s when they won the London Senior Cup in 1923 and the Isthmian League in 1929 and 1930. They were also runners-up in 1920 and 1923. Bromley were overcome 1-0 in the 1923 London Cup final to make up for losing the 1914 final to Ilford 1-2 after a 1-1 draw, and earlier still in 1909, losing 0-1 to Clapton. Continued attempts on both the F.A and Amateur Cups brought a 3rd round exit to Dulwich Hamlet in 1926 in the Amateur Cup, losing the replay 1-2. Round 4, the last 8 would forever elude them. In season 1926-7, Nunhead created a record for a non-league club when they thrashed Kingstonians 9-0 in round 2 of the F.A. Cup. The same scoreline was returned against them in 1932 when they in turn were trounced by Bath City. Nunhead continued on in the Isthmian League after 1939 without any notable success. A year later they seem to have joined the newly formed South Eastern Combination, playing teams like Tooting & Mitcham, Redhill, Wimbledon, Bromley, Dulwich, Sutton and Erith & Belvedere, and at the start of February 1940 were lying 3rd in the table. When the wartime league had finished in April, Nunhead were had fallen back to halfway behind unbeaten Tooting. At the end of April, Tooting beat them 3-1 in the final of the Surrey Senior Cup which seems to have been the last cup match they ever played. At the end of May 1940, promising 17 year old L. Henley signed terms with the Arsenal. Nunhead's final season was 1940-41 and the last result for them I could find was when they won 2-1 on April 26th away to Erith & Belvedere. Once the War had set in, most football club had their players billeted all over the country, and teams were assembled on an ad-hoc basis from whoever and wherever they could borrow players. Eventually amateur football clubs became mothballed by 1942, many clubs never to reform. The Amateur Cup itself was suspended from 1939 to 1945.

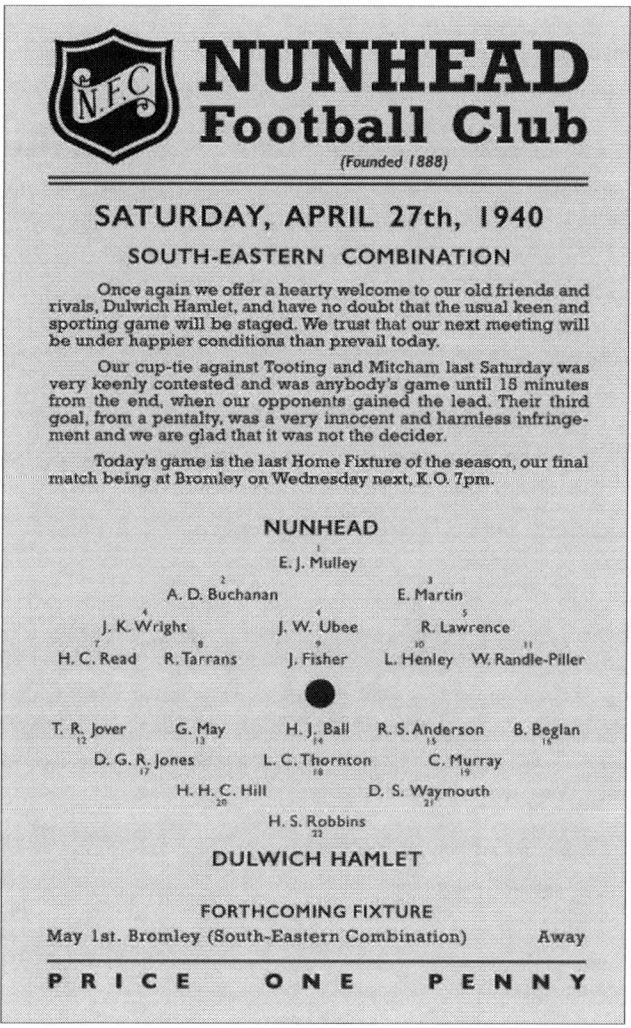

Programme for Nunhead v Dulwich Hamlet 1940. You can still obtain many of these amateur teams' programmes for little money in the football souvenir fairs which tour the country.

Nunhead's most famous players include Dennis Compton of later Arsenal fame, Albert Cadwell and Sidney Pugh. Cadwell (1900-1944) went on to sign for West Ham in 1923 where he spent a decade as their left half, gaining county caps for Surrey and London, as well as playing for the Football League in 1930 against the Irish League. Pugh (1919-1944) was a left back who moved on to Arsenal in April 1936 which began a series of tragic events. He received a kidney injury in his debut game, which ended his career, and then was killed when on training with the RAF at Seighford exactly eight years later.

Compton (1918-1997) was better known as a famous international cricketer. In terms of dual football and cricket careers, his achievements place him at the top of all time greats; 78 Test Matches, almost 39,000 career runs, thrice bowling ten men out in a match, 140 career centuries, the list goes on and on. Suffice to say that he is in the ICC Hall of Fame as one of the greatest of all time. As a footballer, as a left winger, he scored 15 goals for the Arsenal during a 14 year career with them after spending 1934-5 at Nunhead. His career peaked sadly when the 2nd World War was going on, but he still played 12 Wartime unofficial Internationals for England. A knee injury from a collision with the Charlton Athletic goalkeeper finally ended his sporting days.

In 1936, the ground landlords, the Haberdasher school intimated that when the lease ran out in 1941, they would not allow Nunhead to play there and wanted it as the school sports ground instead. Sadly Nunhead never had the funds to find another ground, mainly due to two events, Eddie Marsh, the club treasurer had kept the club afloat for some years with money from his timber-yard business, but when it was hit in the Blitz, he went out of business, and really, so did Nunhead FC. Renowned for his ability to save penalties, goalkeeper Eric Mulley took charge of Nunhead for the final years, but despite support from local politicians and even Sir Stanley Rous, when the last day came, Nunhead ceased to exist although it took until 1948 to wind them up in court.

Their old ground is actually still in use, as part of the Haberdashers Askes school playing fields, with the pavilion (paid for by Marsh) still in use until about 1990. For a complete record on Nunhead, search out a book by Mick Blakeman - 'Nunhead FC, 1888-1949'.

Like many famous amateur clubs, Nunhead players featured on cigarette cards post-war.

OLD BRIGHTONIANS

Founded - 1880 (unconfirmed)
Folded - 1914
Ground - 1. Dulwich 1881
          2. Brighton College sports ground
Colours - 1. Maroon and navy halves
          2. Maroon and navy stripes

The Sportsman paper reported in December 1863 that "the popular game of foot-ball was now being played in Brighton", with a game between students of Brighton college and the school. The game took place on the Queens Park ground, and the players "used the new india-rubber football made by Fred Lillywhite". This students v old boys match became a long-standing annual fixture. The club seems to have been founded (as were the Old Salopians) for their Old Boys residing or working in London, as they would often play there as well as in Brighton.

Old Brightonians opened their 1881-2 season with a 0-2 away defeat to the Pilgrims FC, but *The Graphic* thought it sufficiently important a result to mention it amongst only a handful of matches played that week. Oddly, I could find no earlier results. However they entered the London Senior Cup in November 1882, being drawn away to Kildare, suggesting that they were already firmly established. At first playing in blue and white shirts *(Robin Horton)* at Dulwich, they soon adopted their old college colours.

In 1882, the selection committee of the London team to play its annual match with Sheffield revised its selection rules, choosing only players who had either been born or resided within London. This gave Brightonians' and Upton Park player Norman Leete his first chance to represent London. Oddly, when Oxford University played against Middlesex county in January 1885, two Brightonians, L. Norman and J. Bennett both played on the right wing; presumably their selection was based on residency too. The London Cup became a regular feature of their season, but in 1885, they were eliminated by unknowns United London Scottish, by 4-0 at Barnes.

Old Brightonians entered the F.A.Cup in season 1884-85, much later than most clubs. In round 1 they were eliminated by the powerful Swifts, by 3-0. Acton were beaten 2-1 in the following year, only for Old Westminsters to put them out by 3-0, the game being played at Wimbledon. In November 1886, Brightonians took the scalp of a once famous name when they defeated the Clapham Rovers by 6-0 at East Sheen in round 1 of 1886. On the same day, two former legendary clubs clashed in the first round of the F.A.Cup, when Old Etonians beat Royal Engineers by 1-0. That famous name of the Old Etonians were the visitors three years later and Brightonians beat them 4-1 at the college fields to progress into the 3rd round of the F.A. Cup. Once more, the Old Westminsters were their nemesis, beating them 3-1 after a 0-0 draw in London. The modern name of Swindon Town were overcome 1-0 in the opening round of the 1887-8 F.A. Cup in front of a small crowd, but then came a wonderful result when they beat Old Harrovians 4-0 away in round 2. Sadly, they came down to earth with a bump when top side Old Carthusians beat them 5-0 at home in round 3.

Before a large crowd, Great Marlow were defeated 5-2 in the 4th round in early

December 1888 but Notts County were too strong and beat them 2-0 to move into the last sixteen. Having to battle through the qualifying round put clubs like Brightonians at a disadvantage, but a well-known name was beaten in the 3rd qualifying round, when they won 3-1 at Luton in stormy weather on Saturday 17th November. On the same day, rivals Marlow beat Watford 2-0 away. The Brightonians continued on with playing only friendlies and cup ties after the founding of the Football League in 1888, and the range and quality of the opposition would vary greatly. For unknown reasons, Brightonians scratched to Clapton in November 1889, in the 3rd qualifying round of the F.A. Cup. In October 1891, Brightonians scored possibly their record away win when they defeated Gravesend FC by 8-0 in an F.A. Cup qualifier. In October 1893, a great match was brought of on the college grounds, in a qualifying round for the F.A. Cup. The famous Old Carthusians were the visitors, who went away with a 4-3 victory (*Sussex Agricultural Express*).

After 1889, only Old Carthusians and Old Westminsters would get through to the 1st round proper (last 32) and so clubs like Brightonians would turn their attentions to the new Amateur Cup. Old enemies the Westminsters oddly scratched to them in the 1893 Amateur Cup 1st round proper (it too, had a qualifying competition) but in mid-Wales, Chirk beat them 4-3 to end the inaugural run. The *Wrexham Advertiser* said ' the Brightonians underestimated the capacity of the home team; both sides played admirably but the ground was very slippery and passes went astray. Cotterill was the best man for the visitors but was well checked by Mates who played superbly. The home side gave a very useful display of pretty passing and more than matched their opponents'. Their Amateur Cup run in the following season came tumbling down when the then amateur Middlesborough crushed them 8-0 in round 3, and went on to win the cup. A wonderful 5-2 away win opened their 1895-6 Amateur Cup run, but a name which might surprise you, beat them 6-2 in round 2 – that of Shrewsbury Town. In the following year a 3-1 win away to Cheshunt promised much, but unknowns Kirkley beat them 2-0 at home in round 2. After 1896, Old Brightonians never again made any impact in the Amateur Cup, nor indeed any other old boy's club. It would be fifty years before a southern old boys team would make any impact - Pegasus. The annual match with Brighton College in 1892 was easily won by 8-2.

On Tuesday 4th December 1894, the team travelled to Leytonstone to play the boys of Forest School, but were surprisingly defeated by 4-1. If you read the section on Forest School in the 'Forest FC' section, you will see that Brightonians were just the latest in a long line of victims. In January 1889, as did many other teams, Brightonians went on a small Christmas/ New Year tour, and were beaten 5-0 by Old Westminsters at the Oval. Strangely, when Brightonians entered the 1893-4 Amateur Cup, their well known opponents the Old Westminsters withdrew, giving them a walkover. Maybe the 'pinks' couldn't raise a team.

This was the Old Brightonians team which came from two goals down to win 3-2 at Reigate Priory in October 1895 -

		E.W. Sutton			
	F.W. Goodbody			L. Coll	
	L. Cavendish	N.C. Copper	H.G. Andrews		
W.D. Eggar	W.D. Corbett	W. McCowan		R. Young	A. Harris

When touring side The Pilgrims became the first English team to win the Belgian International Cup in April 1902, two Old Brightonians, goalkeeper A.E. Grisar was their captain, and H. Richards was at right-half. Pilgrims beat Leopold 4-0 in the semi final and Dordrecht (Holland) 4-1 in the final. The Old Brightonians' peak period seems to have been 1886-1896, which is still longer than many teams in this book. Old Brightonians had many fine players down the years and I single out the following for merit, starting with George Cotterill seen below -

George Huth Cotterill (1868-1950) an inside right or centre forward described as having great pace and a powerful build, he averaged almost a goal a game when playing for the Corinthians. A keen member of the Weybridge rowing club, he was an all-round athlete, playing rugby for Richmond and Surrey. He was a Corinthian during 1886 to 1898; he played for Cambridge University from 1888-1891, and football for Sussex from 1886-1890. During World War 1, he rose to the rank of Major in the Army.

Leslie Hewitt Gay (1871-1949) was a well-known wicket-keeper for the England cricket team during 1894-5, and also played golf for the county of Devonshire. He was another Cambridge University footballer, and scored on his England debut against Scotland on 1st April 1893. He played for the Corinthians and Old Brightonians between 1891-1894 and played for Southampton as a stand-in for Jack Robinson, their number one keeper. He played goal for England against Canada (1891), Scotland (1893 and 1894), Wales (1894) and also represented Devon at golf.

Claude Wilham Wilson (1858-1881) described in *Alcocks Annual 1882* as 'a splendid back, a strong kick, very fast and active'. Unfortunately for Alcock, Wilson had died the year before, a sudden death coming at the young age of 23. Wilson gained two England caps, and played for the Oxford University team in the 1880 F.A. Cup final. He was with the Old Brightonians during 1876-7.

This Old Brightonian side beat Marlow 4-0 in October 1890 -

A.C. Stone

S.M. Woods   **A.T. Hay**

P.C. Muspratt   **N.C. Cooper**   **C.H .Bonds**

C. Simmons   H.A .Harrison   G.H. Cotterill   G.L. Wilson   H.C. Holland

In reviewing the possibilities for the 1895-6 season, the *Pall-Mall Gazette* opined that the Old Brightonians would miss the loss of G.I. Wilson and keeper Leslie Gay, who was engaged in his tea plantation company in Ceylon, although stalwart George Cotterill was still with them and in N.C. Cooper of the Cambridge University, they would have a fine new full back. In March 1897, Walter McCowan, of the Old Brightonians, presented a charter of the amateur player's rights from the Sports Club to the Football Association in London. In 1889, Old Brightonians played the Great Marlow club at home, on Saturday 5th October, winning 4-1 with goals from Wilson (2) and Cotterill (2). Played in incessant rain, the attendance was described as meagre.

Formed in 1900 out of the ashes of Brighton United, Brighton & Hove Rangers joined the Second Division of the Southern League in 1900, using Brighton North End's Withdean ground. Finishing 3rd at the first attempt, they were placed behind Grays United, and luckless Fulham, who despite finishing runners-up for two consecutive seasons, had lost the promotion 'Test Matches'. Rovers won 11 and lost 5 of their 16 league matches, scoring 34 against 17. They moved to the County Ground in 1901 and changed their name to Brighton & Hove Albion for 1902. At the time of writing they are a Premier League club.

The Sussex A.F.A. cup was also a happy hunting ground for Old Brightonians, since the county did not have many first class amateur teams. The 1909 competition was won when they defeated Helmston by 5-2 at the Sussex County cricket ground, and in 1911, Eastbourne were defeated 3-2 in the final. By the Edwardian era, Old Brightonians were being left behind, and were reduced to playing for the Sussex Junior Cup. Their March 1914 Sussex A.F.A. cup final, which was drawn 1-1, was the last report I could find on the Old Brightonians. Neither could I find out whether the replay took place, as the Great War put a big shadow on sport for the next four years. A great number of amateur clubs never reformed after the cessation of hostilities, and Old Brightonians were one of them. In the 1930s, Old Brightonians could be found playing rugby and cricket, as they had done for many years, but not, it seems, the association game. Today, football has been revived, and the college plays in the Brighton League, and still has its annual match against the 'old boys'.

Today, the old college sports ground remains as ever, situated at the rear of the college buildings, next to Sussex County Hospital. Sitting between Sutherland Road and Walpole Terrace, with its superb whitewashed Georgian terraces, the sports ground has a wonderful playing surface (with a gentle left to right slope) and its old pavilion makes for an idyllic setting. Still revered for its superb grass surface today, the England rugby team used the college field as a training camp in 2016. Measuring 180 x 150 yards, there is room for three rugby or football pitches side by side, although many other athletics and sports events are held there.

In 1903, Old Brightonians were on the fixture list for Reigate Priory, but I could find no matches reported upon. In the 1890s, several other clubs sprang up in the town such as West Brighton Wanderers, Brighton Rovers, Hornets and Hove. Brighton Athletic were playing at Preston Park, and a Brighton Cup was already under way. In 1898, a new professional club, intending to represent the town started up, called Brighton United, with E.W. Everest as secretary, and support from T. Harrington, T. Sweetman and J.J. Clarke, J.P. By September 1899, not only had they entered the F.A. Cup, but were able to defeat Notts County by 3-1 at the Hove County Ground, and with attenances of over 3000, were admitted into the Second Division of the Southern League, and soon went up into the First. In 1900, however, they resigned after playing 22 of their 30 league games, the champions that year being Tottenham Hotspur! By 1901, Brighton Rovers had become Brighton & Hove Rovers, and then Brighton & Hove Albion. The rise of the new principal town club coincided with the demise of the Old Brightonians.

Old Brightonians. Back row: P. Cobbett, C. Simmons, A.G. Cavendish, F.W. Goodbody, W. McGown, P.M. Cooper, C. Mackintosh. Front row: C.R. Fort, A.C.S. Stone, H.A. Harrison (Capt.), N.C. Cooper, R. Young.

OLD CASTLE SWIFTS FC

Founded - 1892
Folded - 1895
Grounds - 1. Dunotar Park, West Ham (1892)
          2. Temple Meadows, Wakefield Street (1892-94)
          3. Hermit Road (1894-95)
Colours - Light blue shirt, white shorts, red socks

Although this relatively unknown team was in fact the district's first professional side, I did not think that I would be able to find enough about them to include them in the book. However, with three grounds and a colourful if brief history, they certainly attracted attention. The football team was founded in September 1892 when wealthy Scotsman Donald Currie decided that the workforce of his Castle Shipping Line would benefit from playing as well as working together. In this way, they were a precursor to Thames Ironworks, who evolved into West Ham United. The day to day running of the club was done by Robert Cook, honorary secretary. Playing in colours of light blue shirts, their first 'ground' was in Dunottar Park, which faced West Ham police station, but before the year was out, they had found a better spot at Temple Meadows in Wakefield Street, West Ham. The land was within the grounds of Temple House, and the team used the nearby Denmark Arms as headquarters and for changing rooms. Today, the Denmark Arms is a regular pre-match meeting place for fans of Fulham FC.

Success came quickly at local level, and they won the West Ham Charity Cup in 1892-93 when they came from two goals behind to beat Barking Woodville 4-2 with this team :-

			Lewis				
		A. McFarlane			Benbow		
	Leith		W. McFarlane			Baird	
Murray		Mitchell		Frazer		Taylor	Grundy

The McFarlane brothers had joined from one of London's leading amateur clubs, Upton Park, which had reformed in 1891. Greater things were to follow, when they competed in the London Senior Cup in 1894-95 season, having strengthened their team with new players, including Cunningham, Lindsay, McCulloch and Willing from Millwall Athletic.

At the end of the 1893-94 season, Castle Swifts merged with Old St. Lukes FC, and moved into their ground in Hermit Road. In September 1894, the *Sporting Life* thought that good things lay ahead for the combined club in Canning Town. I found nothing before 1890 for Old St. Lukes. A similar sounding but different club, the ambitious St. Lukes continued on until 1896. The Hermit Road 'ground' as it was, lay surrounded by marshland and was of no commercial use, so lay barren. The name was merged too, with Castle Swifts adopting the 'Old' part. Old St. Lukes, despite their bad ground, played in the Middlesex Cup and opponents included the Old Westminsters, the Scots Guards, the

Grenadier Guards, and West Herts. The last Old St. Lukes eleven I could find, from April 1894 was -

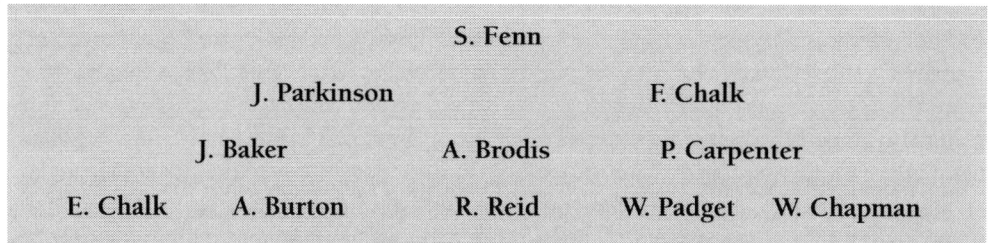

		S. Fenn		
	J. Parkinson		F. Chalk	
	J. Baker	A. Brodis	P. Carpenter	
E. Chalk	A. Burton	R. Reid	W. Padget	W. Chapman

The Hermit Road 'ground' did in fact belong to a Mr. Wilkinson, who presumably unaware that Old Castle Swifts were drawing paying crowds of around 250 to it, eventually realised that fact after the demise of Old Castle Swifts which led to the Thames Ironworks FC moving there, and erecting a stand and charging gate money, needed to do something to recover his land from the footballer 'squatters'. The London FA were still very twitchy about professionalism even as late as November 1893, five years after the commencement of the Football League. Old St. Marks were thrown out of the Junior Cup on account of a player, Cunningham, who was also turning out for Millwall, was decreed not to have been a resident of London for the required six months. At the same hearing, Tottenham Hotspur were suspended for a fortnight simply for providing a player with a new set of football boots, an action deemed to make the player a professional on the thinnest of definitions in that he received an item of monetary value for his services! The first match under the new name saw them defeat City Ramblers by 6-1 at Hermit Road, a game watched by a better attendance than usual of five hundred. This team is almost completely changed from that given above from a year before -

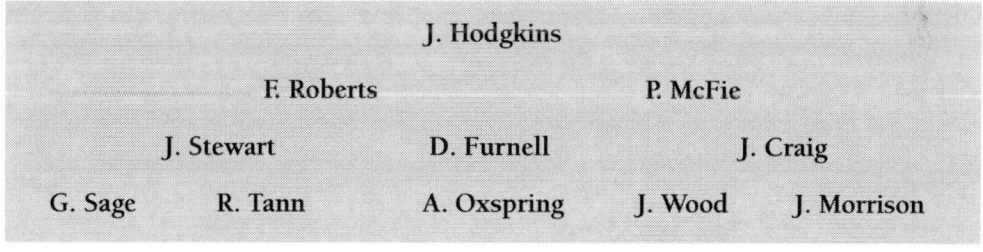

		J. Hodgkins		
	F. Roberts		P. McFie	
	J. Stewart	D. Furnell	J. Craig	
G. Sage	R. Tann	A. Oxspring	J. Wood	J. Morrison

The Tann and Furnell brothers were late from the Old St. Marks first team, and presumably all other players formed the 2nd and 3rd teams. Morrison, Furnell, Wood, Sage and Stewart had come from the Old St. Lukes club. Old Castle Swifts applied and got memberships of the F.A. in October 1894. Playing only friendlies and cup ties, including losing 0-3 to Wolverton in the 1st round of the FA Cup in October 1894, they defeated a team yet to rise to fame – Arsenal - by 4-0 in January 1895. Of the few matches reported, I found that they also beat Royal Ordnance Depot 2-0, City Ramblers 3-1, Ealing 3-3, Swindon (1-1) and Evelyn by 8-1, all in February and March 1895. Other opponents at this time included West Croydon and Kings College Hospital. During season 1894-95, they competed in the prestigious London Senior Cup, but were knocked out by Millwall Athletic by 4-0, another club which turned professional. Again, their 1895 first team bore no resemblance to that of 1894, with only Morrison and George Sage remaining. On Easter

Monday 1895, a France XI nipped across the channel and play Folkestone FC and Old St. Stephens, although no-one seemed to thing it was important enough to cover the results.

The demise of Old Castle Swifts came suddenly in the summer of 1895. Only 12 months earlier, on November 7th 1894, they had announced to the Essex County FA that they had turned professional. This mean straight away they Old Castle Swifts were expelled from the various cup competitions organised by that authority, something which I don't think that Robert Cook had thought through. Both Essex and Middlesex County F.As were staunchly pro-amateur, and when, in 1896 all county F.As were ordered to put the names of all professional players and teams on their membership roll, they both refused to do. Thus, the Old Castle Swifts suddenly found that they were severely limited as to finding opponents within a close radius. There must have been some sort of internal wrangling, as owner Donald Currie withdrew his support in September 1895, and the bankroll that went with it. Old Castle Swifts, faced with a choice or returning to amateur status or folding, chose the latter, with at least three players joining the St. Lukes club. St. Lukes, at Beckton Road, thought that with another club now defunct, that they would have it all their own way in the district, but they did not reckon on the rise of the ambitious Thames Ironworks, who would evolve into West Ham United, and by 1897, St. Lukes too had folded.

OLD ST. STEPHENS FC

Founded - 1880
Folded - 1915
Grounds - 1. Westminster
              2. Raynes Park 1889-91
              3. Champion Hill in 1892
              4. Nunhead 1894-5
              5. Denmark Hill 1896
              6. Wormholt Farm, Uxbridge Road 1901-04
              7. Loftus Road 1904-1915
Colours - 1. Red and white stripes, black
              2. White shirts, black shorts 1892-3

Old St. Stephens FC were predominantly a team of the 1890s, as they spent the 1880s 'under the radar' and I could find no match reports for them. Their ground on Denmark Hill does not show on any old maps, but would have been very close to the Ruskin (now Kings College) Hospital, as there was a cricket ground which became built over by hospital extensions, and that may have been a probable location. A further large field across the road became Ruskin Park in 1907, named after Denmark Hill's most famous resident, John Ruskin. A team called St. Stephens (Westminster) who were surely their origin, became Acton FC in 1879 (Robin Horton) played in scarlet and navy jerseys with monograms, and caps and stockings to match, and they played on Battersea Park.

The earliest match report was from October 1889 when they beat the Polytechnic FC 3-1 away on their Merton Hall ground, the OSS being called the 'Westminster' club. Their eleven that day was – W. King (goal); T. Hughes (captain) and R. Clarke (backs), J. Ashworth, W. Wilson, J. Mahoney (half-backs) and forwards H. Edwards, H. White, A. Lomax, A. Thomas, W. Knight. In the following month, a reasonable indication of St. Stephens' place in London football came when they met the Old Westminsters in a 3rd round London Senior Cup tie at the Oval. With the 'Pinks' two men short at kick-off, Old St. Stephens held a one goal lead at the break, at which point, the two missing men arrived, and the Westminsters turned it around and went on to win 3-1. When OSS played Old St. Paul's at Leyton in January 1889, it wasn't clear who was the home team, but players were advised to "change their dress at The Eagle Inn, Chobham Road".

A Boxing Day friendly away to Newbury that year ended badly when they were defeated by 7-3, now captained by H. Edwards. In November 1891, Old St. Stephens trounced local rival Queens Park Rangers by 7-1, the match being played at Brondesbury. Old St. Stephens were declared winners of the short - lived Southern Alliance League in 1892-93 even though not all clubs completed their fixtures, but they could not have been caught. Observe the once humble Spurs in third place! Slough were a descendant of the famous Swifts FC. Most of these teams were those who were rejected in 1893 when the formation of the Southern League was being discussed.

		PL	W	D	L	F	A	Pts
1.	Old St.Stephens	12	10	1	1	44 - 15		21
2.	Erith	11	8	1	2	29 - 14		17
3.	Tottenham	12	7	2	3	29 - 21		16
4.	Polytechnic	8	4	0	4	18 - 12		8
5.	Slough	11	2	2	7	21 - 33		6
6.	Windsor & Eton	10	2	1	7	14 - 37		5
7.	Upton Park	10	1	0	9	7 - 36		2

Their usual first team of 1892-3 ran -

E. O' Hare (goalie-secretary)

M. Wallace   **James Pryor**

E. Pope   **F. Doland**   **J. Ashworth**

W. Applebee   E.L. Chapman   T. Callaghan   H.C. Edwards   James Read

The team wore a white shirt at this time, monogrammed with a large "OSS" badge, which unfortunately looked more like "SOS". Their committee consisted of W.W. Powell, J. Mahoney (assistant secretary) and A.G. Thompson. Edwards was captain, and Clarke the vice-captain. Their centre back Doland, was over six feet tall.

In 1894, Old St. Stephens entered the Middlesex Cup and hedged their bets by entering in both the senior and junior sections of the London Cup. Old St. Stephens players were often selected to play for Middlesex county, as were V.E. Smith, a full back, A. Mayor, a half back, J.F. Pollard and A. Murray, both backs, in December 1895. When the Southern League was finally established in 1895 after two years of stop-start antics, Old St. Stephens' W. J. Wadhams was elected to the management committee.

The 'Old Saints' entered the first Amateur Cup competition in 1893-4, and did quite well, not quite reaching the last eight. A 1-0 away win over the Old Foresters put them up against another famous old boy's side, the Old Wykehamists in round 2. Another great away win, by 4-3, put them into round 3 where unknown side Warrington St. Elphins scratched to them. The then amateur Shrewsbury Town held them to a 2-2 draw in London, but the long return trip resulted in a lacklustre performance in the replay, and the Shrews won by 4-0. After qualifying rounds were introduced in the following season, Old St. Stephens never again appeared in the competition proper. One of their worst defeats came on September 23rd 1893, when they lost 8-0 to West Herts, who would soon alter their name to the present day Watford.

In October 1895, Old St. Stephens met and defeated (1-0) the club that would later move into their shoes at Loftus Road - Queens Park Rangers. In September 1896, the 'Saints' F. Thomas was appointed auditor to the London Football Association, and their Thomas Gunning was elected to the committee. On the night of Monday 16th December 1895, Old St. Stephens played the Thames Ironworks club under 'electric lights' with the iron-workers winning 3-1 at Canning Town. Sadly the floodlights were a flop as the generator being insufficient in horsepower, failed near the end of ninety minutes and the game was cut short.

In 1898, Old St. Stephens changed their name and became the more modern - sounding Shepherds Bush FC, but not before their reserve team had won the Middlesex Junior Cup. Season 1901-02 saw a near success as Shepherds Bush reached the final of the London Cup but were defeated 2-1 by the Civil Service Club, who themselves had won it for the first time in their long history (f.1863). At this time, they moved into the football ground at Wormholt Farm, which lay down a lane set back off the Uxbridge Road. Several teams over the years had and would use this location, which was little more than acres of flat fields with almost nothing in the way of facilities. The London side West End FC (f.1868) also played there, using the nearby Princess Alice public house as a base. In the 18th century the 360 acres of Wormholt Barns was divided up into Eynham Farm and Wormholt Farm,but in 1911 when the land was sold for development, only seven acres were retained as a park.

In 1904, the 'Saints' built a new ground on waste land in Loftus Road, and moved out of the Wormholt Farm ground on the Uxbridge Road which they had occupied since the autumn of 1901.Their ground was used to hold the 1905 Amateur Cup final between West Hartlepool and Clapton when 4,000 saw the northerners win a thrilling match 3-2. Shepherds Bush FC folded in 1915, and their ground at Loftus Road was soon taken up by Queens Park Rangers (1917), who remain there to this day.

I naturally thought that the name Old St. Stephens referred to old boys of a private school, hospital or college. I found no such suitable establishment in London. The hospital of the same name in Fulham was only named such after 1930; the only other candidate I found was an exclusive gentleman's club in Westminster, founded in 1870 on the corner of Bridge Street and Embankment, now called Portcullis House after 1962 when the club relocated in Queens Anne Gate. If this is the place, then membership was very costly indeed: Charles Dickens informs us that in 1879, membership after ballot cost £21, and annual subs were ten guineas, which was identical to the Garrick Club fees. Such sums represented the annual pay of servants. Connected to the Conservative Party, founder members included Prime Minister Benjamin Disraeli.

After some sleuthing, I worked out that the Wormholt Farm ground lay behind the church of St. Lukes, just off the Uxbridge Road near the Q P R ground at Loftus Road A large rectangular field of about 8 acres is now covered by the junction of Wormholt Road and Aldbourne Road, and the junction of Askham and Aldbourne roads would have been in the centre of the pitch. For a while, many other teams rented football fields at this location, which had room for at least four pitches.

OLYMPIC FC (LONDON)

Founded - By 1876
Folded - By 1910
Ground - Wormholt Farm grounds, off UxbridgeRoad
Colours - White shirts, black shorts

Olympic were a late Victorian junior club , whose only notable success came when they won the London Junior Cup in 1892, beating the reserves of London Caledonians by 5-3 in the final. Despite the rather generic name, they were in fact a club formed by workers at Hitchcock & Williams Co. Ltd in London. Founded by George Hitchcock as a general drapery warehouse in St. Paul's, Williams became a partner in 1855. Hitchcock died in 1863, leaving Williams sole proprietor, who was succeeded by his sons. The company expanded across the UK and abroad by 1900, and survived until 1984 (*Mark Matlatch*). They became a leading London fashion house in Edwardian era, and published catalogues and posters of their latest ranges. Other junior clubs founded from London businesses, such as the Vulcan FC (Shoolbreds & Co.) formed the West End Association. I found some of the Olympic players - H. Oliver, K. Oliver, G.A. Johnson, and D. McDonald - competing in athletics events as sprinters at the end of the 1870s. In an age when clubs of any level could enter the FA Cup merely by paying the entry money, Olympic entered in season 1881-82 but were unfortunate to draw the well known Old Harrovians away from home. A 2-4 defeat was no disgrace, and undeterred, they entered again the following year. It was around this time that the various London hospitals saw the benefits of playing football, although for most of them this meant the rugby version. Falling again at the first hurdle, London Olympic were knocked out 3-0 by the United Hospitals team, which seems to have been the last time they took part.

There were few 'works' teams who would later be able to say that they competed in the FA Cup proper. As the company grew, their workforce must have been substantial, as they were soon putting out four elevens each Saturday. These were Olympic's usual teams for season 1888-89 -

1st team - W. Monkton, J.D. Campbell, R. Baingeman, F. Kirton, J. McNaughton, J.W. Kemp, R.B. Kerr, W. Ellis, H. Hookway, W. Rant and captain R.H. Trueman.

2nd team - J. Jarron, E. Shaw, E. Campbell, Ino Mace, Bert Mace, J. Palmer, C.H. Bidlake, F. Catford, H. Simmons, A. Carter, G. Taylor (captain).

3rd team - Adcock, Read, Milford, Blagg, Leets, Oldfield,Banks, Pearson, Upsdale, Gordon, Parker (captain).

4th team - R.Jones, T. Middlemiss, A. Southam, F. Pinchbeck, J. Jenkins, A. Woodbridge, H. Reynolds, G.R. Parker, A. Dobson, F. Berkley

Reports were few and far between for Olympic during the 1890s. They generally contented themselves with friendlies, and cup ties in the West End, London Junior, Middlesex County and Amateur Cup competitions, without notable success. With so many footballers to chose from, Olympic rarely fielded the same eleven twice. Captained by Purcell, this was their 1st team of 1895-96 :

	H.Abbott	
T. Davis		A. Hill
A.Scott	A. Bastock	G. Evans
D. McNaughton	S. Hooper	C. Purcell	A. Perkins	G. McNeil

Regular opponents in the West End and London cups included Cavendish, West End Rangers, Polytechnic, Clarence, Vulcans, Unity, Minerva, Gresham, Crouch End, Edmonton Albion, Cedars, Eltham House, Belmont, Barnet, and London Caledonians.

Of the few reported matches I found for Olympic in 1897 were when they played the West End Cup final in March against the Vulcans, winning 2-1, and a 0-3 reverse to Polytechnic in December that year. I found a team called Olympic losing 0-7 to St. Michaels at St. Quintin's Park, London, but cannot say if they were the same team.

When the West London Association played the City of London Association at junior football in February 1899 at Olympic's Wormholt Farm ground, the London side was comprised mostly from the Olympic club – goalie A.W. Chester, full back A. Wade, half back E.G. King, forwards J.F. Hornblow, C.H. Purnell and A. Perkins. Even the linesman, R.B. Kerr, was an Olympian player. Locally, they were members of the West End Cricket & Football Association, whose senior cup they won again 1899, and were presented with it at a dinner ceremony at the Banqueting Hall of St. James Restaurant, Pall Mall.

When forward Hornblow received a severe blow to the knee in a cup tie against Clapton Orient in November 1899, it was stated that the "St. Paul's Churchyard man would be off work for six weeks as it was much worse than at first thought", adding that Clapton had won the replay 6-4. Olympic FC continued on into the 20th century at Wormholt Farm and began to enter the Amateur Cup, but by now, their team ran as (*West London Observer*)-

	Howgego	
J. Clarke		Perry
Brooks	Hicks	F. Ward
Anderson	Rowley	Dullear	S. Hicks	E. Fulford

Olympic were now playing more well-known opposition, including Upton Park, Ilford, West Hampstead, and began to enter the Qualifying Rounds of the FA Cup itself. I was surprised to see that they knocked out Ilford FC by 2-0 away, after the two sides had drawn 1-1 at Wormholt in October 1900, to progress to the 3rd Qualifying Round. Their opponents would be a team who had only just altered their name from Thames Ironworks to West Ham United. Played by mutual agreement in November at Canning Town Memorial ground, Southern League side West Ham scraped through by 1-0 in Olympic's most important match yet in their history. Compared with the above eleven, a different set of players met West Ham that day – Meates (goal), Wade and Roberts (backs); Maidman, Sands, Hooper (half-backs), and forwards Saunders, Purnell, Malone, Roesi, Wenman.

197

1905 found them still alive, but now having moved to the much-used Lea Bridge grounds on Elm Park Road, and competing in the London Business Houses Cup and the London Postal League, suggesting that their parent company had their own delivery service. Their annual sports were still held at the old Wormholt grounds however. Olympic were now competing in the London Senior Cup. By 1908, a team called Olympic Postal were playing in the London Postal League, suggesting that Olympic may have changed their name after 1907. I found no news of Olympic FC after 1910, although their athletes continued to compete in the athletics events of the London Business Houses A.S.A until the Great War of 1914.

Olympic FC (London)

PANTHERS FC

Founded - November 1873
Folded - Unknown, circa 1880-1
Ground - Sturminster Marshall and Blandford Downs, Dorset
Colours - Chocolate brown and yellow hoops
Founder - Edward Farquharson

For a village team who never won anything, you may well ask what they are doing in this book. There is one simply reason - I was so intrigued by the name, and the fact that they felt confident enough not even to prefix it with their place of origin, I was determined to find out more about them. It was two years before I even discovered their location, believing, that like many other single titled teams such as Dreadnought, Greyfriars, Rangers, that they came from the environs of London, but I couldn't have been more wrong. Luckily, Panthers entered the F.A. Cup in the 1870s, and after following the scant match reports, I spotted that they came from the village of Blandford Forum in Dorset. Now today, we see an image of picturesque villages set in countryside and go there in our cars perhaps to enjoy a holiday in that area, with Bournemouth, Weymouth and the seaside nearby. Imagine then in December 1876, how you would make the journey from Surrey to Dorset in the age of gas lamps and horse drawn vehicles. Fortunately, even by then, the train had made incursions from London to all the principal seaside resorts and inland towns, but it was still a two day journey for the Pilgrims FC who had to find Blandford for an F.A. Cup tie on Saturday 9th December, possibly when it was snowing. The Pilgrims players took a Friday evening train from London to Southampton, where they stayed overnight, and thence to Wimbourne, reaching Bailey Gate station at the village of Sturminster Marshall, where the Panther's ground was. They would have been met at the station, perhaps at lunchtime, fed and watered at the nearby Churchill Arms, and then taken to the Panthers ground. Well I say 'ground' but of course it would merely be either a borrowed field or a nearby recreation ground, of which the candidates are a four acre field by the police station, a three acre field next to the vicarage (Baillie House, burnt down 1893) on Poole Road which measures out at barely 100 x 80 yards, or a five acre field next to St. Mary's church at the other end of the village on Mill Lane. Still used today as the village's main recreation ground on Churchill Close, a five acre field 350 yards from the Churchill Arms and the Newton Road, must also be considered as a candidate for the Panthers' ground, although before the Great War was a very large 12 acre field. The fact that a vicar was their goalkeeper leads me to favour the fields by Bailie House or St. Mary's church. The Pilgrims, comprised of experienced footballers, won more easily than the 1-0 scoreline suggests, and made the two day trip back to Surrey perhaps after further refreshments from their hosts. Thanks to the notorious Beeching Report, that entire stretch of the Somerset & Dorset Railway, and the stations including Bailey Gate, no longer exist.

Despite being remote from other great footballing centres, such as London, or Sheffield, and with a sparse and rural population, football (but of the rugby type) was being played in Dorsetshire as early as 1864, when a team representing Weymouth took on fifteen gentlemen of Dorchester but were beaten 4-0 on a field opposite Weymouth grammar school. Soon, other short lived clubs sprang up notably at Chard, Bridport, Portland,

Blandford and Poole. It seems that the association game was not popular in the county, for almost every report of a match, or a new club being founded across the 1870s and 1880s, turned out to be the handling code. When a South Hants & Dorsetshire Association cup was put in in 1884, only five teams entered – Blandford (with E.O. Richards), Bournemouth, Wimbourne, Ringwood and Portland, and the county FA was resuscitated more than once.

Almost no Panthers' matches were reported upon, only a few reports found in the *Western Gazette* gave a glimpse into this mystery team who probably only survived from the early 1870s until the early 1880s. At the end of my research, whilst checking any reports of escaped or exhibited panthers in Dorset during the 1870s, I stumbled upon the founding date of the football club. The *Bridport News* of Friday 19th December 1873 reported briefly that 'the return match had taken place between Blandford School and a club recently formed by the exertions of E.G. Farquharson playing to the rules of the Football Association', and 'with a ground at Sturminster Marshall'. After a closely fought game, Panthers won 1-0 on Saturday 13th.

Panthers travelled to play the soldiers of the Portland 4-60 Regiment on Saturday 4th March 1874, winning there on Blandford Downs by 3-0, the *Dorset County Herald* giving no further details. Played on 29th December 1874, Panthers accepted a challenge from the Breamore club to appear on their ground for a 3pm kick-off on a frozen ground. Evidently superior, Panthers scored after a few minutes when Edward Farquharson put the ball through the posts. A second goal was soon obtained, a peculiarity of the times saw teams *change ends after every goal scored,* yet a goal scored when R. Fort chested a bouncing ball through the posts was disallowed. Edward scored a third for a 3-0 victory, captaining the following side -

		E. Cave		
	E.W. Parke		E. Penny	
		E.O. Richardson		
R. Fort T.A. Fort A. Cave E. Farquharson S. Daniell T. Penny J. House					

Played in the same week, Panthers went over to play the Dorchester club at Poundbury, the match attracting numerous spectators," including Sir Molyneux Neapan and a fair sprinkling of the fairer sex". The result – three tries and a touchdown to nil – to Dorchester clearly shows that Panthers had to play both codes in order to get a game. From the dates of most of these matches, it seems clear that the football team only assembled around Easter and Christmas-time, probably when the various Farquharsons returned to Blandford from their London business appointments.

A match played on 9th January 1875 at Sturminster Marshall between Mr Edward Farquharson and Mr. C. Paget's Wimbourne teams took place under rugby rules, with Panthers comfortable winners. Mr. Ronald Farquharson appeared to be 'man of the match'. The Panthers side was-

Edward Farquharson (captain), Lacey, Ronald Farquharson, Captain Barton, Parke, C. Caddie, H. R. Farquharson, F. S. Farquharson, R. Fort, T. A. Fort, E. Cave, E.O. Richards, T. House, J. Garland, Caddie, Luckham, Lacey.

From the parish census records of 1871, we discover that Eddie Cave was 26 in 1875, and living with his farmer parents Edward and Mary at Almer Farm in Fordington. There were also four Cave daughters, aged between 11 and 23, and none of them were yet married. Edwin Richards was a 22 years old land surveyor from the hamlet of Chaldon Herring, with brothers George, Arthur, Robert Gale and Frederick all living with their extended family at Winterbourne Kingston.

The annual match with Beamore next took place "at Baileys-gate" on 2nd April 1875. This location falls within 200 yards of the present recreation ground. Goals from Eddie Farquharson, Woodhouse and House saw a comfortable win, and a possible fourth was not disputed since they had a three goal cushion. George Richards was in goal on this occasion, but scarcely touched the ball, in game watched by a large body of spectators. (*Southern Times & Dorset County Herald*)

Panthers took part in the F.A. Cup of 1874-5, the fourth season of its existence, when only five entrants came from outside the greater London area. That was quite a brave decision for a village team remote even from any others in Dorsetshire, although up to this point I could not see that Panthers had ever conceded a goal. A tough draw brought them up against one of the competition favourites Clapham Rovers. They were beaten 3-0 at the first hurdle in a match played at Winchester College sports ground, used as a compromise on travelling. The *Dorset County Herald* thought that the first goal had brushed against the tape, and gone over and not under, and with the third goal coming from a hopeful long range punt, that Dorset people should take pride in the commendable efforts of a small countryside football team. Clapham were then put out 2-3 by eventual winners Royal Engineers.

In the following season, 1875-76, in a game watched by about five hundred spectators, Panthers scored the only goal of the game against Woodford Wells to enter round 2, where they were drawn away to cup holders Royal Engineers. The Woodford Wells match was again played at Winchester on Saturday 6th November (*Sheffield Telegraph*) presumably as some sort of compromise due to the fact that the two clubs were over 100 miles apart. Comment was made that "Panthers were merely a countryside club, whilst Woodford Wells had a metropolis from which to draw their players". The Panthers however, seem to have drafted in some new men, with the names of Vidal (scorer), J. Brymer (goalie), C. Pagett (defence) and Drewitt (wing forward). I am tempted to speculate that winger Drewitt was none other than Montague Druitt, a leading candidate (for some) as being none other then "Jack the Ripper" himself. Druitt was born in 1857 close to the Panthers ground, at Wimborne Minster, Dorset, and after attending Winchester College went on to Oxford University. A barrister schoolmaster, the various stories about him include being dismissed for 'irregular behaviour' (with boys), or that he had a mother complex and committed suicide a fortnight or so after the final Ripper murder in December 1888. His father William was a governor of the local grammar school and a Justice of the Peace. Residing at Westfield House, he had three brothers, the elder William and the younger Edward and Arthur. In 1876, Montague would have been 19 which fits the age as a footballer, although his main sporting prowess lay at cricket (he played for Hampshire) and rugby.

In the early years of the Cup, the first out of the hat did not automatically have home advantage, but merely had choice of venue, although naturally, most teams would chose their home ground. Sometimes, however, a neutral venue was agreed upon either to help the travelling team, or perhaps to play the match in a nearby town where a much bigger attendance could be attracted. Panthers promptly gave the 'invincible Engineers' a walkover, but the Sappers were surprisingly eliminated by the Swifts in the 3rd round.

On Monday December 19th 1875, E.W. Cave, O.E. Richards, E.O. Richards, and R. Farquharson were in a team selected and captained by A.C. Rogers which played Milton Abbas school XI, no score resulting. This suggests that football was only played at around holidays, when scholars could return home from their colleges and universities. Two months later, when Panthers played Bournemouth Rovers in that F.A. Cup tie, Milton Abbas school captain G.S. Pollard was borrowed in the Panthers team. Nine days later, the Panthers went to the Breamore FC ground on the village green, "kindly lent for the match by Sir Edward Hulse, Bart". Play was delayed when players arrived late, but "spectators were rewarded with an exciting game". A 1-0 reverse seemed a fair result, with Panthers' the Reverend J. Brymer defending his goalposts valiantly. One of the three Bury brothers scored for Breamore after twenty minutes, but an 'equaliser' for Panthers was ruled out for offsides. Breamore then met the Fordingbridge Turks on New Years Day resulting in a goal-less draw.

Of their six local match reports, three of them were to rugby rules, and only one match was won, against Bournemouth Rovers, by 4-0 on Saturday 19th February 1876, having played out a goal-less draw at their Dean Court ground on the previous weekend. From those two games, not only do we learn that Panthers played in chocolate brown and yellow hoops, and that Bournemouth were in blue and white hoops, but we get to find out the Panthers' names -

	Reverend G.R. Dupuis			
	E.O. Richards			
	A.J. Farquharson			
R. Cave	**O.E. Richards**	**(missing)**		**Brown**
E. Cave	**E.G. Farquharson**	**H. R. Farquharson**	**Pollard**	**C. Caddie**

As you can see, everyone wanted to be a forward, with double wing-men and five players awaiting crosses in the centre. The description of the first Panthers' goal is clearly the result of a free kick 15 yards out from goal as a result of a rouge being obtained. When a shot at goal is attempted and wide, instead of today's goal-kick, whichever side first got to the ball then took possession. If it was the attacking team, the ball was brought in a line to a point 15 yards from goal, almost identical to a modern day conversion kick in rugby. The venue for the football match was given as Sturminster Marshall, which is six miles back down the track on the Somerset & Dorset Railway, a village surrounded by fields, any one of which could have been used for that game. A letter in the *Dorsetshire County Herald* written by a curious spectator who went along to witness a football match for the first time, said that he saw no sign of the "dangerous and brutal game so often mentioned by headmasters and fathers" and expressed the opinion that the healthy pursuit he witnessed would ensure that young men did not turn out as milksops. Another Christmas match was recorded for Panthers in 1876 when they played the Cambridge Old Shireburnians on their school cricket ground. The *Western Gazette* simply stating that the old boys were victorious.

Season 1876-77 saw Panthers once more victorious in the 1st round of the English Cup, when they defeated Wood Grange by 3-0 in October. This brought them up against the Pilgrims FC, the match was played at nearby Sturminster which was said to have drawn a crowd of 700, who saw a Watson goal win the tie for Pilgrims. It was said that the Panthers eleven 'included a number of notable Oxford men'. This did not mean they borrowed star players from Oxford University (who were one of the three best teams in England at the time), but that young university men returning to their home villages turned out to put the Panthers at full strength. This may have been a reference to the Farquharson brothers. Nearby Sherbourne School sent over a dozen young men to Oxford that year, and other boys from private schools would also have gained scholarships there. Thus, it is probable that the Panthers FC were founded by returning scholars, with local enthusiasts making up the numbers. From match reports, we know that the brothers Farquharson and the Caves made up half of the team, with the Reverend Dupuis as their usual goal-keeper. The Panthers played football to both rugby and association codes, as did many out-of-city teams, who would have found it difficult to find opponents had they limited themselves to one code.

At Easter 1877, Panthers met the Breamore FC on their ground, by now an annual challenge,and came away with a 1-0 victory. Had Breamore's well-known defender Lindsay Bury (Old Etonians FC) turned up, the result might have been different, although his brother, F. G. Bury did play. Again, the heavier weight of the Panthers players seemed to be decisive, presumably in the scrimmages which took place in front of goal. The Panthers eleven was once again assembled around the Farquharson, Cave and Fort brothers, with Richardson, Roberts and Lagdon assisting the attack.

The following year saw Panthers once again enter the F.A. Cup, but this time, on 1st October 1877 they were drawn at home to the most famous name in the whole football world at that time - The Wanderers. Even by 1877, Wanderers had won four cup finals, and the fifth was in the waiting. A dazzling array of elite upper-class footballers faced the Panthers on Wednesday November 7th. The Wanderers had uncharacteristically had a wobbly start to the season, with a shock 3-1 defeat to Clapham Rovers, but had bounced back with a big 7-0 win over Runneymead and an impressive 4-1 win against Royal Engineers only 48 hours earlier. The game was a formality, Wanderers winning 9-1 without counting the usual disputed goals. Neither the *North Devon Journal* or the *Western Gazette* felt obliged to even mention the game, and neither could I find it in any of the London papers which usually gave Wanderers' matches a report. As the Wanderers' name came first out of the hat, they would have had choice of ground, and theirs was the Oval cricket ground, and all events there were always reported upon by Charles Alcock himself, as he was not only head of Surrey C.C., but also editor of The Sportsman magazine. This absence of a match report led me to believe the game was played on neutral ground, and not reported in the local paper. Finally, I found a report in that most excellent of football periodicals, the *Sheffield Daily Telegraph*. My deductions were correct- the match had been played at Farnborough near Aldershot, Hants, a spot about halfway between the two clubs' bases. Wanderers' superiority was such that they were 6-0 up by half-time, with goals from Hubert Heron (2), Henry Wace (2), Kenrick and Wylie, all internationals. In the second half, Heron (2) and Wylie increased the agony to nine goals before Panthers captain Eddy Farquharson scored a late consolation goal. But this had been a true Goliath v David fixture, but with the inevitable steamroller result. The Swifts took advantage of the vacant

Oval ground (usual home of the Wanderers), and played their cup-tie with the Leyton club on it.

On Saturday 7th December 1877, the Panthers travelled to play the boys of the Dorset County School, but despite their considerable weight advantage, fell behind to a goal after about a quarter of an hour. Panthers claimed a second half equaliser when following a ruck in front of the school goal, the ball was driven through although a back standing behind the goal returned the ball into play. At the end of the match, the *Salisbury & Winchester Journal* gave the match to the school as being "one goal and three corners to one disputed goal". Oddly enough, the Blandford newspaper never carried a report on any Panthers matches.

On the following Saturday, Panthers played the Milton Abbas school football team under rugby rules, and were beaten by 'one goal and three tries to nil'. Played on Blandford Downs, addition players to the above eleven for the Panthers were E. Leverett, H.E. Corbett, J.H. Garland, G. Flux, H. Scutt, W. Birch, H. Ingram, T. Cox, and W. Burt. Only captain Henry Farquharson and the Cave brothers from their 'F.A. Cup team' played, suggesting that all the others were working-class locals. From the Sturminster census of 1871and 1881, I discovered several of the Panthers footballers. William Burt (b.1868) was a dairyman's labourer, Frank Brown was a thirty-something bachelor; Richard and Edwin, the Cave brothers were the sons of a farmer Edward who had 1,200 acres and employed 25 men and 10 boys at Almer Farm, and brothers Owen and Edwin Richards were sons of farmer and auctioneer Henry. In Blandford Forum, G.T.H. Scutt was a corn merchant in Railway Station Yard, and the Ingrams lived in White Cliff Mill Street as Agricultural Ironmongers. There was no trace of an E. Leverett but the Everett family were bakers and millers employed at White Mill. Of the Reverend George Richard Dupuis, he had a son Richard baptised there in 1875, although he is not listed as living there.

On Boxing Day 1873, Panthers travelled to Dorchester, where three touchdowns and a goal' to the home side in a game played on Poundbury and watched by numerous spectators 'who included Sir Molyneux Neapan', a surname I associate with the Charles Neapan who played for Oxford University in the 1874 Cup Final. Sir Neapan (1814-1895) died without issue and thus footballer Charles Neapan (1851-1903) was instead the grandson of Sir Evan Neapan, baronet and Canon of Westminster.

On Friday 18th December 1877, the Panthers again travelled to play the return game with Dorset County School on their ground at Charminster, where once again, Panthers "'lost by the smallest of margins"after a spirited and keenly-matched game, when it seems that the fitter physique of the school team was the deciding factor in their 1-0 success. A scrimmage under the school posts saw Panthers claim a goal, but if it did cross the line, was booted back out just as quickly, so it remained inconclusive. There arrived a new vicar in Sturminster Marshall in 1877 when Reverend James Cross arrived, at Baillie House, remaining until 1931. He allowed the village cricket team to play in the three acre grounds, suggesting that it is probable that the Panthers did to.

Undeterred, Panthers again sent off their entry fee for the 1878-9 national competition, and were rewarded with a home tie against Runneymead who promptly scratched to them. In round two, they were drawn away to the strong and experienced Old Harrovians, who won as expected, 3-0. Not played until 21st December, three weeks after Cambridge defeated South Norwood in their 2nd round cup-tie, the Harrow men "worsted the Panthers to the tune of three goals to none to the delight of their old school fellows" (*The Graphic* 1878). In 1879, many new entrants from the North and Midlands swelled the F.A.

Cup so that a 5th round was added. No longer could London area clubs expect to have things all their own way. Unfortunately, several provincial teams now found themselves drawn away to new teams who were great distances away. And so when Panthers were drawn away to the Birmingham Cricket & Football Club in October, there was little chance of the match taking place, although Birmingham's other club, Calthorpe, did arrange to travel to their away tie with Maidenhead despite 'losing' their best men to a political rally in Birmingham. It was a pity that Panthers declined to make the journey, as I think they would have been in with a chance as Birmingham's best days were already behind them. This seems to have been the Panther's final throw of the dice, as they never again played on the national stage. Nothing was found for Panthers after 1880, which dovetails with the founding of the Blandford Association club circa 1883, which we know at least E.O. Richards had a leading role.

It is clear that the Farquharson, Richards, and Cave brothers made up the nucleus of the Panthers side. Having the local vicar in the team often meant that a field belonging to the church was used. But why call themselves the 'Panthers' ? It is possible that the twelve-year old Henry Farquharson was taken to see Wombwells Menagrie of Animals when it came through Dorset in 1869 and that creature caught his imagination above others, although the late Victorian period was sadly the era of big game hunting in Africa; either way, Victorians were getting used to seeing in the flesh the various big cats from the Americas and Africa. Today, we think of the panther as being black, but close up they are really a chocolate brown, with yellow eyes, and here I think is where the shirt colours came from, since the Farquharson family crest feature instead colours of red and white. Interestingly, when Wombwells Menagerie came around Dorset in December 1870, *a black panther escaped and got among the spectators but was speedily recaptured.* Perhaps the young Farquharson brothers witnessed this and the creature stayed in his mind for some time. In total contrast to the 21st century doctrine of protection for wild and endangered animals, the late Victorian period saw a trade in wild animals, both dead or alive, and the more dangerous, the higher the price. With frequent reports of villagers and Europeans being killed by tigers and lions, locals were encouraged to kill these 'wild beasts' and paid about a pound per animal. A trade in live big cats flourished, and one dealer was charging £30 for a lion or tiger, but the ultimate prize was a black panther, which fetched £150 or more. An estimated 1,000 people were killed a year by big cats in India alone, and in retribution, 898 panthers were killed in an average year in the 1870s.

The Panthers' 1-1-8 formation was typical of the age of leisured amateur footballers who all wanted to join the attack! With E.G. Farquharson as captain, he and his brothers are likely to have founded the Panthers. The Farquharsons were noted members of the Kennel Club in the 1880s, from whose records I discovered that E.G resided at 'Huish', Blandford, and that his brother Henry Robert at Eastbury House, Tarrant Gunville, Blandford, along with half a dozen servants, butlers and nannies, where he was described as a landowner from Brighton. An H.E. Farquharson was a judge at the national dog show of 1883 held at the Aston Lower Grounds in Birmingham, specialising in imported Newfoundlands, he was host to several spring meetings of the Kennel Club field trials. The Farquharsons of Langton House were Master of the Hounds even in 1835 (*New Sporting Magazine*) and owned 'an immense estate' in the district. There was not a committee within five miles that did not have their name in it. With much land of their own, I am surprised that the Panthers did not play in the grounds of Eastbury House.

Illustrative of the difficulty in which the association game had getting established in the county was shown when most matches reported under the banner of 'football' in the 1880s turned out to be of the rugby code. A match billed Blandford v Old Shirburnians played on the Fairfield on Good Friday 1883 also turned out to be a 15-a-side rugby match, although H. Ingram and E.O. Richards, once of the Panthers, had switched codes and were playing rugby for Blandford. Landowner James John Farquharson allowed a cricket match to take place on his Langton cricket ground in June 1880, when Durweston were the visitors. One S. Burt, relation to W. Burt of the Panthers FC took part in the match. On the 1891 census for Blandford Forum, the Burts are listed as being agricultural labourers, and Eddie Richards is now a wine spirit merchant living in Mill Street, White Cliff.

Christmas holiday friendly matches are easier to arrange when you can work dates around the availability of your best men, but no doubt when the entered the F.A. Cup, with time constraints set by the F.A. committee, Panthers would sometimes have to play important matches without their best men. Association football seemed to be quite backward in Dorset even as late as 1888, when a six a side tournament was held for the first time in Bridport, when 4 points were awarded for each goal scored, and 1 point given for each corner obtained!

A new association team, Blandford United, then started up in the town. Said to have been founded in 1882, (although no results before 1891 can be found), they still play this day on Blandford Recreation ground, although their original home, built around 1890 was at the rear of the Crown Hotel. I would imagine that the Panthers FC were the short-lived fancy of the three Oxford educated Farquharson brothers who reformed the team around Michaelmas and other college holidays, when they returned home to Blandford. After attaining the age of 21, they were probably given duties commensurate with their position in the town, such as in the recently formed Volunteer Rifle Corps, and

Henry Farquharson, Member of Parliament for Blandford.

the football club was allowed to fade away. Indeed, Henry Richardson Farquharson (1857-95) became Member of Parliament for West Dorset, standing for fair trade and the plight of the lowly paid rural farmworkers in a town often blighted by outbreaks of foot-and-mouth disease. As a keen Ripperologist I was surprised to find the subject constantly cropping up in my research for the Panthers. After the Ripper murders of the autumn of 1888, it was M.P. Henry Farquharson, who publicly named a fellow Blandford man, barrister and schoolteacher Montague Druitt as the man he thought to have been Jack the Ripper. In another twist of fate, the man well known for being put in charge of the Ripper case, George Frederick Aberline, also came from Blandford!

Edward G. Farquharson became secretary to the South Dorset Hunt along with friend Cave who sat on the committee of 1887. Despite almost weekly reports nationwide of deaths and serious injury on the football fields, the nearest I came to an injury to a Panthers players was when one Hwia Williams, married to Florence, sister of H.R. Farquharson, was accidentally shot in the leg with a pistol at close range in Pall Mall, London in November 1883 by his friend Frederick Moriarty (a name which brings Sherlock Holmes books to mind) as they exited the United Services

Club ! Eastbury House, the Farquharson family seat, became infamous as one of Britain's most haunted houses (*The Haunted Homes & Family Traditions of Great Britain, John Ingram*). Commissioned by Lord of the Admiralty George Doddington in 1709 and completed after his death by Budd Bobbington (later Lord Melcombe) in 1713 at the outrageous cost of £140,000, its vast site was later much demolished until only one wing remained and it subsequently fell into the hands of J.J. Farquharson, where stories of ghosts and vampires remain to this day.

The long gone railway station of Blandford Gate at Sturminster Marshall, where teams visiting the Panthers' ground would have alighted.

Bailey Gate station (1863-1966) fell foul to the Beeching axe, having been pivotal in sending milk and cheese from the United Dairies plant at Sturminster Marshall to London. Until closure in 1978, it was the world's largest cheese making factory.

207

PEGASUS FC

Founded - 1948
Folded - 1963
Ground - Iffley Road ground, Oxford
Colours - White shirts, black shorts

Although football saw a resurgence of interest after the Second World War had ended, and attendances at professional League matches had increased noticeably, the 'golden age' of the amateur had been left behind. Even though nine out of every ten teams were amateurs, the gulf between even the best amateur sides and the Football League sides had grown wider. The glory days of even the Corinthians had been left behind since they had amalgamated with the Casuals in 1939, and there was a need for a strong new amateur team, especially since Oxbridge had faded from the scene after being pioneers in the 19th century.

Harold Warris Thompson, a professor at St. John's College, Oxford came up with the idea of Pegasus, a side drawn from the best footballers at Oxford and Cambridge Universities, and young men returning from the war provided much of the initial team. The early debate of where to base the club was settled when the joint Oxford University sports ground on Iffley Road was chosen. This was the same venue where Roger Bannister famously broke the four-minute mile world record. Playing in a white shirt featuring a badge of Pegasus, the fabled winged horse, it represented a meld of the centaur and falcon motifs of the two universities. Elected as first president was the Reverend Kenneth Hunt, a former Corinthian and Wolves player, and it was said that they modelled themselves on the style of Tottenham Hotspurs, a club with which they had connections. Vic Buckingham, who had played for Spurs for 17 years, became manager of both clubs. In 1950, L.H. Blaxland, a Derbyshire county cricketer, was elected as vice-president. One of the problems facing Pegasus was that due to team loyalties, Pegasus players did not return to the fold until after the annual Varsity football match. Under the guidance of Buckingham and Bill Nicholson, Pegasus became a push-and-run team, and were a very fit bunch of undergraduates. In their debut match, they defeated Arsenal reserves by 1-0.

On 18th December 1948, Pegasus competed in the Amateur Cup for the first time, beating Enfield, in the 4th Qualifying Round, with goals from Tanne and Insole. Smethwick Highfield were despatched 4-1, and then Brentwood & Warley 2-1, followed by another squeak when they edged past northerners Willingdon 3-2. They had progressed to the quarter-finals where a big crowd of over 11,000 saw them go out 3-4 at home to Bromley on February 26th 1949. The following season, they disappointed with an early exit when Walthamstow beat them 3-1 in round 2.

The following year, however, they achieved their ambition by winning the Amateur Cup, beating one of the legends of the era, Bishop Auckland 2-1 at Wembley Stadium. An incredible full house of 100,000 saw the match, won 2-1 by Pegasus. This was the winning side that day :-

Pegasus Winners 1950-51. Players only, back row: Sutcliffe, Bower, Laybourne, Brown, Dutchman, Carr, Richards, Maughan. Front row: Pawson, Potts, Shearwood, Saunders, Cowan, Tanner, Platt.

The team line ups for the final played on Saturday 21st April 1951.

With the trophy to defend, Pegasus just failed to reach the final in 1950-51. Drawn away in every round, they won 4-3 at Gosport with brace from Carr and Tanner, and then 3-1 at Slough with two from Tanner and one from Pawson. They came back from two goals down at Brentwood & Warley to win 3-2 thanks to Lagbourne, Sutcliffe, and Carr. In round 4, they 'travelled' to the ground of Oxford City where they won 3-0 before coming unstuck against Hendon in the semi-final. The first game ended 1-1, and the replay was held on the old Crystal Palace ground, where Hendon edged home 3-2.

In the next season, 1951-52, there was an early exit at home when Crook Town scored the only goal of the game, but a year later, it was glory time again. Another large crowd of 9,000 saw then beat Slough 2-0 in the semi-final, and they were through to the Wembley final to face unfancied Harwich & Parkeston. Experience counted for a lot, as Pegasus equalled the highest score when they won 6-1 in front of another 100,000 full house. Quickly a huge success, Pegasus were getting crowds as large as many Football League sides. This winning side had truly captured the public imagination :-

		Brown		
	Alexander		**McKenna**	
Vowels		**Shearwood**		**Saunders**
Pawson	**Carr**	**Leybourne**	**Lunn**	**Sutcliffe**

Defending the cup in 1953, they failed at the 4th round stage. After wins against Clevedon 3-0, Gedling 6-1, Willingdon held them to a 1-1 draw before Pegasus came through 4-2 in the replay. However, Brigg Sports caught them on an off day, and beat them 3-0 in Oxford to end their run. The 4th round would be the furthest that Pegasus ever reached for the rest of the club's life. Solid win s against Dagenham 4-0, Stevenage 5-2 and West Auckland 4-1 saw them come unstuck against rising Wycombe Wanderers, who held them 0-0 in Oxford before winning the replay 2-1. Season 1955-56 saw Barnet overcome 2-0, only for Wycombe to return to Oxford and win 2-1. The following year was even worse, as Romford won 2-1 in Oxford at the first hurdle. Walthamstow proved troublesome in 1957, and Pegasus needed a replay before winning 3-1, only for Ferryhill Athletic to win in Oxford by 2-0 in the second round. Pegasus had now gone out losing at home for four years on the trot. By the late 1950s, several teams had begun to stand out, and Kingstonian of London and Durham's Bishop Auckland were two of them. Kingstonian were beaten 1-0 in the 1958-59 Amateur Cup, but after an epic three games, the 'Bishops' put Pegasus out when the only goal after 300 minutes was scored in the second replay at Sheffield Wednesday's Hillsborough ground. By this time, Pegasus were fading, in a new age where college men found other pursuits instead of football, and Sheffield side Norton Woodseats put them out of the 1959-60 competition in round 2. Erith FC held Pegasus to a 3-3 draw before being overturned 2-0 at Iffley Road, but Bromley put an end to further progress when winning the replay 2-1 after a 1-1 draw at Iffley. Season 1961-2 saw the dying embers of a club crash 1-6 to Hendon in a replay, following a goal-less draw. Pegasus were now no longer a leading amateur side, and they were obliged to now battle through the qualifying rounds in 1962. Before an attendance described as 'small' Windsor & Eton beat them 3-1 at the 4th qualifying stage to signal the last ever game played in the competition by the twice cup winners.

Pegasus, like the Corinthians and Casuals before them also went on annual tours. Not all their games were reported, but in 1950 I found that they lost 1-4 to Torquay United on a tour of Devon & the south west, and in 1952 they met a select Leeds XI at Elland Road on a Yorkshire tour. Distance was no object, and in 1951 they toured Switzerland in December, and then the Far East in 1954, where they played in Singapore and Hong Kong. No matches were won, and the following results are thanks to Neil Morrison of the Rec. Sports Soccer Statistics Foundation :-

1.1.1954	Hong Kong	4-1	Pegasus
2.1.1954	Hong Kong XI	1-0	Pegasus
5.1.1954	China XI	4-1	Pegasus

A Pegasus team in 1952 was :-

P.R. Leydon

F.C.M. Alexander   G.H. McKinna

K. Taylor   K.A. Shearwood   D.F. Saunders

H.A. Dawson D.B. Carr J.D.P. Tanner J.S. Leybourne R.G. Lunn

Alexander, Dawson, Saunders and Tanner were England amateur internationals, and Tanner had also turned out for Huddersfield Town in the Football League.

Pegasus quickly faded as a force by the end of the 1950s, due to changes in university culture brought about by the new sixties decade, and several of their best men had defected to the Corinthian-Casuals. However, several other trophies were added to their cabinet, with success in the Oxfordshire Cup 1948, 1950; the Cambridge Invitation Cup 1960, 1961; and the A.F.A. Invitation Cup in 1952, 1954, 1955, 1957. Running teams costs money – even amateur pure at heart ones- and thus, when Pegasus played the legendary Sheffield Club at the end of 1952 at Bramall Lane, it enabled both clubs to share the £500 gate money, which in Sheffield's case paid for two season's rent of their Abbeydale ground. When Pegasus played Portsmouth in October 1954, they were already famous, and the local Portsmouth Evening News printed a special evening edition on sale outside the ground, with full team and individual player photos and profiles. In August 1957, aged 36, Ken Shearwood departed Pegasus to take up the coaching role with Lancing FC in the Sussex County League.

In January 1959, the Birmingham Mail reported with delight that "Professor A.P. Thompson, Dean of the Faculty of Medicine of Birmingham University and President of the British Medical Association, receives a C.B.E in the New Year honours list". They went on to say he was born in British Guyana and educated in Dulwich College and Birmingham University. He went on to have a glittering medical career which included Consultant Physician to the Children's Ear, Nose & Throat Hospital, and chairman of the Regional Hospital Board. Nine years later, as Foreign Secretary to the Royal Society, he received a knighthood. They also thought he was the founder of the Pegasus FC, but they had the wrong Thompson, for our man was born in Sheffield, educated at Trinity College Oxford, worked under Max Planck in Berlin University, was a chemical physicist who later taught a certain Margaret Thatcher, and was the disliked administrator who sacked Sir Alf Ramsay and made sure that Brian Clough was never made England football manager. Apparently, in life, he was a bully.

Naturally, Pegasus players caught the eye of many a Football League scout, and some went on to play League football, like King, a forward who assisted Colchester United in 1959-60 season. It was said that Pegasus had a style which copied Tottenham Hotspur, and some say it was the other way around!

At the end of the 1962-63 season, Pegasus were finally wound up after a brief but successful 15 years. Their Iffley Road sports ground, still famous as the venue for Roger Bannister's four-minute mile, continues to be used as the Oxford University general sports ground. When the Football Association dropped the Amateur Cup in 1974, and a decade earlier when the golden era of the famous amateur clubs had passed, the name of Pegasus,along with Wanderers, Corinthians, and Oxford University were being held up as best examples of the pure ideal of simply playing for the honour of representing one's town or country, without financial gain being the motive for trophy winning.

For further reading on Pegasus, try Ken Shearwood's book, published in 2011 by Kennedy & Boyd, simply titled *"Pegasus FC"*.

Ultimately, the duffle-coat wearing undergraduates belonged to another age, they wanted to light up the optimistic bright new Elizabethan era, and for a short while, lit up dull and grey post-war Britain with their pure amateur principles recalled from a different era.

Founded - 1. Circa 1871-2
           2. New club 1907 when Corinthians resigned from the F.A.

Folded - 1889 (original club)
           1915 (Edwardian version)

Colours - 1. Broad Black and white hoops, white knicks, black socks and tasselled caps.
           2. Black and white halves 1880s
           1907 reformed club : White shirt, black shorts when on tour.

Ground - 1. Hackney Downs
           2. Croydon at 1877
           3. Copper-mill Lane, Walthamstow at 1880-81 (now the Water Works)
           4. Greyhound, Dulwich at 1882
           5. Ritherdon Road, Balham 1885-92
           6. No home ground after 1907

The Pilgrims were not what you would call one of the leading teams, with a range of early opponents which included St. Georges College, Woodford Wells, Upton Park, Forest School, Trojans, Phillestines, Swifts and Notts County. The earliest report I found for them were in January 1872 *(The Sportsman)* when they met Leyton Harrow and later, Brondesbury, Forest, and Lausanne, suggesting a possible 1871 formation date. Twelve months later, they lost 0-2 to South Norwood, 0-4 away to Crystal Palace, whilst their reserves beat the Leyton team 1-0 at home on Hackney Downs, captained by C.A. Hampton. They also went the way of many other when they lost 1-2 on the Georges Lane ground of the Forest School in November 1872. Van Summer and captain H. V. Andrews rotated the goal-minding duties. A leading influence when the Pilgrims started out was president George Gowland, a well-known philanthropist in the Hackney area.

    I stumbled across the end of season set of results for the Pilgrims in the June edition of *Bells Life* which remarkably gave the results of every match and venue of their 1873-74 season, when they won 11, drew 6 and lost 9. All home matches were at Hackney Downs and were as follows -

9th October	1-0	v	Great Marlow FA Cup
11th October	1-1	v	Surrey Rifles, venue Camberwell
18th October	2-1	v	Phillistines
25th October	8-1	v	Trojans
1st November	1-2	v	Forest School, George Lane
8th November	1-4	v	Maidenhead
15th November			Wanderers failed to show (!)
22nd November	0-1	v	Sheffield FC (FA Cup) The Oval
29th November	1-1	v	Windsor Home Park
6th December	4-2	v	Brondesbury at Notting Hill
6th December	1-0	v	Prairie Rangers
13th December	1-1	v	Woodford Wells
20th December	4-0	v	Crystal Palace

3rd January	1-1	v	Woodford Wells at Woodford
10th January	1-1	v	Herts Rangers
17th January	1-0	v	Letchfords XI and 0-6 v Southall at Southall
21st January	0-1	v	Crystal Palace at Camberwell
24th January			Forest School failed to show
24th January	0-3	v	Prairie Rangers at Wormwood Scrubs
31st January	0-2	v	Maidenhead at Maidenhead
7th February	1-1	v	Windsor Home Park at Windsor
14th February			South Norwood failed to show
21st February	3-0	v	Trojans at Leyton ground
28th February	3-1	v	Phillestines at Leytonstone
28th February	2-0	v	Southall
7th March	0-1	v	Herts Rangers at Watford
14th March			Wanderers again failed to show
21st March			Won away to Reigate Priory
28th March			Brondesbury failed to show, also South Norwood failed to show
4th April			Reigate Priory failed to show

Notice how often visiting teams failed to show up, especially the Wanderers (twice). This 1875 ten man Pilgrims side beat South Norwood in October 1874 to progress into the 2nd round of the English Cup -

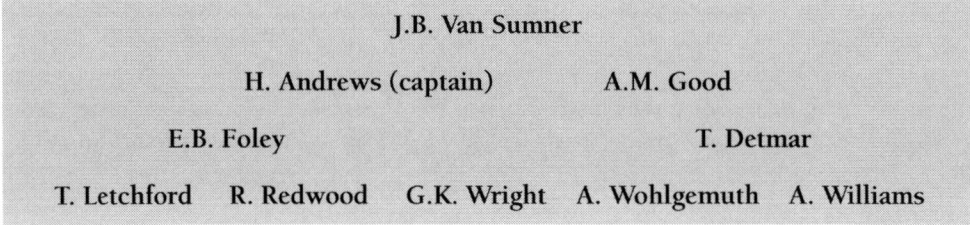

The players' names also allowed me to wonder if the team hitherto called Clapton Pilgrims was one and the same club, because when they played on 15th February 1873 on Hackney Downs, four of the above were in action (*Bells Life*). A month later, Pilgrims were no match for the Old Etonians in the opening round of the English Cup when they were beaten 4-1, with Tom Letchford getting a consolation goal at the Oval. The *London Standard* praised the 'spirited effort' of the Pilgrims side. Other first team players included Charlie Spraggs, John Drummond, John Thomas, Yetts, C.A. Hapton (vice-captain), H. Foley, C. Child, M.J. Phelps and A.M. Airley.

Detmar and Williams were the Pilgrim's best players two years later, when they lost 0-1 to the Swifts on the Dolphin Ground at Slough. Either Pilgrims didn't have a ground of their own, or they moved around a lot, as they were reported as playing Hackney Downs in the early 1870s, in Leytonstone in 1874, at Slough in 1875, Croydon in 1877, Walthamstow in 1880, and the Oval in 1882. Forest school seemed to be on everyone's fixture list, and in February 1877, the Pilgrims played them 'at Tottenham' (*London Standard*) and comfortably won 3-0.

Studying Victorian maps of the Croydon area in the 1870s, I was surprised as to how built up it already was. There were the usual countless fields on the west and south side, but I spotted two likely candidates for the Pilgrims ground of 1877. A cricket ground near the town cemetery, which was soon built over, or more likely, a ground marked 'football |& cricket ground' on Wellesley Road (now the site of Tugella Road) by Selhurst railway station.

Now known simply as the Pilgrims, they first entered the FA Cup (then known as the English Cup) for season 1873-4. Defeating Marlow 1-0 in round 1, they did very well to give the Sheffield club a hard game before losing 0-1, Sheffield at that time being one of the best teams in the country. The following season saw them beat South Norwood 2-1 away, only to lose 0-2 to the Clapham Rovers. They were unfortunate to be drawn against double cup finalists Old Etonians in the 1875 competition, and were beaten 4-1. The following season, however, saw Pilgrim's best effort, when captained by J.K. Wright, they reached Round 3 after beating Ramblers 4-1 and Panthers 1-0. The *Lloyds Weekly* paper gives an insight to the perils of football outside one's own town in 1876 when Pilgrims left London on the Friday night of the 8th December and making for Southampton where they stayed overnight. The next day they continued on by train via Wimbourne to Bailey Gate, Blandford (Dorset) where they played the Panthers who "played up well, their side containing a number of Oxford men". The match probably took place on the three acre grounds of Bailie House on Poole Road, being the vicarage where the local cricket team played.

When Pilgrims played a new team Runnymeade from Eton, on the Saturday before the trip to the Panthers, the game ended goal-less at a venue simply given as 'Tottenham' with Detmar, Wright and Litchford drawing praise for their endeavours. Sadly, they came up against the strongest side in London, if not the country, in the Wanderers, who had some difficulty in beating them 3-0 at the Oval to put them out of the 1876-7 FA Cup. Pilgrims held the Wanderers off until the 75th minute when Frank Heron chested the ball through from a cross, and two more were added in the last ten minutes. Pilgrims were still playing with six forwards, who generally were - Mott and Gibson (right side), Detmar and Frank Lloyd (left side), with Good and Tom Letchford as twin centres. When Pilgrims went over to play the Reading FC in October 1876, the *Lloyd's* newspaper said that it was the first time a club from London had been to Reading. A close game was won when Tom Letchford scored the only goal in the second half, and both teams retired to a post match supper at the Queens Hotel.

Pilgrims once again beat Ramblers in the following season's national cup, but were outclassed when the Royal Engineers humbled them 6-0 in round 2. Now having ditched the black skullcaps, Brentwood were despatched 3-1 at the end of 1878, only for the Remnants to overcome them by 6-2 in round 2. This Pilgrims side played lost 5-2 to Southill Park on Saturday 9th February at Hampstead - Wohlgamuth, Ramsey, Horner, Maynard, Poland, Grieve, Gledhill, Fole, Moore, Tidd (goalkeeper). The role of goalkeeper seemed to have rotated around several players, although it was usually Wohlgamuth or Henderson. In 1878, new players Horner, Lloyd, Watson and Gladhill joined the ranks. The Pilgrims and Surrey Rifles seem to have been well matched in 1878 when they drew both their matches 1-1 and 2-2. Friendlies against Upton Park (1-1) and away to Barnes (2-3) were also played in early 1878.

One tragic occurrence happened on Saturday 25th October 1879, when Pilgrims travelled to play the Reading club. The home captain Henry Rogers *'was seized with a fit and expired on the ground having hardly touched the ball"* (Lloyds Weekly). No doubt the game was immediately brought to a close. The result was not to hand, but in the previous week, Pilgrims had beaten Ware Rangers by 6-0. A few weeks later on the 7th November, crack

Scottish club Queens Park travelled down to London, and amongst other games, played the Pilgrims on Kennington Oval, winning comfortably 2-0. For a friendly match against such illustrious visitors, indicates that the Pilgrim's were rising through the ranks, and a key factor would be new goalkeeper Harry Swepstone, *The Graphic* stating that Swepstone's excellent goalkeeping had prevented a possible rout. Harry Albermarle Swepstone (1859-1907) became the Bob Wilson of the era in London, and was in great demand, also turning out for Swifts, Corinthians and Ramblers, but I believe his first club was Clapton. Swepstone was capped six times between 1880-83. A solicitor by profession, he lived variously in Stepney, Hackney, Leyton and Lewisham, and served on the FA Committee during 1883-4 *(Doug Lamming)*.

There was now a noticeable presence from the provinces in the English Cup, as Nottingham Forest, Wednesbury Strollers, Sheffield and Darwen made their entrance. Pilgrims at last got through to round 3 in 1880, when they overcame Clarence 5-2 and then had a walkover against Herts Rangers. One of London's strongest clubs, Clapham Rovers trounced them 7-0 to end Pilgrim's hopes, and went on to win the Cup themselves, beating Oxford University 1-0 in the final. In March 1880, Pilgrims travelled up to Aston to play the Birmingham football club on the Aston Lower grounds, and departed as 3-1 winners. Unrelated to either Villa or Small Heath, this Birmingham FC were formed as a hobby team for workers at the pleasure grounds, which was the principal weekend attraction for West Midlands, with its permanent circus, fair, skating, zoo and fireworks displays. Sometimes, leading Aston and Birmingham footballers such as Eli Davis, Howard Vaughton, Jack Devey or Arthur Brown would turn out for them when visiting teams might prove too strong.

Season 1880-1 saw a quick cup exit when, following a 1st round walkover against Old Phiberdians, a single goal by Massey on Saturday 11th December at the Oval was enough to eliminate Pilgrims at the hands of the Royal Engineers. Strangely, when the south Birmingham side Calthorpe came down to play Maidstone in Kent at the end of February 1882, I spotted the name of Harry Swepstone turning out for Calthorpe (Birmingham); also the game was refereed by Pilgrims player John Henderson. Normally, when a visiting team arrived one or two men short, the home side would loan them some substitutes, drawn from their reserves, and the newspaper would always comment on this. However, on this occasion, there was no reference, so perhaps Swepstone had a business connection with Birmingham, since Swepstone had qualified at the bar in 1881, and Calthorpe FC were founded as Birmingham Law Clerks FC. The south Birmingham side were defeated 1-0 when their defence stood still thinking that Blackwell was offside, and making no attempt to stop him, he went on to score, much to their annoyance. Queens Park of Glasgow, the Scottish cup holders, were Pilgrim's visitors to the Surrey Oval on Saturday 19th February 1881, and their class was evident as they ran out easy 4-1 winners in front of a large crowd *(Lloyds Weekly)*. In January 1882, when the London XI went up to play Sheffield XI in the annual fixture, no less than four Pilgrims' were involved: Harry Swepstone as usual, in goal, and R.L. Escombe and J. Last in the role of twin centre forwards, and London took Pilgrim's C.E. Hart as their umpire. At this point Pilgrims were using the popular Greyhound ground at Dulwich, and had for bedmates the Greyfriars FC (f.1876), who also used the Greyhound Inn as headquarters. In April 1882, the Pilgrim's president George Gowland passed away, and several players gave tribute to a generous man who had been with the club in that capacity "for more than ten years". Gowland had been a philanthropist to several organisations in Hackney.

Pilgrims recorded their biggest win in the national cup when they trounced another ground-sharing side, Mosquitoes (f.1870) by 5-0, only to lose in the now traditional 2nd round when Old Foresters beat them 3-1 at Leytonestone at the start of 1882. A month later, this Pilgrims eleven met Midland visitors Notts County at the Oval on Saturday 2nd February but were outclassed and beaten 5-1 in a match played under terrible weather conditions of freezing fog ;-

Harry Swepstone

A.W. Ramsay (capt.)   **E.A. Young**

C.H. Last   **E.H. Puttock**

A.J. Vincent   H.R. Knowles   A.J. Last   R.L. Escombe   E.C. Mott   S.W.Scott

Goalkeeper Harry Albermane Swepstone (1859-1907) is credited with inventing the name for the Corinthians football club in 1882. He also played as an amateur for Clapton, Ramblers, and the Swifts and was capped six times for England. His nickname was 'little Pilgrim'. The powerful Notts County side contained the three Cursham brothers and Widdowson, and once more, the name of Charles Alcock as referee was seen. The *Chelmsford Chronicle* reported that in October 1882, Pilgrims had arranged to play every week, all of them away to clubs including Forest School, Dreadnought, St. Barts Hospital, Bruce Castle, and Grove House. The Pilgrims eleven which lost 1-6 at home to ascendant Reigate Priory on Saturday 15th December 1883 is almost entirely different to the above side, comprising -

J. Roberts

R. Shannon   **C. Stone**

C.H. Last   **E .Mantle**

W. Colebrook   E. Graham   J.H. Bennett   Whatley   F. Edwards   W. Stringfield

My initial belief that (Clapham) Pilgrims and the Pilgrims were the same club began to evaporate in 1882 when I saw both teams play on the same day, with completely different elevens. The version with well-known names (Clopton-Jones, Holden-White and R.A. Ogilvie) met Clapham Rovers whilst Clapham Pilgrims 1st team met Orion FC. But when the Pilgrims held their AGM in September that year, it was at the Downs Hotel, Clapton, announcing fixtures against Old Foresters, Forest School, Upton Park, Dreadnought, Minerva and Clapham Rovers, Cambridge University, and Barnes. That did not sound like the fixtures for Clapham Pilgrims. When the draw was made for the 1885-6 London Charity Cup, the name of Clapham Pilgrims was pulled out, yet when the final was contested against Ashburnham Rovers in the following February, the beaten finalists were listed simply as the Pilgrims. Clarity was brought to the issue when, in April 1886, the *South London Press* stated that the "Clapham Pilgrims, having started out six years ago (1880) have flourished since their inception, and both 1st and 2nd team games are played in Ritherdon-road, Balham every Saturday". I could now concentrate on the original Pilgrims club.

I was delighted to read a vivid description of a hare & hounds paper-chase through Walthamstow in 1882, for the route went " twice straight through the Pilgrims football field" after coming down Black-horse Lane, turning left into Copper-mill Lane and down across the fields to Lea Bridge Road, one of which was the Pilgrims ground. I followed their route on a map of 1880 and I'm pretty sure that the ground was facing Copper-mill farm on Watery Lane, gone by 1910, which makes the Waterworks our site. Watery Lane lived up to its name, for by 1890, the area had been turned into a reservoir.

The touring Pilgrims travelled up to Sheffield on Saturday 20th January 1883 and met the Sheffield FC at Bramall Lane. In advertising the attraction, the *Sheffield Independent* said that Pilgrims would be bringing Harry Swepstone, the England goalkeeper, and Andy Watson the Scottish international. Sheffield, in reply, were going to borrow Harry Cursham from Notts Forest to strengthen their side! Forest School were an annual fixture for the Pilgrims, and a tough nut too on their own ground. On the afternoon of Tuesday October 21st 1884, despite the efforts of Couts, Lamont and Jessop, the school ran out 3-1 winners. Pilgrims appeared to have sent another eleven to play the Royal Military Academy on the same day, and they were beaten 2-1 at Woolwich. The Forest school team had even beaten the Swifts 6-2 on the previous Saturday, although all the 'Birds' best players were playing for their 'other' teams in the F.A. Cup on the same day.

The Old Carthusians proved much too strong an outfit when the two sides met in the opening round of the 1882-3 English Cup, and ran out 6-0 winners. Carthusians, in their multi-coloured shirts of maroon, pink and navy, almost made it to the final, but this was the year when the Cup famously 'left town for the first time' when Blackburn Olympic edged past Old Etonians 2-1 in the final after extra-time. Mosquitoes got their revenge over Pilgrims when they knocked them out 1-0 at the first hurdle of the Cup at the end of 1883, and the same fate awaited them in the following year when Dulwich - soon to be at the forefront of the national amateur revival following the creation of professional clubs in the Midlands and the North - had the better of a five goal match. Goals from Excombe and Shaw were not enough on Saturday 8th November, and Pilgrims' run in the national cup was finally over. That proved to be the last season in which the Pilgrims entered the English Cup, by which time, most of the independent amateur sides had folded, and the amateur flag was mostly carried on by the Old Boys' sides who were of course institution based. By the late 1880s, as with Wanderers, Swifts, Rovers, there were also 'Pilgrims' clubs around the country, such as the Arbroath version in Scotland, and at Cheltenham. The Pilgrim footballers continued to be good members of society and gave annual dramatic performances at the town hall. When Goalkeeper John Henderson married Mary Campbell Loftus, of Hereford House, Ilfracombe on 26th June 1883, he was given an illuminated scroll thanking him for 8 years' service as honorary secretary to the Pilgrims FC.

Pilgrims competed in the London Senior Cup in the late 1880s, and one of their biggest wins came on October 17th when they thrashed Vikings FC by 14-0 in round 1. I could not find their name in any of the London finals, but on Saturday 20th February 1886, they missed their chance to appear in the London Charity cup final, when they were beaten 3-1 at the Oval in the semi-final by team of the season Ashburnham Rovers. Attendances were typically around 2,000. The Pilgrims FC seem to have faded away by 1887, and the last matches I found for them were the London Cup semi-final 1-3 defeat against Ashburnham

Rovers (a side comprised of Old Westminster men led by Ralph Squires) when Pilgrims had to put out virtually their reserve side with so many 1st team men unavailable. Played at the Oval in February 1886, having overcome United London Scottish over Christmas (1-1, 4-1) and with Swepstone being criticized for constantly rushing too far out of goal, this team missed out on a cup final appearance -

		Harry Swepstone			
	G. Mitchell			A. Roberts	
	E. Mitchell	R. Lamont		H. Mortice	
H. Holman	R. Escombe	Dr. Smith	G. Goodliffe	F. Robertson	

Hinting at things to come, matches in February and March against Cambridge University and Forest were called off when Pilgrims couldn't raise a team. A few matches were played in April, but when the 1886-7 season started up, Pilgrims were again arriving at grounds with eight or nine men, and went out of the London Cup to Clapham at the first hurdle. The Sportsman reported on the sixteenth annual fixture between Forest School and the Pilgrims played on Tuesday 6th December 1887 at Georges-lane, won easily 7-0 by the visitors led by W.E. Fry , Warren Leete and Dr. Smith. Most matches in 1887 turned out to be for the Clapham Pilgrims. In the *Sportsman* on New Year's Day 1890, the Clapham version appealed for opposition for the following Saturday as they had an open date. Their ground was stated as being Ritherdon Road, Balham, and their headquarters and changing rooms were at the Coffee Tavern, Bedford Road (3 minutes from Balham station). I assume he meant the nearby Bedford Hill as the Bedford Road is well over a mile away, unless visiting players hired a cab to the ground from there. The advert was placed by secretary G.J. Blower of 27 Broomwood Road, Wandsworth Common. A similar advert placed in the following August stated that they had since amalgamated and absorbed a team called Druids, but were still playing at Ritherdon Road, as they had done for the past five years. However, maps for that street in 1895 show much new housing being built all over that district and the fields of Ritherdon Road are no more, and so the Clapham Pilgrims had to find a new home. Prior to 1880, Ritherdon Road was a winding lane which principally led to to the 17th century Bedfordhill House, its Priory Lodge (f.1822) and the grounds. All the fields had trees, except two near the junction with Balham Road, so I would say that Clapham Pilgrims played where is now Foxbourne Road, accounting for the fact that the bend of Ritherdon was straightened out in the 1890s, having originally started where is now Brook Close. I found no mention of the Clapham Pilgrims FC during the late 1890s, suggesting that the loss of Ritherdon Road had caused the club to fold. I found no results for either Pilgrims or Clapham Pilgrims in 1889, and I could not tell which one of them it was which won the Reading Junior Cup final in April 1888 by 1-0 over Reading St. Mary's (later Minster). When John Henderson acted as a referee in a match in September 1889 he was described as being "formerly of the Pilgrims".

The name, which had lain dormant for over a decade, was used again for the Edwardian touring team which again made the headlines in the new century. In August and September of 1905, Sir Charles Kirkpatrick took "the new Pilgrims FC" on a short tour of the USA and Canada, where of course, they met little opposition, but achieved its objective of raising the awareness of the association game over in North America. This, I believe to be a resurrection of the old name. At the same time, many London amateur clubs were going on annual short tours to the Continent, particularly Holland, France and Belgium. Invited over by Theodore Roosevelt, who was conducting a campaign to eliminate the brutality of the American version by popularising the Association game, a series of trips proved a great success. Winning nearly all their matches, and impressing many thousands of curious onlookers, these were their results -

5-0 v Montreal, 8-2 v Hamilton, 5-2 v Niagara, 1-2 v Berlin, 3-3 v Galt, 10-2 v Detroit, 10-2 and 6-0 v St. Louis; 1-2 and 6-0 v Chicago; 6-0, 4-1 and 5-0 v Philadelphia; 4-3 v Fall River (U.S. Champions), 5-0 v Boston, 7-1 v New York and 10-0 v Pennsylvania University. The 17 game tour included 14 wins, one draw and two defeats, across September and October.

The 3-3 draw against best Canadian side Galt FC drew the best attendance there of 5,000. The goalkeeper position rotated between Kirkpatrick, Coopland and Milton (Colin Jose). The team, featuring Vivian Woodward which toured with such success was generally-

Sir Charles Kirkpatrick (goal)				
F.H. Milnes (Blackburn Etrusians)			F.H. Walmsley (Etrurians)	
W. Storer (Leeds City & Corinthians)		J. Barnsdale (Nottm For.)	W. Nuttall (Rovers)	
J. E. Raine (Sheff. Utd)	J. Bryning (Northern Nomads)	T. Fletcher (Derby Co.)	C. Coopland (Sheff. Utd)	V. Woodward (Tottenham)

Others in the squad were E.A. Milton (Sheffield Wycliffe), F.O. Wright (Notts Magdala) and F. H. Milnes (Sheffield United).

Sir Charles found himself given the goalkeeper's gloves at the last moment when C.E. Wilson pulled out, and he surprised everyone, including Lady Kirkpatrick, as to how good he was. They thought that the Chicago club were the best team over there, but had mixed receptions from the colleges and universities, who thought that they were out there tying to stamp out the American handling (and bashing) game. The Berlin club gave them a hard time, and did not hold back with the crunching tackles and bad sportsmanship, once kicking a dead ball into the Pilgrims goal when play had stopped for an injured man, and a goal was awarded!

Despite a total of 40,000 people watching the two St. Louis games, the tour made a loss of some £2,000 which was covered by a Mr. C. H. Murray. They then watched with mirth at an American football match, and saw one player break his leg despite "everyone padded up from head to toe" and learnt of two others who had died on the field during their stay. On return home, they were treated to a dinner celebration evening by Sir Ernest Cochrane, and then threw out a challenge to the Corinthians. I believe they went out again on 1906. In 1907, the Pilgrims were once again assembled by Kirkpatrick, this time at the Royal Victoria Hotel in Sheffield, where Fred Milnes played for the amateur Sheffield Club. I detected a snub towards London and the F.A with this move out of the capital, and later,

Milnes stated that they wanted nothing to do with the squabbles which arose between the FA and the new AFA.

In 1909, a 15 player Pilgrims touring team comprised of a combination of leading amateurs and semi- professionals toured the U.S.A again in an effort to raise the profile of the game over there, although we now realise, in the 21st century that it may never rise above 3rd favourite sport over there behind baseball, basketball and American football. The tourists who arrived appropriately in Philadelphia, were – W. Stanser (Rotherham), J. Brown-Sim (Queens Park & Sheffield FC), H. J. Eastwood (West Ham & Ilford), goalie H.M. Lemoine (Arsenal & Shepherds Bush), H.C. Littlewort, George Simon , Fred Houghton Milnes (captain & founder), W.O. Clemson (Newcastle Utd), E.J. Coton (Dublin Bohemians), J.J. Bayley (Clapton), William Davidson (Queens Park), T.T. Fitchie (Woolwich Arsenal), A.K. Campbell (Glossop). All of course, leading amateurs even if they played for top League sides. Scoring freely, with 128 goals netted in 22 games, many by double figures, only Fall River (1-1, 1-2) and Hibernian (0-1) game them a decent game, with Mount Washington (14-0), All Baltimore (11-0) and St. Louis (13-1) being walked all over. Several games attracted attendances in five figures. At this point, Pilgrims were an ad-hoc celebrity touring side, and as with many others, never reformed after the end of the 1st World War. In an interview given by Fred Milne in October 1907 confirmed that the Edwardian touring Pilgrims were not a continuation of the earlier Victorian club of the same name. The club was open to all amateur players he said, they had got all the amateurs currently playing for First and Second Division clubs on their roll, and were about to replace the ostracised (by the F.A.) Corinthians in their traditional annual match with the Queens Park and Newcastle United clubs. They intended to step into the role once held by the Corinthians, and to this end, were relocating to a ground of their own *in Sheffield.* I was puzzled by this remark, but it seems that in 1907, the Football Association were tightening down on amateur players, and stringent definitions suddenly many that many Corinthians players like Woodward, Herbert Smith, Bob Hawkes, and Harold Hardman, having played alongside professionals were being castigated. County Associations were ordered to admit professionals into their ranks, and some, like Middlesex and Surrey refused to do so. The old rows of 1884-5 were starting up again. In response, leading amateur clubs resigned from the FA and started up their own Amateur Football Defence Federation, causing a rift between the two organisations. This quickly became renamed the AFA, and, led by Clapham Rovers and Corinthians, marched forward with the banner of amateurism held high. Various organisations became forced to declare behind whom they stood, the Universities were with the AFA, but the Army and Navy, Essex and Leicestershire came out supporting the FA. The four home countries national associations were ordered not to recognise the AFA causing further rifts, and the schism lasted until the outbreak of the First World War, when rather more pressing matters were at hand. At the end of 1909, the Pilgrims were starting to make themselves unpopular around the British Isles. First came a complaint from Scotland when their advertised team comprising "leading amateurs" was comprised of mostly professionals, and when Thomas Jackson of the recently formed Northern Nomads challenged Pilgrims to a match, "anywhere on a League ground in mid-week" I detected a fair amount of animosity from the North-Western club. I found no activity for the new Pilgrims beyond 1910.

READING MINSTER

Founded - 1876
Folded - 1896
Grounds - Oxford Road (1878)
          Western Elms Avenue (1882)
          Prospect Park (1883)
          Caversham cricket ground (1890s)

During the 1870s, the town of Reading had several half decent football clubs, although of course only the present-day Reading FC have survived. A likely source of footballers was the ancient Reading Grammar school, said to have been founded in the time of Edward VII, and with pupils moving on the the universities, then returning home at Easter and Michaelmas times, as in other towns, the well educated young men of Reading started up football clubs in their home town. The Prince and Princess of Wales came to lay the foundation stone of the 'new' grammar school buildings in 1870, coinciding with when Reading FC, Reading Minster and South Reading clubs were founded. In 1860, Huntley & Palmers cricket club was set up, and the company gave them 12 acres of land known as Kings Meadow to use. In the spring of 1870, the long established Reading cricket club opened a new ground and a fund was set up to erect a new pavilion. Several hundred interested locals donated nearly £300, led by J. Hargreaves who gave a significant sum of ten pounds. In autumn 1871, the *Reading Mercury* began to report on football matches played at nearby Maidenhead, Farringdon, Swindon and Windsor & Eton, and this may have sparked a desire for the town to have its own team, especially when attendances of over a thousand had been reported in nearby towns. The Reading Football Club was founded on Christmas Day by Joseph Edward Sydenham, and acquired the nickname of the "Biscuitmen" as the main employer in town was the Huntley & Palmer Company. Playing on the town recreation ground, they played a series of matches against the grammar school in February and March 1872, suggesting, as with Forest FC and the Forest school, there was an old boy connection. Ending goal-less, it was said that the school had better skills but lacked the greater weight and strength. The club v school match became a traditional season opener, and Readings' first outside opposition came from Henley FC. Reading were playing in blue and white halves, dark trousers at this time. In November 1872, Windsor Home Park came onto Readings' fixture card.

With no prior announcement of their birth, the *Reading Mercury* gave notice on the 1st March 1873, that "a football match would take place this afternoon on the recreation ground, Kings Meadow, *between the town's two football clubs*". Mechanics and tradesmen from the Royal Victoria working mens' club had started up a football club at the end of January, but no title was given, although R. Silver, Reading's mayor, was voted in as president.

Both the Reading and Reading Hornets opened their 1874-5 season on the first Saturday in October, and both were using the town recreation ground. Comparing the two eleven in October, it seems that two or three men played for both clubs.

Reading FC 1874 - Longman, H.F. Rodgers (captain), Miller, Hayne, Wakeman, Cooke, Wells, Mullins, Barnet, Threlfall, Gibson

Reading Hornets 1874 – G.J. Gibson, Miller, A.H. May (captain), F. Boyce, Ewart, Day, Rodgers, Marks, E. B. Haygarth, Sillence, C. Miller (goal).

In January 1875 the Reading FC held a ball at the Englefield House, home of the local Member of Parliament, Mr. Benyon. When Reading FC played the Swifts at Slough in January 1875, E.B. Haygarth was now the Reading captain. I was starting to think that Reading and Reading Hornets were one and the same team, until the two clubs actually met each other on 25th January 1875 on "Mr. Heelas' meadow on the Oxford Road". The Hornets eleven was G. Sillence (captain and goal), K. Mullins and J. Allway (backs), J. Suddaby, H. May, H. Lucas, A. Margrett, L. Simpson, G. Gibson, J. Day, C. Miller, with J. Foster being their umpire. Hornets were no match for the town club, who won 3-0. While Reading FC continued to meet clubs like Maidenhead, Great Marlow, Pilgrims and Marlborough, the Hornets went off the radar, presumably since their low key matches were against working-class opposition. By 1876, another local club, St. Lawrence sprang up in the town, from the school of that name. When Reading FC held their 1876 AGM at St. Mary's parish rooms, president Jasper Simmons declared they had almost ten pounds in the bank. By the end of 1876, two further clubs had been founded, St. Mary's and Reading Strollers. When Reading St. Mary's beat Henley 1-0 in January of 1876, the 'Saints' team were praised for their speed and excellent centres. Captained and founded by the Reverend Charles Mackarness who played half-back, they had only A. Whichelow and W. Hilliar behind him acting as back and goalkeeper, with the rest of the men being forwards - H. Bilson, A. George, H. Hatswell, W. House, C. Hall, C. Thatcher, E. Thatcher, F. Read, and G. Morffew. For some reason, the Reading Mercury newspaper was unobtainable for 1877, just when Reading clubs began to organise themselves for better things. The new Bucks & Berks Cup, made by Messrs Bracher & Sydenham Co., saw entries from Reading FC, Reading Hornets and 'Reading Minster', who suddenly appear out of nowhere. I suspected that the St. Mary's club had changed their name to Minster in 1877. With clubs like Swifts, Marlow, Windsor, Wycombe and Maidenhead now playing strongly, the Bucks & Berks Cup provided a catalyst for football clubs in the area, many of whom had begun to enter the FA Cup.

Oddly, the first Reading club to enter the FA Cup was Reading Hornets in October 1876, and despite being drawn away to the Swifts, only lost 0-2 in Slough. Hornets entered again in 1877, but were demolished 10-0 by Maidenhead FC who had been going since 1870, and were much more experienced. Reading Hornets appear to have been founded in 1873, although I found nothing about them until that FA Cup match. They also seem to have disappeared within a couple of years.

My suspicions that Reading Minster used to be St. Mary's was confirmed when Reading Minster played the Reading FC in February 1878 and the Minsters' had their old name in brackets. G. Sillence was now playing for Reading having left the Hornets, and for the first time, we see the full Minster eleven, which includes well-known superstar athlete Alfred Lyttleton -

H. Bilson

Rev. C. Mackarness

Honourable A. Lyttleton   **C. Thatcher**

E. Winter   A. Wychelow   W. House   F. Wilson   H. Hatsell   A. George   F. Read

Some suggestion that the Minster players were still not altogether *au fait* with Association rules, came near the end, when umpire George Tull awarded Reading a free-kick for 'hands' and the Minster players booted the ball into goal instead, which of course was wiped out! The venue was again Mr. Heelas' meadow on the Oxford Road. When Reading FC opened their 1878-9 season with the traditional match against Pilgrims, they seem to have opted now to play on Reading cricket ground. A great tragedy occurred to the Reading FC, when captain Henry Francis Rogers, was killed on the football field when he suddenly collapsed to the ground without warning, and expired. He was carried into the pavilion tent where three spectator doctors were unable to save his life. The Reading Mercury said "with so many of his friends on the ground, a deathly silence hung over the ground". The post-mortem revealed the 25 year old had a history of fits and an epileptic fit was given as the cause of expiry.

Reading FC's record for the previous season had been 11 wins, 6 draws and 7 defeats in all competitions, and were pleased in reaching Round 2 of the FA Cup. Reading Ramblers were still alive and well, according to secretary A.H. Cane at their 1879 AGM held at the Foresters Hall. The rest of their team going into 1880 was – Jeffries (goal), Osborne and Batten (backs), Barker, Barley, Fox, Cox (four wing-men) and centres Withnall, Plummer and Stock. This 1-2-7 formation was long since out of date in other parts of the country.

In February 1879, the Honourable Alfred Lyttleton may have departed his curateship of St. Mary's, when he took the wardens post at Selwyn College, Cambridge. At the same moment, the St. Giles church football team of London Street, amalgamated with the Christ Church FC to become South Reading FC, as a result of their Church of England Society of Reading membership falling to below 100 persons. Also making an appearance at the start of the 1879-80 season were the Reading Wanderers FC, and South Reading. Initial interest was weak, with secretary J.H. Smart complaining that only three matches had been played from October to Michaelmas, and that the footballers did not keep up their practice sessions.

At the Minster's AGM in July 1879, when forty invited guests sat down to a long supper, concluded by many toasts and speeches, vice-chairman the Reverend N.T. Garry remarked that if, instead of having a rotating goalkeeper (where the nearest man to goal is allowed to use his hands to save a goal attempt) that they should keep one man in that fixed position, then they would not have lost as they recently did, to the Remnants of Slough. This is quite odd, because the position of having a fixed goalkeeper had been established since 1872.

In May 1880, the Reading Minster FC held their AGM dinner at the Upper Ship Hotel, where forty members were dined by Mr. Bailey. Including their captain, E.S. Hillard, all their leading players and officials were vicars, which answers the obvious question! After many toasts to the Church, the State, and Queen Victoria, the Rev. Mackarness recalled how he and a Mr. Kiddle and Mr. Parsons went walkabout in search of a suitable field for use as a ground. Mr. Walter House said that of 10 matches played, they had won 8 and lost 2; the second team had won 5, drawn 1 and lost 1, and the third team had won all five matches. A fourth XI played five but won only once. When the draw for the 1880-81 Bucks & Berks Cup was made at the Queens Hotel, nearly half the entries were from Reading with Minster, South Reading, Reading FC and Ramblers now being joined by the red and blue shirted Reading Abbey club. After a while, I determined that Reading Abbey used to be the St. Lawrence club, led by C.O. Fullbrook. Reading FC may have struggled to find a ground for season 1880-81 when some games were played on the Park House ground. In

December that year, Reading defeated the young Reading Abbey team 2-0 to knock them out of the Bucks & Berks Cup. The Abbey must have continued to improve quickly, as the long established Maidenhead FC could only beat them by 1-0 that year. October 1880 marked Reading Minster's first foray into the FA Cup, along with other Reading sides. Abbey overcame St. Albans 1-0 to progress, but when drawn away to Romford, Minster scratched, probably on account of distance.

In February 1880, Reading's ground was "under much water and the match against Remnants transferred to Mr. Bartholomew's field". At Reading Minster's AGM in May 1881, it was announced that the town now had no less than thirteen football clubs. Sadly, they were now not one of the best, as their 1st eleven had sought out the best and been thrashed. The 2nd eleven had a better year, winning all five matches, scoring 20 goals, and the 3rd and 4th teams did equally well. They played sports all year round, cricket, athletics, but at present they had no ground to play on, and hoped this would soon be remedied.

October 1881 saw the FA Cup come around again, and Minster did well to beat Windsor Home Park 1-0, and were joined in the 2nd Round when Reading Abbey (who used Huntley & Palmers cricket ground) beat Woodford Bridge 2-0. Abbey were eliminated 4-1 by Hotspur, Reading FC had a walkover against West End, and Minster defeated Romford 3-1 to reach the dizzy heights of the 3rd Round. Reading FC went out in the 4th Round without even playing a match after beating Hendon 5-0 in Round 1! A combination of byes and walkovers saw them throw in the towel when drawn away to Great Marlow.

When the Minster met the Reading club in November 1881, the older club comfortably won 4-1 to put Minster out of the county cup. The Minster team was little changed except for the Rev. S.E. Miles in goal and S. Earles at centre forward. When Minster went to play London Hotspur (not Spurs) in the 3rd round of the FA Cup at Christmas 1881, the match was played in a field off the Uxbridge Road at Acton. Played in torrential rain and sleet, the ground resembled a duck-pond, and it was no surprise when no goals were scored. After the match, Minster were given a hearty meal by the father of the Hotspur captain, the vicar of Ealing. Sadly, Minsters were beaten 2-0 in Reading in the replay a week later, played in Prospect Park. By 1881, Minster seem to have caught up on other and were playing a 2-3-5 formation. 1882 saw Reading Minster still fielding four teams each week, but they still didn't have their own ground. At the Reading FC AGM in 1882, it was claimed they were founded "13 years ago" which would make it 1869. Football practice was before office hours, said captain Edgar Field, "and the club nearly died out when initial enthusiasm waned." Reading FC now had 60 players and was a very strong organisation. Young club South Reading were congratulated on winning their first cup in 1881, the Reading Challenge Cup. For the 1882-83 season, it seems that the Minsters secured a ground on Western Elms Avenue, when they defeated Eagles at home in December, on a day when Reading FC found their place in the national hierarchy when the Royal Engineers FC thrashed them 8-0 in the FA Cup at Aldershot. Minster should have been playing Great Marlow in the FA Cup 2nd Round that day, but scratched, after themselves gaining a walkover over the Remnants in the 1st Round.

Season 1883-84 saw an embarrassment for Reading Minster in the FA Cup. Drawn against the powerful Old Carthusians, they were demolished to the tune of 10-1. On the same day, Reading got past South Reading 2-0 to represent the town in the next round alone. March 1884 saw success for the Minsters when they beat Caversham 2-1 in Coley Park to win the Reading Challenge Cup, the final watched by around 1,000 spectators.

The Minsters were again overcome in the opening round of the 1884-85 FA Cup when Hanover United scored the only goal of the tie. Reading FC got past Rochester , and the improving South Reading scored an impressive 4-1 win over the Casuals. South Reading went out out 2-3 in the next round to the Swifts, and Reading were put out by Upton Park to end the town's FA Cup interest for another year. Minster may have resorted to playing on the recreation ground at this time, along with Reading Strollers. December 1883 found them playing at Caversham Place Park. November 1884 saw them play on the Coley rifle range ground, which if it was Coley Park, was sometimes home of Reading Strollers. By the end of 1884, Reading Minsters were forced to field weak 1st elevens when several key players had business commitments. The Reading Cup was retained in April 1885 when Minsters again met Caversham, this time walloping them by a record score of 7-0, with only A. Bilson remaining from their team of the late 1870s, which was now -

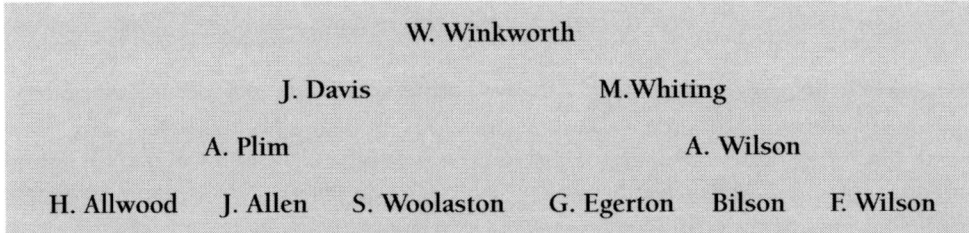

Their efforts in such a brilliant win may have been a tribute to their captain, H.M. Foster, curate of St. Mary's who tragically died from typhus a few days before the final, aged just 27.

September 1885 saw Reading Abbey drop senior football and become Reading Athletics Association, although continued to play in the Temperance League. The popular Reading Challenge Cup gave the town's various junior teams a good competition during the 1880s, with Reading FC deeming themselves too 'senior' to take part. Between them, Minster (1884, 1885) and South Reading (1883, 1886, 1887, 1889) dominated the event during the decade, with Reading Albion successful in 1888.

Season 1885-86 saw Reading FC walloped 6-1 at Rochester in the FA Cup, but South Reading edged past Dulwich Hamlet 2-1 away, with no entry from Reading Minsters that year. Remarkably, South Reading got through to the 4th Round, when both Clapton (disqualified after a 1-1 draw in Reading) and Clapham Rovers (also disqualified) gave them passage in the next two rounds. Brentwood ended South Reading's journey when they beat them 3-0 on 2nd January 1886 at Reading. This was the season when several clubs got thrown out of the FA Cup on the suspicion of having paid or professional players in the team. Many disputed this allegation, but others, like Preston North End held their hands up and said "so what?" By 1885, half the clubs north of Watford were secretly paying their best imported men.

There was no entry from Reading Minsters in 1886 either, as Reading and South Reading seem to now be the top two clubs in that town. South Reading were at this time sub-letting a part of the Caversham cricket ground, the other part being also home to the Reading club. They were also playing in navy or black shirts, as I discovered when they trotted out to play the Swifts one day, and Swifts obligingly returned to the pavilion and changed into whites. Reading still went out at the first hurdle, to Old Carthusians, and

South Reading capitulated to Maidenhead 2-0 at home on 30th October. The same two clubs were again eliminated in the following season at the first stage. 1889 saw an obstacle placed in front of Reading football, when the local squire F.B. Monck, forbade any further playing of football on his Coley Park, "due to excessive rowdyism" and Reading FC and other were suddenly forced elsewhere.

Minster were still struggling on beyond 1890, but many of their players were old hands, and they fell down the town rankings and teams like South Reading began to overtake them, and thrashed them 9-0 that year on their ground by the barracks. With a season's record of won 5 drawn 4 lost 9 for 1890-91, South Reading still had room to improve. They had a big support however, for when they were playing a cup-tie in a field adjacent to the Reading v Marlow match, only fifty people were watching Reading, while over a thousand preferred to turn around and watch South Reading. Strange then, that according to the *Berkshire Chronicle* for September 1891 "South Reading FC have ceased to exist, and that their cup tie clashes with Windsor will be missed". This, despite South Reading winning the Reading Junior Cup only 4 months previously.

The usual Minsters' first eleven at this time was – Knott (goal), Collins and Plim (backs), Blake, Mace and Wilson (half backs) and forwards Baker, Woollaston, Green, Woodland and Hewett.

In 1892, with Reading FC's ground at Caversham cricket club doing them no favours, Reading Minster seem to have fallen down somewhat, as I found them soundly beaten 7-2 by Culham College in March that year, although on the same day, Reading Abbey could only just beat the boys of Newbury Grammar School 4-3. Reading Minster and the Reading FC fell out at Christmas 1893 when Reading tried to cancel a long-standing fixture with them and go off and play the Newbury FC in a cup-tie stead, resulting in letters in the Berkshire Chronicle from W. S. Crake, "Curator of St. Marys' and captain of the Minsters FC". It seems that the Minster and South Reading teams were evenly matched in 1894 when they drew 2-2 in October. In 1894, I noticed that Reading Temperance FC allowed *their* Elm Park ground to be used by Reading FC, whose ground was under water.

Frustratingly I found no reports for Reading Minster or Abbey in 1895, but I discovered that by turning professional that year, the Reading FC alienated themselves from much of the town's older sportsmen. The club was split into two, and those who were anti-professional formed the Reading Amateurs team. They began to play on the newly created Palmer Park grounds, but soon switched to the Caversham ground. With a new ground at Palmer Park, a president James Simonds who was a local Justice of the Peace, they chose colours of amber and gold stripes, and a bright future seemed to beckon them.

As elsewhere, some amateur players began to refuse to play against professionals, as did Slough when drawn against Marlow in the county cup. I then found a report that the Reading Minsters had folded but reformed at the start of 1894, but wins over Abingdon and Wantage showed that they were back on good form. Minster announced a modest fixture card for 1894-95 at their September AGM, appointing W.H. Knott as secretary and the Reverend Sturges-Jones as 1st team captain. Matches were fixed against Abingdon, Wantage, Henley, Basingstoke and Reading reserves, as well as competing in the 7 club Temperance League.

The Huntley & Palmer sports ground had been greatly refurbished with running and cycle tracks, and provision to offer bowls, quoits, tennis and other sports for their employees, and a suggestion was made that all four of the town's amateur teams might play there. I wondered if several of them elected to merge. The park was given over to public use in 1889 (and not 1898 as reported by the University of Reading website) by William Palmer, and a further 20 acres in 1891, after a pavilion by William Ravencroft was erected. There were other parks in Reading, notably Coley Park and Courage Park. By 1900, Huntley & Palmers, the world's biggest manufacturer of biscuits, employed 5,000 people, a tenth of the town's workforce.

This Minster eleven were beaten 4-2 by Wokingham in January 1896:

	Hart	
Murrel		Dahse
Collier	Collins	Dahse
Gilligan House	Plym	Merrett Rossiter

The *Berkshire Chronicle* reported somewhat anticipatory in August of 1896, that the Reading Minsters and Redlands FC (Temperance champions in 1895) have both become defunct due to an inability to consistently raise a good eleven. Collins, Murrel and the Dahse brothers "threw in their lot with Reading Amateurs, along with some old Redlands players" so reported the *Chronicle*.

I found a few matches for the Minsters towards the end of 1896, but think they called it a day at Christmas. December 1896 was the last Reading Minster game I found, when they competed in the Henley Cup. In the middle of that year, I found Reading Abbey FC celebrating winning the Temperance League, with South Reading finishing in 3rd place, having won 14, drawn 2 and lost 7 in all competitions. South Reading then promptly resigned from the Temperance League in the following July. Meanwhile, professional Reading FC, drawing crowds of over 3,000, finished 3rd in the Southern League, against opposition which included Southampton, Tottenham Hotspur. Millwall, Luton and Swindon. Reading Amateurs, playing out of Cavendish Park, now began to enter the FA Cup and Bucks & Berks cups. South Reading FC and Reading Minster were still going in 1889, when I found them drawing 3-3 in a Bucks & Berks Senior Cup tie played at Reading rifle range grounds.

REMNANTS FC

Founded - Circa 1875
Folded - 1883
Colours - Unknown
Grounds - 1. Aldin House, Slough
          2. Wormholt Farm, Shepherds Bush

The Remnants were, if you like, as sort of 'Wanderers rejects' comprised of ex-public school men who were either not quite good enough to get into teams like Wanderers and Swifts, or perhaps took their football a little less seriously than the keenest men. They were based at a field behind a private school in Slough, which itself backed onto the Dolphin Ground of the Swifts FC.

Founded by the Hawtrey family around 1875, their ground was a level and flat four acre field at the rear of Aldin House, which lay at the corner of Langley Road and the London Road. There seemed no obvious reason why the Remnants would rent a meadow from a school, until I delved deeper. On September 22nd 1869, the new headmaster of St. Michael's school was none other than the Reverend John William Hawtrey, formerly an assistant master at Eton college. He was allowed to form his own school, and moved a group of pupils to his new location in Slough, but maintaining connections with Eton College. Several high-flyers of the age were schooled at St. Michael's, including the later Prime Minister Stanley Baldwin, Lord Hawke, Percy de Paravacini, and three who would later own racehorses who won the Derby : Sir James Miller (Sainfoin 1890), Major Loder (Spearmint 1906) and George Baird (Merry Hampton 1887). John Hawtrey's brother Charlie, would find unlikely fame as an early Hollywood film star, and better known as Sir Charles Hawtrey.

Studying old maps of the period, it seems that the pitch must have been turned around ninety degrees in some years, as I found them variously "kicking into the sun" i.e. east to west, or again "playing towards the school goal" which is due south. When later drawing the team players from London, having a home ground in Slough may have proved in itself enough barrier for the club to be successful, as players probably never trained, and simply turned up on the day of the match. The buildings had seen many uses over the years since it was built as a residence for the Baroness Burdett-Coutts (reputedly the wealthiest woman in England who apparently never bothered to live there), and then re-opened as St. Michael's school in the autumn of 1869 . When the school relocated in 1884, the building was bought by Jesuit monks, then in 1897, it was bought by some Bernadine nuns and renamed St. Bernards and used firstly as a convent, and then as a school again from 1906.

When Remnants played Upton Park in January 1878, they were described as being comprised of 'heavy built men' but they still went down 0-3 in their 3rd round tie of the English Cup with this side featuring the still old-fashioned 1-3-6 formation -

		Rev. W. Blackmore		
		Rev. H.T. Wood		
	H. Blackett	**F.H. Rawlins**	**A. Flowers**	
F.A. Govett	**R.D. Anderson**	**W.P. Phillips**	**A. Dear**	**E.M. Hawtrey**

The brief match description lay surrounded by fixtures for hunting appointments in the Berkshire papers which shows that football was very much of small interest in the Home Counties at the time. The casualness with which the team was assembled is reflected when Remnants defeated Reading 3-0 nine months later with an almost completely different eleven, with goals scored by Prior (2) and Fuller. Reading returned the favour in November by beating them at home.

Remnants' name did not appear in the English Cup until season 1878-79, by which time, most of the amateur teams from the London area were seasoned veterans. In round 1, Remnants drew a team called Unity who scratched to them. In round 2, Remnants trounced the Pilgrims by 6-2 and met 'foreign' opposition in round 3 when the location of Darwen had to be discovered on a map of Lancashire. Featured in Keith Dewhursts' book *Underdogs* where he sees the match as the romantic story of the Cup's first working-class heroes, the unknowns of Darwen came back to win the match 3-2 after extra-time to record a famous victory. Dewhurst makes much of the angle of underfed and undersized working-class paupers defeating the aristocratic and moneyed Remnants on their own ground, which further increased Darwen's fame when they took the Old Etonians to three games in the Quarter Final before luck and funds ran out. The story of the Darwen FC is so widely known that I will add no more, except to remark that it was Darwen, not Remnants who contained at least two well paid professionals of some experience. Darwen had moved John Duxbury from full back to goalkeeper, it was his hash-up which led to E.M. Hawtrey opening the scoring for Remnants. However, Darwen equalised on the stroke of half-time when Bury headed home. As the rain turned to wintry sleet, Dear put Remnants ahead once more, only for Will Kirkham to score a second equaliser near the end. Sensing Remnants were tiring, the Darwen captain 'Jem' Knowles pressed for extra-time to be played. Darwen had two pressing factors for the game to be settled there and then; Remnants were worn out and here was the best chance to beat them, and could they take the risk that Remnants might not be better should they come up to Lancashire for a replay? The Remnants captain sensed their tiredness, but he knew that he could not assemble to same team together again for some time, and so he agreed, despite the wintry conditions. Within minutes of the restart, Darwen went ahead when a Jimmy Love shot was deflected through the posts, and that was that: 3-2 to the northerners, and Remnants had become the Cup's first 'giant-killing' victims.

Remnants again entered the Cup in 1879-80 season, only to meet a strong Upton Park side who beat them 5-2 at Tuffnell Park in the replay after the first game had been drawn 1-1. This was the Remnants' line-up at the start of 1879-

Rev. W. Blackmore

T. French   **E. Cooper**

W. Hichcock   **J. Flowers**

A. Dear W.M. Hawtrey Hon. N. Hawke E.M. Hawtrey L.B. Keysar A. Dibbar

Other players utilised in 1879 were – A.G. Hutchins, A.G. Beatson, J.H. Savory, C. Griffiths, W. Blythe, and J.P. Hawtrey. Goalkeeper the Reverend William Blackmore was selected to play for England in their first match against Wales in January 1879, *but failed to turn up!*

His place was taken by stand-in 19 year old Etonian Rupert Anderson, the match abandoned after an hour played in a snow blizzard, to complete a farcical day.

A sometime Remnant was the superb player R. Walpole Sealey-Vidal, a schoolboy prodigy. He was the Victorian 'George Best', and was nicknamed the Prince of Dribblers. He was captain of the Westminster school team, and actually played in an FA Cup Final *whilst still at school* - the only player ever to do so. A superb all-round sportsman, he was a rugby blue, and a good oarsman and golfer, and played county cricket for Devon. Later, active in the world of politics, he rose to prominence on Bideford Council. Obtaining his M.A in divinity, he later became Dean of Hartland. Another sometime Remnant, was Edward Parry (1855-1931), who also played for Wanderers, Swifts and Windsor. Born in Toronto, and following a Charterhouse and Oxford education, he became a schoolmaster at Felsted public school.

Two of the best sides in Buckinghamshire were drawn together in the Berks & Bucks Cup in early 1880 when Remnants were placed against the Swifts . Played on 17th February at the Dolphin Ground, the tie was drawn 1-1, but in the replay at Aldin House a fortnight later, the Swifts stole the match when Hubert Heron (a Wanderers player) sent in a shot out of reach of Hawtrey in goal. Three Bambridges (Swifts) and two Hawtreys (Remnants) took the field, and Swifts had a powerful eleven which included Keith-Falconer (Oxon), Wawn (Civil Service) and A.J. Parry. It sounds as if the Aldin House ground was one of the finest fields

The rear view of Aldin House, in which lay the field used by the Remnants football club. The grounds are currently used as a Catholic Grammar School sports ground, with a running track marked out across where the Remnants played their matches.

on which to play football, described as perfectly flat and protected from the wind. A very fast game ensued, but both goalkeepers were on top form, and chances few and far between.

When Remnants arranged to play the Reading club on the following Saturday 21st February 1880, the players on arrival discovered the Reading ground under several inches of water! So as not to disappoint the visitors, the game was played on the grounds of the nearby Park House thanks to the 'kindness of Mr. Bartholomew' (Newbury Herald). Played in 'torrents of rain and mud' a first half Remnants goal won the game despite Reading having much of the play in the second half. Remnants proved a difficult opponent for the Royal Engineers when the two sides met in the 1st round of the English Cup in November 1880. The first two games had been drawn 0-0 and 1-1, and the Sappers only just edged through in the third game by 1-0, in a game described as 'fast and well contested'. Engineers were still a force, and progressed through to the 4th round, where they were edged out 1-2 by eventual winners, the Old Carthusians. The navy and red hoops of the Engineers and the maroon, pink and light blue colours of the Carthusians must have set a pretty scene for the spectators!

Reports on the Remnants were scarce after 1880, but I found them playing rivals Marlow on Thursday 2nd December of that year, at home. A snippet of information tells us the orientation of the pitch, when Marlow chose to defend the 'house goal', meaning that the pitch was marked out at ninety degrees to Aldin House. Now featuring no less than four Hawtrey brothers – E.C., W.M., A.P.,W.S. - the side included Savory and Cousins at half back, Childs, Keyser, Bird and Dear in attack, with W. Ackerman at full back. Despite winning 2-0, the Remnants' defence was chastised for being "very weak at the back". Competing each season at this time for the Berks & Bucks Cup, Remnants' opposition came from Reading, Reading Abbey, The Swifts, Old Etonians, Windsor Home Park, Grosvenor, Marlow, Maidenhead, South Reading, Wycombe, Chesham Town, Maidenhead Excelsior and Reading Ramblers.

Remnants v. Old Harrovians.

This match was played at Aldin House, Slough, on Saturday, and resulted in a victory for the Remnants after a very fast and well-contested game by two goals to none. The first was obtained by E. H. Parry after a well-combined rush of all the forwards just before half-time, and the second by Dear, who was well backed up by E. M. Hawtrey and A. Parry. For the visitors W. H. Churchill, Davidson, and Colbeck were most conspicuous forwards, while R. de C. Welch kicked very finely. The Remnants played well together, their back play being very strong. The Old Harrovians played one short. Sides :—

Remnants.—W. F. Hawtrey (captain), A. Dear, E. H. Parry, A. Parry, E. M. Hawtrey, and A. R. Hutchins (forwards) ; J. F. Flowers and H. Blackett (half-backs) ; T. French and C. M. Cave (backs) ; Rev. W. Blackmore (goal).

Old Harrovians.—R. de C. Welch (captain) (half-back) ; W. H. Churchill, H. O. D. Davidson, C. J. Colbeck, E. E. Bowen, G. Gordon, and A. J. Whittaker (forwards); A. W. Welch and A. Chater (backs) ; E. S. Gibney (goal).

A typical match report from 1878, giving a very condensed version of the events, the primary objective seeming to be the naming of all who took part. No shirt colours were ever given in 99% of reports, but unusually, the precise location is given, instead of the stock phrase of "played at the ground of the home team".

A county cup tie played at Christmas 1880 saw Remnants call up the services of R. deWelch, J. Hughes, H. Hutchins, W. Currie and A. Scoombs to secure a 3-0 away win at Maidenhead Excelsior.

Remnants play-anywhere and co-founder John Purvis Hawtrey was selected to play for England against Scotland in March 1881 *in goal*. Older brother to the famous actor Sir Charles Hawtrey (1858-1923), J. P. Hawtrey (1850-1925) was also a regular with the Old Etonians, and played for them in the 1879 FA Cup Final against Clapham Rovers. Remnants reached the final of the Bucks & Berks cup final on April 16th 1881, in a game played on Maidenhead cricket ground. A thousand spectators saw a close match where opponents Marlow emerged victors by the only goal of the game. *The London Graphic* remarked that Remnants were fully represented 'with all the Hawtreys'. It is believed that nine generation of Hawtreys went through Eton College. Indeed, John was actually born at Eton College on 25th July, where his father John was lower school master. John, in private life, was a tutor at first and then a journalist, and latterly a writer under the pseudonym of John Trent-Hay.

The Remnants persisted with the English Cup, but were put out 3-2 at the first hurdle by short-lived team West End in 1881. The following year, Remnants scratched when drawn away to Reading Minster, possibly due to travel difficulties, or they were unable to raise a team. They would probably have won that match, since Reading were thrashed 10-1 the following year by Old Carthusians at the same stage. Remnants never again took part. It seems that Remnants folded in the early 1880s which seems to coincide with the time that St. Michael's school relocated and Aldin House was taken over by the Jesuits. One of their last matches was reported in the *Reading Mercury,* when Remnants went play West Reading and the Eagles teams on Saturday 4th February 1882, losing 1-3 on Reading Rec and 0-1 on the Eagles' Coley Park ground. The Remnants eleven were -

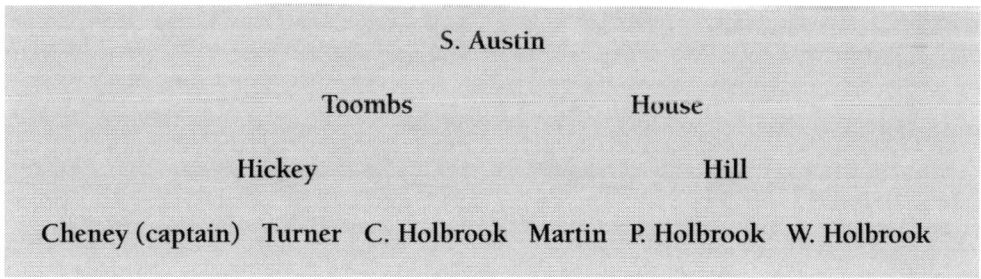

S. Austin

Toombs   House

Hickey   Hill

Cheney (captain) Turner C. Holbrook Martin P. Holbrook W. Holbrook

With many of their well known men no longer in the team, I wondered what became of them. I found two Hawtreys and A. Dear now turning out for the Windsor FC club in January 1883 for their FA Cup tie with Clapham Rovers.

When the Berks & Bucks FA held a general meeting at the Queens Hotel, Reading in December 1884, there were no representatives from either the Remnants or the Swifts. I could find no announcement that the Remnants had folded or even amalgamated with another club, although the Hawtreys did start to play for the Swifts in the next field. Meanwhile, by Christmas 1883, a new club, Slough AFC had started up. From the history of Aldin House as a school, and the school's departure in either 1883 or 1884, and the fact that John Hawtrey was both headmaster and football club captain, it seems evident that the Remnants FC ceased to exist when St. Michaels school was moved away by John's son

Edward to Westgate-on-Sea. When Edward died, the school was re-named Hawtreys and again relocated far away to Oswestry, Shropshire under the wing of wealthy landowner Sir William Wynn-Williams (who had connections with the Ruabon Druids FC). After the War, Hawtreys School moved yet again to Tottenham House, an imposing Georgian mansion house in Wiltshire.

Remnants ground rear Aldin House Slough

The Remnants' ground is still in use today.

SOUTHILL PARK

Founded   -   1876 ?
Folded   -   Unknown, circa 1881
Colours   -   White shirt, navy knicks, scarlet socks (Alcocks annuals)
Ground   -   Green Leaf Lane
Headquarters   -   Rose & Crown Inn, Green Leaf Lane, Walthamstow

Southill Park were a short-lived Berkshire amateur team who competed in the early years of the F.A. Cup, never progressing past the opening rounds. As was the entitlement of the day, any team which became a member of the Football Association, and paid its entry fee could take part in the English Cup. The difference between the weakest and the best was often more than ten goals. The earliest match I found for them was a friendly with the similarly named Southall FC on Saturday 9th December 1876. With R.T. Hughes in goal, and Lloyd Clopton- Jones in attack, Southill Park "played a fast and furious game, attacking throughout, and were unlucky not to score more goals" (*The Sportsman*). Leyton FC provided the opposition when the two sides drew 2-2 on the following weekend, when Southill started the game with only 8 men. Captain E. Mantle scored both Southill goals, who did well to hold on when so outnumbered. Demonstrating that they were becoming a force in junior football, the 1st Surrey Rifles were beaten 4-0 on their own ground in October 1877, but there were stronger opponents to be had. Thankfully, when Southill Park went to play the Cambridge University team in the opening round of the FA Cup at Kennington Oval on 7th November 1877, a defeat by 1-3 was no disgrace against an institution which had pioneered many facets of the early game in the South. New friends must have been found, for they soon arranged a friendly return game, played on St. Johns ground, Cambridge saw a comfortable 4-0 Cantab's victory against this eleven -

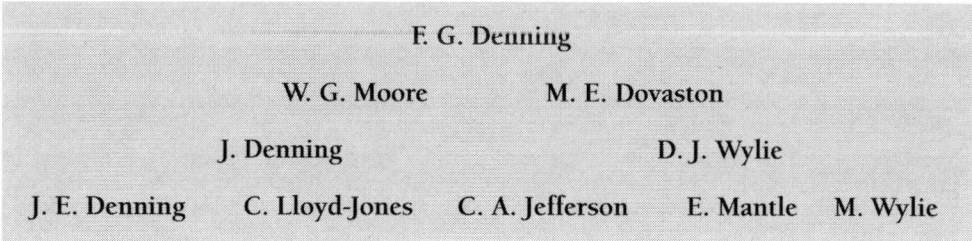

F. G. Denning

W. G. Moore   M. E. Dovaston

J. Denning   D. J. Wylie

J. E. Denning   C. Lloyd-Jones   C. A. Jefferson   E. Mantle   M. Wylie

In February 1878, D.G. Wylie (a name usually associated with The Wanderers) was listed as a Southill Park player when selected to take part in the trials match for the England v Scotland selection committee. Maidenhead FC were visited on 11th October that year , and Southill Park emerged 3-2 winners, although they did play 12 men to Maidenhead's usual eleven (*Reading Mercury*). At the end of the year, the full extent of the gap between strong established clubs and small sides like Southill Park was illustrated when the Old Harrovians thrashed them 8-0 to end their FA Cup run at the first hurdle. The *London Evening Standard* stating the obvious that "it soon became clear that the Harrovians were much too strong, and by half-time had scored five goals, three more being added in the second half ". All six Harrovian forwards scored that day, but no names were given from the

Southill Park team. I did not trace any further results in the English Cup other than those two matches. Bizarrely, the *Nottingham Evening Post* thought it was more important than a single paragraph report, and gave a fuller account. Regional newspapers often simply copied original reports from London papers, but I don't know where they got this match report from. "Southern kicked off for the Southill Park but Harrovians, who had choice of ends, gained little from it. It was soon evident that Harrovians were superior on every point, especially in defence. Bowlby scored on 11 minutes following two corner kicks; Howell, Lowis and two from Prior following series of corner kicks gained by Harrovian pressure brought the score to five-nil. On the change of ends, Southill played much better and until fifteen minutes before time, no further goals were scored ". Thankfully, at the end of the report, a full set of Southill Park names were given as -

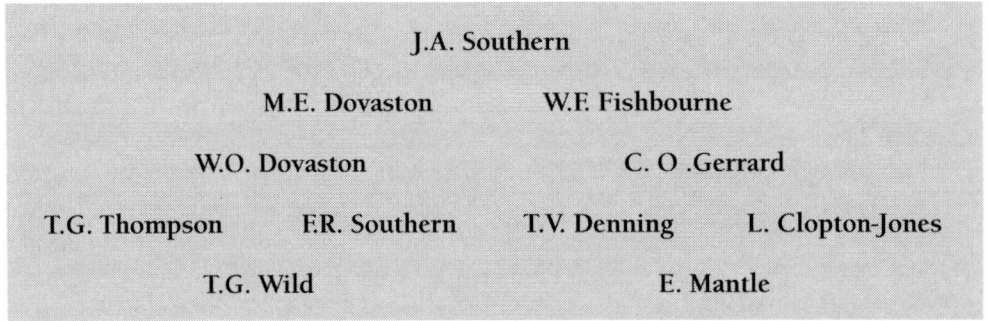

J.A. Southern

M.E. Dovaston   **W.F. Fishbourne**

W.O. Dovaston   **C. O .Gerrard**

T.G. Thompson   **F.R. Southern**   **T.V. Denning**   **L. Clopton-Jones**

T.G. Wild   **E. Mantle**

Well-known Clapham Rovers player Lloyd Clopton-Jones briefly played for Southill in 1878, indeed he captained the team against the Old Harrovians that year. The *Lloyds Weekly Newspaper* tells us that when Southill Park defeated the Pilgrims FC by 5-2 on Saturday 9th February the same year, this was their team, captained by E. Mantis -

W.F. Fishbourne

M.E. Davastone

D.J. Wylie   **W.D. Davastone**

E. Mantis   **Clopton-Jones**   **R.T. Hughes**   **T.G. Thompson**

F.V. Denning   **F.R.Southern**

One wonders whether D.J. Wylie was related to (or indeed was the same man) the John Wylie who played centre for the Wanderers? Notice how Dovaston has become Davastone, and Mantle is now Mantis! A fortnight later, the South Norwood club were beaten 2-1 on their own ground. Season 1878-9 was brought to a close with a 0-6 defeat away to the strong Upton Park club. Yet only a year before, at Christmas 1877, the roles were reversed on the Hampstead ground, when Thompson shone in a 7-0 win over Upton Park. Both teams also played each other in a second eleven game. Southill Park FC simply disappear off the radar when we get to 1880, with nothing being found for them. A sudden folding of a football team usually means an unexpected loss of their ground (which was only rented by the season).

According to Charles Alcock's book of 1879, their ground was "a ten minute walk from Hoe Street railway station", which defines a limit of perhaps a radius of 800 yards. Their base, the Rose & Crown on Hoe Street North (then Green Leaf Lane) is happily extant, resplendent in red and white amidst a street full of shops and curry houses of every kind, and is now well-known for its folk music scene. The Rose & Crown itself is 800 yards from the railway station and at 1876 there were many fields across the road, where now stand Green Leaf and Pearl Roads. A recreation ground was created sometime in the 1880s by the railway station and still exists for the most part, although Walthamstow bus station was built on one half of it. If Southill Park were still active going into the 1890s, they may well have used it, since by then nearly all the fields off Hoe Street North had been built over. Prolonged study of maps around the Rose & Crown across the period 1865-1900 show no obvious reason as to why they disappeared, since at 1895, there were still fields facing the Rose & Crown, where Pearl Road was built. I did trace that an auction of lands to be known as the Green Leaf Park estate was held at the Foresters Arms Coffee Tavern on Hoe Street in April 1881, when one James Pousty sold off 98 plots of land (each for four dwellings), with the money being repayable over 18 years, and interestingly, particulars viewed inside the Rose & Crown. It seems then, that the fields used by footballers were being sold off in 1881, even though it took up to fifteen years for the whole estate to be completed.

1st SURREY RIFLES

Founded - 1867
Folded - Circa 1890
Colours - 1) Royal blue shirts, with gold 'epaulettes', scarlet cap, white flannels
(1873)
2) Red and Black (1876)
3) All White, red and black hooped stockings and cap (1877-8)
Ground - Flodden Road Drill Ground, Camberwell

In 1861, the Volunteer Battalion of the 1st Surrey Rifle Brigade were formed, with headquarters at Brunswick Road, Camberwell, with General Sir George Pollock in command of eight units spread across Camberwell, Putney and Peckham. Based around the Peckham Rifles, members were recruited from the nearby Hanover Sports Club (see Hanover United).

A new railway line had been built through their original drill ground at Hanover Park in 1863, and a new barracks were built on Flodden Road in December 1864 and opened in the following July by the County Lieutenant, the Earl Lovelace. The unit went through several name changes until their departure in 1961.The soldiers' uniform was "rifle green with red facings", and they were conspicuous in the Boer War and the Middle East in the First World War. By 1867, officers and ranks had formed a general sports club, which at first concentrated on competition rifle shooting and athletics. A swimming race was held at Teddington in June that year, where winner of the quarter mile race, G.M. Craufurd (Crawford?), 'won' the captaincy of the team. No records exists of the forming of a football team, and the first time they 'appeared' on the football map was when they entered the English (F.A.) Cup in the winter of 1872. They seem to have reached a good standard, presumable, like the Royal Engineers at Chatham, they were able to practice frequently on the Drill Ground. Again, as at the Chatham barracks ground, where the persistent marching and manoeuvres had worn all the grass away, and a hard earthen surface produced, the Surrey Rifles' drill ground was probably hard earth too. The drill ground was barely of sufficient size as a regulation football ground, just about 100 yards long but its boomerang shape meant that it was probably no more than 60 yards wide, and they may have instead used the adjacent field at the junction of Flodden and Knatchbull Road, being now the houses of Calais Street. Army teams have several natural advantages over civilian teams: they virtually live together, so that tactics and team roles can easily be discussed, and as exercise was encouraged by the military, they could practice on their own ground several times a week, and of course, they were generally fitter than civilian teams. The Flodden Road barracks were half a mile south east of the Surrey Oval, being further along the New Camberwell Road, and the Rosemary Branch and Denmark Hill grounds were also only half a mile away. The parade grounds were sold off around 1952 and the Charles Edward Brooke school built on the site (now called St. Gabriel's College, named after the original Victorian women teacher's training building on nearby Common Road)).

Their English Cup journey began in November 1872 when promisingly, they overcame Upton Park by 2-0, but were put out by Maidstone 3-1 in round 2. The following season saw an early exit as Barnes beat them 1-0 at home. Something must have gone awry in 1874, because they did not enter the Cup that year. Returning in the winter of 1875, they had the misfortune to be drawn against the country's top side, the Wanderers, and were trounced as expected, by 5-0 at the Oval on Saturday 23rd October, with the *Graphic* saying that the Wanderers 'gave them a terrible dressing'. Few 'Rifles' games were reported on other than English Cup ties, but when they travelled to Chorley Wood to play the Herts Rangers on Saturday January 1876, they were beaten 2-1 by the Watford team. In November of 1876, another army team, the 105th Regiment, beat them 3-0 to knock them out of the national cup on the 11th. Played " in mud and fog, conditions under which the footballer seems to revel" *(Graphic),* perhaps the fact that they had only just played the Ramblers at home 48 hours earlier had contributed to their being out of condition. A hat-trick from Hooper for Surrey and a single reply by Ramblers' Swepstone gave them a 3-1 win at the expense of being better prepared for the cup tie. A fortnight later, they hosted the Reigate Priory FC who played in rather splendid chocolate and blue quartered shirts (halves). A Woollaston hat-trick and a fourth from Allport gave then a 4-0 win in a match which *Lloyds Newspaper* described as 'a very fast game'. This could well the same Woollaston who was a regular for the Wanderers, as one private F.W. Sparks was also stationed there, he being a member of the Herts Rangers club.

Surrey Rifles progressed through to round 2 of the national cup for only the second time in season 1877-78 when they overcame the plucky boys of Forest School XI in November. Forest School had been a breeding ground for many public schoolboys who went on to become leading players of the top teams of the day, including Wanderers. The Old Harrovians were a different proposition however in the next round, and when they came to Camberwell on Saturday 29th December 1877, the visitors thrashed this side by 6-0 :-

R.L. Allport (goal & captain)

M.H. Featherstonehaugh

W.P. Haskett-Smith   **E. Maynard**

K. Kirkpatrick   **R. Green**   **P. Shansham**   **J.E. Field**   **E.J. Hooper**

E.C. Thompson   **W.J. Maynard**

Featherstonehaugh, I believe is one of those wonderfully eccentric old English names which is believe it or not, pronounced " Fanshaw". To any American readers, I offer no explanation.

When William John Maynard made his England debut in March 1876 against Scotland, the *Athletic News* said of the new man "he is a very powerful and strong forward". Born 1853, Maynard spent 1878-9 playing with the Wanderers, later becoming County Durham Registrar in 1903, dying in office in 1921. Of the cup-tie, the *London Daily News* had nothing to say, but the *Lloyds News* said that 'the Riflemen played a plucky game but were over-matched against their opponents'. On Saturday 1st December 1877, Surrey Rifles obtain what I think is their best result, when they defeat a Wanderers side by 1-0 at home. A winner from Maynard, and good performances by Allport, Kirkpatrick and Stransham saw then overcome a below strength Wanderers.

Almost no more is heard from Camberwell for a while, except that Surrey Rifles played host to the Pilgrims FC on 2nd February 1878, in a game which finished level at 2-2. The *Lloyds News* said that for the Riflemen, Thompson and the Maynard brothers played well. A fortnight later, once again at home, Surrey Rifles were surprisingly beaten by 3-0 by Runneymede, a side containing some Oxford University men. Despite the home loss, Boucher, Maynard, Thompson, Stransham, and 'Fanshaw' were singled out for praise. I managed to find the playing record for Surrey Rifles, buried in the Kentish Mercury for January 1879, giving their statistics for the previous calendar year. They read – played 17, won 5, drew 1, lost 11, no goals scoring details were given.

One can only speculate whether the football team was disbanded at this point, or whether they were busy in action in Egypt and the Transvaal, but Surrey Rifles did not again enter the English Cup until the winter of 1885. A similar thing happened to Warwick United in 1901 in the Midlands, when, formed as an army team, they were suddenly whisked away to fight in the Boer War, and the club disappeared overnight (*Lost Teams Of The Midlands Revisited, 2020*). This delay turned out to be a bad idea, as they were drawn away to the now ascendant Clapham Rovers who embarrassed them by 12-0. For two once (almost) evenly matched teams to be twelve goals apart suggests that Clapham had improved throughout the 1880s (which we know), but that Surrey Rifles had fallen well back from their previous standard. This adds weight to the idea that their once competent side had folded and reformed with

inferior men. I did find that Surrey Rifles were still competing in the London Cup in 1885, as they were beaten 2-1 at home by St. Judes in October.

The winter of 1886 probably finally convinced them that they should either finally call it a day, or stay out of the national scene, when they were again humiliated in the English Cup, when Upton Park thrashed them 9-0. On the known assumption that they played home games on the Drill field at the side of the barracks, as opposed to a field facing the barracks, then today, that site is occupied by the St. Gabriel's College buildings and sports courts. The old Surrey Rifles barracks are still in use, now home to the London Regiment T.A. and the London Irish Rifles. For anyone wanting to delve even deeper into the lives of the men of the 1st Surrey Rifles, their complete records are held at Lambeth Archives.

THAMES FC

Founded - 1928
Folded - 28th May 1932
Ground - West Ham greyhound stadium, Prince Regent Lane, Custom House, London E16.
Colours - Red and blue quarters, white shorts

Thames FC was a short-lived London club of the late 1920s and early 1930s. They, like Chelsea and New Brighton Tower, were formed by a group of businessmen who decided a professional football team would draw in the crowds to their stadium, in this case, the vast West Ham Stadium , used for greyhound racing and later speedway. The Athletic News calculated that the stadium capacity was 96,144, split between covered and standing (32,798) and open terracing (63,346). They never even got one tenth of that to turn out. The short-lived venture proved a financial flop, as there were too many teams nearby such as QPR, West Ham United, Charlton and Millwall. It was odd before they had even kicked a ball to see their name in the draw for the London Senior Cup when the draw was made in July 1928, placing them away to Millwall. According to the *Star Green 'Un* paper, they were formed in May. The football field was laid out by Kent & Brydon of Darlington. The directors quickly signed players from here, there, and everywhere in a race to assemble a team squad during the summer break. James Martin was signed as a centre forward from Falkirk FC, who scored their first goal in a 2-3 away defeat at Millwall's New Cross ground. Entry into the Southern League (East) in 1928-29 began with a 0-1 home defeat to Brighton & Hove Albion, and this was the usual eleven for Thames that year, with the teams they signed them from in brackets -

	Kelly (Crystal Palace)	
Gilroy (Falkirk)		Phizackerlea (PNE)
McIveney (Bradford)	Hirst (QPR)	Tonner (Orient)
Martin (Falkirk)		Springett (Walsall)
Jones (Swansea)	Gibson (Charlton)	Swann (Huddersfield)

Playing opposition which included champions Kettering, Millwall, Brighton, Peterborough, Bournemouth, Northfleet, Aldershot, Sheppey Utd, Poole, Dartford, Chatham and Grays, Thames finished a fairly woeful 14th (*Folkestone Herald*).

Jack Hebden was signed in December 1929 as a reliable full back, although rather prone to injury, and Donnelley (QPR) whilst C. Landgon was offloaded to Tunbridge Wells Rangers. David Buchanan was the manager for 1929-30, joined by A. Pickles as trainer, formerly the Burnley manager, and he also added Manchester United's Rhys Williams as an outside right to the squad, and Prestwick was offloaded to Hampstead FC. As early as April 1929, Thames AFC applied to join the Football League but only polled one vote, the same as Argonauts, a team which didn't actually exist yet! Entry into the FA Cup in November 1929 was brief, when Fulham dispatched them 4-1 at Craven Cottage on the 30th on a rain soaked pitch. An article in the Daily Herald on the eve of the 1930-31 season stated that Thames had 32 professionals and 3 amateurs on the books, which seems excessive to me considering their shoestring budget.

An improved second season saw them finish 3rd, which gained them entry into the Football League Third Division South in 1930, taking the place of outgoing Merthyr Town from Wales. Their application was backed by West Ham United and Millwall, and their immense ground carried further weight. Sadly, pathetic crowds meant no income, and being in a national League meant much more travelling expenditure. With escalating costs, and no new players to strengthen the team, it was no surprise when they finished 20th and 22nd in their two League seasons. In only their third League season, the directors decided to cut their losses and fold the club, despite an offer from Clapton Orient of a merger, and their place was taken by Aldershot from Hampshire. In April 1931, manager Buchanan was replaced by team captain Jack Donnelly in a surprise move.

Season 1930-31 saw them gain only 34 points, and narrowly missed being relegated anyway, with only Norwich and Newport (on 28 points) below them. Leading scorer in the division Peter Simpson of Crystal Palace, with 46 goals, scored almost as many himself as Thames did (54), and a worrying 93 goals were conceded. Their FA Cup run was limited to ninety minutes when Queens Park Rangers thrashed them 5-0 on 29th November. Thames hit an all time low attendance when just 469 people saw their match with Luton Town on 6th December 1930. It did not help with six rival London clubs also in their Third Division South. Norwich were re-elected but Newport lost their place to Mansfield Town. A public appeal at Canning Town Hall to raise £5,000 of funds in March 1931 fell on deaf ears, but it didn't stop them signing the Notts County captain Haydon Kemp and H. Brown from Newport in August, and sell Fred May to Watford on the eve of the next season.

Season 1931-32 was a disaster of some magnitude, with only 7 wins from 42 League matches, and a terrible 109 goals conceded, all added up to the wooden spoon position. To add insult to injury, free-scoring (111) Fulham won the Third Division, with Crystal Palace and Brentford both in the top five. Once more, the FA Cup 1st Round barrier proved beyond them, drawing 2-2 at home to Watford on November 28th, and losing the replay 1-2 four days later. A crisis meeting was held in December, where voluntary liquidation was on the agenda of secretary H.R. Millbank, who announced in December 1931 that all the Thames players had accepted a hefty pay cut to enable to club to carry on. Trouble was, there had for some time been a trade depression in the docklands, and no orders meant thousands of men laid off or on short time. On the 28th May 1932, Thames announced that they were to resign from the Football League. Secretary Millbank said " lack of funds prohibits us from continuing in the League and we will not compete in any other competition. It is with great regret that the decision to disband has been arrived at but there was no alternative" (Hartlepool Mail).

Thames resigned instead of waiting to be voted out, and Aldershot (35 votes), Newport (36) and Gillingham (41) got back in. They disbanded altogether in May 1932, which was covered in all the regional and national newspapers. Six months later, reported as far away as by the Dundee Courier, all the first team were put up for sale, and auctioned like Roman slaves to the highest bidder. Dimmock, Handley, Kemp, Lennox, Mann, McCarthy, Pritchard, Smith and Spence were all sold, and ten other players were given free transfers.

Their brief record in the League thus ran: played 84, won 20, drew 17, lost 47, goals for 107, goals against 202. They did employ some once famous players, notably ex-international Jimmy Dimmock (1917-1972), who played some 400 games for Tottenham, scoring a hefty 100 goals, a record still held today. He scored the winning goal in the 1921 Cup Final, a competition in which he also scored a further 12 goals. Dimmock moved on to Clapton Orient when Thames were disbanded.

Struggling from the outset, attendances were too low to sustain a professional football team in a city with many others in competition. Crowds over their short life averaged out at just 2,469 - a figure surpassed by several amateur sides. Their biggest attendance being only 8,000 against Exeter City in August 1931. December 6th 1930, saw the largest ground ever to host Football League matches (capacity estimated between 100,000-120,000) achieve

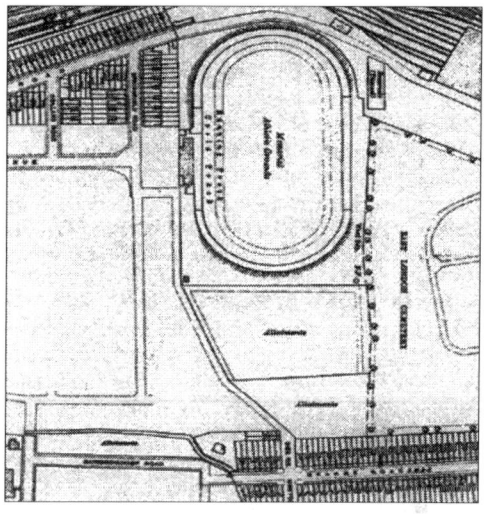

the lowest recorded Saturday attendance for a League, when a minuscule 469 people paid to watch Thames versus Luton Town in the old Third Division South.

The West Ham stadium remained in use until 1972 when it was demolished, causing the famous greyhound race the Cesarewitch to move home to Manchester's Belle Vue stadium. It is now a housing estate, giving no clue as to the fact that it rivalled Wembley Stadium at its height. The vast stadium stretched from Coleman Road to Churchill Road, with Nottingham Road alongside its western edge, the general location being at the junction of the A13 with Prince Regent Lane at Canning Town.

The huge arena which was the West Ham stadium, once home to Thames FC.

THAMES IRONWORKS FC

Founded - 1895
Folded - 1900   (reformed as West Ham United)
Ground - 1895-96 Hermit Road, Canning Town,
         1896-97 Browning Road
         1897-00 Memorial Grounds
Colours - 1895-96 All navy blue with union flag badge
          1896-99 Light blue shirt, white shorts, featuring red sash, red socks
          1899-00 Light blue, white shorts, claret socks

The Thames Ironworks & Shipbuilding Company was London's biggest shipyard, and many of England's largest ships had been built there, including the world's first iron-clad ship, the HMS warrior, and I.K. Brunel's Royal Albert Bridge over the river Tamar in 1850. The ship yard lasted from 1857 until 1912, having built 144 warships for navies all over the world. The last such vessel built at Thames Ironworks being the HMS Thunderer in 1911.

After a period of industrial unrest at the shipyards, foreman David Taylor suggested to owner Arnold Hills that forming a football team would improve worker-management relationships and in July 1895 the football club was announced in the company newsletter, the Thames Iron Works Gazette. Backer Hills did have some football background; he had played for the Old Harrovians, and had played for Oxford University in the 1877 Cup Final, which is probably where the dark blue colours came from.

The club was financed from member subscriptions of half a crown per year, backed up with funds from the company, and soon they had over fifty members, and a large workforce who lived in the vicinity. Ted Harsent became the club's first secretary. The club crest was a pair of crossed riveting hammers, from which comes the familiar West Ham nickname of 'the Hammers'. The first ground was at Hermit Road, when they moved into the vacant ground left behind by the defunct Old Castle Swifts, although, 'ground' was probably a polite description. Variously described as 'a cinder heap' and 'a barren waste land' it was also surrounded by a moat, and the club had to erect a 'fence' made of canvas supported by poles. The word 'moat' suggests some sort of medieval ruins, but in fact the whole area had been marshland for a long time, and what I took to be lanes laid out in an American-style grid, turned out to be drainage channels. The opening game at Hermit Road was a handsome 5-0 win over the deliciously-named Vampires FC from Crouch End, who are still active today. Their opening season saw them compete in the London League and the South Essex League, with their reserve team in its Division Two. Regular opposition included Leyton, Leytonstone, Woodford Wells, Romford, Manor Park, Brentford, South West Ham, St. Luke's, and in the London League, Ilford, Crouch End and Barking Woodville.

Four players were picked up from the Swifts: James Lindsay, George Sage, George Furnell and notably, Bob Stevenson who became the 'Irons' first captain. A leading player was Charlie Dove, who could play anywhere on the pitch. As early as 12th October 1895, the Irons entered the F.A. Cup, but were put out away to Chatham 0-5 after Hermit Road was declared unfit for F.A. Cup use. The start of 1896 saw a successful period when ten straight wins were recorded. Gainsborough Trinity man George was signed, and he went on to become one of their top scorers over the next four seasons. Early success came when the Irons defeated Barking to lift the East Ham Cup in March 1896. It took three games, however to separate the teams: the final was a two goal draw at the Spotted Dog ground in Upton. They returned another twice before the Irons finally won 1-0. Their first season ended most satisfactorily, with 30 victories from 47 matches, scoring 136 against 68.

In November 1896, the *London Standard* reported a court case brought before Mr. Justice Kekewich, listed as Atkinson v Hills. Atkinson was the owner of 'a piece of building land' in Canning Town. Also brought into the court action was Francis Payne, Thames Ironworks Athletic & Football Club secretary, and John Henry Bethel, formerly mayor of West Ham. Atkinson's Q.C.s alleged that the Thames Ironworks AFC had, without permission, turned the land into a football ground, with goal posts and a pavilion erected within a perimeter fence, and posters had gone up advertising forthcoming matches. The defendants' counsel said that the land had lain waste, and that leave of permission had been obtained from Bethel to use it, as he was representing Atkinson charged with selling the land. The judge found in favour of the plaintiff (Atkinson) and granted an injunction against Bethel and Payne. Although the location was not given, the description fits Hermit Road, and if so, then 'the Hammers' would have been forced to quickly find another home, and dismantle and re-erect the stand and fencing there. No mention was made that another team - Old Castle Swifts - had used the ground in the previous year. Perhaps, as they made no 'improvements' on the land, it had gone un-noticed!

The Hammers quickly went from strength to strength, and by the end of 1897, they were top of the London League with only 5 goals conceded, and three of those came in one match. Progress was also being made in the F.A. Cup, as the team won their way through the qualifying rounds which had been introduced in 1888. On the 15th January, the Iron recorded their biggest win of the season when they defeated Bromley by 7-3, and as the end of the season approached, Thames were top of the London League. The big clash came however, in the penultimate match, and when Brentford beat the 1-0 on their Shooters Field ground on April 23rd 1898, the Bees leapfrogged over them at the top by one point. It was all down to the final match. Thames won away to the Grenadier Guards, then heard that Brentwood had been beaten by Barking Woodville, which gave the Iron the title. (*Chelmsford Chronicle*). A great season ended when their application to join the Southern League Division 2 was accepted, and the Iron were on their way up. The Hammers also competed in the London Senior Cup during the late 1890s, but never made a mark.

In January 1897, Arnold Hills found a piece of waste ground on Browning Road, but this proved to be a bad move, as no-one went to see them play there, and soon, they were on the move again. Also, by charging an admission fee and erecting their grandstand, they had violated the terms of their lease, and were given their eviction orders in October. A few months later, and Hills put his hand deep into his pockets and spent some £20,000 on developing the Memorial Grounds into a fine ground, featuring a cinder running track, a large swimming pool, and a cycle track. It is now home to the Phantoms and East London rugby clubs. The new ground was christened by beating Brentford 1-0, and the club stayed there until 1904, by which time they had become West Ham United.

Season 1898-99 marked the club turning professional, somewhat against owner Arnold Hills' principles, but he agreed that it was an inevitability to secure continued success and growth. Hills was a former public school old boy and in fact played for Oxford University in the 1877 F.A. Cup final, lining up alongside such luminaries as Henry Otter, William Rawson, and Edward H. Parry. His brother in law was solicitor Harold Lafone, a player with the Upton Park club. As was often the case at the time, when a one year contract was as much as anyone could hope for, new players came and went in droves. Goalkeeper George Furnell was replaced by Tommy Moore from rivals Millwall Athletic, and practically a whole new side was brought from clubs such as Chatham, Warmley, Grenadier Guards and Inverness Thistle, notably centre forward David Lloyd. Another great season began by beating Shepherds Bush away, and although the Iron fell away somewhat in October, they won 17 of their last 18 matches. With the Second Division title in the bag thanks to 10 straight wins, the Iron showed no mercy to Maidenhead who were thrashed 10-0 to finish the season on a high.

Automatic promotion was not yet universal, and they had to play off against the bottom teams from the First Division. Cowes (I.O.W) were beaten 3-0 and Sheppey United were held 1-1. However, after all that, the Southern League management decided to increase the First Division to 19 teams anyway, and Thames Ironworks were promoted, along with Q.P.R and Bristol Rovers. At this time, Ironworks increased their ground admission prices to 10/6d in the stand (53p) and 7/6d in the ground (37p). Attendances were sometimes into five figure figures, but bigger rivals Tottenham and Chelsea were sometimes getting over twenty thousand. There was a backlash to this price rise, as for the next match, only 1000 people turned out.

For 1899-1900 season, Thames Ironworks obtained a new kit, of claret and blue. This was 'donated' by Aston Villa, who knew nothing about it! The story goes that Charlie Dove's father, a well-known sprinter, was in Birmingham; he challenged some Villa players to a race and won. The Villa men wouldn't 'pay up' and instead gave William Dove a spare kit set which he had the responsibility of washing. The Villa man later reported that they had been stolen off his washing line ! Good job Thames Ironworks didn't draw Villa in the Cup that year ! Thus, when Thames folded, and re-emerged as West Ham United, they unwittingly wore the Villa colours! Most people know that Juventus adopted the Notts County kit, but perhaps this one is a new one to you! Whether this kit was regularly used is hard to say, but when they won 5-3 away at Luton Town in January 1900, Thames were in blue shirts, white shorts and red socks, which the *Luton Times & Advertiser* thought was most patriotic. This was the Ironworks' team that day :-

		Moore		
	Adam		King	
Gilmour		Turner		McEachrone
Allan	McKay	Joyce	Connelly	Walker

On a fine sunny day, a pathetic 300 turned out to see a miserable Hatters performance, going into the break already five goals down.

As a thank-you for how well his club was doing, owner Hill gave a money-pot of £1000 to club secretary Francis Payne, who brought in several more experienced players to bolster the squad. Tom Bradshaw, Bill Joyce Kenny McKay and were obtained from Tottenham. Bradshaw had been capped whilst at Liverpool FC (then a new team only seven years old) , but in all this excitement, the Irons got into trouble with the F.A. and were accused of paying an agent to poach players for them; the agent was suspended for two years and the Iron were fined £25. Payne resigned, and was replaced by defender George Neill. The player in question, Bunyan of New Brompton FC, I believe to be the same Charlie Bunyan who departed from Walsall Town Swifts in 1897, as a goalkeeper; if so, he was also the man between the posts in 1887 when Hyde conceded 26 F.A. Cup goals against Preston N.E.!

The qualifying rounds of the F.A. Cup were battled through, with wins against Royal Engineers (6-0), Grays United (4-0) and Dartford (7-0 away). Their league form was suffering though as a result, and they were trounced 7-0 at Tottenham on 4th November. New Brompton (later Gillingham) were beaten 2-0 in the cup, and only Millwall stood in the way of a 1st round proper appearance. However, in front of a huge 13,000 crowd on December 9th, their cup run came to an end with a 2-1 home defeat. Sadly the Irons' captain Tom Bradshaw died on Christmas Day after a long illness due to 'consumption'. The real reason was more likely a kick to the head he had sustained four years previously which had left him with regular headaches. He was only 26 when he died, from a blood clot to the brain and left a widow and two children. The loss of their talisman seriously affected their performance, and with 7 consecutive defeats they plummeted down the table to finish bottom but one with a playing record of played 28, won 8, drew 5, lost 15, for 38, against 45, giving 21 points. They kept their division one place by winning the Test Match against Fulham by 5-1.

Season 1900-01 saw a radical change. Hill's Ironworks company took over another, and became a public limited company and floated further shares, bringing in more wealth for Hills. Technically resigning from the Southern League in June 1900, they were accepted back into the same, under the new name of West Ham United on 5th July, with Len

THAMES IRONWORKS
FOOTBALL CLUB 1895

Bowen, a works clerk, appointed as secretary. Most of the first team were kept on, save the departing Bill Joyce and Kenny McKay who went to Portsmouth and Fulham, and Albert Carnelly who joined Millwall. Those forwards had scored 45 goals between them that season. The dark blue shirts were replaced with a light blue one, with white nicks and black socks. In the following season, a claret chest hoop was added, which resembles the West Ham shirt from the 1970s. By 1903, the familiar 'Villa style' shirt of claret with blue sleeves was the established kit for the next 110 years.

Hermit Road appears still to be there today, as the Hermit Road Recreation ground, only a few hundred yards south of the Memorial Ground. Of the Browning Road ground, the area behind St. Barnabas church was all fields in the 1890s, and Byron Road was extended across Browning Road and built through that 5.5 acre field. The Memorial Recreation grounds still exist, next to East London cemetery by West Ham railway station. Memorial Avenue led to the ground from the west, which had allotments to the south, and the railway engine sheds to the north, and the cemetery to the east. Entrance gates led to turnstiles into the grandstand on the west side of the ground.

Thames Ironworks circa 1900 in their light blue shirts, with presumably, Arnold Hills in the top hat.

THE CASUALS

Founded - 1883
Folded - 1939 (amalgamated with the Corinthians FC)
Grounds - 1. Upper Tooting 1883-90
          2. Wormwood Scrubs 1890-04
          3. Tufnell Park 1905-14
          4. Essex County Ground 1919-20
          5. East Molesely cricket club 1920-21
          6. St. Joseph's Road Guilford 1921-22
          7. Crystal Palace grounds 1922-25
          8. Richmond Road, Kingstonian 1925-39
Colours - Chocolate and pink halves, navy shorts

Founded in 1883, the Casuals were originally comprised of old boys from Eton, Charterhouse and Westminster only, but soon this widened to other public schools. They based themselves at the Surrey Tavern public house, on the edge of Wandsworth Common, and played there until 1890. The two likeliest sports fields used are the cricket ground in front of the Surrey Tavern, which still sits at the crossroads of the A21 and the B229, or a five acre cricket field with its own pavilion which used to be between the county lunatic asylum and Beechcroft Road, facing Brenda Road. The asylum is now the hospital, and the cricket field is now Pavilion Square, off Beechcroft Road. In the 20th Century, the Casuals were nomadic, and shared grounds all over London.

Their chocolate and pink colours were obtained from the racing silks of the Churchill family, who were benefactors, and not, as I once thought, derived from Westminster school (pink) and navy from the Charterhouse colours. Although generally able to compete with professional clubs, an early severe defeat came on Wednesday 7th January 1885 when Bolton Wanderers trounced them 12-1 at home. A few days later, Casuals went to Nottingham and were beaten 3-0 by Forest club at Trent Bridge. Two years later, Casuals returned and beat Forest 4-1. These were risky and ambitious fixtures for a club only two years old, and rarely able to field its best eleven. On Boxing Day 1887, saw a visit to play Derby County but things went badly from the off. Turning up a man short, Fox dislocated his shoulder and Derby ran out 5-1 winners in front of a 2,000 crowd, who saw Casual's centre Dr. Smith open the scoring. In 1888, Casuals went on what would become a regular feature - a holiday tour- when they played three games against Sheffield teams, winning 4-2 against the original Sheffield FC. Another famous club was met in December 1887, when the Old Etonians came to Upper Tooting, upturning a 1-2 arrears into a 4-2 win, with Jackson and Humphrey scoring for Casuals.

The late 1880s saw disappointments as Casuals lost a series of London cup finals. Swifts beat them 3-0 in the 1887 Charity Cup final, and again by 1-0 in 1888, who themselves found what it felt like when Old Westminsters beat them 6-3 in 1889. In a repeat series, Westminsters were then too beaten by Arsenal in the 1890 Charity Cup final. In 1887, the final of the prestigious London Senior Cup was reached for the first time, but the Casuals had to share the cup with Old Westminsters after a 1-1 draw. Veitch opened the scoring on 40 minutes, but Ingram equalised for the Pinks. After no decision from two hours' play, the cup was shared. The final had already been postponed from the 28th to the 31st, because *no ball had been provided by the Oval authorities!* In the following year, the same clubs again contested the final, with Westminsters winning 1-0. 1889 saw a third consecutive final defeat, when Clapton beat them 4-2. Indeed, further losing finals were played in 1893, 1895, 1896, when Westminsters and Carthusians beat them 3-0, 6-0, and 3-1 respectively. Never before have I heard of a team losing all six cup finals. However, in April 1891, the Casuals got revenge when they beat Old Carthusians 5-2 in the final of the London Charity Cup at Leyton, with goals from Knox (3), Sandilands and Clarke, although the *Morning Post* said that the scoreline was flattering to the chocolate and pinks. Clearly then the top four amateur clubs in London at this time were Swifts, Casuals, Westminsters and Carthusians.

In January 1889, Casuals travelled north to meet Newton Heath, and were just beaten by 1-0. In October that year, the *Sunderland Echo* made much about their team's trip to London to play the Casuals at the Oval, claiming they were the first north of England team to do so. Sunderland were at full strength, and Casuals had borrowed the Walters brothers (Cambridge Univ.) as full backs, and the rest of the side included such luminaries as Charles Wreford-Brown, C. Holden-White, J.G. Veitch, and George H. Cotterill. A month later, Casuals played Everton, who were riding high in the new First Division at the time, who not unexpectedly ran out 7-2 winners at the 10-acre Leyton county cricket ground. Always subject to late withdrawals more than most, Casuals were only able to field two of their advertised eleven, namely W.R. Moon in goal and P.M. Walters. Other top class opposition in the 1890s included three games against Sheffield United in 1892 (3-0, 2-7, 3-1), Lincoln City (2-3), Sunderland (1-2, 2-3), Preston North End (3-4), Old Etonians (2-0), Third Lanark (3-3), Millwall (2-0) and Arsenal (0-8), when a weak Casuals eleven were forced to play centre back Charles Burgess Fry at centre forward. Still, to have the world's greatest all-round athlete in one's team was luxury enough. Another final defeat came in the 1894 Amateur Cup when the Old Carthusians once again proved their masters, edging home 2-1 on April 7th in front of a 3,500 crowd at Richmond Athletic Grounds. It had been the inaugural competition, and had attracted 81 clubs. Their team that day was -

			Harrison			
	Lodge				Hatton	
Richard Barker		Arthur Topham			Grierson	
Robert Topham	Carlton	Perkins		T. Rhodes		W. Rhodes

In a strange move in 1890, Casuals and Old Carthusians fielded a joint team in the F.A. Cup.

In 1891, Casuals won the London Charity Cup for the first time, and went on to win it in 1894, 1897, 1901, 1904, and 1905, and became a dominant name in amateur London football.

In 1905, along with Civil Service, Caledonians, and Ilford, Casuals were founder-members of the Ithsmian League, whilst continuing to play friendly and exhibition matches far and wide, sometimes four or five times a week, more than once fielding different sides in different counties on the same day! The strong amateur principles were upheld, with the league champions receiving *no medals or cups*. The Ithsmian League was recognised as the top league for amateur sides, although one level below the semi-professional Southern League. The Corinthians were very much against professionalism, to the extent that they fell out over the matter with the F.A., when they allowed professional teams into the ranks. Corinthians, Casuals, and other leading amateur clubs then formed their own Amateur F.A., and for some years there existed a rift between the two organisations.

The *Cambridge Independent Press* reported the sudden death on Friday 28th February 1902 of well-known Cambridge & England international player Arthur T.B. Dunn at his home at New Barnet on the previous week. Whitby born in 1860, and educated at Eton and Trinity College, he obtained a Masters Degree, and gained soccer blues in 1883-4, playing alongside William Cobbold (then thought of as the greatest ever centre forward) and J.P. Rawlinson, he also played in two F.A. Cup finals for the Old Etonians. In 1892, now a back, he captained England. Dunn was instrumental in setting up the first stable Cambridge University AFC in 1884, and was its first secretary. Today, leading amateur London area clubs play for the Arthur Dunn Trophy. Famous footballers of the age attended his funeral, and they included Gilbert O. Smith, William Cobbold, W. J. Oakley and W. Gosling. Over a hundred floral wreaths were sent from family and representatives of many regional football associations.

The Casuals in their chocolate and pink shirts, featuring legendary Victorian all-round sportsman and athlete Charles Burgess Fry in the centre of the middle row. Gilbert Smith, an outstanding forward sits on the far left.

In 1908, Casuals lifted the A.F.A. Senior Cup, and repeated the trick in 1913, when they beat New Crusaders 3-2 in the final, which made up for losing the 1909 final. This was a competition put up in opposition to the F.A's own Amateur Cup. February 1925 brought a rare big defeat when they went to Redhill and were trounced 8-1 by the home side, although the *Surrey Mirror* said that Redhill never played so well. After 1925, the Casuals ground-shared with the Kingstonians until 1939 when they joined forces with the Corinthians, at which point they technically became defunct. A nine goal thriller in November 1926 saw Casual lose 5-4 at home to Cambridge University. For the Casuals, Parkes, Jansen, Bird, Adshead and Barnie drew the plaudits. In 1930, the Surrey Senior Cup was added to the trophy cabinet, when they beat Nunhead 2-1 on the Guilford ground, their first trophy for a generation. The first ever Surrey cup final was played on the Reigate ground, where they were later converted (as at Queens Club in Kensington) to tennis courts.

In 1934, Casuals got to the semi finals of the Amateur Cup. After wins over Ilford, Tufnell Park, and Bournemouth Gas, they were beaten 2-1 at home by winners Dulwich Hamlet. Finally, after years of trying, Casuals won the elusive Amateur Cup in 1936 when they defeated Ilford 2-0 (Shearer and Webster) at West Ham in the final on 2nd May, after the first game had ended 1-1 on the Crystal Palace ground a fortnight before. This would have been a very popular victory for all fans of the amateur game across the country. A massive total of 52,064 fans watched both games, when the Casuals side was -

			Huddle				
		Whewell			Evans		
	Allen		Bernard Joy		Couchman		
Shearer	Howard Fabian		Clements		Webster		Riley

Bernard Joy was also playing for Arsenal in the First Division at that time. In their last season as an independent club, Casuals finished as runners up in the Ithsmian League for 1936-7. Their 3rd round 3-0 win over I.C.I was watched by 7,000 spectators. By the 1930s, Corinthians and the Casuals had seen most of their best men retire from the game, and weren't able to replace them with men of the same calibre, and both teams went into decline. A notion that the two sister clubs should combine forces was carried through. On Wednesday 23rd June 1937, a statement by F.G.J. Packington of Palmerstone House, Old Broad Street, E.C.2, said that the Casuals and Corinthians would henceforth be run by a joint committee, of which he was now the joint honorary secretary. Following a meeting on 4th January 1939, the two 'sister' clubs made it formal, by co-joining their names, and were henceforth known as the Corinthian-Casuals. The Corinthian-Casuals have played at Tolworth since 1988. Their Brazilian namesakes, Corinthians (Paulista), continue to play the Corinthian-Casuals in remembrance of their heritage.

THE SWIFTS

Founded   - 1868 (claimed but more likely January 1871)
Folded   - 1894
Colours   - See text
Ground   - The Dolphin Ground, Slough (1873-94)
Secretary - E.C. Bambridge, Bridge Cottage, Shepperton, Surrey

This famous, and almost legendary football club were based at Slough in Berkshire, and their home for many years was the old Dolphin Ground which later became home to various teams representing the town of Slough. Initially comprised of eight members of the Bambridge and Hawtrey families, membership, like the Wanderers, was open to public school old boys. In reading well over 100 match reports, I doubt the Swifts ever played the same eleven twice!

Their home ground for over twenty years, the Dolphin Ground was originally a field behind the old coaching inn of the same name, which lay at the junction of the A4 and the Uxbridge Road. Sadly, it is now underneath the Sainsbury's car park which was built when the Dolphin was demolished to make way for the Premier Inn. The ground had been developed during the middle of the twentieth century, with stands down the flanks, and raised terracing behind the goals, and had a capacity of perhaps 8,000. The Dolphin Ground ended life more associated with greyhound racing than football.

Brainchild of William Samuel Bambridge (1819-1879) who probably had the idea at Christmas 1870, the Swifts were basically a middle class plaything for his sons, although only three of them were really interested in football. Edward Charles 'Charlie' (1858-1935), Arthur Leopold (1861-1923), and Ernest Henry (1848-1917) were the three Bambridge brothers who played for the Swifts and later, the Corinthians. The 1868 date goes out of the window, as 'Charlie' would have only 10 at the time ! Having said that, in a match against Marlow in November 1875, with all three Bambridge brothers on the pitch for Swifts, it would make him 17 at the time. I think that a foundation of January 1871 is more likely, as I found Swifts playing away to Windsor in Home Park in February that year. When the Swifts played Uxbridge in October 1873 to start their season, the *Reading Mercury* said it was the first match on their new ground at the Dolphin Inn. Swifts at this time wore all white with a swift on the left breast and black stockings (*Robin Horton/ Alcocks Annuals*).

Having previously found a Swifts v Windsor match from 1871, then Swifts must have played elsewhere for their first two seasons, although I found nothing on this matter. Mitchell and Butt were the only other named Swifts players from 1871. The return match, played Saturday 11th March, ended in another 0-0 draw. The Swifts' players were said to be the bigger eleven, but a gale spoiled the match, watched by a large number of fashionable spectators in Home Park. Ernest Bambridge was also playing for Windsor (Home Park) at this time.

When Swifts went over to the Maidenhead cricket ground and played the home team there later that month, another goal-less draw was fought out, but a remark which puzzled me was when the reporter said that "the young Maidenhead FC did well against such experienced hands". I could not tell whether he was referring to the individuals of the Swifts, several of whom had been playing for Windsor Home Park, or the Swifts club itself.

According to *Windsor & Eton Express* of August 1872, one William Crowhurst applied to Slough magistrates to move the licence of his Dolphin public house in Langley Marish, to a newly built premises on the Uxbridge Road, which he would call the New Dolphin Hotel. The original building, a house, seemed to have come into the ownership of Mr. Aldin, who erected his St. Michaels school-house in 1865 (see the Remnants FC), and for some reason the building became taken over as part of Mr. Aldin's land and property. Immediately, the Slough & Upton cricket club began to use the field at the rear for their matches, as of 24th June, as they had been looking for a new ground that year. Rental was to be £20 per annum, the ground to be fenced in, with cricket club members given a key. None of the cricket club members seem to tally with any early Swifts FC men. Cricket was still being played as late as the end of October 1872 at the "New Dolphin ground". In December 1872, the Dolphin ground was already in use for football, and I believe the first match ever played there was a cup-tie between Windsor Home Park and Maidenhead. Interestingly, I found the Bambridge brothers and A. Joll playing for WHP that year, while the other Swifts stalwarts, the Heron brothers, were turning out for Uxbridge FC as well as for the Wanderers. Very quickly, clubs and societies made the New Dolphin their base, and it soon became a focal point for the neighbourhood. Proprietor William Crowhurst apparently did not ask any rental fee from some of the small local teams which later played on his ground.

The Swifts players' cultural and social elevation was no better illustrated when they held a meeting at the Literary Institute in April 1875 when 'a large and brilliant attendance' listened to musical performances by soloists and musicians of the works of Beethoven, Donizzetti and Mendelsshon (*Bucks Herald*). The founding father, William Samuel Bambridge had a remarkable life in which money and position provided the opportunity. Born in Windsor, William became a teacher and then went off to be a missionary in New Zealand where he remained for a few years. Returning to England and marrying Sophia Thorington, he resided in Sheet Street, Windsor and then after the children were born, in Adelaide Place, Kings Road. He became associated with the studio of pioneering photographer William Fox Talbot and many of William's photographs adorn the walls of Buckingham Palace. His son William Samuel became Professor of Music at Marlborough College, and George became private secretary to the Duke of Edinburgh.

Affectionately known as "Charlie Bamm" by his fellow footballers, son Edward Charles had a glittering career, both on and off the football pitch. Working for the Lloyds Insurance Co. of London, he gained eighteen England caps and went on to serve on the F.A. committee from 1883 to 1886. As a Corinthian (founder, Nicholas Lane Jackson in 1882), he scored seven goals in 27 appearances for them, and went on to become their honorary secretary from 1923 to 1932. Of Charlie Bamm, it was said 'there was never a finer left-wing player'. Of the other brothers, educated at St. Marks School, Ernest Henry became a merchants clerk on the Stock Exchange, and his football career saw him play for Windsor, Swifts, East Sheen and the Corinthians. He was capped once for England in 1876, and in retirement, moved to Hove, Sussex (1900) and Southend (1910). Arthur Leopold was capped three times for England (1881,1883,1884), played for Upton Park during 1879-84 as well as the Swifts. The census for 1891 finds him living with his family at 57 Bedford gardens, Kensington, and at 12 Edith Villas, Fulham in 1901. It seems he was a widower by 1911 as he alone resided at Norfolk Cottage, Pinner.

As time went on, public school old boys were introduced into the Swifts' team, until it no longer represented Slough (which it never intended to do anyway). Of many celebrated players, possibly the greatest ever Swift was the centre forward William Neville Cobbold (1862-1922), known as "Nuts" by his fellow Corinthians. A wonderfully balanced athlete, Cobbold was regarded as he the 'finest ever dribbler' even decades after his playing days were over. Fellow Corinthians remember his extreme measures in order to avoid picking up any sort of injury, as he would take the field "swathed in rubber bandages and ankle guards" and his perfect balance and peculiar shuffling run resulting in shots of uncanny accuracy from every possible angle. Along with Vidal, the Old Westminster and Wanderers forward, Cobbold was nicknamed "the Prince of Dribblers".

A third legend of the Swifts was Corinthian George Brann (1865-1954). He was an all-round athlete, football being only one of several sports in which he excelled. His main interest however, lay in cricket; he played county cricket for Sussex for twenty years and his career aggregate exceeded 11,000 runs. Other prominent Swifts men included William Crispin Rose (5 caps whilst also turning out for Preston and Wolves), William Francis Pawson (1 cap - and a Royal Engineer), Andrew Watson (3), Edward Brownlow Haygarth (1), and Frank Etheridge Saunders (1 and for also played for Gloucester City), all of whom were also leading players with the Corinthians club. Three of the Bambridge brothers were selected to play for England against Ireland on 23rd February 1884, a unique honour which will probably stand for all time. The casual nature of the middle class amateur game of the 1870s was illustrated when the Swifts put South Norwood out of the English Cup in December 1875; their team included four players borrowed from the Old Etonians FC! Nearly all Swifts' matches for their first three years ended goal-less.

Taken from a group of 1880s footballers, all in different costume, I think that this shows one of the Swifts players from an early Corinthians line-up, when the photographer must have asked the footballers to wear the kit of their own club instead of the white Corinthian shirts.

When the Swifts played out yet another draw against Maidenhead in March 1873 -this time 1-1 – George Turner scored for Swifts, with the others in the team being : Frank Mitchell (captain), F. Bird, Percy Chamberlain, George H. Bambridge (a rare appearance), W.M. Gardiner, Frank Heron, F. Aldworth, H. Ive (goal), G. Turner, H. Wright, W. Case. *The Windsor & Eton Express* made a most interesting remark; "when other clubs are thinking of repose, the Swifts come into active life". This suggests that they never played before the New Year, either because their men turned out for other teams, or were unavailable until after Christmas. UxbridgeFC came to the "new Dolphin ground" on 5th April 1873, and drew 2-2 with the Swifts, with both sides exhibiting good football. Swifts were lucky to get away with a 0-1 defeat when the visitors returned stronger and fitter to the Dolphin in October 1873. The visitors had already played two or three matches and were sharper. The Swifts eleven was much the same as for the Maidenhead game, except that Frank Heron played with his two brothers for the visitors, and Ernest Bambridge took George's place.

The Swifts entered the FA Cup for the first time in October 1873, and were placed at home to the Crystal Palace club. Captained by W.S. Bambridge at half back, and with goalscorer Jeans winning the match, the rest of the team was: E.B. Haygarth and H. Ive (backs), G.H. Bambridge, E.H. Bambridge, A. Joll, M. Jeans, P. Chamberlain, W. Nicholls, G. Pinniger, H. Wright. Edward Brownlow Haygarth (1854-1915) was another cricketer-footballer, who played cricket for his native Gloucestershire and also Hampshire. He also played for the Reading FC, and was a tall, robust figure with a splendid moustache. A 2-1 win (given as 2-0 in most books) over Woodford Wells on November 23rd put them into the 3rd Round, at a time when there only seven clubs left in, although the 'big' names of Wanderers, Oxford University and Sheffield were still in the hat.

Arriving nearly an hour late, Woodford Wells, featuring Tom and Will Spreckley, seemed happy to let Hubert Heron officiate the game. The Swifts got an early measure of the Wanderers, when they met in a friendly in November at the Oval. The final score of Wanderers 0, Swifts 5 raised my eyebrows in amazement, so I searched out a match report and soon discovered the main reason for a woeful Wanderers. They arrived (as they often did) with only seven men, and Swifts lent them forward Maurice, but 11 v 8 proved too much of a handicap. The Swifts also had the three Heron brothers in their team, names who often featured in Wanderers' later FA Cup-winning sides. Swifts' fourth goal, a hopeful punt from the centre circle by half back J.A. Wild, bounced over the Wanderers' goal-keeper's head. Shortly before, another Swifts goal had been ruled out for offside. Luckily, Swifts drew the bye into the semi-final where they came up against previous finalists Royal Engineers, who proved too strong, and ran out 2-0 winners to go into the final for the second time. Played in constant rain at the Oval, yet watched by a sizeable crowd, Engineers scored on five minutes, but it was another hour before they settled the game. Swifts had their chances, once hitting the post, but worse, a centre which eluded the Sappers' keeper only needed prodding over the line, but the slippery ball was altogether missed. The season ended late, in May, with an in-house match between the players of the Swifts. The Heron and Bambridge brothers continued on as the committee for 1874-75 at their September AGM, with W. Nicholls continuing as their goalkeeper. Joll seemed to be the top goalscorer at this time.

In the following season's FA Cup, Swifts unluckily were paired with the Old Etonians, who would go on to be beaten finalists in 1875 and 1876. It took three games to separate the two teams; a 0-0 draw in Slough on 5th November was followed by a 1-1 draw a week later. In the third match, played on the 26th, Swifts were well beaten 3-0 back at the Dolphin. The Wanderers were party-poopers again on Wednesday 7th January 1874, arriving at the Dolphin ground five men short, and were despatched accordingly 3-1. The Wanderers frequently failed to come up with an eleven (even at home), and it seems that all their fame came from mustering their best men only on Cup Final day! A concert given that month put on jointly by Slough cricket club and the Swifts, raised funds to cover the recent expense of re-laying the turf on the ground. Another Wednesday afternoon match a fortnight later saw Swifts lose 1-0 away to Maidenhead.

In January 1875, the Swifts invited the renowned Sheffield FC down to their Dolphin Ground. The Sheffield players were given a reception on arrival by Hubert Heron and one of the Bambridge brothers, and taken on a tour of Windsor Castle prior to the game, which was watched by a crowd of 500 who stood unprotected in pouring rain. After a hard fought match in which both goals withstood many an onslaught, the match ended goal-less with spectators and players running for cover at the call of 'time'. The after match dinner, speeches and toasts received five times the column inches as did the actual game itself, but the gist of it was that Swifts were very grateful for a northern club to come down and play them so that they could measure their own progress to date. This gave an opportunity for Charles Clegg to discuss both their similarities and difference regarding the playing rules. Clearly, rules were not yet universal, since comments were made about handball offences, and that Sheffield play just one man for off-side, whereas London said three. The Swifts' president thought that if offsides were dropped down to one man, it would encourage 'sneaking' (where a forward loiters about the goals, waiting for the ball to come up-field to him). These were the two sides for that important match, refereed by none other than old man George Bambridge who had been a key figure in promoting football in the Slough and Windsor area since the late 1850s.

Swifts :
Hubert and Frank Heron, William and Ernest Bambridge, W. Wright (goal), H. Blackett, H.B. Haygarth, A.H. Stratford, G. Turner, W.B. Fassnidge, H. Talbot.

Sheffield FA XI:
W.E. Clegg, W.H. Stacey, Jack Hunter, A. Wood, W. Orton, E. Bowling, R. Gregory, W.H. Carr, John G. Wylie (a Wanderer), W. Wilkinson.

Admission was set at 6d (2.5p), with carriages at 2s/6d, and admission to the dinner afterwards at the Dolphin Hotel would set you back five shillings (25p). The Sheffield team were regular members of other clubs, such as Exchange, Perseverance, Albion, Heeley,with Wylie often turning out for the Wanderers in London. Their record to the end of January 1875 was played 13, won 10, drawn 2 and lost 1, scoring 29 against 6. A friendly match away to the powerful Oxford University team in March that year, showed that the improving Swifts were near to the best, when they only lost 1-2, after George Bambridge had given them the lead.

The Swifts almost reached the FA Cup final in season 1875-76, when they were edged out by 2-1 in a close semi-final on the Surrey Oval against the 'celebrated' Wanderers, who proceeded to win it for the next three years, thus becoming the first 'folklore' team of English football. In the opening rounds, Great Marlow were defeated 2-0, and South Norwood away by 5-0 on 7th December, which put Swifts into the last eight. In probably their finest result yet, Swifts went to the ground of the Royal Engineers on 29th January and came away as 3-1 winners to reach the semi finals. After eliminating the cup holders, many newspapers gave Swifts as much a chance of winning the FA Cup as any other team. I thought the Swifts did well to hold Wanderers to one goal, but reading match reports, it could have gone the other way. Wanderers must have 'called rank' because Frank and Hubert Heron turned out for them instead of their own club, the Swifts. How Swifts felt about this I can only imagine, luckily no Heron scored that day. Wanderers' opener was fluky and against the play, but Swifts, after making it 1-2, came several times close to an late equaliser.

Swifts opened their 1876-7 season with a friendly away to boys of Eton College, where they ran out comfortable 3-0 winners with this team-

Charles Denton, Edward Parry, G. Talbot, Edgar Lubbock, S. Savory, A. Joll, J. Evans, Philip Novelli, J. Bright, W.E. Bambridge, Charlie Bambridge.

Edward Parry, Edgar Lubbock and Phillip Novelli had all played in F.A. Cup finals for the Oxford University or the Old Etonians, and Parry also played for the Old Carthusians in the 1881 Cup Final.

George Cotterill played for the Swifts against the Canadian XI touring team in 1888.

Cunliffe Gosling, sometime Swifts forward.

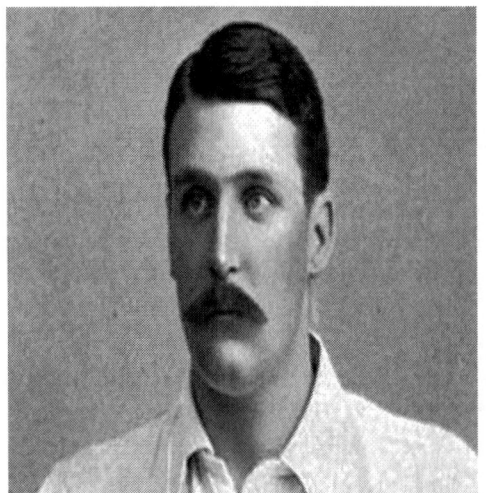

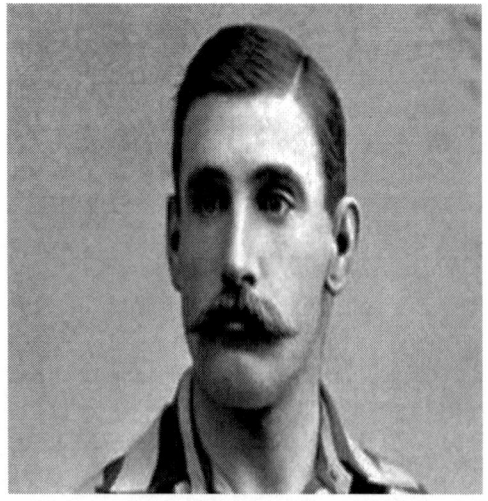

Arthur Walters (above) and Percy Walters (above right), Corinthians, Cambridge and Swifts full backs. They were universally acknowledged to be the finest defenders of the era.

Lubbock was also a regular for the Wanderers. The Sheffield Association had started a tradition of travelling down to play the London FA in 1875, and a year later, following their game on New Years Day 1876, elected to play the Swifts at Slough to make the journey more worthwhile. Fielding a side seemingly half comprise of Wanderers men (Stratford, Otter and the Heron brothers), the *Morning Post* only described the Swifts' goal ten minutes from time when Hubert Heron converted Parry's cross and the match ended 1-1 without further description. When Swifts went over to Eton College to play the school XI on the afternoon of Thursday 31st October 1877, the Eton association game still seemed to be stuck in the past, as 'rouges' were counted in the score. Played on the 'Timbrells' field, Eton won by two goals and two rouges, to the Swifts' one goal. Eton College, needs no introduction, suffice to remind that England's wealthiest sent their sons there to be thrashed - I mean to be educated - to within an inch of their lives (*I think Stephen Fry may have said that*). With such wealthy patronage and long history, you will not be surprised to learn that Eton College owns over 300 acres of the surrounding fields, although much of it floods being adjacent to the Thames, and its several rivulets and brooks coming off it, such as Willow brook and Colenorton. Whilst the old and 'new' college buildings straddle the High Street (then called Slough Road), and the famous 'Eton Wall' backs onto the High Street near to Fellows Pond, 'Timbralls' sits on the other side, between Common Lane and Fifteen Arch Bridge on Colenorton brook. Today, the famous 'playing fields of Eton' are superbly manicured, although I doubt that they were so back in late Victorian times, and as ever, subject to flooding. At this time, 1878, Swifts had 'flipped' their colours and were now in a black shirt with a white swift on the left breast, white knickerbockers and black stockings.

A further indication of the Swifts' ascendancy was when they defeated the Casuals by 2-0 at home on New Years' Day 1879. Captained by A. J. Stanley, Casuals included E.H. Topham and E.M. Hawtrey of the Remnants in their side. A 2-0 away win on the Hendon ground on the following Saturday saw the Wild brothers take the plaudits for Swifts. Entering the FA Cup (then simply known as the English Cup), Hawks were beaten 2-1 in the opening round at home, and Romford by 3-1 in the 2nd, and when they received

The Dolphin Ground shortly before demolition. Photo by Bob Lillyman.

a bye in the 3rd round, Swifts must have thought they could possibly make the final for the first time. A 3rd Round FA Cup match away to Clapham Rovers, played at the Oval on 7th March 1879 turned out to be a disastrous day for Swifts. Captain and talisman E.C. Bambridge received a severe blow to the knee and left the field early on, leaving Swifts to play virtually the whole game with ten men. Clapham were three up at the break, and never looked back, piling on the agony with relentless attacks, and a further five were added, with only a single from Henry Leaf for Swifts' efforts in an eleven that included all four Bambridges.

Two games could not separate the Swifts from the Old Philbertans in the final of the Bucks & Berks cup, at the end of April 1880, and so the trophy was shared, although the Graphic could not understand why they couldn't play a third match. No doubt, the Swifts could not assemble an eleven capable of winning. On Saturday 8th January 1881, Swifts once again met the cup holders, when they faced Clapham Rovers at the Oval in their 3rd round tie. The Morning Post however, merely stated that Rovers- whose team included Norman C. Bailey, Sparks, Parry, Birkett (Wanderers) and Woollaston (Wanderers) - edged through by 2-1 past this Swifts side-

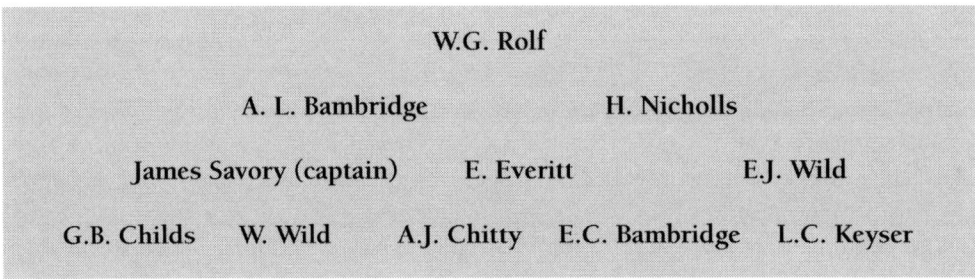

A year previously, when they edged past the Remnants 1-1, 1-0 to enter round 2 of the Berks & Bucks Cup, the side was entirely different to the above, with only Charles and Arthur Bambridge present, in a Swifts side that included Wanderers' men Hubert Heron and Cecil Keith-Falconer. Successful clubs such as the Swifts, Wanderers, Casuals, and Corinthians, drawn from the public school system, would often have up to a hundred members from which to select a team, although of course, as many of them were city merchants, bankers, solicitors, or even clergy, team selection was more a case of who was available as much as who was on form. A 2-0 win over Barnes at Christmas 1881 was marred when midfielder A.G. Paske slipped badly on the icy ground, and players agreed to call time early.

Swifts had a good FA Cup run in season 1882-83. A comfortable 4-1 win over Union was followed by two close games with Upton Park in the 2nd round. Comfortably two goal up in Upton Park, Swifts let it slip and the game finished 2-2; indeed the Uptonians had a third goal wiped out for offsides. Swifts scraped home 3-2 in the replay to enter the 3rd round, where they luckily drew a bye. In Round 4, they met Cup holder the Old Etonians, who had just too much for them, who won by 2-0.

This Swifts side demolished the Old Carthusians by 9-0 at Slough on Thursday 11 th January 1883 -

Arthur Bambridge

T. E. Hughes   P. C. Parr

H. Nicholls   W. Crowhurst (Dolphin owner)   R. Scoons

A. Watson   H.H. Barnett   R. Taylor   E. Wheatley   J. Biffin

At this time, both Bambridge brothers, E.C and A.L, were England regulars. As Swifts players, Charlie amassed 18 England caps, Arthur 3, and Ernest 1. The Swifts probably lost the services of the Hawtrey brothers when the Aldin School closed down in 1883. Full back Percival Parr was better known as the Oxford University goalkeeper, and appeared for them in their F.A. Cup final of 1880 against Clapham Rovers. Capped for England against Wales in 1882, he was for some odd reason, tried out at centre-forward, and must have been a success, as he scored three goals for Swifts against Marlow in their F.A. Cup tie later that year. An old Wykehamist, he was often selected for the Kent county team, but was a barrister in professional life. He later became a partner in the publishing company H.W. Allen & Co.

The team travelled up to Glasgow on New Years Day 1884 to face the formidable Queens Park, who were probably still the world's best team, save for Blackburn Rovers. A 1-5 defeat was no disgrace in front of 8,000 people, for many others, including Aston Villa, had gone the same way before. Swifts men were called up for international duty on 21st March when Will Rose (goal) and Charlie Bambridge (wing) played for England against Scotland at the Oval, with Bambridge scoring on the hour to get England a draw. Billy Rose went on to play in goal for Wolverhampton Wanderers in the 1893 FA Cup final at Manchester.

Turning up on Parkers Piece with only five players is not the way to expect a result away to Cambridge University, and with more than half the Swifts comprised of borrowed men, they could have no complaints when a record score of 0-13 was the end result on 1st November 1884. Five of the Cambridge men – Percy Walters, Frank Saunders, Arthur Bambridge, Frank Pawson and Neville Cobbold were also members of the Swifts club, but Cambridge had first call on their men. By the end of the year, Arthur Leopold Bambridge had to retire from football before he was even 24, due to a knee injury, and he decided to travel and see the world and become a painter, although the 1881 census has the four Bambridge brothers living together at 23 Spencer Road, Battersea.

Their 3rd round January 1885 FA Cup tie with the Old Westminsters went to three games before it was decided. The first match was a 1-1 at Slough, and the replay was a 2-2 draw played on the Oval cricket ground, as Westminsters didn't have a ground capable of holding the several hundred who watched the game. Swifts players singled out for merit included goalie William Rose, Scoons, Rawson and Bambridge. The London Morning Post reported on their third meeting, once more played at the Oval on a cold and semi frozen pitch. A counter attack by Westminsters saw Heath open the scoring, but soon after Swifts were level when Watson delivered a free kick into the goalmouth, and it went in off a Westminster defender's head. Before half-time, a shot by Jones was returned by Sandwith, but only to Swifts' forward Brann who delivered the ball between the posts to put Swifts ahead. No further scoring in the second period saw Swifts progress by 2-1. Swifts unluckily were put out 1-0 by one of the province's rising stars- Nottingham Forest, who went on to reach the semi-final, where Queens Park needed two games to get past them (1-1, 3-0).

Swifts once again played their annual fixture with Forest School at their Snaresbrook ground, when they easily won by 7-1 on the afternoon of Tuesday 3rd November, with E.C. Bambridge getting four of them, including the opening goal which saw him dribble the ball for fifty yards before sending in a powerful shot which went in via the underside of the bar.

Amateur footballers were often all-round athletes who would turn up around the country and take part in athletic events. C. Daft and W. Sheppard were two Swifts players who competed in the April 1885 sports day of the Nottingham Forest club at Trent Bridge.

It was a return trip for the Swifts men, who had played Notts County on the same ground a month previously, beaten 3-0 by the future League side, watched by 3,000 spectators.

The Swifts' journey into the English (F.A.) Cup of 1885-86 saw them become the surprise team of the season, when they trounced the Casuals by 7-1 in the opening round on 3rd October. A 5-1 win over Rochester from Kent on 21st November put them into the last 32.

After a walkover, from Old Harrovians, there came a bizarre ruling from the clueless FA in London who, in attempting to reduce 18 teams down to 8, gave 2 clubs byes, made four teams play each other, and even though 12 clubs were paired off (Swifts drew Notts County) *all twelve were allowed through into the next round.* After 14 years, the FA still hadn't worked out how to eliminate teams down to 32,16,8 etc. One hundred and thirty teams entered, so why couldn't the FA eliminate them down to 128 by playing off four teams in an extra preliminary round, and then the numbers would reduce mathematically down to two? Swifts then found themselves in round 5 where they easily despatched Lancashire village side Church away by 6-2. South Shore proved a difficult opponent in round 6, but a 2-1 win saw Swifts into the semi-finals for their one and only time. However, the other three sides were all powerful clubs from their own regions; West Bromwich Albion and Small Heath from the West Midlands, and the by now legendary Blackburn Rovers, who had won three of the last four cup finals. The Swifts' side at this point was their best ever, featuring Dr. Smith, Lockhart-Mure in goal, E.C. Bambridge, and three star Corinthians in Saunders, George Brann and Holden-White. They put up a terrific fight, but Rovers edged past them 2-1 and went on to beat Albion in the replayed Cup Final. I gained the impression that it was the greater fitness towards the end which tipped the balance for the Rovers.

There were no such stars in a Swifts eleven which got beaten 4-1 in February 1886 on Vincent Square when the *schoolboys* of Westminster outran them with future stars of their own, Ralph Sandilands and C. Page in their eleven. In the following November, Swifts were said to have "eased off" against Swindon Town when the 7th goal was put through the posts in a friendly match where the visitors were clearly outclassed.

The London Charity Cup was a popular vehicle for many old boy's clubs in the late 1880s, at a time when the balance of power in the land had moved away to professional clubs from the Midlands and the North. Swifts became the first winners of the London Charity Cup in 1886-87, and retained it the following season to confirm their status as one of the country's premier amateur sides. Swifts met another leading club, the Casuals, to contest the final of the 1887 London Charity Cup when they met at Kennington Oval on Saturday 22nd March in front of a 1,500 crowd. In a game which did not live up to the expectations from the assembly of star players present, goals from Cotterill and Spilsbury (2) secured a 3-0 Swifts victory. Cobbold and Mills-Roberts (in goal) for Casuals and Challen and Spilsbury for Swifts were 'men of the match' with both sides also having a goal wiped out for offside. Comparisons were clear to be seen, when on the same day, Preston beat Bolton 3-0 to lift the Lancashire Cup, with an attendance ten-fold that of the London Charity cup final. Swifts went on to appear in the next two London finals, beating Casuals 1-0 in 1888 but losing 3-6 in 1889 to the Old Westminsters. Swifts played a combined Oxford & Cambridge universities side (which would famously be resurrected in the 1950s as 'Pegasus') on the afternoon of Wednesday 22nd March on the Renelagh ground at Barnes on the banks of the Thames. A close match remained scoreless until fifteen minutes from time, when Brann opened for the Swifts, but Street soon equalised. A goal by Hewett five minutes from time sealed a 2-1 win for the Swifts.

When the Swifts (by now nicknamed "the Birds") played the Old Foresters in November 1887 at home, star players Holden-White and E.C. Bambridge were away playing for London against Sheffield, and even without the Guy brothers, Foresters inflicted Swifts' first defeat of the season, wining 2-1 at the Dolphin. At Christmas 1887, Swifts played the Forest School on their Snaresbrook field and the boys did well to make a 1-1 draw, with Dr. Smith scoring for Swifts. A seemingly run of the mill fixture in the English (F.A.) Cup played at the Queen's Club Kensington on Saturday 17th December 1887 turned into a moment in football history. At a time when the game still hadn't shaken off the annoying habit of losing sides constantly appealing to the authorities to have their game replayed for a range of frivolous reasons, the visiting Crewe Alexandra team, having been beaten 3-2, protested about the height of one of the goals. Measured by an F.A. official, they were eight feet high to the top of the cross-bar, but the distance should have been to the underneath of the cross-bar (!) and thus, Crewe not only got their way, but Swifts were thrown out of the FA Cup too. This does seem odd to me, as the Queen's Club (now a famous tennis venue and a pre-Wimbledon event) was frequently used for football in the late 1880s and 1890s, principally by the Corinthians, so I would expect that the goalposts were permanently in situ. Anyway, the game became known as the 'two foot rule' match (a wooden ruler which hinged out to 24 inches) and served as a stern reminder to other clubs to check that their grounds met with current regulations.

No one expected anything much when in September and October 1888, a Canadian XI touring team managed by David Forsyth toured Great Britain, but judging by their results, they certainly knew what they were doing. Winning all games in Ireland, it needed Queens Park (3-1) to beat them before they went on to record wins over Sunderland (3-0), Middlesborough (3-2), Hearts (3-0), Newton Heath (2-0) before respectable results against Aston Villa, Blackburn and Notts County. When the Swifts met them at the Oval on Saturday 13th October, I was more interested in a hint as to the Swifts' colours than the result, so when the Sportsman said that you could barely tell the two teams apart, so similar were their costumes, I thought I was on to something. Despite having men like Tinsley Lindley, Holden-White, George Saunders, Harry Swepstone, George Cotterill and Charles Aubrey-Smith on the field, a 2-2 draw was said to have been a representative result. I then found a photo of the Canadian XI which of course, was in black-and-white, but I estimated they were in either all blue or all red. Canada is nowadays associated with red and the maple leaf emblem, but I doubt if they had red trousers back in 1888. In what seemed to be a very promising lead on a website by a Canadian Colin Jose giving a detailed description of all the tour results, and a potted biography of all the Canadians, half of whom were doctors from Ontario district, he didn't manage to state the Canadian colours. A second game with the Swifts took place on 31st October, when the "Birds" sneaked home 1-0, and the Canadians returned home having created for themselves quite a new reputation. Again played at the Oval, opportunity was taken before they departed for home, for some royal patronage to attend, in the form of the Prince Of Wales, the Governor of India and the High Commissioner of Canada, along with Viscount Oxenbridge. The two sides were very evenly matched, and the Canadians were unlucky to lose to a goal scored on thirty minutes by Challen. There was still no mention of colours, nor the resolve of the colour clash which had occurred in their first meeting. No doubt Swifts changed into a white shirt this time, but never in reading over a hundred Swifts' match reports had I found their colours mentioned. If I use a "Famous Footballers" drawing from 1881, then they played in all-white, for Sparks and Charlie Bambridge are depicted in those colours, although Sparks is as much associated with Clapham Rovers, who wore cerise and grey. However, when Swifts played South Reading, the report said that as the two sides wore identical colours, the Swifts *changed into an all white strip*. All this told me was that they *didn't* play in all-white. I was then indebted to a report on the Canadians' match in County Antrim, where the local paper said the visitors entered the field "dressed in dark blue". Thus it appears then, that the Swifts did in fact wear a very similar colour, which could have been navy blue. After countless hours of research, I chanced upon the Bambridge family coat of arms. It was completely in royal blue depicting a suit of armour with yellow detail. This, however, proved a 'red herring'. On the eve of publication, *Dave Moor* of *Historical Kits* and *Robin Horton*, fellow historian informed me that their post-1877 shirts were black!

The touring Canadian XI which played the Swifts, and clashed by turning out in navy blue shirts, when the Swifts wore black, although Swifts generally wore white trousers.

The Swifts' run in the FA Cup was short-lived in 1888-89. They overcame Wrexham in the opening round, but when drawn away to the mighty Blackburn Rovers in the next, Swifts scratched. The Football League season had just commenced, and the dozen professional clubs involved were beginning to pull away from the rest, and Swifts would probably have been on a hiding to nothing. That year onwards, only 32 clubs were permitted in the 1st Round Proper of the FA Cup, all others having to wade through qualifying rounds. The League sides were exempt, but Swifts and Old Westminsters, along with Chatham and Old Brightonians, were the only four Southern clubs who appeared in the 1st Round Proper.

When the Swifts returned to the Forest school grounds on Saturday 10th November in the following year (1888), they arrived with only 6 players. Many old boys teams were under the same sufferance in that, having players who were teachers, lawyers, doctors et al, that they often found themselves struggling to make up an available eleven. Received by the Old Foresters, they had to borrow three men, but were placed at a serious disadvantage when forced to use a schoolboy as their goalkeeper. It only took a few minutes for the Foresters to start scoring, with the poor lad too feeble to save a grown man's shots, and at the call of time, Swifts had conceded seven. The season had started badly with two 0-3 defeats in September, and looking at their eleven, few recognisable names were to be found, save for Piele, Holden-White and O.B. Parry. Presumably professional reasons kept away the Bambridge and Wild brothers.

1888 seems to have been a bad year for the Swifts, who suffered a big defeat in October at the hands of the Old Westminsters. Played at Vincent Square on Saturday 14th, Swifts were leading 2-1 at the break but were beaten 6-3 at the end, despite having England goalie Harry Swepstone and George Brann and E. Charlie Bambridge up front. Westminsters had their own stars too, with Norman Bailey and Ralph Sandilands in a Westminsters team that was having its golden period. Worse was to come, as a fortnight later, Swifts went to Oxford and were thrashed 8-1 by the University side. The last day of the year saw a reversal of fortunes when Swifts got their biggest win for many years, beating the Old Wykehamists by 8-0 with E.C. Bambridge in "International form", scoring several goals, and was well aided by M.M and H.C. Barker in attack. It appears that only some of the Bambridges were now available, and only then at holiday times.

There were no 'big' name now in the Swifts team, save for George Brann, H.E. Morice, and the Rev. F.W. Pawson, and when one of their brothers died in a football accident in the 1889 London Hospitals Cup final in 1889, the Bambridge family gave up football altogether. The fate of one super club – the Wanderers- had already been sealed when the old boys teams called their former players to heel, and clubs like the Etonians, Foresters, Westminsters, and the Varsities began to have their best men back. The Swifts would suffer the same fate and I found their ex-players playing on the same day in other old boy matches.

Some stability must have returned in 1889, with George Brann now the captain and Edwin Sampson in goal, as they drew 2-2 away on the Oxford University Parks ground. Once more, the dark blue halves of Oxford were mentioned, but not those of Swifts. Due to the introduction of Qualifying Rounds, the usual round-per-month system of old was bumped up by two months, and the main competition didn't get underway until the new year. Welsh opposition was met and defeated on Saturday 2nd February 1889, when Wrexham were the visitors in an FA Cup tie. Played for some reason at the Oval, a 3-1 win (given as 3-0 in most books) put Swifts into the last sixteen. Wrexham's reputation caused

Swifts to assemble a powerful eleven, including Swepstone, N.C. Bailey. Holden-White, Brann, Saunders, Wilson and Eddy Bambridge, but Wrexham proved a disappointment, and Swifts were so confident of victory that they did not appeal against a clearly offside Wrexham goal late in the game (*Sporting Life*).

A remarkable match took place at the Oval in October 1889 when Swifts took on the Casuals in a 2nd Qualifying Round FA Cup tie, when a final score of 8-3 was recorded to the "Birds". This was followed by another easy 5-2 away win on the ground of Watford Rovers on 16th November. Next came a result which the history books will find hard to accept, but on December 7th, Swifts went to play Royal Arsenal and won 5-1 at Plumstead's Invicta Ground. Sadly, the high scores were returned in January 1890, when Swifts were trounced 6-1 away to Sheffield Wednesday, who went on to reach the final. Swifts' reputation caused over 7,000 fans to assemble at the Olive Grove ground. Despite a strong eleven, the Wednesday "outmatched them at every point", had a further two more struck off for offsides, and if it wasn't for the goalkeeping of Harry Swepstone "the finest ever seen in Sheffield" then it would have been more, and he got a standing ovation as he left the field.

A thrilling encounter took place at the Dolphin on 27th September 1890, when the Swifts and the Old Wykehamists drew 5-5 in a game of unbridled attacking play which must have delighted the spectators. Two once famous amateur teams found themselves face to face in October 1890 when the Old Etonians met Swifts on the 4th in a humble 1st Qualifying Round FA Cup tie. Eton won 4-1, but got no further, being trounced by Caledonians 6-3 at the next stage. By 1890, a wide gulf had opened up since professionalism had been legalised, not just between Football League clubs and the rest, but between the semi-professional or well supported clubs and the smaller and older amateur sides, who constantly lost their best men to those who had money. Less so, in the South, where only Millwall (1893), Arsenal (1891), Tottenham (1895) and West Ham (1898) went the professional route, from which there was no turning back, as a professional player could not revert back to amateur status then.

In 1891, on Wednesday 4th February, Swifts played Oxford University on the neutral but strangely named Philberds football ground near Maidenhead, the Oxonians scoring the only goal of the game. A large attendance saw a 'fast and interesting game' (*London Standard*). Swifts entered the FA Cup for the last time in autumn 1891, but when drawn away on 3rd October to Wolverton (a railway team who joined the Southern Amateur League), surprisingly scratched. Three days before the scheduled date, Swifts were playing the Royal Military Academy at Woolwich in Charlton Park where they made a 3-3 draw. I can only assume that Swifts couldn't raise an eleven against a side they could have beaten. On that FA Cup day, both Old Westminsters and Old Etonians successfully won Qualifying Round matches when I spotted several Swifts men in action for them instead.

When Swifts defeated Cambridge University by 5-2 at Queens Club on Wednesday 11th February 1892, the *Morning Post* mourned that little was now heard of from this famous old club, suggesting its days were numbered. The re-emergence of leading old boys clubs had led to Swifts' men choosing to play for their traditional clubs, and when the Amateur Cup came along in 1893, teams like Carthusians, Harrovians, Foresters and Etonians intended to have their best men available. Back in their home town, a new club, Slough FC had been formed in the early 1880s and almost immediately joined the Southern Amateur League, where opponents included Windsor & Eton, Tottenham Hotspur (!),

Upton Park, and Old St. Stephens. They don't seem to have set out to rival the Swifts, but with Swifts playing rarely after 1892, no doubt the owner of the Dolphin ground wanted some steady rent from a team that at least was playing at home twice a month.

The earliest matches in Slough were for the Slough Rangers, formed in 1877 with their earliest reported match in February 1880. Slough FC soon appeared and had their own reserve and third sides too. When the "Slough Cricket, Football & Tennis Club" held their *thirteenth* annual sports day on Easter Monday 1890, the venue was the Dolphin ground, so it seems that they probably did play there since 1881, as an offshoot of the cricket club. When another Slough club, the Albion voted to amalgamate with the Chalvey and the Friendly Society clubs in September 1889, it was remarked in the *Windsor & Eton Express* that "at present Slough does not have its own football team, and we suggest a name of Slough & District football club for the new venture". This I fear, is where Wikipedia sources its information about the founding of the team which became Slough Town. In 1887, I found Slough FC, Slough Rangers, and The Swifts all playing concurrently. Slough Rangers changed their name to Slough Athletic in 1882, but must have reverted back a few years later. Old Remnants' men E. Hawtrey and E. Charsley were at the helm of the new club, with Dolphin Hotel owner on the committee.

1893 saw few matches arranged for the Swifts, although they met the 2nd Scot Guards FC on their Brigade ground, Barton-court, Chelsea on 21st January, with a result which showed how far they had fallen. Arriving once more with only nine men, with one a last minute substitute, they were steamrollered 9-0 by a fit and well trained team on a sodden ground covered with pools of water. This was the Swifts side that day -

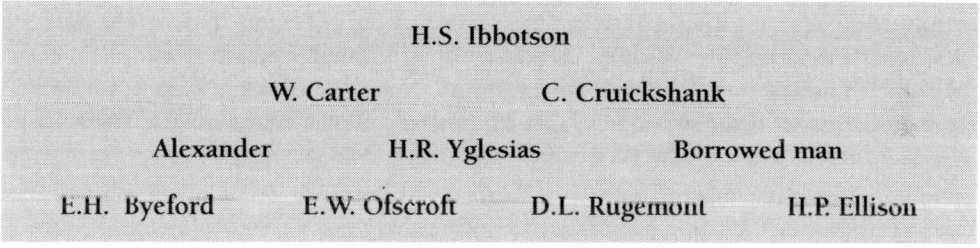

On the 4th March, Swifts played the Military Academy again, the game switched from Slough to Sandhurst. On a firm ground and full sun, an eleven completely different form the ones above and below were defeated 3-1, save for Ellison, but George Brann made a welcome appearance. Presumably arranged when they realised that they would all be present at the annual Boat Race on 22nd March, the Swifts arranged to play a combined Oxford & Cambridge eleven at the Ranelagh Club, Barnes, on the morning of the race, and then presumably walked across the field to watch it. On Saturday 14th October 1893, Swifts suffered another one of those embarrassingly large defeats, consistent with fielding a random eleven, when the Old Westminsters hammered them 13-3 at Wembley Park. Only Yglesias, Idle and Fawlkes were names I recognised, and their goalkeeper- of- the -month was James Wheeler. Swifts seemed to wake up at ten-nil down, as there was still twenty minutes to play.

Noticing that Swifts never seemed to play at home anymore, they went over and played the Old Brightonians on the Elms ground at Walthamstow on November 19th. Originally intended to have been played at the Barnes ground, Swifts fell away badly at the end, and

2-2 became 2-5 when they fielded this team : H. Joseph (goal), T. Wilkinson and J. Wheater (backs), A. Gordon, F. Corbett, A.L. Bambridge (midfield) and forwards E. Cooper, L. Pallairet, J. Davidson, D. Rougemont, and A. Adams. It was the first time for some years that a Bambridge (and especially Arthur) had turned out for the team they had founded.

A traditional fixture with Cambridge University was kept up, and an almost completely different Swifts eleven went to the Corpus ground in November that year. Carter was in goal, with F. Anderson, G. Groves, E. Hilleary and H. Yglesias forming the defence, whilst the attack line was H. Hewett, R. Fawlkes, J. Idle, E. Idle and R. Hilleary. Beaten 3-0, Swifts' failure to score was put down to erratic and weak shooting (Sporting Life).

Reverting to pastures of old, Swifts went to the grounds of the Forest School in December, when at last they won a game, and by 3-1 with goals by Brann and Idle. With the Rev. R.C. Guy returning to the team defending the sticks, and the Idle brothers and George Brann in attack, the team was better than of late.

The same annual fixture with the Cantabs took place in February and November 1894, confirming that they were still an active club. Played at Queens Club, Kensington on 14th February, Swifts surprisingly won 2-1 in a very poor game where it seemed neither set of players exerted themselves too much despite the fine weather. Once more the Swifts' 'pick any eleven from fifty' side contained only Yglesias and Cruickshank of note, with the others being Ibbotson in goal, Pickering at back, Deane and Lorraine at half backs, with Ferney, Bay, Skurray, Groves and 'A. Cantab' in attack (a borrowed Cambridge man).

The Swifts were seemingly still trickling along in September of 1894, when I found their name as being drawn away to a little club called Tottenham Hotspurs in the draw for the London Junior Cup (Division 4) when it was made on 10th September 1894. Listed simply as "Swifts", it turned out to be the Matlock Swifts of Leyton. That Wednesday 7th November 1894 game then, against Cambridge, may well have been the Swifts' final game. With the founding of the Corinthians and the Casuals, players like George Brann and R.C. Gosling now had new teams to play for after the demise of the Swifts. The name of the Swifts was absent at the start of the 1895 season and when the draw was made for the various London cups in September, a list of clubs which were no longer members (i.e. were defunct), included the name of Swifts.

Some sources claim that Swifts were gone by 1890, having amalgamated with Slough Albion to found a new club, Slough Town, but as I have shown above, that cannot be correct.

The demise of the Swifts has more to do with the founding of the Corinthians FC in 1892.

Any merger, which also included the Y.M.F.S. team, did not include the Swifts. It's clear from my findings that a team called Slough Rangers began in 1877, to be joined in town by the football team from Slough Cricket Club by 1880, but they folded around 1887-8 and Slough Rangers, renamed as Slough Athletic also folded at the same time, leaving the town without a local team by 1890. The Swifts had never been intended as a 'team of the people'; they were founded purely for the pleasure and enjoyment of the Bambridge family, the same as the Remnants in the next field for the Hawtreys. It seems that after 1890, Swifts only played random friendlies, and all away from home. A new Slough club (the one to which Wikipedia refers) was formed out of a merger between Slough Albion, Chalvey and the Young Mens Friendly Society as a 3rd version of the town team. This new Slough FC started to play at the Dolphin ground from 1890, entered the new Southern Alliance and became Slough Town. The ground's new owner George Bennett made improvements which included a perimeter greyhound track and the sport became popular. In 1936, Slough Town themselves were evicted from the old Dolphin ground when the 3.35 acre venue was sold to a consortium called the New Clapton Stadium Company, who changed the name to the Slough Stadium. They had no interest in football, only in greyhound and speedway racing, which drew much bigger crowds, and three years later, in 1939, football left the site it had occupied for over fifty years. Slough Town then ground-shared the York Road ground with Maidenhead United, and Slough merged again with Slough Centre FC to become Slough United. Slough then reverted to their previous status and once more returned to the empty Dolphin ground during 1947 to 1973. Once more forced out, they ground shared with Windsor & Eton at their Stag Park ground, but departed for Holloway Park in 2003.

THE WANDERERS FC

Founded   -   1864 (possibly at the end of 1863)
Folded   -   1882
Colours   -   Violet/Orange/Black hoops, white trousers, black socks, caps to match
Grounds   -   Various including Battersea Park, Middlesex county cricket ground, Kennington Oval, Crystal Palace park.
Secretaries -   Alfred W. McKenzie (1859-64)
                 Charles W. Alcock (1864-75)
                 Jervis Kendrick (1875-79)
                 Charles Woollaston (1879-83)

For the average football enthusiast, should you ask them to name a famous football team from the Victorian era, probably the names of the Wanderers or the Corinthians would be the first to come to mind. Wanderers- that legendary yet short-lived team of assembled aristocrats – won the FA Cup five times in a decade to become luminati in their own lifetime. Yet, as we shall see, they were far from invincible in friendly matches, for their trick was to assemble the strongest eleven they could muster for when it really mattered – Cup Final day. During the 1870s, when the Wanderers rose to fame, the team with the actual best playing record were the Royal Engineers, beaten only 3 times in over 80 matches, and two of those were Cup Finals. The Wanderers may well have had the pick of the best footballers from the universities and public schools in the early years, but as time went on, clubs like the Old Etonians, Old Foresters, and Oxford University set out to win the FA Cup by demanding that old boys show allegiance firstly to their *alma mater*. By the late 1870s, some Wanderers' men were now playing *against* them for their other clubs.

When the Wanderers famously threw down the gauntlet and challenged any football club in the world to a game of football, at that time - the mid 1860s - their view of the football world was a very insular one from their lofty position at the very top of the London elite social circle. With strong connections to the military and government, the Wanderers evolved out of the earlier Forest FC who were from Leytonstone on the edge of the Epping Forest. They were initially a club for old Harrovians, but soon sought out the best men form all public schools. Their 'squad' of over a hundred qualifying old boys were from the upper classes and even the aristocracy. The Honourable, and later Lord Kinnaird was in the company of the 1st Baron Knaresborough (Henry Mersey-Thompson), the 3rd Baron Montcrief (Robert Montcrief), the 1st Baron Fitzmaurice (Edmund Fitzmaurice), Baronet Sir James Kirkpatrick, the 1st Baron Kenneth Muir McKenzie, Baronet Sir Samuel Roberts, Francis Pelham the Earl of Chichester, and Bishop Henry Montgomery, and many other lesser titled men, including the son of the prime minister (William Gladstone) and philanthropist Quintin Hogg. Small wonder they almost never fielded the same side twice.

The Forest public school, along with Harrow, Eton, Westminster and Charterhouse, had been playing their own version of football since the 1850s, although due in part to limitations placed upon the boys from the geography of each school's playing field or arena, the game was played to different styles and different rules at each place. Out of that cradle of football sprang the Forest FC, the Old Foresters, and the Wanderers, as well as the capable school team itself. Forest School were one of only eight carefully chosen opponents on the Wanderers' fixture card for season 1865-66, the others being Charterhouse School, Crystal Palace FC, Westminster School, No-Names of Kilburn, Harrow school, Reigate Priory and the Civil Service FC. The season at that time ran only from the start of November till the end of February. Wanderers FC began the 1865 season with 43 members, and were only defeated once in sixteen games.

The Forest FC are said to have changed their name to Wanderers in 1864, although the name of Forest was still playing matches in 1869, so either the name was revived by old Forest players, or the Wanderers was formed by the leading Forest players only. In 1863, this Forest side played Walthamstow in December :-

J. Pardow, F.E. Adams, R. Edmunds, C. Biglands, J.F. Alcock, C.W. Alcock, C.D. Jackson, C.M. Tebbut, W.B. Standidge, A.M. Tebbut, A.L. Cutbill.

Wanderers' first ever game was against the No Names club from Kilburn in 1864, at which point Alcock had decided that they would forgo the expense of running their own ground and make the team a roving one, a nickname which the papers tried to give them in the early years, but it did not stick. Roving was not a universally accepted decision, which seems to have led the dissenters keeping the name of Forest alive, by sometimes turning out under their old name. Secretary Alcock, from his 155 Fenchurch Street, Aldgate address arranged for outfitters Gann, Jones & Co., from number 171 from 16 doors further along the same street to become the suppliers of the Wanderers uniforms. Old maps of Fenchurch Street show that the numbers ran from 1 to 90 on the station side and ran up in consecutive numbers on the opposite side. Alcock's abode is easy to find since it still has "155 Fenchurch Street" emblazoned across the frontage, and more recently was split into several retail and office units, including a Carphone Warehouse shop. Gann Jones seems to have become Gann and Root by 1879 when the Football Association purchased their England football jerseys from them at a cost of £7/2s/0d (£7.10p). Sadly, Gann & Root went bankrupt in 1883, and their location at the corner of Gracechurch Street had been swallowed up with the Marks & Spencer building.

Charles Alcock, famously the originator of the F.A. Cup and the Football Association itself, was 19 at the time, and his older brother John was the team captain. All the other players were of the same age, perhaps except for Standidge who in 1863 was sporting a full length ginger beard. Charles Alcock came from a Sunderland family whose values allowed him to accept the idea that there was nothing wrong with a man earning a living at football as he might as a clerk or mill-worker. It was Alcock doing all the hard work to keep Wanderers at the forefront of the London scene, but after about 1866, he was finding it increasingly difficult to maintain the standard, with players declaring themselves unavailable to play, as their own high flying careers filled their social and business diaries.

When Wanderers met Herts Rangers for the first time in December 1867, *The Sportsman* paper went into poetic overdrive, pouring out quotes from military-inspired stanzas, likening the match to a battle, with the ball being the weapon. Much was made of the distance in miles between the two clubs, and the fact the yet again, Wanderers could only muster seven men, it being clear that everyone else they contacted was either suffering from hangovers or had Christmas parties to go to instead. The result was yet again, a goalless draw. Frustratingly failing to give their true names, some of the Wanderers players were described in familiar style, such as 'Snowball' 'Busy Bee' and 'captain here-there-and-everywhere'! I would guess that 'the latter was Charles Alcock. The goal was defended admirably by a player described as 'N.N's finest'. This again could only be Arthur Pember.

At the start of the 1868-9 football season, *The Sportsman* reported a list of all the association and rugby fixtures arranged by the leading clubs of various codes (teams like Forest School still stuck to their own rules), and the Wanderers played three matches on three consecutive days in October. The Etonians would be met on the 16th, Harrow on the 17th and Charterhouse on the 18th, with even another match scheduled for the 21st against Harrow School. Even this was eclipsed a year earlier when Wanderers, basing themselves in Cambridge for the week in October, arranged a match for every day of the week! Hardly any real goals were scored, most matches ending goal-less and decided on rouges (obtained when a ball crossed the goal-line but outside the posts, and an attacking forward touched the ball down first, as in a rugby try today). The purpose of the 'tour' seemed to be to attract some more players into the ranks of the Wanderers from the Cambridge men, but this proved fruitless. In the match against Eton College, with Kinnaird on the Eton side, the Etonians were the better side; the match against Charterhouse being won with a goal by Charles Alcock after a long dribble. Following a 'week of football' Wanderers then based themselves in Oxford for a week in November, when they played Harrow Chequers, Harrow School, Corpus College, and Oxford University on consecutive days. For the remainder of the season, Wanderers just played once a fortnight against teams such as C.C.C, Harrow Chequers, Hitchin and Charterhouse. Next time a Premier League club complains of two matches in a week, I'll remember this fact!

It seems unbelievable now, but when Wanderers met the Royal Engineers on Wednesday December 2nd 1868 at the neutral ground of the Midllesex county cricket ground, the game almost never took place. Wanderers only brought 8 men, as the absentees believed that the fog and mist prevailing would have cancelled the game, but even worse, no-one had brought the ball. One was eventually purchased from *a toy shop in the town* (Islington). A goal from Lieut. Johnson and a scramble involving Alcock and Baker saw the game end 1-1 amidst dense fog.

FOOTBALL.
WANDERERS v. HITCHIN.

This match was played at Hitchin yesterday, and resulted in a victory for the Wanderers, who scored two goals to nothing. The toss was won by the Hitchin captain, who chose the upper goal with the wind. The superiority of the Wanderers soon became apparent, as the ball was flying about on all sides of the Hitchin posts, which, after about half an hour's play, surrendered to a kick by C. W. Alcock. With the wind and hill the Wanderers immediately commenced once more to pen their opponents, who shortly afterwards witnessed the second overthrow of their goal, a good side kick by H. Emanuel achieving this second score. For the Wanderers W. Rigden and L. Ogden were most conspicuous, and Shillitoe and Parker did good service for Hitchin.

The following were the players :— Wanderers.—C. W. Alcock, H. Elliot, H. Emanuel, H. Head, A. F. Kinnaird, L. Ogden, Hon. T. H. W. Pelham, W. Rigden, C. M. Tebbut. Hitchin Club.—F. Shillitoe (captain), Rev. J. B. Parker, W. Hill, W. O. Atkinson, G. Lewin, E. Logsdon, T. Mainwaring, F. Lucas, G. A. Passingham, L. Thompson.

A typically brief but very much concise match report in the Pall Mall Gazette of 21st February 1868 for the Hitchin v Wanderers match.

Few Wanderers matches from the mid 1860s were reported on in the London press, as such events were of very minor concern to the everyday sporting public, who were much more interested in racing in all its forms, rowing, cricket, horse racing, pugilism, and gambling. When the *Morning Post* of March 1869 already called them 'the celebrated

Wanderers' in its match report of their 3-1 away success against the Old Westminsters played at Vincent Square, they were not referring to the team that had yet to win anything. They were referring to the individual players of the Wanderers' ranks, each of whom came from the elite of London society, many of whom were already either rich or soon to be famous in the world of politics or the government. You were no-one special in the ranks of the Wanderers camp if you were merely a 'right honourable', no doubt those players simply called each other by either their first names, or a nickname gained at public school which would be retained all through their adult lives, within a close circle of friends. In that Old Westminsters match -who were known as the 'Pinks' - goals from Arthur Kinnaird (2) and Neapan overcame a Rawson effort which had halved the half-time advantage. A fortnight later, Wanderers edged home 3-2 against Charterhouse School with a brace from Kinnaird and one from Lubbock. Interestingly, Neapan and Dunn, who had played for Wanderers in the Westminsters game, now turned out *against them* playing for Charterhouse. This would become a common theme which Wanderers would have to take in their stride; comprised as they were of young men and old boys from Westminster, Harrow and Charterhouse public schools, they would frequently find that allegiances were divided from their 'pool' of players, and that men who played with them one week would play against them the next.

Although through Wanderers' pioneering efforts in the greater London area, matches were becoming more standardised in terms of eleven-a-side and the elimination of handling, I noted that when they played the Old Foresters at their Woodford ground on April Fools Day 1869, the game was played 'for the usual hour and a quarter'.

Many of the Wanderers' home games in the late 1860s were played on the Middlesex cricket ground on Caledonian Road. Running north to south from Camden Road to Pentonville Road, no cricket grounds appear on any maps of Holloway in central London from 1850 to 1890, but in 1895 when the whole area had been populated by a network of streets, a large field remaining at the corner with Mark Street by the Caledonian Asylum, now better known as HMP Pentonville Prison, looked the likeliest spot, until I discovered that the prison had been there since 1842, unmarked as such. Studying their results from the 1860s decade, they were not noticeably successful, although rarely beaten, with many games being goal-less draws. One exception to this was when they defeated the Old Bradfieldians 6-2 at Caledonian Road, Islington on the afternoon of Thursday 14th January 1869, with goals from Alf Baker (4), G.G. Kennedy, and C.H. Booman. Just two days later, they were playing at home to the Old Etonians, when this side were held to a 1-1 draw:-

C.W. Alcock, E.E .Bowen, A. Baker, W.F. Higgins, Vere Shaw, R.E.L. Wade, J.M. Yates, T.C. Hooman, C.L. Higgins, G.G. Kennedy, with goalie J. Kirkpatrick notably absent being unavailable.

Results for 1869-70 suggest that Alfred Baker and Charles Alcock were the leading goalscorers. With a roll call of the highest of flyers who quite naturally had better things to do than play football, such as running the country and protecting Queen Victoria's overseas Empire, the Wanderers' team almost never saw the same eleven run onto the pitch one week from the next. A month before the above two games, Wanderers were beaten 2-1 at home by the boys from Chartehouse School, with only Alcock, Tebbutt, Baker and Dixon present in a nine man team from what one would call the Wanderers first eleven.

On Thursday September 23rd 1869, all members of the Wanderers F.C were summoned to attend a general meeting at the offices of the Sportsman magazine at Boy-court, Ludgate Hill. A curious command of 'attend at 4.50pm' was issued, by the club secretary, Charles Alcock, who just happened to work in that same office; later meetings and banquets etc would be held at the luxurious Pall-Mall Restaurant, the Strand. The meeting may have been to inform members that home matches were henceforth generally to be played on the Surrey Oval ground, since Wanderers were involved in 15 of the 18 matches which took place there in season 1869-70. Wanderers were still a way off their best, and the season opened with two 0-2 home defeats, to West Kent and Old Etonians before a run of three wins against Rochester (3-0), Upton Park (2-1) and Royal Engineers (2-1) steadied the ship. A goal-less draw with Gitanos was followed by wins over Civil Service (4-2) and Hampstead Heathens (2-0) before further home defeats came against Crusaders and Desperadoes (both 1-2). In the new year, Wanderers again drew with Gitanos, this time 1-1, before finishing the season on a flourish with wins against Harrow Pilgrims (1-0), Civil Service (3-0), Forest (7-0) and Hampstead Heathens (2-1). Two matches, against Crystal Palace and West Kent, were never played due to frozen ground.

I gain the impression, having read dozens of Wanderers' match reports across a decade, that it was only in the Cup that they defended their honour and reputation fiercely. Ordinary friendly matches were another matter; with a large pool of players to draw from, they were unfortunately subject to their members' other more socially pressing engagements, with many of their players in the military and Civil Service or the Foreign Office. After the initial few years of excitement, Wanderers found it ever more difficult to persuade their far-flung members to turn out, especially on bad weather days. With a season of just November to the end of February, central London would see many dense foggy days to go with the rain and sleet. Little wonder that players could not be coaxed from their country seats! Although most Wanderers' sides featured a backbone of what you might call 'cup final men', they would sometimes field teams with either unknown players, or play games with as few as seven men. And get away with it.

A goal-less draw (a frequent Wanderers' result, which whilst meaning they didn't win as many as you might think, also allowed them to say 'we were rarely beaten') with the C.C.C.C team on Clapham Common on 9th October 1869 featuring G. Lubbock in goal, saw the Penny Illustrated paper say of Wanderers : 'they exhibited an erratic nature of kicking....a lack of direction...and displayed no dribbling'. When Wanderers lost 2-1 at home to Charterhouse School at the M.C.C ground on Caledonian Road, they fielded this weak nine-man side:-

Alcock, Tebbutt, Cutbill, Baker, Dixon, Reid, Carter, Hurley, Yates. When they played the Gitanos at the end of November 1870, Wanderers fielded only 8 men, having said that, they still won 5-0. Wanderers only mustered 7 men when they travelled to play the Upton Park club in the same month, but came away with another 0-0 draw. In 1875, Wanderers actually assembled at Charterhouse to play the School XI with only five men ; Alcock, Emmanuel, Stewart, Gibney and Borwick. This meant that they had to ask the school to make up their numbers, and Burrows, Page, Curran, Reeve, Todd and Lucas duly obliged. At least they were 'qualified' to play for the Wanderers, perhaps they didn't expect to do so whilst still at school!

When Charles Alcock dribbled the ball from the halfway line and sent the ball between the posts for the winner in the game against Hampstead Heathens played on Saturday 4th December 1869, it was said to be 'the best goals seen at the Oval all year'. It was also typical of the Wanderers' low scoring averages, with many games ending 1-1 or 1-0. One exception was in the 'high scoring' 4-2 home win against the Civil Service FC played three days earlier, when Huggins and H.P. Stephens got a brace each. Once again, two Wanderers men - Kirkpatrick and Giffen- played for the opposition against the Wanderers.

I was surprised to find that when Wanderers met the Old Harrovians at the Oval, a week before Christmas 1869, it was the first time that the two sides had played each other. Harrow school had been on the Wanderers' fixture card for five years, but it seems that their old boys team had only recently been formed. Walker scored for the visitors, and Alcock got the equaliser, and the game seemed to be heading for the usual draw, when Openshaw scored a Harrovian winner with five minutes to go.

The Oval cricket ground had no stands when the Wanderers used to play there in the 1870s.

Wanderers' fixture card for the 1869-70 season was published in the Sportsman, with home and away games against extra teams including Gitanos, West Kent, Hitchin, Upton Park and Clapham Rovers, being added to the usual fixtures against the schools and college sides. 1870 seemed to be the year that Wanderers took their game more seriously, and with the advent of the English Cup in 1871, they entered their golden period. A 3-0 win over Civil Service saw the appearance of R.W.S. Vidal, later to become the Reverend Vidal, and christened the 'Prince of Dribblers' by his contemporaries. Notably, three Wanderers men were on the Civil Service side, J. Kirkpatrick, J.F. Giffard, and Quintin Hogg, a philanthropist whose career in politics saw him found the London Polytechnic. The end of February brought the Forest club to the Oval, but Wanderers were too strong, both physically and in age, and ran out 7-0 winners, mainly due to a hat-trick by Baker. The *London Standard* remarked that this was one of the first games played under the strict no-handling rule recently introduced by the F.A. At a meeting of the F.A. Council on Wednesday 24th February 1870, two new rules were pushed through, proposed jointly by Wanderers and Civil Service. The first, and critically important, which drew a deep line between the association and rugby games, was that there would henceforth be a complete ban on handling, the Sheffield F.A. proposing a free kick at the point of offence. The second, was that teams should change ends at half-time *if no goals had yet been scored*. This rule would soon become 'to change ends regardless at half-time'. Previously, ends were changed at the scoring of every goal. This could produce a kaleidoscope of silliness in games with a glut of goals. Amusingly, Alcock 'swapped sides' when the score got to 5-0 to help the Forest boys out! The other very noticeable feature of the game was the bizarre outfit worn by the Forest club, being described as 'all black at the rear, yet bright scarlet at the front, including their caps'. You may recall that the Wanderers were thought to have been an evolution of the Forest FC, circa 1863, but by playing against them in 1870, suggests that Forest had reformed.

Saturday March 19th 1870 saw a demonstration of the Wanderers' strength in depth, when they played two opponents on the same day simultaneously. One Wanderers XI drew 1-1 away to Charterhouse school, whilst another eleven beat Hampstead Heathen 2-1 at the Oval. Forest school held their 1870 sports day in October, and Thomas C. Hooman went along to his old school and competed in the events, winning the 220 yard sprint. Held on a large well turfed area facing the school, Major General the Right Honourable Sir H.K. Storks presided over the events. Kidderminster-born Hooman (1850-1938) was a Charterhouse man who became a merchant shipping broker, rowed for England, and was said to be the fastest dribbler of all time. The 1870-71 season would prove to be Wanderers best yet with only five losses in 37 games.

An interesting game took place in December 1870 against 'Harrow Rovers', a team selected only from the boys of the school. The Harrow game allowed ' a fair catch' and knock-ons with the hands to bring high bouncing balls under control, but the Rovers had to play under association rules, and they were disadvantaged, their two backs frequently forgetting this and constantly conceding free kicks. After Wanderers took a 4-0 lead, the remainder of the game was played to Harrow rules, but the Rovers, possibly overawed by the Oval venue, never played together as hoped for.

Wanderers held their sports day of 1871 on Saturday 8th April on the Lillie Bridge grounds of the Amateur Athletic Club. Every football book states that 'Lillie Bridge is now buried under railway sidings' but studying O.S. maps across 1870-1890 shows a different truth. On the south side of Lillie Bridge Road, West Brompton, lay the sports ground of the AAC, but there were two fields, at right angles to each other. The cricket ground lay hemmed in by Ongur Road where the road crossed the railway by Brompton station. That is probably where the 1873 Cup Final was played; however, Wanderers sports day would have been held on the athletics ground which lay parallel to Lillie Bridge Road. At around 1890, a school was built on the athletics ground, and railway sidings were brought through the cricket ground. Seddlescombe Road was built alongside the former athletic ground, parallel to the railway, which split the athletics and cricket fields apart, and in modern times it has become the IBIS Court Hotel for Earls Court. Around about 1960, the railway sidings were torn up, and the old cricket field became a lorry and coach car park, and the site of the new Fulham Ambulance Station. Location-wise, Lillie Bridge grounds lay 500 yards due north of the present day Chelsea FC home of Stamford Bridge.

As we enter the 1870s, the Wanderers were using Battersea Park as a home venue, but the gas lamps which lit the walkways for afternoon promenaders were of little use to the many rugby, football and other sportsmen who were using the wide open spaces in the winter when the light would rapidly fade in mid-afternoon. More than once, a park-keeper would inform the Wanderers men that he was about to shut the gates at 4.30pm, and that their game must quickly be brought to an end. Kick-off times were usually about 3.15pm, but in an age before public transport, when solicitor footballers couldn't get away from court on time, no match could guarantee any watching public that it would commence on time. The weather too, played a significant part, as the infamous 'London fog' would interfere with games played on low open spaces. When Wanderers somehow beat Brixton 4-1 on Wednesday 9th November 1870, the fog was so dense that "players rushed around like phantoms and no spectator had any idea where the goals were situated" London Daily News. The London fog again featured when Wanderers went over to play the Civil Service FC at Battersea Park in January 1875. This time, the fog won, and the game was abandoned after about forty minutes with no side having scored.

Despite a reputation as a club which did not have its own ground, Wanderers played so often at Kennington Oval (151), that they must have known the ground intimately, and it clearly became their main 'home' ground. At that time, the Oval was merely that, a tree lined ovoid field with a pavilion, a few benches, and a six feet high wooden fence, and bore no resemblance to the modern stadium at all. Vincent Square was also played on over thirty times, although several of them were away to the Old Westminsters or Westminster school, and the Wanderers also travelled to Harrow school about forty times. Battersea Park saw about a dozen Wanderers' appearances.

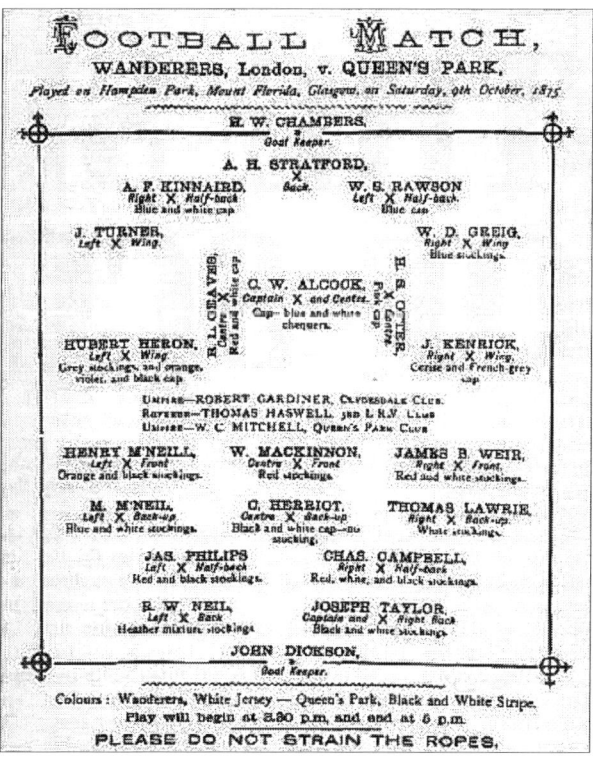

The Queens Park v Wanderers match programme from 9th October 1875, from which we can glean quite a bit of information, particularly regarding the Wanderers' men who wore stockings and caps proclaiming the colours of their primary football club. Kinnaird wears the blue and white cap of the Old Etonians, Alcock the blue quarters of Harrow Chequers, Kenrick the cerise and french grey of Clapham Rovers, Otter the pink of Old Westminsters, and so on.

Wanderers' five F.A. Cup wins in one decade must mean that they were the best club in England, surely? Well actually no, for that accolade goes to the Royal Engineers who only lost five matches in an 85 game run, and two of those were Cup Finals. Indeed, the Royal Engineers defeated a full strength Wanderers team by 2-0 at their favoured ground the Oval on 23rd October 1874. These two giants were the Manchester United and Arsenal of the 1870s, with Oxford University and Old Etonians being the 'Chelsea' and 'Liverpool' of the era. Wanderers bounced back from that surprise home defeat by caning the unknowns of Farningham FC in the F.A.Cup by a staggering 16-0. In an age when goals were not easy to create, this must rank as the biggest win in British football at the time. Who was this 'rubbish' Farningham side? did they even know how to play football? Well, actually, the team was entered into the Cup by Wanderers' own player W.D.O. Grieg, who turned out for them as goalkeeper, which suggests it was a team he had assembled to represent his home town. His brother Albert was in the Farningham attack, with the Piggot brothers. Captain Kingsford helped himself to five Wanderers' goals, with Charles Woollaston getting four, and it was said that without the splendid goalkeeping of Greig, it would have been many more.

Where the Wanderers held the advantage was that, when it really mattered - in the Cup Finals- they could muster their best available eleven, now that all the other sides had been eliminated, and Old Boys' allegiances could be put aside. There was no such concept of being 'cup-tied' in the early decade of the FA Cup, although the Sheffield FA had followed that principle for years. The first F.A. Cup was, in all honesty, a bit of a shambles. Half the games were never played, wildly hopeful no-hopers from schools and the countryside all withdrew or scratched, and even Wanderers' long awaited clash with Queens Park ran out as a damp squib as neither side could score in London. Even the Cup Final winning goal was scored by a 'ringer'. The huge distance involved from Glasgow, which probably took an entire day and night by train and carriages, probably exhausted the best out of the 'Spiders'. Even a whip-round from Wanderers players was not sufficient to permit an epic return journey from Queens Park, who reluctantly had to scratch and allow Wanderers into the final to face Royal Engineers. Betting money was 7-4 on to the Sappers on Cup Final day, 16th March 1872, but a single goal by Morton Peto Betts after a run by R.Walpole-Sealey Vidal secured the first ever cup final for the Londoners. Betts had earlier played for Harrow Chequers, and so played under a pseudonym of 'A.H. Chequer'. I found several different published line-ups for the Wanderers that day in regional newspapers. Whilst several list Morton Betts as 'A.H. Chequer', the knowledgable *Sheffield Independent* gives his real name, as did *Bells Life*. The *Morning Post* names R.C. Wilson and H.E. Crawford when it seems that Edwin Bowen and Robert Walpole-Sealey Vidal played instead. No doubt, those two men became unavailable on the morning of the match and were substituted. Another man listed to have played was unknown Rev. Henry Stewart (but didn't), but since he played in an earlier round for his Cambridge University team, would have been disqualified if his name had come out. The attendance at the Oval was a disappointing 2,000 but with the admission set high at a shilling, few ordinary people could afford it. Ordinary matches in Sheffield and Birmingham cost just 2d or 3d by comparison *(for younger readers, there were twelve old pennies to a shilling and twenty shillings to a pound)*. Most newspapers thought it an even match, except the *Morning Post* who said that "Wanderers had it their own way from the start and that it was a one-sided match, Wanderers taking it comparatively easy defending their goal (once they had scored)" They also thought that " a great crowd watched the match including many ladies in the enclosure and those on open landaus (carriages) around the ground". Ever the watchword on football matters, the Sheffield Independent observed that the Chequers' goal was scored on thirty minutes, but uniquely recorded a goal by Morton Betts for Wanderers on the hour which was disallowed "for clearly being off-side". Interestingly, it seems that the Wanderers also sent out their 2nd and 3rd teams on Cup Final day, for according to Bells Life, scheduled to be played the same day were Forest v Wanderers at Woodford, and at Chatham, Royal Engineers v Wanderers !

Having failed to beat both Crystal Palace and Queens Park, Wanderers now held the English Cup. Wanderers had it even easier in 1872-3; they exercised their right to only be challenged in the final itself! This loony concept was immediately abandoned in the following year. Wanderers' opponents in the 1873 final were Oxford University, which took place at Lillie Bridge, and not the Oval. In an age when footballers, and not the FA decided what happened and when, the final kicked off early at 11.30 so that they could all rush over to the Thames and catch the (far more important) annual Boat Race. Oxford had nailed their credentials to the mast by beating Royal Engineers, but were without star player Neapan for the final. Having said that, in Cuthbert J. Ottaway, they had one of the finest all round sportsmen of the age, a man who excelled at football, tennis, cricket and racquets. Wanderers themselves could not obtain the services of either Thomas Hooman, William Crake, Wilson and Albert Thompson. If the team listed in the morning edition of the Morning Post is to be believed, then one R.C. Cambrian was due to play in goal, failed to appear, his position taken by the reliable Eddie Bowen, and Reginald de Courtnay-Welch drafted in at the last moment. Scheduled to commence at 11am, there was a half hour delay, which leads credence to the above, which caused players and spectators alike to have to scurry over to see the Boat Race on the Thames. The London Evening Standard must have been at the wrong Lillie Bridge ground, for they reported that "due to the hazy weather, only about 150 persons were present" ! Their report did make an interesting comment, for the year, when they said that "Maddison (for the Sappers) sent in a regular purler" a phrase not often associated with 1870s football.

In the final Oxford were the better side in the first half hour, but gradually Wanderers woke up. Arthur Kinnaird broke away and went on a long run and put the ball under the bar to give Wanderers a 1-0 lead against the run of play. Wanderers improved in the second half, had a goal ruled out by Kenyon-Slaney for the ball having gone out of play (Morning Post). Bells Life thought that Kinnaird's old-fashioned (even by then) long mazy dribble, with his red beard and white cricket flannels flashing past man after man, left an indelible scene in their minds. Oxford then threw caution to the wind, and played without a goalkeeper in an effort to draw level. According to the Morning Post's correspondent, Oxford once more gained the upper hand, but a goal by the dark blues was ruled out after 50 minutes, but until the 80th minute, looked likely to draw level. However, Woollaston scored a second when he broke free on the left, and finding the goal unguarded, sent the ball through the posts. The Sporting Life attributed Oxford's failure in not delivering crosses from the wings, instead relying on dribbles through the centre of the field. Both the Boys of Westminster school and the Old Westminsters were strong at home on the public space known as Vincent Square, but Wanderers took a one-sided victory there on Wednesday 4th March 1874 when goals from Robert Kingsford (2), Woollaston and John Edwards gave them a 4-0 win.

The two greatest teams in the world met at Hampden Park, Glasgow on Saturday 9th October 1875, when the Wanderers made the long overnight train journey to play the Scottish champions Queens Park. The match, simply billed as a challenge match, was quite simply a battle of the best two teams anywhere at the time, and its seemed that the entire population of Glasgow wanted to see the outcome. Not used to calculating such vast assemblages, estimates of the attendance fell in the range of ten to thirteen thousand people inside the ground, with half as many again locked outside perched on the surrounding vantage points. As when Queens Park did the return trips, the long journey drained the players who suffered travel fatigue, and although most would agree that Queens Park were unofficial world champions, it was clear that the Londoners weren't at their best. Apart from the 'Spiders' goalkeeper, the Wanderers were on average over two stones heavier than their hosts. A goal down after just 7 minutes, it sounds as if the Wanderers forwards were indulging in old fashioned and selfish dribbling again, when attack after attack broke down due to a lack of backing up, with Otter, Alcock and Heron all guilty of dribbling straight into a brick wall. A 4-0 defeat (some reports give 5-0) merely demonstrated to the Wanderers that this was clearly the best way forward, but they were unlikely to copy the 'team-combination' game, as a team of individuals was never likely to change. Afterwards, the Wanderers captain admitted that a finer game as played by Queens Park has never graced a football field, and in the customary style, all concerned enjoyed a splendid supper evening at the Glasgow Crown Hotel, George Square.

Wanderers proved they would not shy away from the best opposition available, when they clashed with the team with the best actual playing record of the 1870s- the Royal Engineers FC. They met on the afternoon of Monday 20th December 1875 at the Oval, when neither side could score a goal, in a match played under very blustery conditions where it was reported that the two teams were evenly matched. They also clashed on the opening game of the 1876-77 season, which saw goals from Woollaston (2) and Wace score a decisive 3-0 victory over the Engineers at the Oval, although the Chatham side were not at full strength, and a piercing side wind made scientific football difficult.

On the eve of the England-Scotland International of March 1876, the *Athletic News* gave these description for the competing Wanderers' players- Alfred H. Stratford: "can play back or forward, but best at back as he is a good and strong tackler". Of Hubert Heron "as a wing player he is very useful, at times brilliant, he is also fast and dribbles skilfully although can be rather selfish, although improved of late", and of his brother Francis Heron "dribbles well but is rather light(weight)".

In 1876, Wanderers again reached the Cup Final, where they faced a side they knew well- Old Etonians. Although Eton College had been playing football of their own variety for longer than the Wanderers, their Old Boys team had seen a stop-start history, and had missed out on the benefits which a continued existence brings. Moreover, many top players of the day belonged to both clubs. Allegiances would have to be chosen on the day. Quintin Hogg, Alexander G. Bonsor, William S. Kenyon-Slaney and the Hon. Edward Lyttleton chose to play under the *eu-de-nil* colours (pale blue with a hint of pale green) of the Etonians, with the Heron brothers, Charles Wollaston and Jarvis Kenrick featuring for Wanderers, captained by Francis Hornby Birley. The Honorable Edward and Alfred Lyttleton came from a family home in Hagley, Worcs, and were just two of a large and talented family. They played for the Etonians in both matches of the 1876 Cup Final and also for England soon after. Edward, two years the elder, became headmaster of Haileybury school and then Eton College. Alfred, was an exceptional athlete : English champion at real tennis for a decade, an M.C.C cricketer, and later its president, he was a barrister who became M.P. for Warwick, and served as Colonial Secretary under Prime Minister Balfour.

One giant of the game with whom they would be without, came with the shock news on Saturday 29th January 1876 in *The Graphic* that the founder of the F.A. and the F.A. Cup - Charles W. Alcock himself had withdrawn. He had announced, that, with regret, he was to retire as captain and honorary secretary of the Wanderers Football Club. The Graphic said " with honours bestowed thickly upon him as the man whose achievements and endeavours had raised the game today to its loved position". Alcock was Wanderers' most famous and probably best footballer; in 200 appearances he scored 82 goals, scoring a best 17 in season 1870-71. Over 3000 spectators at the Oval saw a drawn game in which Sporting Life newspaper remarked that the superiority of the Eton men did not manifest itself in a superior team performance, which was lacklustre. Wanderers played in 2-2-6 formation, Etonians with an already old fashioned 1-2-7 set-up. Wanderers kicked off late at 3.30pm with the sun and a stiff wind at their backs. A Charles Wollaston goal gave Wanderers the lead, but Eton's equaliser can only be described as bizarre. A general rush resulted in the Wanderers' goal posts being trampled down, and as they fell to the ground with the tape torn, a body of men from both teams fell through where the posts stood moments before, and the ball was carried over the line, and a goal given. Imagine such happenings in today's Wembley Stadium ! The replay, a week later, saw a different outcome as unchanged Wanderers took advantage of three missing Etonians, their places being filled with three who were out of condition, although the familiar name of Edgar Lubbock was one of them. Two goals ahead by half-time, Wanderers saw a spirited effort by Eton, but a third goal finished the game off. If the reports of the *Illustrated & Dramatic News* are correct, then the three goals by T. Hughes is the first ever cup final hat-trick, although some reports give Woollaston as the man who prodded home the opening goal from the melee under the Etonian posts.

In a match which had been eagerly awaited, Wanderers invited the famous Glasgow side, Queens Park, down on Saturday 4th November 1876. Played on the Kennington Oval, the lack of fitness of the Wanderers' men soon became apparent, as did the match fitness of the 'Spiders'. In a result which must have shocked the large attendance, Queens Park ran out 6-0 winners. In a fixture instigated in the previous year, Wanderers were dismayed to be beaten 5-0 in Glasgow in front of a massive crowd of 10,000, but gained some respect when the return match in London was won 2-0. It was then Queens Park's turn to be shocked, for in nine years, it had been the first time they had tasted defeat. They were known in Scotland as the Unbeatables. Unlike Queens Park, the Wanderers never did anything which resembled training, they found it hard enough to get their best men just to even turn out from their professional, civic or military duties!

The following year saw Wanderers once more into the final, this time to face Oxford University who were slight favourites to repeat their 1874 triumph. Wanderers' trait of being slow starters gave the advantage to Oxford who pressed them well in the opening half hour. However, when they took the lead, it was put down as an own goal by Kinnaird, who caught a Waddington shot, only to step back over the line with the ball ! Even Kinnaird had returned to his old college calling when he left Wanderers for 1875-6 to play for the Old Etonians, but a year later he was back. Most of the second half saw Oxford continue to press to no avail, and with five minute to go, Kenrick prodded home a Heron centre, and the game went into extra-time. Before long, Wanderers' Morgan Lindsay sent in a cross which was headed out, but he ran onto the ball and sent his second effort high under the tapes and out of the reach of Edward Allington in the Oxonian goal. This was the year of the infamous 'dead heat' in the University Boat Race, an event given over to acres of newsprint, while the Wanderers' Cup Final success was, in many papers, reduced to a single paragraph.

Wanderers' 'friendly match' performances were on show again when they played the Old Harrovians two months before the end of the 1876-7 season, when they were embarrassed 2-6, one of their heaviest defeats. Wanderers again met head on with the Royal Engineers on Saturday 3rd November 1877 at the Oval, winning by the decisive score of 4-1. Goals came from Wace (2), Denton and Wylie, with Lt. Ruck scoring for the Sappers. Bizarrely, the Lloyds Weekly congratulated Tower and Hawkins for their goalkeeping for the Engineers! Sounds like they alternated as being the last man by the posts. It was credited with being Wanderers' best performance of the season. Marindin, at this time, was of the rank of Colonel.

Scottish Cup holders Vale of Leven were invited down to London as a fitting end to the 1877-78 season on April 13th. Fielding almost the same team which had just beaten Royal Engineers to win the FA Cup for the 5th time in a decade, Wanderers kicked off at 3.30pm to defend the Harleyford Road end and did have the best of the opening half hour. However, two breakaway goals from Ferguson gave the all-blue Scots a 2-0 half-time advantage. Woollaston pulled one back, but Ferguson again scored for the visitors to give them a momentous 3-1 victory in front of an attendance described as 'disappointing'.

March 23rd 1878 saw probably Wanderers' best cup final performance when they once again clashed with the Royal Engineers at the Oval in front of a 4,500 crowd. They had outclassed Panthers FC and High Wycombe in the early rounds, putting nine goals past both, and did well to beat Sheffield FC 3-0 in the 4th round, when a large attendance at the Oval saw goals from Wace, Wylie and Denton defeat a Sheffield side which included the Clegg and Sorby brothers, and Cursham. Charles Denton (1852-1932) was one of the unsung players of the Wanderers, and one of the few who regularly turned out beyond 1878, having played more frequently since 1875. A solicitor qualified at the bar in 1880, he became assistant secretary at the Union Bank of London and later Secretary of the London Assurance Corporation. His first love was cricket, and played for Bradfield College during 1870-72, and was a member of the M.C.C. He passed away at the Grand Hotel, Folkestone, whilst having an address at Grosvenor Place, Westminster. The Bells Life newspaper concluded that, with fine passing, their play against Sheffield was Wanderers' best performance ever. They were clearly gearing themselves up for the little tin pot again. Whilst the Royal Engineers were being given a hard time by the Old Harrovians in their semi-final, the Wanderers actually drew a bye into the final. And this after nearly a decade of 'organising' by the Football Association.

Back to the Cup Final of 1878. The Oval ground was in fine dry condition, with the usual cross-wind present. This time, Wanderers were first out of the starting blocks, and within five minutes, Wace centred and Kenrick sent the ball between the posts. The 'Sappers' retaliated, and it was no doubt in the usual style of shoulder charging the goalie that Kirkpatrick in the Wanderers goal, sustained a fractured arm. Contrary to popular reports, he remained at his station for the rest of the match. Wanderers increased their lead early in the second half when following a Kinnaird free kick, the ball was sent through the posts. The Sappers seemed to have reduced the deficit when Hedley scored, but it was ruled out for offside. As the match wore on, the Wanderers improved and Kenrick scored a third from a dribble by Hubert Heron. The Sappers continued to press for the last 25 minutes, but Wanderers were resilient, and held out to win 3-1. The oft cited fact that the Wanderers, who were entitled to keep the original cup as three times outright winners, offered the trophy back to the FA on condition that no club could henceforth keep it, may not strictly be true, for several London newspapers stated that the FA refused Wanderers' offer, as they "intend to purchase a new cup for next year" . Interestingly - or should I say – disappointingly - not one newspaper ever mentions the Wanderers' colours in any of their cup final appearances!

The Wanderers were by 1877, a very successful institution. Their membership had grown to a staggering 1,378 members, and membership was then limited to a further 200. To become a member, expense had to be irrelevant. In an age when an office clerk might do well to earn a guinea a week (£1.05p), city members paid 8 guineas, countryside members paid 4 guineas, members abroad, 1 guinea, and there was an additional 10 guineas entrance fee, which meant entrance by way of introduction or recommendation (*Daily Graphic* 1877).They may, by this point, have seen themselves as more of a gentlemans' club who happen to play football rather well than a viable football team. Their opening match of the 1878-9 season saw a weak Wanderers eleven drubbed 5-1 at home at the Oval by Clapham Rovers, with Sparks bagging a second half hat-trick.

The following season 1879-80 saw a shock result as Wanderers were trounced 7-2 by the Old Etonians to exit the English Cup at the first hurdle. It was possibly bad luck to have drawn the eventual cup winners in Round 1, but the Etonians, having been reformed in 1878 in an effort to make an impact in the Cup, would go onto to have a wonderful next few seasons where they reached four Cup finals in five years. The match was supposed to have taken place on the Vincent Square playing field, of the Westminster School, who put a notice in *Reynold's Newspaper* on Sunday 1880 saying the match, due to have been played on Friday night inst., was not allowed by the authorities, and the game was held over until Saturday 24th at the Oval. One wonders whether a stronger Wanderers' eleven would have been available on that ill-fated Friday night? Wanderers suffered in the late 1870s from several of their best men being given the 'party-whip' by their old colleges, particularly the Old Etonians, who got stronger as a result. One such example was Herbert Whitfield, a tall, fine dribbler, who 'defected' to the Etonians. A fine cricketer, he notched up 2,400 runs for Surrey as captain, and became an M.P.

The Vale of Leven side returned to play a top English side in the following December of 1879, when after defeating the Old Harrovians 5-3 in Scotland, also won the return match in March 1880 in London. Leven's claim to now be World Champions seemed entirely justified. Another Scottish club, Renton would later defeat English Cup winners West Bromwich Albion in a specially staged match to claim the same title.

The opening match of the 1879-80 season saw a shock as Wanderers were thrashed 2-8 at home by the Clapham Rovers. Played on Saturday 11th October in cold, damp, foggy weather, Woollaston's brace did little to make the scoreline respectable as Clapham were already 6-0 ahead mainly thanks to four goals from Barry, with Sparks, Tayloe, Stanless and Rumball adding to the agony. The campaign improved with a 2-1 win over the Old Foresters at the Oval a fortnight later. Few matches were played between then and their 4-3 win over old friends the Old Harrovians on Saturday 3rd January 1880 when they nearly let a 3-0 advantage disappear. A week later they mustered a stronger eleven to defeat the Old Carthusians by 1-0 to progress through to the next round of the English Cup in a game which the *London Graphic* described as 'fast and interesting'. Wanderers' love affair with the 'little tin idol' ended forever when - of all teams - the Old Etonians beat them 3-1 in the 3rd round.

Wanderers' connections to the military could not be better illustrated than when, to the background of men fighting abroad against the Zulus and the Afghans, they held a banquet on the evening of Friday 17th October 1879 at the Pall Mall Restaurant. Several Wanderers' men had excelled themselves at the battle of Rorke's Drift, when 120 British men of the 24th Regiment held off an estimated 4,000 Zulus, resulting in 500 Zulu deaths. The banquet, in honour of Major General Sir Hastings Doyle and Lord Headley, was attended by one hundred guests, most of whom had titles, both civic and military, and the long list of attendees included many 'Lords',' Colonels', and men with V.C or K.B.E at the end of their double-barrelled names. This then, was the stock of the Wanderers, although this would prove to be the twilight of their existence as a club, and their heady days of cup final successes was behind them. Within a couple of years, they would virtually cease to exist.

By the end of the 1870s, Wanderers were no longer the powerful club they once were. Almost no 'Wanderer' turned out exclusively for the side, and everyone held joint, or sometimes, triple allegiances. Now having first call on their old boys was the prep school, Eton, Harrow, Westminster or Charterhouse, and each of them subsequently formed their own Old Boys team. These Old Boys clubs got stronger in time, and many Wanderers men felt the tug of their alma mater an irresistible pull, and they began to play instead for those teams. Additionally, as the years went by, many players felt that they could not play much past the age of thirty, although famously, Alcock was one who did. For many Wanderers men, in important political or social positions, as the years went by, came with it greater responsibilities, and the call of the War Office and the Houses of Parliament would mean that they would have to retire from the field of play. The Wanderers would never again feature in the English F.A. Cup. After entering the competition for 1880-1, they scratched without playing a game. Drawn to play London Rangers (the team for which Frederick Wall played), they withdrew. Again, in October 1881, when drawn to meet St. Bartholemew Hospital, they withdrew, unable to raise a team. The Wanderers had taken a great part in the hard work of establishing football, and they had set an excellent standard, and to play against them was the secret hope of every club in the country.

In their last two seasons of proper existence as a football club, seasons 1879-80 and 1880-81, one home and away challenge in particular illustrated the fact that they had long since vacated the throne of football. Teams such as Queens Park and the Vale of Leven in Scotland, and clubs in Lancashire and Staffordshire which would soon become professional were beginning to forge a new direction. Wanderers began the 1880-81 season, but I doubt whether they finished it in the following Easter. The opening match of the season gave no hint of a club about to call it a day when they walloped the Old Harrovians 6-1 at the Oval, although three weeks later, the Upton Park FC beat them 2-0 on the same ground. On the same day, over at Chatham in Kent, the Royal Engineers, without a single player remaining from the 1878 Cup Final, trounced the Old Etonians by 5-0, with Marindin and Kinnaird turning out for the light blues.

No Wanderers players were in the side selected for the England international side to play Scotland in March 1881, or even in the reserve list. This seems to be a demonstration that the Wanderers' flame had finally been extinguished. Pomp and ceremony still continued though, when a testimonial gala was held at the Freemason's Tavern on the evening of Monday 11th April 1881 for the most worthy Charles Alcock. Described by

Major Marindin on the night as 'truly the father of modern football, and for whose zeal and energy in forging the establishment of the popular winter game, we are forever indebted'. An illuminated scroll depicting his achievements for the Football Association and the F.A. Cup were presented in addition to a velvet purse containing 300 guineas. Interestingly, Alcock's club was given as the Old Harrovians, and Marindin's as Royal Engineers, with the name of the 'celebrated Wanderers' absent. The Wanderers may have still existed at Christmas 1881, the only 'evidence' I give is that when Charles R. Woollaston umpired for the Old Etonians in their 2-2 draw with Clapham Rovers on November 5th, his club was given as 'Wanderers'. At this point, the only time Wanderers appeared in the sports press was for their annual match against Harrow School.

For the most famous club in London, a supreme irony came about in February 1882. In the year in which the Wanderers' brilliant flame finally died out, it was announced that the London Football Association had been formed, with the purpose of assisting amateur clubs within a 12-mile radius of the city. The Lord Mayor of London was its patron, with Arthur Kinnaird (soon to become 11th Lord Kinnaird in 1887) as president, and Robert A.M.M. Ogilvie (nicknamed Ram for obvious reasons) of Clapham Rovers as vice-president. Ogilvie, educated at Brentwood School, had two years with Upton Park FC before joining Rovers in 1873. In private life, he was a member of Lloyd's of London and served as an underwriter with the Alliance Assurance Co.

Surprisingly, after Wanderers left the national stage at the start of the 1880 decade, I found evidence that they continued to exist almost a decade later. A week before Christmas Day 1888, they played the Harrow School XI at the Oval, winning 3-1. The *London Standard* said that for Harrow, it was their traditional annual visit. Harrow, *alma mater* to many of the old Wanderers' men, such as Charles Alcock, Morton Peto Betts and Reggie de Welch, had been on Wanderers' fixture card from the beginning, and perhaps, when the Wanderers fell back into occasional matches, retained their ties with Harrow to the end. The huge change of the times however, could no better be illustrated than to remind you that in 1888, the top twelve clubs - all professional with large followings and grounds to match - had formed the Football League, and another match at the Oval in March 1889 set a totally different scene. In contrast to the one hundred who turned out to see Harrow School play Wanderers, the Corinthians met and defeated the mighty Preston North End 2-0 in front of a crowd of 8,000.

When Middlesex met Surrey at the Oval in December 1889 at the Oval, there was no mention of any Wanderers' names, and indeed only one 'old boy' mentioned at all. On the previous weekend, the Royal Engineers were still active, as they played the Royal Military Academy at the Oval ground. The other principal old boys sides - Etonians, Swifts, Westminsters, Casuals, Oxford and Cambridge, continued to fly the amateur flag into the 1890s, along with the 'new Wanderers' of the age - The Corinthians.

After only knowing for many years that the Forest/ Wanderers' played on a field 'near to the Merchant Seaman's Orphanage Asylum at Snaresbrook near Leytonstone, Essex, I finally decided to track that field down. Internet searches led me to the wrong building, as there were two asylums and I ended up searching land by the council offices and the Crown Court by the lakes. I finally spotted the Seaman Orphans Asylum on the other side of the main road, by what is now Wanstead Hospital. The Asylum lay right next to Nightingales Farm and I had the old chapel as a reference point. That chapel today is the Reform Synagogue, and the five acre square field next to the Asylum lay due east of it. After many mental 'overlays' of maps through the decades, I now say that Cranbourne Avenue, from the bend halfway along, down to Rooney Road (honestly), including the whole of Orchard Close, occupy much of that football field where legends began 155 years ago.

Comprised as they were of *illuminati* any attempt to describe the achievements and lives of Wanderers players would fall well short unless it was a book of several hundred pages. Team captain Arthur (later Lord) Kinnaird is so well known that I will in fact leave out that hard-tackling football-mad scallywag altogether, and offer an insight into some of the other leading men.

Cuthbert Ottaway (1850-1878) uniquely represented Oxford at five different sports, and was seen as a contemporary of the Hon. Alfred Lyttleton. Son of a Dover surgeon, Ottaway became a barrister in 1873, and married a Canadian lady. Described as a poised and speedy winger, his football career was curtailed when he took a severe ankle injury in the 1875 Cup Final. Having captained England in 1874, he also turned out for Oxford, Marlow, Crystal Palace and the Old Etonians.

Edgar Lubbock (1847-1907), a tall and spindly back, had "no rival in that position, possessing an accurate kick" said Charles Alcock. Son of wealthy Sir John Lubbock, a banker, Edgar also became a governor of the Bank of England, and a partner in the Whitbread Brewery Company. Following an Etonian education, he became a lawyer, and went on to become Lieutenant of the City of London, and Master of the Blankney Foxhounds. Two of his daughters married earls and the other married a baron. Affectionately known as 'Quintus' he also played for Gitanos, West Kent and Crusaders, and was a Wanderers regular, alongside his brother Alfred.

Edward Ernest Bowen (1836-1901), a forward, was made Master of Music at Harrow in 1859 following an education at Blackheath school and Cambridge, he became a lawyer. Playing alongside his brother Charles, Albert was described by Alcock as 'one of the best half-backs of the day'.

Gilbert George Kennedy (1844-1909) was an early Wanderers' player who even by the time of their first Cup Final in 1871, would have been approaching thirty. Born in Bath, his father was the Charge d'Affaires for Naples, and his great-grand-father was the 11th Earl of Cassilis. His brother Sir William was a Commander-in-Chief, and the other brother Sir John, was an eminent diplomat. Educated at Harrow and Cambridge, where he excelled at football, rowing and athletics, he joined Wanderers in 1866, going on to play 41 times, scoring 8 goals. He became a barrister and a police magistrate. He died in Thanet, Kent, having lived in Kensington and Broadstairs. As a footballer, he was described as "no mean forwards and very great in front of the enemies goal".

Alexander Bonsor (1851-1907) was an Old Etonian and was able to play for either team. Winning FA Cup medals in 1872 and 1873 with Wanderers, he was in the beaten finalist Old Etonians team of 1875 and 1876. Twice capped, he also scored England's second-ever international goal when playing against Scotland in March 1863.

Lindsay Bury (1857-1935) was born in Withington near Manchester and went to Eton College, and was another of the dual-club players, turning out for Etonians in the Cup Final of 1879 against Clapham Rovers at full back. When up at Cambridge, Bury gained a blue at football and cricket and was a noted sprint runner. He played cricket for Cambridge University in 1877-78 and sometimes turned out for the Swifts, as it seems that Bury was one of the more available players. He later emigrated to Florida to become of all things, an orange grower, but returned to England in old age, and became a Justice of the Peace in Bradfield, Berkshire.

Herbert Whitfield (1858-1909) played more so for the Etonians, but also was the Sussex County cricket captain during 1883-84, with a career total of 2,400 runs. Born at Hamsey, East Sussex, Whitfield went to Eton and on to Trinity College, Cambridge, where he excelled as a sportsman, gaining blues at football, cricket and real tennis. A tall but somewhat tubby dribbler, he was capped against Wales in January 1879, but a snow blizzard ruined the fixture, which was curtailed to just one hour's play. In professional life, Whitfield became a director of Barclay's Bank in Lewes, East Sussex and a Member of Parliament, but died relatively young aged fifty.

Francis Marindin (1838-1900) was the son of the vicar of Chesterton, Shropshire. Characterised by his long full side whiskers, Marindin rose through the ranks so that variously, he was called captain and major, and was in fact, later knighted. Educated at Eton and the Royal Military Academy, Woolwich, he fought with the Royal Engineers in the Crimean War of 1854-56. The son of the vicar of Chesterton, Shropshire, Marindin's profession was as an Inspector for the Board of Trade, with a specialised interest in railway safety. Equally well known as a Cup Final referee, Marindin kept goal for both Royal Engineers and the Old Etonians, famously playing for neither in the 1875 Cup Final. Along with Charles Alcock, Betts, Stair, Marindin was a leading early official of the Football Association.

Alfred Baker (1846-1900) was an unsung hero of the early Wanderers' teams, sharing equal billing with Charles Alcock as leading scorer with fifteen goals from 58 appearances. An auctioneer by profession, Baker was a champion athlete, once winning the 100 yards title at the AAA championships.

Thomas Bridges Hughes was rarely available due to spending much of 1876-80 obtaining his law degree at the Bar and then becoming a teacher. A former head boy at Winchester College, Hughes played often during 1876 but it was 1880 before he returned to football. He also sometimes played for Oxford University and the Swifts. Hughes played for Wanderers in the 1876 Cup Final against the Etonians, where he scored twice, and

Above - left, Charles Alcock, secretary to both Wanderers and Surrey Cricket Club.

Centre - William Kenyon-Slaney, who married the daughter of the Earl of Bradford, was M.P for Newport, Shropshire and a Colonel in the Grenadier Guards.

Right - The Honorable Arthur Kinnaird (later Lord Kinnaird) was Wanderer's most fervent player, playing in any position as long as he got to play a match five times a week to keep fit

again in the final of 1877 against Oxford. On his return in October 1880, he scored twice against the Old Harrovians.

Charles Clerke (1857-1944) a sometime Wanderers forward from a leading family. Son of Sir William of Tipperary, the 10th baronet Clerke, Charles received an Eton and Oxford University education, and thus was qualified to play for several teams as he wished. A Hampshire landowner, he played cricket variously for Herfordshire, Shropshire and county Radnor. An Old Etonian, he played for them when they won the 1879 Cup Final against Clapham Rovers, and indeed scored the winning goal from a centre from Goodhart on the hour.

Henry Waugh Renny-Tailyour (1849-1920) owed his swarthy looks to being born in colonial India. As a Royal Engineer, he played on the losing side in the F.A. Cup finals of 1872, 1874, before success came the Engineers' way in 1975. An all-round sportsman, he uniquely was capped for Scotland at both rugby and football, and scored their first ever International goal.

TROJANS FC

Founded - 1869
Folded - Circa 1901
Ground - 1. Walthamstow Park
        2. West Ham park (1870s)
        3. Leyton
Colours - Black and white stripes

A team simply called Trojans briefly competed in the F.A. Cup in the early years of its existence. Well technically speaking, that is. They sent in their entry money in the autumn of 1873 and were drawn against Farningham who promptly scratched (probably on account of distance), and so Trojans were through to round 2. Unlike today, when every minnow club hopes to pull the name Manchester United away out of the hat (to go out with a bang and fill the club coffers for the next two years), in the 1870s, the last team you wanted to be drawn against was the Wanderers at the Oval. And thus, Trojans gave them a walkover and scratched. Wanderers would probably have put ten goals past them, but as upper class gentlemen amateurs, they had no need for gate money, and the two hundred who would have turned out would have merely contributed to the coffers of the Surrey County cricket club who owned the ground. Thus their F.A. Cup record reads : played none, won one, lost two. Three years later, Trojans again entered, and were drawn away to the Sheffield club, probably the 4th best team in the land at the time. Trojans again threw their cards on the table and scratched. And that, ladies and gentlemen, is the brief and entire history of the Trojans' F.A. Cup exploits. So why bother to write about them at all?

As with the Panthers of Dorset, and other such clubs whose names give no clue to their whereabouts, this is enough intrigue for me to begin investigations. Another obscure club, London Olympic FC, a name with hints of grandeur, turned out to be the works team of a London department store, Hitchcock & Williams of St. Pauls churchyard in old London town. Playing in the 1890s, Olympic appear to have briefly been a very competent side, notching up impressive wins against Tottenham Hotspur (6-3), Romford (7-0) and Dulwich (11-0), and played at the 'London Athletic Grounds' at Herne Hill. Sending out three teams each Saturday, they competed in the London Junior and West End cups, and also played water polo, cricket and swimming galas. *(Illustrated Sporting and Dramatic News 1892)*

Imagine my surprise when I find out that the 'Trojans' are alive and well, as a rugby club playing in the London 3 South West division. Playing several age group teams in red & black hoops, their current ground is on Stoneham Lane, Eastleigh, just north of Southampton, and their website tells us that were founded in 1874, a fact of which they are rightly proud. However, they were not the same club, as I would soon find out. I found a match report as early as 30th March 1870, when Trojans played the Leyton club on the cricket ground. gaining mention for plucky play were captain W.F. Fern and E. Frery and W.C. Frery. It was remarked that the players of both teams frequently forgot to abide by the new Association law which forbade handling the ball, and both teams were often penalised for it, the game ending goal-less, although both sides frequently 'touched the ball down behind their own goal-lines'. This technique is still in use today in the rugby game, when a back cannot find a way out from his back line because he is surrounded by opponents, and shows that until the F.A. Cup of 1871, teams were still playing a hybrid mix of the handling and kicking codes. In February 1871 the writer in The Sportsman said that the Trojans had been thrashed 12-0 by Woodford Wells, but as they were a new club, that they wished them better luck next time ! Another source says that Trojans were founded at the end of 1869 and used the Cowley Arms pub at Leyton as their base. Captain for that game was T. Knight, with brother James at back, the others being : W. Ringrose, Scobie, R. Ringrose, Kay, Fern, Pearson, Garstung, Jennings and Gowar. Later, in November 1871 the same newspaper tells us that they played an association match against the Pilgrims of Clapham on Saturday 11th, on 'the ground of the Trojans' - the Leyton cricket ground in London. Played eleven-a-side, mention was made of goalkeepers who were 'difficult to pass' and clever dribbling by some of the players. These Trojans played out a 1-1 draw: W. F. Fern (captain), (Segar?) Bastard, Copely, Gower, Kelmore, W.R. Kay, M. Kelmore, Moore, W. Ringrose, E. Stevens, Dix. The Pilgrims seem to have become an annual fixture, as the two teams met again three years later at Leyton, with Pilgrims winning 3-0. In January 1873, *The Sportsman* gave a long and detailed match report when Trojans went to the ground of the Surrey Rifles, being beaten 1-0, and playing the return match at Leyton a week later, as was the custom of the day. A heavy Trojans defeat was averted by the solid defensive play of J. R. Stephens, and Surrey were again limited to a single goal success. Captained by G. F. Fern, Trojans played with only nine men until the second half had begun, the others being – J. Cobbett, R. Copley, G. Dix, A.F. Gower, W. Ringrose, F.R. Scott, Wilkinson and brothers E.W and J.R. Stephens. It was remarked in the *Sporting Life* on the eve of the 1874-75 season that "Trojans, Gitanos, Surrey Rifles and Amateur Athletic Club do not complete in this season's Association Challenge Cup, their places taken by Harrow Chequers, Windsor Home Park, Panthers and Hitchin". Captain for the season was Copley, with a forward line of Hall, Middlebank, Farnie, Middleton and Crockett, backed up by defenders Brown, Dawson, Ringrove, Cramphorn and Collins. This Trojans twelve man side drew 1-1 with London Olympic in February 1876 -

		W. Ringrose			
	D. Ringrove			W. Cramphorn	
E. Cramphorn			Millbank		Neil
J. Hall	G. Hall	Collins	Daneson	Scott	Millbank

Scott and Hall gained praise for their fine dribbling skills. We know they were active in 1876 as that was the year they scratched to Sheffield FC, but Trojans disappeared off the radar soon after that. In a match against Wood Grange played in West Ham Park on 3rd February 1877, an eleven comprised of most of the above played out a 1-1 draw, although the name Daneson becomes Dawson, J. Collins is captain and J. Allsop is now in goal. They also met Clarence and Olympic at West Ham park that season. Nothing could be traced for the London Trojans for the next twenty years.

1896 saw the name of the Trojans reappear after a gap many years, when *Lloyd's Weekly,* a valuable source of football results of minor teams, listed matches played in each public park and ground across greater London, and a match against the Forest club in 1899 was lost 0-3 at Wadham Lodge. In September 1900, the name of Trojans once more surfaced when I found them playing at Walthamstow, London. *Lloyd's Weekly News* gave scores of the Walthamstow area friendlies, and opponents included Hackney, Leyton Rovers, Remington Athletic, Peel, Lower Clapton, St. Peters Athletic, St. Michaels Rovers, Malvern Rovers, Toynbee, Springfield, and Albany, when most were generally beaten, and it seems that the Trojan side of 1900 was one of the better ones in the area. Sadly, the last report for Trojans I could find was in December 1900, a classic time for a football club to decide to either call it a day, or amalgamate with another club.

Founded - 1907
Folded -   1950 (amalgamated)
Grounds - Tufnell Park, Holloway, North London
Colours -   Amber and yellow stripes, black

Sport at Tufnell Park, of one kind or another, goes back perhaps to the 1860s, when cricket was played there, and later, in the 1870s, rugby, athletics and association football was played at Holloway. A sports day at Tufnell Park, held in the summer of 1867, was put on by the Red Rovers football club, and attracted hundreds of entrants and spectators. Founded in 1865, Red Rovers were one of London's oldest clubs; after a match against the Carlton Hill FC in 1871, the latter club were amalgamated with Rovers and Carlton's Bob Clement became the new club's captain.

Then known as W.J. Pages' cricket ground, entrance was confined to members of clubs who used Tufnell Park, University men, or 'gentlemen introduced by a Tufnell Park member' (*Bell's Life*). William Page handily lived in the adjacent Tufnell Arms Hotel, and he had a business making cricket equipment. Many different sporting clubs used Tufnell Park as a base including the T.P Athletics Club, Excelsior United cricket club, the German Gymnastic Society (who had a decent football team too), several schools and football and rugby teams, and Stamford Hill and Peckham Rye cricket clubs, who simply hired a portion of the ground for the day, or a whole season. Situated between Huddleston and Campdale Roads and near the station, the ground was said to be "accessible from all parts of London and is well drained". The original entrance seems to have been between 142 and 144 Huddleston Road. Page seems to have obtained the 14 acre ground circa 1867-8, and developed the original cricket ground by extending it and adding facilities for quoits, bowling, and providing a pavilion and refreshment facilities, all in all, creating a general sports club for those who could afford to use it. Later, in the 1890s, by which time housing encroachment had reduced it to less than seven acres, it was home to even more teams, such as the Casuals, Vampires, Scots Guards, London Caledonians, and in September 1899, following the decision from the Leyton county ground to ban football on its grounds, the London FA XI, who moved its headquarters to Tufnell Park.

Founded in 1907, Tufnell Park FC competed in the Spartan League from 1910-1912, then the Athenian League from 1912-1914, finishing 3rd and then as champions as war broke out in Europe, After 1919, Tufnell Park stayed in the Ithsmian League until they amalgamated with Edmonton Borough FC in 1950. This team played away to Aylesbury on their Printing Press ground in March 1912, losing 2-4 :

			Evan			
		Wood			Osborne	
	Wood		Grosch		Beckerley	
Clarke	Newton	Goodman		Bush		Battersley

An early off-shoot from Tufnell Park were Tufnell Spartans who formed in 1911 and later became Wood Green Town in 1920. In their first league season, Tufnell Park finished runners-up in 1911, with just 2 defeats from 18 games and with a goal tally of 57-19 (*Football Club History Database*). They left the Athenian League in 1914 as champions, on 33 points, with 15 wins, 3 draws and 4 defeats, scoring 61 against 24. After the Great War, they moved to the Isthmian Legaue where they started brightly there too, never out of the top three for the first two seasons. Then came a period where they fell back into lower mid-table positions until 1930. Only 1925 saw a top four position, although they somehow achieved this with 11 wins, 11 defeats and 4 draws. An improvement came about in the first half of the 1930s when they finished 7th, 6th, 4th, 5th, but apart from 1938 when they finished 3rd, they had slumped to the bottom of the table. After the Second World War had ended, and league football resumed, Tufnell Park had one bright season where they finished 5th, with 12 wins to 10 defeats, but after that, they once more fell to the bottom of the table for several years. In 1948-9, only one league win was recorded, and in the following year, they let in 91 goals in just 26 matches. It was time to either fold or merge.

The F.A. Cup was entered from 1921, but Tufnell Park never got through all the qualifying rounds to the 1st Round Proper. They almost made it in 1922, but Grimsby put them out in the 6th Qualifying stage. In 1945, they hammered Welwyn Garden City 11-1, only for Barnet to beat them 1-1, 1-2. The Amateur Cup became a happy hunting ground in the Edwardian era. Entering in 1909, they reached the semi-final at the first attempt, beating Romford 2-1, Barnet Alston 1-0, Hereford City 3-1, and a great away win by 5-1 at Barking to meet the Royal Marines Light Infantry of Gosport at Portsmouth, where they were beaten 4-0 by the eventual winners. The Romford match, originally won 2-1 had to be replayed on the silly appeal that Tufnell had used two men who played Sunday football for a parks team. A brace each from Wiseman and Parker, and Adam had done the damage at Barking, which had left them as favourites to reach the final. Another military side was met in the following season, when Shoeburyness Garrison were defeated 5-2, but then they were beaten 4-1 at Bromley for an early exit. In 1911, they needed a replay to get past Luton Clarence, but wins against Basford and Dulwich Hamlet, once more put them into the semi-finals, where they met Eston United on Stockton's ground, a round trip of over 400 miles, only to lose 0-1 by a goal from Hollis in front of a remarkable attendance of 20,000. 1914 saw them reach their third semi-final in four attempts, as Tufnell Park overcame Luton Clarence once more (4-2), and then a great 3-1 win over rated London Caledonians put them up against Dulwich Hamlet once more. Dulwich at this time, were getting huge crowds for an amateur club, sometimes over 10,000 - a figure many Football League sides would have been happy with. However, following a goal-less draw, Tufnell Park won the replay 3-1, Northern Nomads stood in their way to the final, but once again, they were bridesmaids, losing 0-2 at Terne Hill. In 1920, Tufnell Park finally got to that elusive Amateur Cup final, having beaten Wycombe Wanderers 6-2, GER Romford 3-2, a revengeful 1-0 over Northern Nomads, and a narrow win over Stanley United in the semi, with a winner from Hannaford. They faced Dulwich Hamlet in the final, who by now were beginning to become a nuisance team to them, and so it proved in the final held at Millwall, in front of a whopping 25,000 crowd. In a very close game, with nothing between the two sides, it was probably the hobbling off of striker Hannaford before half-time which swung the balance. Late into extra time, Dulwich's Kail scored what proved to be the winner. This was the Tufnell Park side that day -

		Leese		
	Butcher		Evans	
Goodman		Read		Swayne
Fricker	Lloyd	Hannaford	Williams	Elkington

After that, Tufnell Park never again got past round 3 (last 16), and indeed, in 1946, were trounced 6-1 by Leavesdon Hospital in round 1. Four years later, as Tufnell Park Edmonton, they had already lost their identity.

The Tuffnell Park ground still exists today, defined by Campdale, Huddlestone, Tuffnell Park Roads, and the rear of London Metropolitan University (Tuffnell Park House) on Station Road, and is generally turned over to rugby, soccer and tennis, and there is a children's play area. On a site visit in 2016 when virtually empty, it seemed hard to imagine crowds of perhaps three thousand spectators assembled around the two football pitches, which saw teams like Casuals, Caledonians and Tuffnell Park play there nearly a century ago.

The ground was developed very little over the decades, just a pavilion at each end of the grounds, and two small stands, one at the Tuffnell Park Road end, the other being little more than planked terracing along Campdale Road, after the ground was divided into two circa 1925. Today, one mile due east stands a somewhat larger football ground- the new Emirates Stadium of the Arsenal FC.

Tufnell Park FC in 1924, from an old cigarette card.

UPTON PARK FC

Founded - 1866   reformed 1891
Folded - 1887   again in 1912
Grounds - 1. West Ham park
Colours - 1870s Red and black hoops
          1880s Red and black halves
          1900s All white
          1910s Green shirts (unconfirmed)

Upton Park were one of London's earliest and most famous amateur football clubs, and were one of the original entrants in the first ever F.A. Cup competition. It is said that the first ever goal scored in the F.A. Cup competition, came in Upton Park's 1st round match when Jervis Kendrick scored for visitors Clapham Rovers on 11th November 1871, a game re-enacted on 5th November 2017 when enthusiast Billy Jenkins revived the name of Upton Park FC after a century since they folded. The 'new' Upton Park wore a kit of all-white with a red and a black chest hoop, and 'Clapham Rovers' wore a red and grey striped uniform, and the game took place in West Ham park, Upton Park's original home ground. Further re-enactment matches were arranged against Royal Engineers, Clapton and in the Channel Islands. Despite an apparent connection with West Ham's (then known as Thames Ironworks) Upton Park ground, there was none except that some Upton Park men also turned out for Thames Ironworks. Upton Park were responsible for introducing two of the most important rule changes in 1870; that of the abolition of all handling of the ball, and a year later, making the position of goalkeeper a fixed position allocated to one player only (previously, any defender nearest to the goal-line could punch the ball away to prevent a score).

One of their earliest matches was when they travelled to Snaresbrook to play the redoubtable Forest School on Saturday 6th April 1867. It proved a costly mistake to agree to use the school rules, and sixteen-a-side, as the boys ran out 6-0 winners, mainly due to their enigmatic captain Harry Tubb who had the boys train at football every day. The Upton team that day was-

H. Barnet, H. Alexander, T. Anderson, B. Barnet, C. Clutterbuck, J. Cobbold, S. Curwen, A. Evans, M .Gardner, W. Gardner, A. Jones, M. Jutsum, A. Morris, S. Morris, A. Stair, C. Wilson.

I traced Upton Park's results during season 1869-70 which were as follows -

October 16th	0-0	Forest	
October 30th	4-1	Gitanos	(F.Wilton, H.Wilton, M.Jutsum, A.M.Jones)
November 6th	1-2	Wanderers	(F.Wilton)
November 20th	2-0	Brentwood Schoo	(F.Wilton)
December 4th	1-1	Brentwood School	(M.Jutsum)

December 7th	3-0	Forest School	(P.G.Barnett, C.W.Alcock, C.E.Wilson)
January 1st	2-3	N.N.Kilburn	(P.G.Barnett, H.Wilton)
January 7th	0-0	Clapham Rovers	
January 26th	1-0	Crystal Palace	(M.Jones)
February 5th	3-0	N.N.Kilburn	(P.R.St.Quentin, F.Wilton)
February 19th	P-P	Gitanos	(not played)
March 12th	0-3	Wanderers	
March 16th	0-0	Crystal Palace	

The season's record thus was : played 12 won 5 drawn 4 lost 3 goals for 17 goals against 10. Their secretary at this time was Alfred Stair of Surinam-terrace, Stratford, London, and the club had a large committee. Their annual sports day at Upton park went on for many years. Upton Park took some time to gradually become a force, and until the 1880s, were just an average side. This 1874 side lost 0-3 to Barnes at 'West Ham park, near Plaistow':-

Conrad Warner (captain & goalkeeper), T.C. Curwen, E. Curwen, S. Preston, J.B. Hunter, T. Micklem, F. Kitson, F. Wilton, F. Burnett, R. Bastard, H. Compton.

Up until 1874, when the council took over the running of the park, it had been the grounds of Ham House, belonging to John Gurney (1845-1887), until it was demolished in 1872 and handed over on the condition the 77 acres became a public open recreation space.

Curiously, when Upton Park held their annual sports day in April of 1872, the event was held by the generosity of Gustav Pagenstecher "who lent his grounds for the occasion" which implies that Pegenstecher was connected with Ham House. A German physicist by the same name (improbable but true) who found later fame as an early pioneer of psychiatry turned out to be a different man. I unearthed our Gustav on the E7 website to which I am indebted. He was born 1828 in Germany to French and Caribbean parents which gave him a rather odd appearance, if I am not being too unkind. His wealthy parents educated him at the Universities of Bonn, Berlin and Halle, reading classics and languages, where he got a degree in Latin. On arriving in England, he secured a position as tutor to the sons of Sir Edward Buxton in Norfolk. When Buxton moved in with his relatives the Gurneys at West Ham, Pagenstecher went with him. He continued to gain friends in high places, but left Buxton's employ in 1869 to become private secretary to banker William Gibbs until 1874. When the Gurneys fell into financial difficulties and wanted to sell the house and estate, I expected to hear that Pagenstercher had snapped it up at a bargain price – but no; Pagenstercher was merely the broker for the sale to West Ham council, who frankly hadn't got the funds even when the price was dropped by ten thousand to £15,000. The council scraped together £10,000 and friends of the Gurney family came up with the rest, and our Gustav Pagenstercher ended up as deputy chairman of the West Ham Parks committee, so in saying "I grant you permission to use my grounds", he was rather outstepping his authority. A later description of him being pompous falls in line with this. In later years Pagenstercher became many things, including financial secretary of the new West Ham Hospital where he raised much funding. He may also have been a founder of Upton Park FC since he was an occasional player and secretary to Upton Park cricket club and a member of the Sussex C.C. Finding himself back in Germany when war broke out in 1914, he fled back to Forest Gate, London, where he was compelled to report as an alien to police on a weekly basis, something which he said broke his heart, and probably contributed to his death before the year was out. His work in promoting and documenting the history of West Ham has never been recognised.

1874 marked the departure of Alfred Stair who joined them in 1867. He would become better known as the man who refereed the first three F.A. Cup finals at the Kennington Oval. Stair was head of the Inland Revenue Services based at Somerset House, and several of his subordinate officers were fellow footballers, such as J.H. Giffard and K. Kirkpatrick. Of the West Ham park ground, which was merely a chosen area of the park on the Ham Park Road northern end, the cross winds played a part, and Upton Park matches were more at the mercy of the weather than most. With a free football match to watch, attendances soon grew to about a thousand. Upton Park had extra neighbours in the 1880s, when Dreadnought FC (f. 1875), and Upton Rangers also began to play there. Upton Park attracted a good crowd until West Ham United were formed out of the ashes of Thames Ironworks, and people flocked to see them instead. Being staunchly amateur, Upton Park had no desire to charge the public to watch them play (which they couldn't anyway in a public park) whereas Thames Ironworks, once they had funds in their coffers, could begin to pay for better men to join their ranks.

When the Football Association Cup was inaugurated in season 1871-2, Upton Park, having played a good part in the formation of the F.A., had the misfortune to meet Clapham Rovers in the draw, and were put out by 3-0. In the following year, the Surrey Rifles put them out by 2-0. 1873 saw them trounced 4-0 by Oxford University, who went on to beat Royal Engineers in the final, and it was Barnes again in 1874 (0-3) who prevented them from making their first 2nd round appearance. Finally, in November 1875, they did just that when beating Southall by a single goal, only for them to scratch when drawn away to the Sheffield FC. The dizzy heights of the 4th round were reached in 1878, when Rochester (3-0), Reading (1-0) and Remnants away (3-0 *Williams, R. Hunter, J. Hunter*) were overcome. Hoping that their next opponents wouldn't also start with an 'R' (Royal Engineers), instead they found their match in the Old Harrovians who beat them 3-1. Played at the Oval on Saturday 9th March, the teams were level at 1-1 at the break, but Harrovians improved in the second period and scored twice. It would be the only time the once famous Harrovians appeared in the semi-final but they lost 1-2 to Engineers. Hopes of another good cup run in 1878-9 were dashed when, after trouncing Saffron Walden 5-0, they were edged out 3-2 by Barnes. Remnants, an old boy's club based in Slough, proved difficult opponents in November 1879, and it took two replays before Upton Park came through by 5-2, only to get knocked out 1-4 by Royal Engineers. A team called Mosquitoes were swatted (sorry) 8-1 to open the 1880-1 F.A. Cup season, followed by a 3-0 win over Weybridge in round 2. They were lucky enough to draw a bye in round 3 (their first) but were unlucky in round 4 to lose a thrilling match by 4-5 to Clapham Rovers. Played on Wandsworth Common, cup-holders Clapham expected an easy ride, and indeed opened the scoring in the 7th minute and romped into a four goal half-time lead. However, the Uptonians came storming back and had scored three times within twenty minutes of the restart. Clapham got a fifth, but Upton weren't done, and scored again before the end. Clapham had their full cup winning team out and were helped by Woollaston of the Wanderers, although Clopton Lloyd-Jones had to retire hurt at the break.

All previous efforts were eclipsed in 1881-2 when they reached the 5th round, the F.A. Cup entrants now numbering well past a hundred. St. Albans (3-0), Hanover Utd (3-1) were beaten before Upton Park drew a 3rd round bye, in which Swifts, Carthusians and Notts County were eliminated. The name of 'Hotspur' was then drawn out of the hat. When Upton Park defeated Hotspur 4-0 in the 4th round of the F.A. Cup in 1882, thanks to goals from Bastard, Lafour, Mitchell and Barnard, they had not crushed 'the Spurs', but another London amateur club who confusingly had the same! The 5th round contained some serious big names, and it was little surprise when Sheffield Wednesday cruised past them 6-0. In the following season, drawing a 1st round bye, they were edged out by the Swifts 2-3. Silverware was captured that season however, when Upton Park became the first ever winners of the London (Senior) Cup when they beat the Old Foresters in the final by 4-0. Almost no newspaper gave a report on this game, except for the *London Morning Post* who merely said that it was a one-sided game, refereed by Major Marindin (president of the F.A.), and umpired by O. Ogilvie (vice-president) and H. Hart (F.A. treasurer). Captained by Segar Bastard, the winning team, still playing an outmoded 2-2-6 formation was -

			P.C .Bates				
	H.W. Spreckley				Walter Mangles		
	N. Logan				E.D .Ellis		
Segar Bastard	H.R. Barnett	T.G. Thompson	C. Mitchell		James Barnard	Harold Lafone

Clem Mitchell was their star player at this time, and went on to gain five England caps. Most of Upton Park's players were from the Forest Gate area which was then distinctly middle class, and the team was populated by doctors, solicitors, dentists, stockbrokers, barristers, tea merchants and so on, almost all ex-public school men. They could afford to play the game for their own amusement, free from the necessity of having to raise an income from charging spectators or sharing out gate money at the end of each match. Sometime player Thomas Freer Spreckley (b.1850, Marylebone) and brother Herbert William (b.1857, Enfield) also had at least four other footballer brothers, Walter, William, and Arthur. A summary of several of Upton Park's longest serving and better known players will illustrate the club's middle-class status -

Horace Augustus Alexander	1866-73	Architect
Cecil Hugh Aylene	1885-87	Surveyor
Charles William Alcock	1869-72	Administrator
Edward Charles Bambridge	1879-83	Lloyds underwiter
James Jeune Barnard	1879-87	Clergyman
Frederick Barnett	1871-87	Ship-broker
Segar Richard Bastard	1873-87	Solicitor
Percy Chadwick Bates	1879-84	School secretary
John Bennett	1884-87	Army Officer

John Brockbank	1878-79	Actor
Charles Edmund Clutterbuck	1867-70	Stained glass artist
Charles Capper	1867-75	Docks manager
John Hill Capper	1867-68	Colonial Officer
John Spencer Curwen	1866-74	Music Publisher
Thomas Cecil Curwen	1872-78	Stockbroker
Augustus Evans	1867-69	Tea Merchant
William Francis	1883-87	Medical doctor
William Biscombe Gardner	1867-71	Artist
Millner Jutsum	1867-79	Solicitor
Charles James King	1877-82	School master
Robert Stuart King	1879-84	Clergyman
Harold Lafone	1881-86	Solicitor
George Alfred Sedgwick	1870-71	Solicitor
John Henry Self	1873-76	
Arthur John Stanley	1883-85	Stockbroker
Edwin Williams	1874-79	Solicitor

I was sent the above information many years ago, but I believe the research work was done in Australia twenty years ago by *Peter Hamerslie.*

The same two clubs played the 1884 London Cup final too, and the result was very similar - Upton Park winning 1-0 *(London Morning Post)* and not 4-1 as reported on Wikipedia. Old Foresters had beaten favourites Old Etonians 1-0 in their semi final. Played on Saturday April 19th, once again, few papers gave it coverage, but the *Pall Mall Gazette* tells us that the final, played at the Oval before 2,000 spectators was scheduled for April 5th, but the Duke of Albany's funeral was that day. 'Had the losers shooting been less wild, the result might well have been different as they missed several scoring chances' remarked the report. For Upton Park, right winger L. Norman had to retire hurt, but soon after, Inglis scored what proved to be the winner *(London Standard)*. Upton then went on the defensive and held Foresters at bay. Foresters were at full strength and their side included well know men R.C. Gay and Percy Fairclough, and Upton had secured the services of the great Edward Bambridge (The Swifts) for the occasion. In the following year, the London Cup final saw the same two teams meet for the 3rd year running, but this time, the Foresters got their revenge by winning 2-1. Upton Park had beaten West End 3-0 in the semi final on April 30th. Just a week later, the final was played at the Oval, and another very close game ensued. Inglis scored for Upton after a quarter of an hour, but ten minutes later Mills equalised for Foresters. With time running out, C.J. Horner scored a late winner for the old boys. In a similar run of fate, the Casuals were beaten finalists in the London Cup finals of 1887,78,and 79.

Returning to the F.A. Cup, in October 1883, they beat Acton 2-0, then got a 2nd round bye, and a big win over Reading (6-1) brought them to face Preston North End in round 5. This is the infamous match which, after a 1-1 draw, got Preston thrown out of the Cup for admitting to being professionals at a time when to be so was illegal, although the practice was widespread in the north. Famously, Preston manager 'Major' Suddell (of the Rifle Volunteers) admitted that they were, and that so was most of Lancashire too. Upton

Park's 'reward' was to be drawn against the county's top club, Blackburn Rovers, who duly beat them 3-0. In the following season, wins over West End and Reading (3-0) got them to round 3, but the Old Wykehamists just beat them 2-1 to move into the 4th round for the first time. The F.A. Cup of 1884-5 saw an explosion of entrants, particularly from the north, and clubs were also entering from Wales, Ireland and Scotland. Season 1885-6 saw United London Scottish defeated 4-2, and then came a shock as Old Carthusians crushed them 8-0 in the second round. Played at Wanstead Common on Saturday 21st November 'in fine weather before a large company' (Sheffield Independent), the old boys were 5-0 up by half-time. The 1886-7 cup run didn't last until Christmas; a whopping 9-0 win over a faded Barnes FC was followed by a 0-4 defeat to Great Marlow. The 1887-8 effort was even briefer; either they didn't enter, or they scratched without taking part. Southern clubs were by now disappearing fast and accounted for only about one-tenth of the entrants. With the founding of the Football League in 1888, the F.A. Cup was revised as it was becoming unmanageable, and was revised with clubs whittled down to a last 32 who contested the 1st round proper, although 12 of those places were automatically given to the new League clubs, the equivalent to today's 3rd round.

On Boxing Day 1882, Upton Park fielded two sides on the same afternoon, as they beat Barnes away 7-1, and then beat a team at home called Foxes 2-1 ! In season 1883-4, Upton Park were only beaten once - by Blackburn Rovers in an F.A. Cup tie - and won 16 and drew 6 of their other 22, scoring 61 against 22. Many of Upton Park's players were chosen to play for the London XI or Surrey and Middlesex. On Saturday February 19th 1881, H.R. Barnett and H. Barnard were chosen to play for 'the South' versus 'the North' at Sheffield, along with comrades from the Swifts, Oxford University and the Pilgrims. On Saturday 24th March 1883, no less than 8 of their players were on active representative duty. J. Barnard, A. Inglis and F. Barnett were on the Middlesex side which played Surrey which contained E. Ellis and R. Barnett, whilst W. Francis, C. Mitchell and A. Inglis all played for London against Oxford & Cambridge. By the late 1880s, several other teams sprang up in the vicinity, such as Upton Ivanhoe and Upton Excelsior, and up to a dozen teams were playing in West Ham park.

Cup final programme showing the Amateur Cup (left) and right, the solid silver London (Senior) Cup which was won in its first two years by Upton Park, who overcame the Old Foresters in both finals.

Famously amateur they may have been, in an age of the early professional clubs, but when Upton Park went up to play Preston North End in January 1884, they demanded a £65 guarantee ! Preston instead offered half the kick-off receipts (crowds often swelled into the ground at half time) which amounted to £81. It was very interesting then, in the November that year, to see Upton Park take Preston before the F.A. committee for playing professional players after Preston had knocked them out of the Cup. This famous event, blowing the lid on veiled professionalism with hundreds of players (especially in Lancashire, and to a lesser extent in Staffordshire) being coaxed down from Scotland with secret payments in either gifts (even houses in some cases) or wages for non-existent jobs, is so well known that I will not insult the readers intelligence by expanding on it, save to say that leading amateur clubs were then in the habit of asking for large guarantees for them to turn out when visiting Midlands and Northern clubs ! A case of a soot-stained kettle calling the pot black, I would say.

In 1887 it was reported that Upton Park had folded, only to reappear four years later. It was only in February 1887 that they had been knocked out of the London Cup in the semi-final 0-1 by the Casuals ; the other semi seeing Old Westminsters beat Clapton by the same score. Their strict rule of ex-public school men only was relaxed and working class shipyard brothers Ernest and Frederick Roberts were allowed to join the team. In 1892, Upton Park became founder members of the short-lived Southern Alliance League but it collapsed before the season was even finished, with Upton Park bottom with only one win. At this time, W. Hammond was club president, deputised by William and Charles Howard. The *Blackburn Standard* was surprised when 4,000 turned out to see Upton Park play Blackburn Rovers at home that year, but wryly added that this was 'in part due to the entry fee of nil pence'. During the period 1896 to 1906, with the oddly-named Money Ingram as president,Upton Park took on the habit of an annual tour to the Channel Islands, and there is today the Upton Cup competed for there,between the champions of Guernsey and Jersey. The excursion was well organised by J.H. Jones, their secretary-goalkeeper, of 9 Brunswick Square, who announced in the Star Newspaper of 23rd September 1897 that the tour would begin by playing Yeovil and then by train to Weymouth where the boat would take them to Guernsey and Jersey.

ESSEX COUNTY CRICKET GROUND, LEYTON.
ENGLISH CUP TIE.
TO-MORROW (SATURDAY, OCTOBER 31),
At 3.0 o'clock.
LEYTON
(South Essex Champions)
v.
UPTON PARK
(Winners Essex Cup 1894-1895).
Admission 6d.
WEDNESDAY NEXT, November 4, OLD FORESTERS v.
CAMBRIDGE UNIVERSITY. [ADVT.]

At the Olympic Games of 1900, held in Paris, the Upton Park amateurs were invited to represent Great Britain in the football tournament, which they duly did, and won, with a team selected by goalkeeper and captain James Jones. This side beat the USFSA team, representing France, in the final:-

James Jones (goalkeeper and captain), Claude Buckenham, William Gosling, Alfred Chalk, T.E. Burridge, Willliam Quash, Arthur Turner, F.G. Spackman, Jack Nicholas, Jack Zeallery, A. 'Harry' Haslam.

It was said that the USFSA team was drawn from Englishmen who worked at the French Embassy in Paris! It was no 'fiddle': any team comprised of 11 Frenchmen at the time would probably have conceded double figures to a side as good as Upton Park. The club had many well-known players over the years, including Conrad Warner, capped 10 times as an amateur, Clement Mitchell, Alf Stair, Charlie Dove, and Seagar Bastard, better known as the referee in many cup finals. He quite literally fitted the chant " the referee's a bastard! ". Reputedly one Charles Alcock is said to have briefly played for them, which is quite likely, as he was apt to playing five times a week (for anybody) " to keep myself fit". Some Upton Park players also turned out for the Thames Ironworks team, which evolved into West Ham United. A match programme away to Oxford City in 1910 sees Upton Park in green and white, with Oxford in navy blue and white, and since Oxford's colours did not clash with the usual red and black of Upton Park, one must assume this was their colours in their final years, when an inability to recruit new players locally contributed to their decline. In 1915, the public turned its back on football, as it believed that every fit man should be instead enrolling with the forces to fight, although some wartime football continued, except that the players could not be paid wages. Many London amateur clubs closed down, such as Caledonians, Ilford, Dulwich, Clapton and Nunhead, and Upton Park. Many never reformed in 1919, and Upton Park were one of them. On May 30th 2016, a game was staged between 'Upton Park', who were dressed in red and black stripes, black, and 'Royal Engineers' to mark the end of West Ham United's Boleyn Ground before it was demolished.

Founded - 1900
Folded   - 1988 amalgamated with Leytonstone & Ilford and then became
            Redbridge Forest
Ground   - Aveling Park 1905-1910
            Green Pond Road, London E.17
Colours - Light Blue circa 1908
            Light and dark blue hoops, white shorts

Reputedly founded as Walthamstow Grange FC, a second name change to Avenue United saw them finally settle upon Walthamstow Avenue. Since others say they began as Walthamstow Boys Club, it is possible that the two teams joined forces to become a united club. The first proper ground was made on land next to Water House, which property and extensive gardens were bequeathed to Walthamstow Council to be used as a public recreational area. The Green Pond Road ground eventually had an impressive main stand straddling the halfway line, which probably held two thousand spectators, although by then, two hundred would have been the usual attendance. In 1989, the ground was sold and houses were built over it, and the last trace of one of England's best known amateur clubs had vanished. The earliest game I found was a 0-6 away defeat to Malvern Mission at the end of October 1901.

As early as Easter 1907 Walthamstow Avenue toured Holland, with games arranged against ODO Arnham (3-2), Dutch Division 2 professional champions Amsterdam (0-2), Willem II (3-3) and Prince Wilhemena (2-0) of Enschede. Players caught the boat-train from Liverpool Station. The fourteen players who toured the Netherlands were – W. Skinner, W. Robinson, C. Dixon, W. Pearce, W. Marshall, H. Golder, A. Gibbard, P. Downs, E. Marshall, W. Taylor, A. Silcock, and officials H. Bradley and secretary H.J. Heyden.

Their first few years were spent in the local Walthamstow League playing teams such as Standard Rovers, Chillingford Athletic University, Imperial, Spartans and Leyton St. Mary's. A reserve team competed for the Tottenham Cup, and the 1st team entered the London Junior Cup within two years of being founded. Football was already well established by 1900 in the area, and as latecomers, Avenue found there were already other teams in town, including Walthamstow Holborn, Walthamstow Town, Walthamstow Grange and Walthamstow Springfield. When Walthamstow Grange of the Middlesex League were at home in Cricklewood on the Royal Standard Athletic grounds in the 3rd Qualifying round of the FA Cup in 1908, Avenue were only competing in the Essex Junior Cup, and Clapton Warwick had put Avenue out of the London Junior Cup. I found Walthamstow Grange playing in the small seven team London League on the even of the Great War and their best men included captain F. J. Warwick, and forward J. Norman. Their secretary was E. Chapman of 16, Whitehorse Road. In 1915, they were playing home games at the Lea Bridge Road stadium. They were still advertising for "first class players" in 1930 now to their Chingford Road address. I found them still playing in the London League, which had grown in both numbers and status, and included teams as Cray Wanderers, Finchley, Mitcham Wanderers, Carlshalton Athletic, Epsom Town and Hendon Town.

After playing in local leagues, the Avenue stepped up and joined the South Essex League playing teams such as Romford, Barking, 2nd Middlesex Regiment, Mawney Institute, Woodford Crusaders and Southend Amateurs. They moved into the Spartan League in 1921, and again into the new Athenian League in 1929-30 where they became one of its most successful teams. Better class Spartan opposition now included Staines, Wealdstone, Maidenhead United, Aylesbury, Wood Green, Chesham United and Polytechnic. The reserves competed in the Second Division against teams like Birkhamstead, Wendover, Finchley and the reserves of the 1st Division clubs mentioned. Their best players at this time included Lucas, Spencer, Embleton and Vango.

The 'Two Blues' had to wait thirty years for their first trophy, when they won the Athenian League in season 1929-30. They rattled in 94 goals in their 26 matches, winning 19, drawing 3 and losing 4. Season 1932-33 was blighted by the loss of three star players, when inside forward Bazin took a job in France, Halerow departed for Dulwich Hamlet, and R.E. White moved on to Leyton FC. A year later, the team was back to winning ways and was quickly followed by more Athenian successes in 1933, 1934, 1938 and 1939, a decade in which they also won the London Senior Cup (1936, 1937), and the London Charity Cup (1934, 1939). A photograph thought to be of Walthamstow Avenue in the 1910s shows them in blue vertical stripes. In 1938, the ground record was set when 12,500 fans watched their 0-0 F.A. Cup tie with Stockport County. Eliminated 3-1 in the replay, the Avenue had beaten Tunbridge Wells Rangers by 4-1 in their 1st Round proper appearance. A setback in 1938 occurred when the main grandstand caught fire and suffered serious damage on 17th September, an event reported as far away as the Aberdeen newspapers.

Their outstanding player of the 1930s was centre forward Forman, who scored over 50 goals for them in season 1938-39, surpassing forward Spencer, who was sold to Aston Villa in 1930. Goalkeeper H.R. Saphin played for the representative Athenian League eleven. In early 1938, when an England Amateur XI toured Australia and New Zealand, four Avenue men were in the squad – half back J.W. Lewis, forwards R.J. Matthews, E.C. Collins and F.A. Davies. Famous Old Carthusian and Corinthian forward Charles Wreford-Brown was the tour manager.

In 1934, the Walthamstow Stadium on Rushcroft Road was in the news when residents formally complained about noise pollution to the magistrates, who found owner William Chandler in breach of public nuisance orders, and forced him to reduce his speedway and greyhound race meetings to 100 a year. More interestingly, it was stated that "the portion of the stadium hitherto used by the Walthamstow Grange FC in that part of the arena owned by a Mr. Webster until 1932, and the other part, used by the Minerva Sports club, had been acquired by Chandler who decided to modernise it and bring new popular events there. The judge had a difficult time trying to balance the noise pollution complaints of nearby residents with the fact that Chandler had laid out some £35,000 in trying to bring popular sports to the area.

More success came the Avenue's way in the 1940s, with three more London Cups in 1940, 1942 and 1944. Their 5-0 crushing of Wealdstone in the May 1940 final was the biggest since when the Old Carthusians defeated the Casuals way back in 1895. The London Charity Cup was again won in 1949 when they beat Leytonstone by 1-0. A further Isthmian League title in 1946, along with four consecutive Herts & Middlesex League titles during 1942-1945 cemented their position as one of London's leading amateur club. These were the heady post-war boom years for football when even amateur teams counted their attendances in five figures, who attended Saturday matches like a religion, wearing rosettes, scarves in team colours, and making a great deal of noise with their rattles and car horns. Their star forward at this time was free-scoring "Bunny" Bernard Groves, whilst their outside right Walters was found turning out for Tottenham Hotspur who were keen to sign him as a professional. The rest of the forward line included G. Brett, Jim Lewis, Don Nolan, and F.A. Davis (*Essex Newsman*). Sadly, Bunny Groves left for rivals Leytonstone in 1947 at a time when top amateur clubs in the capital were drawing attendances averaging well over 5,000. With a wealth of top amateur teams around London, many of whom could hold Football League sides to a good game, Avenue's main rivals in the 1940s were Leytonstone, Romford, Wimbledon and Barnet.

The 1950s saw two more Isthmian League titles in 1953 and 1954, the London Cup again in 1955, the Essex Senior Cup in 1956 and 1958, and the London Charity Cup again in 1951 and 1956. The most important trophy which had hitherto eluded them, was the national Amateur Cup, and in 1952, they overcame Leyton 2-1 in the final on 26th April. Played at Wembley Stadium, the ground was packed to its capacity of 100,000 demonstrating that amateur football was as popular as the professional game, encapsulating a certain element of romance lacking in the senior game. Their journey to the final saw them overcome Hounslow Town 2-0, Southall 4-2 away, Tilbury 2-0 away, Wimbledon after three epic games (0-0, 1-1, 3-0), and Walton & Hersham 3-0 in their semi-final played on Fulham's Craven Cottage ground. This was their cup-winning team that year -

	Gerula	
Young		Stratton
Lucas	Brahan	Saunders
Rossiter	Bailey	Lewis	Hall	Camis

Season 1952-53 was probably the Avenue's finest hour, as they reached the 4th Round of the FA Cup that year. Just to battle through the Qualifying Rounds for non-League and amateur club is hard enough, but to then get past Wimbledon (0-0, 3-0), Watford (1-1, 2-1), and Stockport County (2-1) brought them a plum tie against Manchester United in the 4th Round. A battling performance saw the famous visitors held to a 1-1 draw, but class shone through in the replay at Old Trafford, with United winning through 5-2. The club also went on a tour of Holland that year, although no results could be traced. At this time, their already attractive kit was augmented by red socks. Club officials included T.G. Blake, J. W. Lewis, treasurer J.R. Long, chairman S.L. Green, and vice-president D.H. Davies.

In 1961, Walthamstow Avenue won the Amateur Cup for the second time when they defeated West Auckland by 2-1 at Wembley Stadium. A close match saw the sides level at 1-1 until the rain played a part, when Auckland keeper Bowmaker dropped a greasy ball crossed by Andrews, and Lewis poked the ball over the line for the winner. En route to the final, the Avenue overcame Bishop Stortford 3-0, Hendon 2-0 away, Harwich & Parkeston 7-2 away, Wimbledon 1-0 away, and in the semi-final, played at the White City stadium, Hitchin Town 1-0. In the opening round of the following year, they were shocked when Aetolian Legaue side Ford United departed as 2-0 winners.

After 1961, trophies were fewer in number, and limited to the London Senior Cup (1978) and the Essex Senior Cup in 1969, 1972, 1973, 1974 and 1977, and the minor Essex Thameside trophy was won in 1978 for the 5th time. In 1988, and still in the Isthmian League, the name of Walthamstow Avenue disappeared when they agreed to merge with Leytonstone & Ilford and later become Redbridge Forest.

WALTHAMSTOW AVE.
Amateur Kingpins of 1960-61

Left to right—back row—Ron Bambridge, Stan Prince, Gary McGuire, Brian Edwards, Terry Keenes. Front row—Brian Harvey, Dave Andrews, Alan Minal, Don Saggers, Jim Lewis, Reg Groves.

WEST END FC

Founded - 1868
Folded - Circa 1902
Ground - Herne Hill stadium 1880s
          Wormholt Farm grounds 1890s
Colours - 1. Black and amber stripes
          2. Blue and amber (1880s)
          3. Navy and white halves, white shorts (1890s)

Another grandly-named small London amateur club who sometimes entered the early years of the FA Cup was a team called the West End FC. Expecting to find some kind of society club, I was surprised to find that they were the football players representing their place of work, namely the London drapers and milliners of Marshall & Snelgrove Limited. Founded in 1837 in Vere Street, they opened on Oxford Street in 1851 and branches were later opened in Harrogate and Scarborough. The Birmingham branch eventually became Debenhams, one of the city's largest and best-known department stores. Affiliated to the Middlesex and London FA, by 1890 they had 70 player-members and fielded six teams, although in that year, lost some of their best men (*London Sporting & Illustrated News*). I think their claimed 1868 date may refer to the company, as I found no matches or results for West End FC in the 1870s.

In the FA Cup of 1879-80, West End gained a November walkover against the Swifts, then edged past Hotspur FC 1-0 on 13th December, and then drew a bye into the 4th round, only to be trounced 5-1 by the cup holders, Old Etonians on February 7th. In season 1880-1, they defeated Hanover United 1-0 before bowing out 0-4 to Great Marlow in Round Two. In the following season, they overcame The Remnants 3-2, before scratching when drawn away to Reading. Season 1882-83 saw a fall at the first hurdle when Hendon defeated them 3-1. It also saw their biggest win to date, when they beat City Ramblers by 8-0 at the end of October in the London Challenge Cup.

Undeterred, West End again entered the F.A. Cup in 1883 and with a Cooper goal, overcame Maidenhead 1-0 on 10th November to enter Round 2 where they were pipped 1-0 at Reading FC. The West End team that season given in *The Sportsman* was -

P. Foster

G.J. Scott (captain)   T. Houghton

A. Edwards   A. Edwards

H. Cooper   J. Gill   D. Foster   P. Lawton   F. Elmslie   J. Steele

November 8th 1884 saw West End scratch after drawing 3-3 (not 1-1 as per Wikipedia) against Upton Park, which marked the end of their attempts on the national trophy. It was not clear why West End, after such a good result against the London Cup holders, would withdraw, but player unavailability and captain Scott selected to play for London v

Oxford on the scheduled day seemed to have something to do with it. When the same two sides again drew 1-1 in the semi finals of the London Cup in January 1885, the *Reynolds Newspaper* stated that it was the semi-finals of the FA Cup! The *Illustrated Sporting & Dramatic News (London)*, only a decade after these events, also managed to get all their facts jumbled up, proving that newspapers can never be relied upon to be entirely accurate, however near to the event.

West End's best players throughout the 1880s were J.G. Scott, F. Elmslie and O.H. Cooper, who were selected for London in the annual match against the Birmingham FA. Secretary in the 1890s was E.W. Badcock. Success came in the form of the London West End Cup, in which they were finalists in season 1881-82, winners in 1882-83 (3-0 v Prairie Rangers at Wormholt Farm), and semi finalists in 1883-84, after which time they dropped out. A multi-sporting club, they were very successful at rowing and water polo; their polo team won the London Eights for four years in a row. Also playing at cricket and tennis, their cycling team were West End champions at their Herne Hill Velodrome. They seem to have been a very well organised outfit, with a club members' book issued yearly giving club rules, results from the previous year, and turning out at Herne Hill three times a week during the late Victorian period. I found West End winning 5-0 against St. Marys Hospital in early 1889 in the Middlesex Cup, but almost nothing after 1895, when they were still at Wormholt Farm. I found them playing in the Middlesex Junior Cup against teams like Old St. Stephens, Hammersmith Athletic, Holborn Circus in 1898, and Shepherds Bush in 1900, giving hope that they made it to the twentieth century. Captained by their goalkeeper, this was their first team of 1891-

			H.A. Campbell			
		J.B. Gould		J.B. Dawe		
	J.M. Mollison		J.M. Price		H. Betteley-Cooke	
F.E. Griffiths	C.E. Yorke	R.A. Parker		G. Manton	J. Creadie	

Herne Hill sports ground was predominantly a velodrome, but the football pitch inside the track was used by many teams over the years.

WEST HAMPSTEAD FC

Founded - Circa 1894 (earlier as a rugby club)
Folded - Circa 1913
Ground - Hampstead athletic grounds
          Willesden cricket ground from 1898
          Cricklewood Lane 1902-09
          Lower Welsh Harp ground 1910-11
Colours - White shirts, black knicks

A level playing field didn't seem to bother the players of 'West Hampstead' when they played the Unity FC in November 1884, as their 9 men lined up against the visitor's 13. Ruscoe, Fawcett and Collins were conspicuous in a creditable 1-1 draw. A match played in the previous month, at Turnham Green on the ground of Essex Park FC sounded more like a rugby match, when the score was given as "a draw in favour of Essex by seven touches to three". Possibly it was 0-0, and the goal-kicks or corners were counted. Further games played in the late 1880s also all turned out to be rugby, although a Hampstead RFC and a West Hampstead Harriers running club had both been going for some time.

West Hampstead FC were a relatively short-lived club which gained some notoriety in the early Edwardian era, when they imported four Scottish paid players, and registered them under false names to the FA who later found out. Their secretary-treasurer J.C. Christie and first team captain W. Denham were among several men suspended or banned. They seem to have rankled the authorities from the word 'go' as Hampstead Council wrote to them in October 1896, telling them that they had received many complaints from residents about

The Middlesex Senior Cup, won twice by West Hampstead, in 1901 and 1906.

the noise coming from their ground, as it was too close to the cemetery. The online forum *West Hampstead Life* thinks it was the football ground in a field off Cricklewood Lane (see Hampstead Town at the end of section) shown on a 1915 map, but as you have seen in my section on the Hendon FC, I believe it was their ground instead, and too far away for a crowd of perhaps 500 people to cause a disturbance to the attendees of Hampstead Crematorium. I believe that West Hampstead played on the sports ground a few hundred yards further to the south, one of three fields which backed on to the Hampstead Cemetery. Avenue Farm lay 300 yards north, and all the fields between the farm and the cemetery were turned into sports grounds. The farm itself, gone by around 1920, also ironically became a cricket ground which is still there today and used by Brondesbury

Cricket & Tennis Club. For their few hundred or so spectators to have been a nuisance to the people attending the mortuary chapel, I suggest they would have had to have been in the nearest field, which was a two acre one which is today the University College sports ground tennis courts accessed from Ranulf Road. It has a noticeable slope, although quite level across its width.

In season 1897-8, West Hampstead gained entry into the London League's Second Division. Opponents included Fulham and Clapton Orient, and a reasonably successful season saw them finish in 5th place. The London Cup was entered and they were drawn against the once famous Clapham Rovers, the leading sports club whose footballing strength by then lay in the handling code. Clapham were overcome, but Fulham proved too strong in round two. The West Hampstead team at this time usually was -

R. Muncer or S.E. Gillam

A. Porter   **B. Sutherland**

J. McLure   **H. Greatorix**   **J. Collard**

W. Kirk   **J. McLaughlin**   **F. Beaumont**   **A. Porter**   **H. Simmonds**

Between 1898 and 1909, the Middlesex Cup final was reached several times. Firstly in 1898-99, when West Hampstead drew 0-0 with London Caledonians, only to be beaten 5-0 in the replay. By 1899 West Hampstead were in Division One of the London League. They were soon back, and the same two sides contested the 1900-01 final. The Callies had beaten Crouch End Vampires in 1900 to retain the cup, and once more, West Hampstead and Caledonians played out a drawn final, this time 2-2. The replay however, went Hampstead's way 3-2 to give them the trophy for the first time. During the 1890s, other sports rose to prominence in the area, notably rugby, lacrosse and hockey, and there were several such clubs in the Hampstead area. At 1890, West Hampstead lacrosse club played home games at Gospel Oak, and those old sports, cricket and golf, never went away. Promotion followed the year after, but they found the higher division too strong, and they finished bottom but one of ten London League clubs. 1898 saw West Hampstead FC move into a new ground at Willesdon, two miles south-west in NW10, possibly to Sidmouth Road, which was occupied solely with athletic grounds (now South Hampstead cricket club). If it was to the grounds of Willesdon cricket club they moved, off Church Road (now Curzon Crescent Childrens' Centre), then the same scenario repeated itself, with Willesden mortuary chapel only 150 yards away. I wonder if the two stories got mixed up over time? With nothing to go on, I noticed that when the Willesden cricket ground got swept away with houses circa 1895, I saw the appearance of the Roundwood cricket ground on Harlesden Lane at about the same time. That ground now has Newman Catholic College sitting on it. Either way, it was yet another demonstration of the difficulties involved in tracking down where football teams played, as they would frequently move to another village or district altogether, some of which already had football teams bearing their own name. In the sister book 'Lost Teams Of The North' I found Turton playing in Chapeltown, Church playing in Enfield and Oswaldtwistle, and in this book, Hendon playing in Cricklewood and Clapham Rovers playing in Wandsworth!

Season 1900-01 was a great success, for they won both the Middlesex Senior Cup and the Middlesex County League. The cup was won by defeating Caledonians 3-2 after a replay, and the Edwardian era saw them reach four more finals, although only one was won. In season 1901-02, West Hampstead were elected into the Southern League's Second Division but after only winning 6 of their 16 games, finishing 5th in the small league of 9 teams, they left the league. Opposition this season came from Fulham, Brighton, Shepherds Bush and Wycombe Wanderers. At this time, the team was captained by Herbert Kingaby, who later signed for Aston Villa in 1906 after a season with Clapton Orient. His stay at Villa was a flop, but they retained his papers which prevented him from continuing his career, and after wasted years, ended up back at Clapton. His court case against Aston Villa which held him in suspension was lost, and it nearly bankrupt the Football Players Union. Notable in the team at this time were the four Westerley brothers, Harold, Arthur, Herbert and Francis, and their similar looks and heavy moustaches made them difficult to tell apart.

A small success was gained in the following season, when they won the Middlesex Charity Cup beating Ealing at Boston Road, Hanwell, and the Hospital Shield. The strong Southern League side Shepherds Bush proved to have the edge in the 1903 Middlesex County Cup final, and won 4-1 to take the trophy for the first time. Shepherds Bush reached the following year's final only to lose to the Richmond Association, when after two games, a single goal decided it. By this time West Hampstead's attendances were in the 1-2,000 range, such as at their 1903 Middlesex Senior Cup semi final against Southall at Wormholt Farm, a game won 3-1 watched by 1,800 spectators. West Hampstead were also playing in the Metropolitan Amateur League in the first decade of the twentieth century, playing teams such as Ilford and Shepherds Bush. However, 1902-03 was the season when they were accused of undisclosed professionalism by Shepherds Bush who reported them to the London F.A. The likeliest way this came about would have been if one of the Shepherds Bush players had been approached by a West Hampstead official offering to pay him perhaps five shillings a game.

Even a club simply paying for a skint player's rail fare broke the strict amateur codes prevalent in London at the time. Even though professionalism had been permitted under certain restrictions back in 1885, and the fact that all the top clubs in the land had been run on all fully professional basis for over a decade, the London F.A. were still being very old-fashioned about this, and were blatantly pro-amateur. There were hardly any professional clubs in London even at the start of the twentieth century, so veiled professionals were looked upon with a dim view in London. West Hampstead's secretary-treasurer (effectively their manager) J. C. Christie was ordered to hand over the account books for scrutiny and constantly refused to do so. This got several committee men and players banned or suspended for the rest of the season at the F.A. disciplinary committee meeting held in January 1903. Star player Will Denham was declared to be a professional, and along with J.T. Baggott, was suspended until the following season.

This entrenched and outdated ideology which saw the London F.A. refuse to allow any professional clubs to join its ranks blew up in 1907 when ambitious clubs like Millwall, Arsenal and Chelsea and later Tottenham were starting to dominate the London scene, and the old boys brigade from public schools formed their own Amateur Association, and diverted their efforts into the Arthur Dunn and Amateur Cups. This rift festered on for seven years until the Amateur F.A. settled their differences and joined the Football Association as a body. 1903 marked the only year in which West Hampstead entered the Amateur Cup. Begun in 1893, it was not for some time the success it was meant to be, or the salvation of the thousands of amateur clubs who felt beached up in the tide of burgeoning professionalism. Riddled with protests about the status of certain players who were once professional but now turning out as amateurs, the A.F.A introduced a new ruling clarifying the situation, stating that former professionals who had been re-instated as amateurs could no longer play in the Amateur Cup, i.e. once a professional, always a professional. This ruling 'nobbled' many a team who regarded themselves as amateur, and did nothing to increase the number of entrants into the Amateur Cup. During the competition's first opening decade, entrant numbers had not actually increased, and when West Hampstead were drawn at home to Croydon, there were only 16 matches in round 1. Croydon were swept aside 6-0, but a long trip to Weymouth Whiteheads saw them go out by 4-2. West Hampstead did not enter again, as no doubt they were, by definition of paying even a single player's wages, deemed to be professionals. During season 1904-05 saw West Hampstead go on a 14 match winning streak.

In season 1905-06, the first round proper of the F.A Cup was almost reached, but they were beaten by Swindon Town in Q4, who themselves were dumped 0-4 away to Brighton in the 1st round proper. However, the Middlesex Cup was again won, when they defeated the 2nd Battalion Grenadier Guards 2-0 in the final. At this time, West Hampstead were playing in the South London League Division Two, alongside Eastbourne, Southend United, Chesham Generals, Grays United, Chesham Town, Clapton Orient, Tunbridge Wells Rangers, Redhill and the reserves of Hastings United. In the spring of 1907, West Hampstead met London Caledonians in a 2nd round London Cup tie, and the two sides were so evenly balanced that it took four matches to produce a winner. And even then by just 1-0 in the third replay at Shepherds Bush, after 1-1 at Tuffnell Park, 1-1 at Kendal Rise and 0-0 again at Tuffnell Park. Around a thousand people watched each game. The team was as below except that F.W. Painter was back in goal. 1907 saw yet another Middlesex Cup final, but this time there was disappointment when the New Crusaders beat them by 3-0. With A. B. Porter still in the side after at least ten years' service, this was the team given in *The Sportsman* which lost to Leytonstone in December 1907 -

			R. Alaway			
	H. Ruston				A.B. Porter	
	F. Painter		W. Denham		H. Woodward	
A. Humphries	A. Parker		W. Harris	O. Neale	H. O. Thurman	

What proved to be their last appearance in the Middlesex Cup final came at the end of the 1908-09 season, when the 1st Battalion Grenadier Guards got revenge for their fellow soldiers a few years before, by beating the West Hampstead men by 4-0. At this time, their club officials were president and treasurer H.J. Head, with no less than 18 vice-presidents forming the committee, which seemed to include nearly all their players! W.J. Denham was 1st team captain, with C. Neale as his deputy. Reserve team captain was J. Scott, deputised by W. Mackintosh. They had entered for all possible cup competitions, and home matches were to be played on the Lower Welsh Harp ground, Hendon. Being right on the Brent

Reservoir, this ground was infamous for being flooded, a factor which ended the life of Hendon FC who also played there.

The team was much changed from that above by 1909, with only Ruston, Denham, Parker and Neake remaining, the others being- T. Cutler (goal), F. Smith (back), Downing (half-back), and forwards Walter Guscott, William Guscott, W. Kelly and T. Mitchell. This proved to be the last headline appearance of the club, who were to be found in the London League Division One for 1909-10 season, meeting teams like Finchley, Sommertown, and Catford, and they were also in the Western Section of the six club Middlesex & District League. Their ground being under flood for much of the winter, they were forced to play away for weeks on end, with the resultant loss of gate money, and to make matters worse, star player right back Ruston broke his leg playing against Wood Green. Their end of season record ran – played 38, won 7 drawn 9, lost 22, scored 66, conceded 126. Optimism was held for the following season, with "the English, Amateur, Middlesex and London cups all entered for" (*Hendon & Finchley Times*). Headquarters at this time was the Lower Welsh Harp inn. In September 1910, the same newspaper announced that "West Hampstead will not be making a team this year on account of being unable to secure a ground. They may play as a wandering team".

By 1910, West Hampstead were struggling to make an eleven, with the core of the team being old hands. A disastrous trip to play Tuffnell Park at Christmas that year saw them arrive with only 9 men and were thrashed by 9-0. In 1913, I found them in the Qualifying Rounds of the Amateur Cup, where they never seemed to make through to the competition proper. A.H. Parker and A. Humphries and J.M. Fearn were now playing for Hampstead Town in 1914, and this led me to think that West Hampstead may have upgraded their name on the eve of the First World War. I then found both West Hampstead and Hampstead

West Hampstead FC circa 1903 - The players were (not in order) G.F. Royce (goalie), G.E. Thurman and F.B. Griffin (full backs), J. Gamble, Baggott and Downing (half backs), H.O. Hingby, R. Reid, J. H. Scott (with ball), T. Pickering, E. Hillyard.

Town active in 1910, so they were separate clubs, who may have amalgamated in 1913-14, or West Hampstead folded, and their best men joined the ambitious Town club, who were only competing in the Willesdon League at their Kendal Rise Ground in 1910, but had applied to join the Athenian League. By August 1912, the Hampstead Town ground was on The Avenue, Childs Hill, Cricklewood Lane (*The Sportsman and the Finchley Times*). Reference was made to the new enclosure and club, and the hope that the public would get behind Town "as in the days of the old West Hampstead club". This seems proof that the old club had folded, yet flies in the face of their 1913 attempt of getting through the Amateur Cup qualifying stages. The Childs Hill ground was opened with the visit of Kilburn in a London League fixture.

Hampstead Town emerged with a new patron and colours after the Great War, and the Childs Hill ground was spruced up to include a flagpole. Town changed their name to Hampstead FC in December 1919, and continued to improve. They were losing Middlesex Cup finalists in 1925 and 1931, later calling themselves Golders Green and finally Hendon (*see Hendon FC*).

WEST KENT FC

Founded - 1867 (as football team, 1812 as cricket)
Folded   - 1874 (to concentrate on rugby)
Ground   - Camden Park, Chiselhurst, Bromley
Colours - Orange and black hoops 1867-74
            White shirts with county crest , blue stockings 1874-1882
            Blue and white jerseys 1882
            Blue and amber jerseys from 1883 as a rugby club
Secretary - H.W. Richardson, Court Yard, Eltham, London SE

Founded by old Rugbeans in the same year as were The Wednesday and Queens Park clubs, West Kent was a football development of the earlier cricket club which went back to 1812. Experimenting with both the association and rugby codes, West Kent, and A. G. Guillemard in particular were at the forefront of establishing the Rugby Union in 1871, and became president of the RFU from 1878-1882.

Ousted from their ground when Bromley Common was enclosed in 1821, the Lord of the Manor gave them permission to create a new ground using eight acres of Chiselhurst Common. The original cricket club was called the Prince's Plain C.C and a caveat of the move to the common was to permit other clubs to use it too, an attempt in 1885 to gain exclusive use being denied. In 1822, the name was altered to the West Kent C.C and the ground was opened with a visit by the M.C.C. For the next half century, cricket held sway.

On Saturday 9th May 1868, they held their first annual sports day on land belonging to N.W.F. Strode in Camden park. A committee of E.O. Berenes, A. Lubbock, J.B. Martin, A.G. Guillemard, P. Norman, H.W. Powell, H.W. Richardson, Slade and B.T. Stow oversaw the events. R.E. Gower and C.H. Allfrey were the club's joint honorary secretaries. H.W. Richardson achieved the huge distance of almost 85 feet with his winning hammer throw, with Lubbock winning both the high jump, long jump and the pole vault events. The Imperial Arms at Chiselhurst was used for their headquarters. The cricket ground saw no development over the decades, save a wooden fence and two tent pavilions used as dressing rooms which were superseded by permanent structures in 1899.

West Kent tried their hand at both the rugby and association codes, and later hockey.

In January 1867, they played the Civil Service Club at Battersea Park, although since C.S.C also played the rugby code, it is not certain whether hands were allowed or not. In November 1867 West Kent travelled into the city to play the boys of Westminster School, on their usual ground at Vincent Square, no goals resulting. The three Norman brothers and the two Ferguson brothers making up most of the team. Interestingly, 'boy wonder' Walpole Vidal was on the West Kent side, possibly loaned by his Westminster school to make up the numbers.

This was the West Kent side that day - P. Norman, E .Norman, H.G. Norman, R.W.S. Vidal, J.B. Martin, J. Round, G. Gurdun, R. Ferguson, H. Ferguson, R.M. Curteis.

On Wednesday 4th December that year, an away match was played against Charterhouse

School, whilst it was still in London, not yet moved out to Godalming. When West Kent played the Croydon club in December 1867 at the cricket ground, the match was almost certainly under the rugby code, although Wanderers' player E. Lubbock demonstrated his versatility by playing alongside Guillemard in the West Kent defence. The Sportsman criticized the excessive amount of mauling by the forwards, and expressed the opinion that this feature was ruining the game. West Kent were excusably confused when they went to play the Walthamstow club on Saturday 8th February 1868. The home team won 'by one goal and two tries to none' suggesting rugby rules were used, but then we see a reference to 'the Walthamstow goalkeeper', and the demise of Kent due to their unfamiliarity of the home rules. Rouquette, for Walthamstow, scored a touch-down, but failed with the 'try'. This sounds like the early rules where if the ball was touched own within 15 yards of the goals, a free kick at goal was then permitted with the ball brought back fifteen yards onto the field, just like in modern rugby, except in the association game, the ball would be aimed under the crossbar instead of over it!

On Saturday November 28th 1868, West Kent demonstrated their dual allegiance when they fielded a 'soccer' and a 'rugger' team on the same day. The fifteen went to Ladywell and played Guys Hospital, and the 'footers' played the Civil Service FC at home, winning 1-0 thanks to a goal by Lubbock. The visitors only brought seven men, and spent the whole match trying to defend their goal. This was the soccer side that day -

E. Lubbock, S. Gibbs, H. Powell, E.C. Goodhart, M. Teesdale, M. Guillemard, H. Trollope, J. Tudor, McKewan, J. Blackwood. Most of the above side represented West Kent in November 1869 when they travelled to play the Westminster School on Vincent Square. Losing 0-1, the game was said to have been watched by 'a great many present and past scholars of the school'. In May 1869, the Royal Military Academy held its annual sports day on the lawns in front of the main building, and amongst over a hundred competitors in a variety of events were C.D. Buchanan and H. Crosbie from West Kent FC.

For season 1869-70, West Kent announced a limited set of fixtures , but only one seemed to be against an association team, namely the Wanderers, with other opposition being Blackheath, Wimbledon Hornets, Richmond and Marlborough Nomads, all rugby clubs, suggesting that for them, anyway, the handling code was the way forward. West Kent were again welcomed as visitors to the Vincent Square ground of the Old Westminsters on 30th November 1870, when a large crowd including many ladies were present. Westminster fielded some famous players such as the Vidal brothers, Otter, Rawson and Dixon, and subsequently won 1-0 with a goal from Haden. The West Kent side that day was captained by Fred Miller -

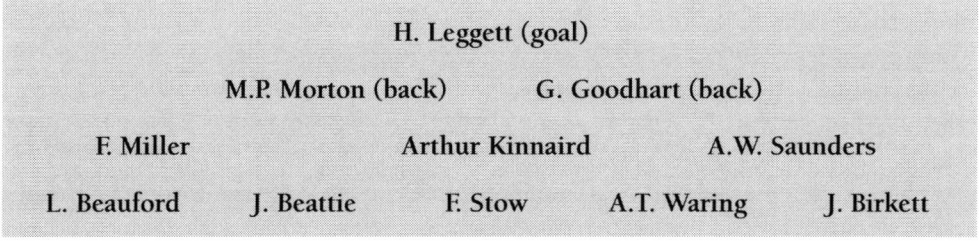

The two clubs had met only a few weeks earlier on October 26th, but West Kent only took two first team men, and were easily beaten 4-0, with Westminster able to give a 'run out' to new players H.D. Vidal, W.S. Rawson and H.S. Otter, and E.H. Ryde in goal 'who had nothing to do' *(The Sportsman)*. A possible lack of that Victorian sporting necessity 'pluck and courage' were decidedly absent on Saturday 10th December 1870, when only five West Kent men showed up at the Oval for a match against Upton Park, who fortunately brought thirteen men with them. Freezing conditions and a layer of snow had sorted the men from the boys, giving an illustrating why Upton Park continued successfully on for many years, whilst West Kent gave up football. With four borrowed men, West Kent had the temerity to win the game thanks to a goal by Hibbert. *The Sportsman* said it showed just how popular the game had become when hardy souls would not just turn out to play a game in such conditions, but applauded those who turned up merely to spectate.

> **WEST KENT v. WANDERERS.**
> This match was played at the Oval on Saturday last, and was well contested throughout. Nepean, as usual, particularly distinguished himself, and obtained the only two goals which were scored. Lubbock, as long-behind, was of course invaluable. The game resulted in favour of the West Kent by two goals to nothing. The following formed the elevens :—
> WEST KENT.—E. Lubbock, T. Beattie, S. Miller, C. E. Turner, C. E. B. Nepean, E. S. Stowe, J. E. Tayloe, J. B. Martin, A. F. Russell, A. C. Wathen, and E. C. Goodhart.
> WANDERERS.—C. W. Alcock, A. Baker, E. E. Bowen, A. Borwick, W. J. Dixon, E. Freeth, C. L. Huggins, J. Kirkpatrick, A. Murten, P. K. Povah, and W. Wallace.

West Kent must have held connections with the highest social classes, for, at their 1872 annual sports day, the exiled ex-French Emperor and about twenty of his court attended the lavish proceeding held as usual in Camden Park, lent for the occasion by owner W.F. Strode. Four years earlier, amongst titled guests was one Sir Robert Peel. The Empress, too ill to walk amongst the 1,000 guests, watched from afar in the estate house. The cricket team, had used a part of Chiselhurst Common known as Hangmans Corner for some years, so it remains unclear whether the footballers used the common or the park. That ground is still there today on Watts Lane, and is still the Chiselhurst & West Kent cricket club grounds. Association football was played until 1874, when West Kent dropped it, and played rugby exclusively thereafter until 1886. When association was dropped in favour of rugger, the team's orange and black hoops were dropped in favour of a simpler white shirt with the county crest, white trousers and blue socks. In 1881, colours were changed again to blue and white (probably hoops), and in the following year, to blue and amber hoops.

Founder-member Arthur George Guillemard (1845-1909) was a prominent player in the development and formation of the Rugby Union organisation in 1871, and became its president from 1878 to 1882. West Kent were one of the original thirteen founder members, and Arthur Guillemard, Joseph Green and Charles Sherrard becoming early capped England rugby players. Two players from West Kent FC were capped for England at football against Scotland when Morton Peto Betts and Edward Lubbock (both also of the Wanderers) took the field on 25th February 1871.

The association game was re-introduced in 1886, as they are recorded as beating the Old Reptonians 5-4 in January 1899 at Chiselhurst. West Kent's social standing became clear when I read that they held their annual sports day in June 1877 at the Camden Park, Chiselhurst "which was once again placed at their disposal by the Empress Eugenie".

WEST NORWOOD FC

Founded   - 1886
Folded   - 1939
Ground   - 1. High View park (till 1902)
              2. Herne Hill bicycle ground (1902-22)
              3. Clapham Common
              4. Goring Park, Mitcham (1920s)
Colours   - Red and white hoops
Nickname   - "The Bantams"

Playing mostly friendly matches plus cup ties in the Surrey Senior Cup during the 1890s, West Norwood made an inauspicious start on the London football scene. In February 1900, West Norwood were one of four clubs being investigated for financial irregularities by the London FA's amateur status committee, concerning how the (finance) books were being kept. The Amateur Status Committee, however, found nothing amiss with their book-keeping records, although Clapton Orient were suspended for a month until they put theirs in order.

Regular opponents in the 1890s included Ilford, Thames Ironworks, Mid Kent, Oxford City, Old Westminsters, Bristol City, Richmond Association, Upton Park, Old Carthusians, Enfield, Chatham, Queens Park Rangers, Grenadier Guards, Reading, Old St. Stephens, Guilford, Ealing and St. Albans, and Clapton Orient. High View park proved difficult to track down, even after knowing the name of the road, for no maps across 1850-1900 name such a place, although until around 1886, much of Canterbury Grove began to be built over as houses from the Norwood Hall end encroached down to the St. Peters church end. By 1890, all that was left of this invisible park were two fields between present day Thurleston and Uffington Roads (which became tennis courts by 1910), and a large open space on the other side where now sits Ivymount Road. There was for some time, an enclosed cricket ground in Pendennis Road with a pavilion, but that was on the other side of the railway cutting, and some half a mile due west, and this did not seem to fit the description of Canterbury Grove. However, I later read that the groundsman had "kept the pitch in excellent condition" and that later, they were forced out because "football did not do the cricket pitch any good". I now feel that the Pendennis Trinity church cricket ground must have been this High View ground.

In 1895, the extraordinarily-named Baron von Reiffenstein, who appears to have been their patron, proposed that the club becomes professional and informed the Football Association that under the name of West Norwood Football Company Limited, this would take place. The club needed to raise at least £250, and planned to do so by public share issue, and looked for a suitable ground. Unfortunately, the Baron imported paid players into the ranks to such an extent that the first team became the second team.

The *Sporting Life* reported on West Norwood's excellent list of high class friendlies at the start of the 1898-99 season, and congratulated the directors on aiming high. Fixtures had been arranged to receive most of the various cup and league winners in London, including London Caledonians, Southampton (Southern League champions), Old Westminsters, Queens Park Rangers, Vampires, Old Malvernians and Ipswich Town. Mr. A. Bacon remained on as chairman with W. Hooton as honorary secretary.

At the end of August 1898, West Norwood played the Southampton club, who were on the ascendancy, and would soon reach their first Cup Final. However even the offer of bringing five internationals in their side only attracted a small crowd to West Norwood of about 300, the visitors winning a thrilling match 5-3. The Norwood goals were scored by Folks (2) and Fitchie *(London Standard)*. The second half play was said to have been 'desultory'. At this time, they were still playing at High View Park. With the Surrey Mirror remarking that " brilliant scraps of play kept the 2,000 spectators cheering" this 1899 side comfortably beat Redhill 3-0, with six other shots hitting the crossbar -

		Bullock		
	Humphries		Smith	
Black		Steven		Fitchie
Bennett	Rainbird	Fitchie	Coppin	Mackenzie

There was a split in the ranks in 1898, after the "A" team had won the West Norwood cup described somewhat insultingly to its sponsor Baron von Reiffenstein as an "insignificant little cup". The "A" team broke away and called themselves Norwood United and set up camp next door to the High View ground of West Norwood. Then what happened was the players of Norwood United passed the cup around themselves for the next few months, and refused to hand it over to the officials of West Norwood, whose name was on it! The local papers gave their backing to the new Norwood United, comprised entirely of local men, as opposed to the Baron's set of 'imported' players from other clubs. Thus, after 1899, the 'real' West Norwood wasn't the team which carried that name on. *(Sporting Life)*. Much of the above was denied by the Baron in a long letter to the same newspaper, counter-claiming that it was more like the other way around, with seven West Norwood first-teamers currently being local men, while half of Norwood United's team were "out of town" men. He further stated that it was his own choice to scrap the West Norwood "A" team, and that this Norwood United had no connection with his club. Citing the whereabouts and circumstances of several players of both teams, he was in a much stronger social position to have his case heard, and the "insignificant little cup" was ordered to be returned to the Baron.

Optimism seemed high on the eve of the 1900-01 season, reported in the *Sporting Life*. Once more having the use of their ground of High View Park, Canterbury Grove, they would field two teams for the coming season, a 'cup' team which will play friendlies and enter local cups, and a 'league' team which will compete in the Suburban League. Secretary Herbert Rainbird was pleased with matches arranged against well known clubs including Old Etonians, Marlow, Wycombe, Old Carthusians, Crouch End Vampires, Ilford and Leyton etc. First team captain would be P. Lingwood assisted by W.W. Read. "The limited company no longer exists and instead is governed by a committee. Secretary Tommy Grimes of 7 Fenwick Road, East Dulwich reports that groundsman Arthur Fincham has carefully nursed the ground during the close season, and is in capital condition, and an excellent season is forecast". Treasurer Digby Marshall reported that funds were sufficient and that the best of last season's men – A. Kent, S. Newman, J. Mandry, J. Watts and C. Lewis – have been retained. They were forced to find a new home in 1902 when it was deemed that football boots did not do cricket pitches much good come Easter-time, and so they relocated to the London County Ground at Herne Hill for the 1902-03 season. J.E. Howland remained as club captain, deputised by A.S. Sothcott. Fixtures were arranged with Tottenham, Brentford, Northampton, West Ham United and Queens Park Rangers and others. Modest success came along when West Norwood won the London Suburban League in 1903. In 1904, they secured a further three years lease on the Herne Hill ground, and club officials at this time were – H. Bacon (hon. Sec.), W.T. Fitchie (1st team captain), and president Alfred Martin. At their May AGM, they were supported by representatives of several south London amateur clubs, with whom they seemed to have a family bond. In Easter of 1906, West Norwood went on a Scottish tour, and actually played Glasgow Rangers.

Entering the F.A. Cup in 1906, West Norwood failed to make it to the 1st round proper. A 6-1 win over Northfleet United in the 4th Qualifying round gave false hopes, as they were embarrassed 1-9 at home by Accrington Stanley in the penultimate stage. Trophy success finally came to West Norwood when they won the London (Senior) Cup in season 1906-07 when they overcame West Hampstead FC by 4-1. They also entered the Amateur Cup from 1907, but never got past the early rounds. Bromley put them out 2-0 after a 2-2 draw that season. Wolverhampton side Old Wulfrunians were beaten 2-1 in the 1910-11 competition, only for little known Sneiton to beat them 3-0 in the next round. Bromley were again their undoing in 1911, and Worthing (3-3, 0-3) the following year. Tunbridge Wells (0-0, 0-4) in 1913 and Catford Southend (2-2, 0-2) in 1914, which brought to an end, their Amateur Cup efforts.

Now using the Half Moon Hotel as headquarters, West Norwood joined the Isthmian League in season 1907-8, until 1924, when they joined the Spartan League for three seasons. Seemingly out of their depth, one remarkable result was when they won 9-1 away against Shepherds Bush in December 1908. A tour of Germany at Easter was claimed as a success.

A report that West Norwood had lost their Herne Hill ground in 1909 seems to have fallen through, although I couldn't find anything about them in 1910-11. However, a period of constant struggle saw "The Bantams" permanently in the basement at this time, when they finished in the bottom three every season, except in 1911-12, when they came 5th out of 11 teams, when it was won by London Caledonians, who strangely had finished bottom the previous year. Founded in 1905-06 season, the Ithsmian League at first had only 6 teams, although they were all top names, such as Casuals, Caledonians, and Clapton. In 1907, three teams left, to be replaced by Dulwich, Oxford City and West Norwood, who finished bottom for the next two seasons, and bottom but one for the following two. When the league resumed in 1919, West Norwood were one of four clubs who did not immediately reappear after the War, the others being Oxford City, Woking and Caledonians. In their final Spartan League season, they conceded 110 goals in their 26 games to finish last again. Even their reserve team finished last in the 13-club reserve section. Norwood were simply unable to compete with teams like Southall, Kingstonian, Uxbridge, Barnet and Enfield.

When West Norwood moved out of Herne Hill cycle ground in 1922, it was said it was due to the Crystal Palace club moving in, who remained there until they built their Selhurst Park ground. This 1925 side were humiliated 10-1 away at Redhill in January, when they spent the year struggling against teams such as Southall, Kingstonians, Sutton,

Barking, Enfield, Uxbridge, Bromley and Barnet, having joined the Athenian League :

		Jones		
	Johnson		Williams	
Sampson		Calhurst		Cole
W. Warnes	Forbes	Sivier	Wulton	R. Warnes

   The loss of their Herne Hill ground after twenty years seems to have broken the back of the club. The Bantams made the news again in 1926, but for the wrong reasons: club trainer Ruben Warren was convicted of assault against a female spectator in January. It seems that as the two teams were leaving the pitch at the end of a hostile game, an affray erupted near the pavilion, and Warren accidentally punched a woman in the face, causing injury. In the following year - 1927 - West Norwood had again folded, having finished consistently bottom of the Athenian, although there was no mention of this at the AGM of the League on Monday 20th June that year, held in the Hertford Rooms of the Great Eastern Hotel, London. It appears that West Norwood had lost their ground, as reported in the *Surrey Mirror* of September 16th 1927, but they were had managed to borrow Sutton United's ground for their FA Cup preliminary round match on the following day. Ironically, it was Sutton United who Norwood drew in the qualifying round for the Amateur Cup a fortnight later, a game they lost 1-3. West Norwood dropped back down a level into the Surrey Senior League for 1928-9. A decade later, they once more dropped down to the Surrey Senior League in 1938-9 at the outbreak of the war. They do not seem to have reformed in 1946.

WEST NORWOOD F.C.

West Norwood, in south London, is better known to football historians as the resting place of legendary Charles William Alcock, founding father of the F.A. and the F.A. Cup.

West Norwood seemed to have too many rivals, even in their own town, with Norwood & Selhurst operating in the late 1890s, Norwood Association at the turn of the 20th century (who had to borrow Leatherhead's ground as they had none of their own), Norwood Wanderers, and last but not least, rivals South Norwood whose demise coincided with the birth of West Norwood, possibly suggesting that 'West' arose from the ashes of the 'South'.

South Norwood FC, founded in winter 1870, wearing red and black bands, played on a field off Portland Road, and Woodside (circa 1875), and may have been an offshoot of the even earlier South Norwood Athletic Club, formed in 1864, and organised by W.G. Stainburn. By 1872, an annual return fixture against the Old Westminsters had been set up, this twelve-man side winning there 1-0 in 1873 - C. Jordan (goal), C.E. Leeds (back), W. H. White (captain), G. Manvell, E. Welborough, T. Viall, C. Barber, G. Fleet, C. Wilson, H. Wilson, H. Hubbard, V. Fletcher. White and Leeds were selected for the Surrey v Middlesex match in November 1875. Ambitiously competing in the F.A. Cup from 1872 until 1880, they never got past the 2nd round. A 1-0 win over Barnes seemed to be followed by the same result against Windsor Home Park, but the match was replayed on appeal, and Windsor men won 3-0. The following season saw a 0-1 defeat by Cambridge University, and 1874 saw a 1-3 defeat against Pilgrims. 1875 was marginally better as a walkover against Clydesdale was followed by a 0-5 drubbing against the powerful Swifts of Slough. Saxons were beaten 4-1 at home in 1876, only for the powerful club Sheffield FC travel down to London and trounce them 7-0 in December. Reading put them out 2-0 at the first hurdle in 1877, but 1878 saw Leyton scratch to them only for once again, Cambridge to beat them 3-0 on Parker's Piece. In their final season of competing in the F.A. Cup, Brentwood were beaten 4-2 at Portland Road in November 1879, before Clapham Rovers knocked them out 4-1 at home in round 2. During the calendar year of 1878, South Norwood played 19 matches, winning only 6, drawing 1, and losing 12, not a great set of figures.

At one point, Scottish International brothers James and Robert Smith (members of the Queens Park FC) played for the club, and also William Lindsay. The Smith brothers were selected to play for Scotland in the first ever official International match when England went up to the West of Scotland cricket ground at Partick on 30th November 1872 in a goal-less draw in which the Smiths 'began to create some fine moves' *(The Footballer).* Since this was the year of South Norwood's foundation, this points strongly to the brothers Smith being the founder members whilst they were working in London. In the mid 1870s, the team captain was W.H. White, with his brother in goal, and the Wilson brothers led the attack. A match against St. Leonards FC, and lost 2-0, was played on *Christmas morning* of 1900. As to the ' field adjoining Portland Road' ground, I could find no such thing within 200 yards of either side of the whole length at any point in the period 1890-1920, only the South Norwood Recreation Ground, by Norwood Junction station, some 500 yards away. The South Norwood Athletic grounds off Auckland Road were similarly some half a mile to the north. Of the many available fields, a 7 acre field facing the Prince of Denmark pub, by the junction with today's Ingatestone Road seems a likely candidate. Both clubs also faced nearby competition, since the Croydon Common 'Nest' and Crystal Palace grounds were less than a mile away.

WINDSOR HOME PARK FC

Founded	-	1869 (see text) and possibly as early as 1854.
Folded	-	circa 1881 (became Windsor FC)
Ground	-	Windsor Park, London, also Dolphin Ground, Slough
Colours	-	1. Scarlet and black hoops (Bells Life, Christmas 1872)
		2. Blue and black hoops (after 1874)
Headquarters	-	Royal Oak Hotel

The *Berkshire Chronicle* remarked in October 1866 that "the popular fashion of football played by men and not boys was spreading out of London into the home counties, and that cricket clubs are now hibernating as football clubs". Windsor Home Park is a section of the greater park which surrounds Windsor Castle, the royal residence. Although upper class pursuits dominated the Victorian social scene there - hunting with dogs, horse racing, coursing, rowing, quoits, polo and cricket, football as a means of local rivalry was already on the agenda by the late 1860s. The royal family would also use the park as a base for pheasant shoots and other social engagements. It was a place where troops paraded, where the Grenadier Guards bands played, and generally, the place to 'be seen' if you were amongst the high society of the district. Public access for recreational use was granted in 1853 when the young Queen Victoria granted that 100 acres be made available, rendering the over-used Bachelors Acre field redundant.

In November 1870, two football matches took place in Home Park between two sides representing Windsor and Eton, two small towns which almost ran into each other. The rivalry would continue on, but in the form of clubs rather than town representative matches. When Maidenhead FC played its first ever opposition on Saturday 17th December 1870, the visitors were Windsor Home Park. The event drew a large crowd, including all the town dignitaries, but as ever, the game ended without a goal being scored. Played on a meadow opposite the Skindle Hotel, and lent for the event by Mr. Bond, the 'superior system' of the more experienced Windsor team was matched by the greater pluck and determination from the home team. The *Reading Mercury* did not see fit to name any of the players, but recited instead a list of the local dignitaries present, amongst which large crowd was a great number of ladies. This report hints at Windsor having been formed for at least several seasons, otherwise they would not have developed 'a superior system' yet. The football team may have been a winter offshoot of the cricket club of the same name which had been active since the early 1850s. The Windsor & Eton Home Park cricket club had absorbed the Windsor Albert & Victoria C.C in August 1853, and used the Swan Hotel as their headquarters. When the Home Park C.C played against a team of professionals in October 1865, one George Bambridge (founder of The Swifts FC) was batting at number five.

I then found an advert in the *Windsor & Eton Express* for October 1854 (!) which said that that W. Runicles & Co. of 9 The High Street, Eton, could now supply the newly invented india-rubber footballs as "they are easy of inflation and readily repaired and do not give off the noxious gases of old leather footballs which used a decayed pig's bladder". Immediately above the advert ran the line "as supplied to the Home Park football club". I will remind you of that date once more- 1854, *a year before even the earliest date claimed by the Sheffield FC.* George Bambridge placed an advert in the *Windsor & Eton Express* on

Saturday 12th November 1853, asking for interested persons wishing to form a football team, to contact him at his Brunswick-terrace, Windsor address. Meetings were to be held at 4pm each Tuesday and Thursday in Home Park. This clearly restricts applicants to the leisured classes, and as his eldest son 'Charlie' proceeded to play for Windsor Home Park, I wonder if this wasn't the year of the foundation of the club. If so, this places them even ahead of the legendary Sheffield FC and would shatter the accepted hierarchy of club foundations of world football! His three sons would later form the nucleus of the Swifts of Slough and become the only instance of three capped footballing brothers.

Football of any sort was bottom of the pile of sporting activities in the Bucks & Berks area, with horse & hounds, cricket, golf, and hare coursing more popular, and thus almost no football was reported in the area before 1870. Windsor Home Park must have been another socially well connected club as, at their Annual Ball (!) of April 1871, at The Guildhall, a hundred invited guests including the mayor, were wined and dined to music played by the band of the Life Guards (*Bucks Herald 1871*). Tickets for a couple costs an astonishing 20 shillings (one pound), about two week's wages for a labourer. Lower classes need not apply!

Later that year, they were one of the original fifteen entries for the first ever F.A. Cup competition. In the 1870s, Windsor Home Park was also used by The Guards for their annual sports day, and by Queen Victoria who inspected the troops who had returned from fighting in the Gold Coast of Africa. It was also used by the Fusilier Guards and the Grenadier Guards for their cricket matches, and horse racing and polo were also popular there. As football would have been a minority event in Windsor Home Park, it was rarely reported.

Mid-March 1871 was a busy time as WHP played sometimes three matches a week, with games on a Monday (Bayley House 5-0), Wednesday (0-1 Marlow) and Saturday (0-0 The Swifts). The Swifts' match drew a good number of spectators, the game being commenced with a 'bully' in the centre of the ground, E.C. Bambridge going closest to scoring with a shot that whistled past the post. The Windsor eleven for the Swifts game included W. Wright, E. Bambridge, Vidler, C. Capes, Nicholls, P. Chamberlain, H. Clarke (back), and C. Sim (back).

Clapham Rovers were visitors in November and departed 2-0 winners with goals from Vansittart and Kendrick. I had heard of that unusual surname somewhere, and recognised it as the name of the actor who plays the lord of the manor in the TV series Heartbeat (Rupert Vansittart). At Christmas 1871, captained by Herbert Wright, 'Windsor' played Maidenhead on Home Park, where it was commented that the ground was 'much better than at Crystal Palace'. WHP included two Bambridge brothers and two Wright brothers, assisted by guest player Hubert Heron of the Uxbridge FC (later also of Wanderers). Several of the best men for both sides were unavailable due to the festive commitments. Bambridge also scored the two goals which beat Marlow 2-0 in February, played on a Tuesday night on a waterlogged pitch. All three matches were captained by H. Wright. The county of Buckinghamshire had few teams, and thus, Marlow were often encountered. When they met in October 1874, captain Joll had already played in one match that day! Played in a fog so dense that the reporter could say little about the play, and won 4-0, both E.H and G.F. Bambridges played under the captaincy of P. Chamberlain. If believed, Marlow thought they had scored when the ball was sent just inside one of the posts; sadly it turned out only to be a corner flag! The WHP side that day was- P. Chamberlain (captain), E.H. Bambridge, A. Joll, J. Harrison, A. Fox, W. Whitfield, G. Dugdale, W.J.

Goodman, G.F. Bambridge, G. Gower, A. Clarke.

Windsor Home Park entered the F.A. Cup in its 2nd year of foundation, 1872, where they defeated Reigate Priory 4-2 in round 1. South Norwood were beaten on the new Dolphin ground by 3-0 to put them into the 3rd round, where there remained only two ties: Oxford University v Royal Engineers (which would have made a good cup final),and Maidenhead v Windsor Home Park. As it was, Windsor and Royal Engineers were both put out 0-1, the *Morning Post* of 23rd December 1872 said of the Windsor v Maidenhead game, played at Slough "despite the unfavourable state of the ground, some good play was exhibited on both sides, resulting in a 1-0 win for Maidenhead". The playing of their FA Cup matches at the recently created Dolphin ground implies that that was Windsor's home ground in 1872. In the only match played in round 4, Oxford defeated Maidenhead 4-0, these being the last two sides standing who had actually played any matches. However, Glasgow Queens Park had been given free passage to the semi final on account of logistics, but then, to make a farce into an embarrassing madness, Queens Park scratched against Oxford, who then met the Wanderers in the final. How did Wanderers get there? Oh, they had a bye straight through to the final, having won it the previous year! Such a ridiculous arrangement surely must have attracted severe comment at the time, as it showed up the organising capabilities of the F.A. in a very bad light, giving one team a free passage to the final, and another a bye to the semi, where they then withdrew!

One curious match took place in November 1874, when Windsor Home Park played the Great Marlow club in conditions so bad that the reporter gave up trying to describe what may have occurred! "Played in a fog so dense, and in a darkness like that in Egypt which could be felt, these two teams supposedly played a match, and I am assured that the following players took part; Joll the untiring (who had already played one match that day) scored two goals, and Clarke one, and that Chamberlain and E. Bambridge again distinguished themselves". Captained by P. Chamberlain and with Harrison, Fox, Whitfield, Dugdale, Gower, Goodman and G. Bambridge reputedly somewhere on the field, Windsor seem to have won by 3-0. For some reason, WHP did not compete in the FA Cup of 1873-4, but were back again the following year, where they never actually played a match; a round 1 walkover against Uxbridge was followed by WHP capitulating when drawn away to Oxford University. Football experimentation took place in December 1874 in Home Park, when a new team 'Swallows' played the 'Antelopes' from Marlow. Those team names may have been public school 'house' names. Two Bambridge brothers (Arthur and Charlie) played in the Swallows team, with the third acting as referee.

This was the Windsor Home Park team of 1876 -

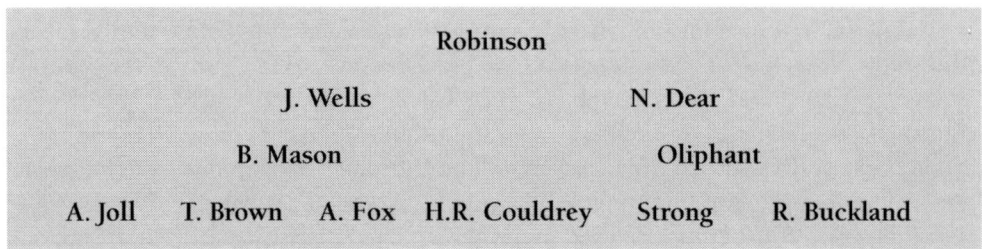

		Robinson			
	J. Wells		N. Dear		
	B. Mason		Oliphant		
A. Joll	T. Brown	A. Fox	H.R. Couldrey	Strong	R. Buckland

Windsor did not again compete in the F.A. Cup proper until 1880, when they were drawn against the Greyfriars FC, who beat them 3-1, in the Section Two of the Metropolitan

Division. Round 1 was again their exit point on 11th November 1881, when Reading Minster scored the only goal of the game. I was thrown back then, when I traced the match report in the *Reading Mercury* which stated that WHP's victors 'in the first round of the Association Cup tie' were called Grosvenor FC ! I wondered if Grosvenor and Minster were one and the same team, since I then followed up by reading the 3rd round report a month later, where the same paper stated that Reading Minster were knocked out at home 3-1 by the London side Hotspur (not Tottenham). The first match, a goal-less draw played in impossible conditions of sleet and ankle deep slush on the Hotspur ground on Uxbridge Road, Acton, the week before Christmas, had seen a Minster 'goal' by Bilson wiped out for off-sides. This was very confusing, since the names of the Reading team did not match those from Grosvenor! The Grosvenor captain was called Powell and their goalie Keeley, whilst the Minster team were led by captain & goalkeeper the Reverend E.S. Hillard. I can come to no other conclusion that *Grosvenor played in Minster's place* and knocked out Windsor Home Park! Is it too late after 135 years for the F.A. to hold an enquiry?

The name of Windsor Home Park never again appeared in the F.A. Cup, but a team simply called 'Windsor' did for the next three seasons before they too disappeared altogether. Considering that many footballers took part in amateur athletics meetings around the country, I was surprised to see that only H. Marriot from WHP entered the Great Marlow sports day of Whit Monday 1877, although many other well known players took part. A football match, simply billed as Windor v Henley was played in that place in January 1878, and this time, three of the famous Bambridge brothers turned out for Windsor – Arthur, Ernest and Edward. Blyth (2),Wild, Bambridge and H. Barnes scored the goals as Windsor won by 5-2. However, in the return game, played on 26th October 1878 and briefly reported in the *Reading Mercury,* said that Henley had beaten Windsor Home Park by 5-1. The full name was back in use again in October 1879 when WHP were beaten 3-1 at home by Henley, although this time, there was no mention of the Bambridge brothers, with Joll, Couldrey, Lochlein and half back Blackett gaining the plaudits. When WHP travelled to meet the Swifts in February 1880, the team had hardly changed since 1876, with Joll, Couldrey, Strong, Buckland, Mason, Oliphant, Dear, Brown and Fox all still ever present, quite an achievement for an amateur side. Only Robinson in goal seemed to be a new player in the 1-2 defeat. In March 1881, WHP knocked the Swifts out of the county cup by 2-0 on their own ground and went on to meet Marlow in the April final. Both goals were scored by a new man, Keyser, and the game was brought to a close by the familiar but curious call of "no time" by the referee.

At a general meeting of the Berks & Bucks F.A held at the Queens Hotel, Reading at Christmas 1884, there were no representatives from the Remnants FC, the Swifts or Windsor Home Park, only from Windsor FC. Considering the continuity, it is almost certain that WHP dropped the 'Home Park' tag and became plain Windsor, who played in light blue & chocolate. They may have also amalgamated with Windsor Grosvenor who were competing alongside them in the Bucks & Berks cup of the early 1880s. Interestingly, when 'Windsor' played Slough in January 1884, their home ground was given as Windsor Home Park, adding further to the probability, compounded by the fact that the 'Windsor' team contained Wells, Brown, Dear, Buckland and Mason, formerly of Home Park. At their AGM of September 1884, held at the Castle Hotel, the following officers were elected – Mr. Richard Gardner, M.P. (president), the Reverend S. Hawtrey (ex-Remnants), Canon Applegarth, and the mayor, J. O. Harris were among the vice-presidents, and J. Rodgers was honorary secretary and treasurer. First team captain was to be T. Brown, deputised by E.C. Kelly, and John Hawtrey was among the large committee elected. A programme of over twenty fixtures were announced to the gathering (*Sporting Life*).

Wherever they played in Windsor Home Park, the matches would have been in view of Windsor Castle.

WHP's most famous two players were probably R. Courtney deWelch, and Edward Charles 'Bam' Bambridge, who also played for the Swifts, and later, Clapham Rovers and the Corinthians. In 1875, Joll was also playing with the Swifts, along with the three 'Bams'.

Left winger Bambridge, was educated at Windsor's St. Marks School before going on to Malvern College. Born in Windsor in 1858, his family lived on Adelaide Road and he became an underwriter with Lloyds Bank. Later, in 1890, it was his suggestion that the south of England should have its own league to rival the Football League, which had no southern sides in it, from which idea was born the Southern and Isthmian Leagues. Of Edward it was said "*he was very fast, had splendid command over the ball, middled with great accuracy and judgement, and to cap it all he was a remarkably good shot at goal*" (Charles Alcock)

Reginald Courtney deWelch (1851-1939) would sometimes play in goal or as a back, but he also turned out for Old Harrovians, Harrow Chequers and Wanderers. Twice capped between 1872-74, he was elected onto the FA committee during the same period. The last match I could find for Windsor Home Park was in September 1881, against Reading Minster FC, in a match where Joll, Couldrey and Lochlein were their best men (Bucks Herald). In October 1883, Windsor FC cried off at the last minute from a match arranged with Marlow, causing the Bucks Herald to say that it wasn't the first time this had happened, and Marlow would now take them off their fixtures list. Windsor had been unable to raise a team yet again. Windsor seemed to have bounced back in the late 1880s though, as they won the Berks & Bucks cup in 1885 and 1887. Oddly, Windsor lost the 1885 Berks & Bucks Junior final 0-6 against Theale 'with their talisman player absent'. Windsor's secretary at this time was E.C. Kelly.

Another player who sometimes turned out for Windsor was Cambridge Etonian and Wanderers footballer Percy John de Paravicini. Better known as a first class cricketer, he was Eton school captain in 1880 and 1881, and one of very few who played for four consecutive seasons. Going up to Cambridge, he was a regular for Cambridge(25) and Middlesex (62) during the 1880s, and turned out for Buckinghamshire in the Edwardian era. Described as a speedy two footed defender, he played in two FA Cup finals for Etonians, and in 1883 played for England in all three home international matches. In private life, he was a Justice of the Peace for Buckinghamshire, and married Lady Cholmondeley, the daughter of the Viscount of Maplas.

Operating at the end of the 1870s, was a club called Windsor Grosvenor; in June 1882, they held their sports day at the Dolphin Ground, Slough. This was the home ground of the Swifts, the team formed around the Bambridge brothers, who also turned out for WHP, so that may have been the connection. Another local team operating around 1886 were Windsor Phoenix, who played on Windsor Rec and Balloon Meadow, Clewer (now absorbed by the racecourse). The name of Phoenix implying a new team arisen from an earlier defunct one.

Marlow and Windsor played in every county cup final during 1880-1890, with only Reading and the Swifts able to break the joint monopoly. I could find no reports of Windsor FC after 1890, when after needing three games to get past South Reading, were then beaten 1-0 by Marlow in the Berks & Bucks cup final in front of a 2,000 crowd, fielding this side -

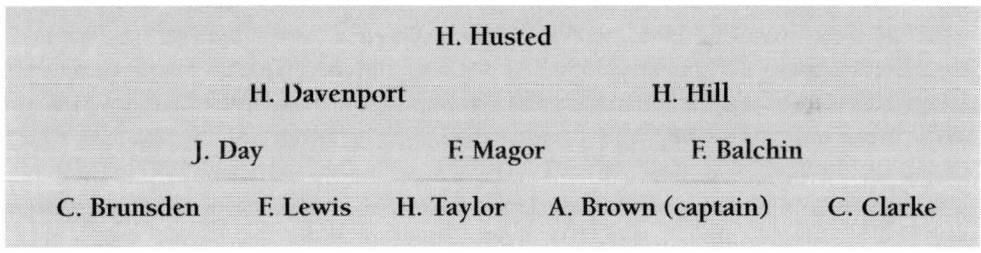

			H. Husted				
		H. Davenport			H. Hill		
	J. Day			F. Magor		F. Balchin	
C. Brunsden		F. Lewis		H. Taylor	A. Brown (captain)		C. Clarke

Windsor Phoenix (and not 'Windsor') were on Marlow's fixture list for 1891-2 season, suggesting the possibility that *they* were now the top club in the district, having earlier won the county junior cup in 1888. Phoenix then won the 1892 county senior cup when they beat 2nd Scots Guards 5-1 in the final, played on the Maidenhead ground, as usual. As H. Davenport was playing for Windsor Phoenix in 1892, this suggests that Windsor FC too had folded and some of their players joined the Phoenix club, which by then was entering the Qualifying Rounds of the F.A. Cup. The leading Phoenix players were F.W. Carlton, J.G. Veitch, H.E. Davenport and C.W. Parry. In late 1892, a new club, Windsor & Eton was formed, which itself was formed out of the amalgamation of Windsor Phoenix and Windsor St. Albans, which then absorbed Windsor & Eton Victoria in 1893, who had only just lost the county junior final in 1892, which arrangement lasted right up until 2011.

WOODFORD WELLS FC

Founded - 1868
Folded - Circa 1876-7
Ground - Monkhams Lane cricket ground (probable)
Colours - Black jersey with white Maltese cross

Located between Walthamstow and Chigwell in north London, the village of Woodford Wells had a short-lived but enthusiastic football club which entered the F.A. Cup in the 1870s, but with little success. Once more, I am indebted to *Robin Horton* for discovering their colours listed for 1873 in Alcocks Annuals. There were several other pioneering clubs on the doorstep - the Forest Club at Leytonstone, South and West Norwood, and Walthamstow to the south was home to several teams by the 1880s, although the early Walthamstow club, led by the Roquette brothers, favoured rugby rules. During Christmas 1869, Woodford Wells were on the fixture list of the Forest Club, pioneering fore-runner of the Wanderers, and the return fixture was played on New Year's Day. When the Wanderers played the Forest Club (having been re-formed by P.G. Rouquette), on 30th October 1869, the venue was given as Woodford in the *Chelmsford Chronicle*. In February 1870, WW travelled the short distance to the Forest school ground on George Lane, where a one-sided game saw the home side win 3-0 with their goal-keeper having nothing to do all match. In the flowery language of the day, *The Sportsman* quipped that "it rendered the office of the Forest goal-keeper a perfect myth".

The three brothers Spicer formed the base of the WW football team, who arrived with only eight men. Checking the Woodford cricket eleven for summer 1868, I noticed footballers W. and T.F. Spreckley, Lloyd, H.L. Davis and W. Bouch all taking part in the cricket club sports day at Buckhurst Hill. On Saturday 11th February 1871, Woodford Wells played host to the Trojans FC, whom they easily defeated 6-0 after *two hours' play*. Again captained by H. E. Kaye, this time the side contained the three Hooper brothers, A.,B., and H. In that game, it seems that the old rule of defenders getting penned in on their own goal-line could touch the ball down behind the goal-line and give possession to the attacking team, perhaps 20 yards out, a rule which soon remained only in the rugby version and known as a short corner in hockey. Few Woodford Wells games were reported in the press, but one of their matches in 1871 against Leyton on Saturday 4th March reported in The Sportsman produced this eleven-man team line-up, who easily won by "three goals and several touch-downs to nil":

> **H.E. Kaye (captain), F.E. Williams, T. Powell, B. Hooper, F. Carter, E. Spicer, F. Robbins, A. H. Tozer, E. Ferrand, A. Hooper.**

Other sides met during 1871-72 season were Leyton (11/11), Hackney Downs (25/11), Brixton (2/12), Forest (9/12), Clapham Pilgrims (10/12), Brixton (6/1/72), Leyton (27/1), Forest Club (3/2), Forest School (10/2), Forest School (17/2), Trojans (25/2).

F. Robbins was a noted athlete who competed in events held at the London Athletic Grounds in the early 1870s. Winning by 3-0 reference was again made in *The Sportsman* to the Leyton men who were often forced to 'touch down behind their own line'. This suggests a still lingering rule from the rugby game, which demonstrates that the association code has still not totally divorced itself from the handling code. The 'three goals kicked under the Leyton goal' confirm that it wasn't a rugger match.

At 1880, Woodford Wells was still surrounded by fields and forest, and with a population of only a few hundred, they were never likely to draw a large crowd. There were two recreational areas in the village, a 4.7 acre field by All Saint's church, which became home to the cricket and tennis clubs, and a 10 acre field behind Bancrofts school (extant as the fortress style Bancroft School sports grounds). Their sports day held on 13th January 1872 was on the Hare & Hounds ground (*The Sportsman*). However, I could find no pub of that name in the Woodford area at that time. The cricket ground, still in use at Buckhurst Hill, one mile due north remains a possibility as being the Woodford Wells football ground, and is three miles up the main road from the Forest School. 'The Green', a strip of recreational land running alongside the A104 and current home of the town cricket club, is another candidate. The field used by the rugby club can be discounted as it used to be part of the grounds of Higham Hall in the 19th century.

For season 1872-73, Clapham Rovers, Pilgrims, Surrey Rifles, Brondesbury and Woodford Wells were added to their growing fixture list. On Saturday 13th December 1873, Woodford Wells played the Pilgrims FC on Hackney Downs, not a helpful description of where it took place ! Fraser opened the scoring for Wells after only five minutes, but Pilgrims equalised when a shot went in via a defenders' head. An evenly well contested remaining hour produced no further scoring and it remained 1-1. On the following Saturday, Beauchamp scored the only goal to defeat Upton Park away. Over Christmas 1873, both matches with the Pilgrims FC were drawn 1-1. A match in 1874 against 1st Surrey Rifles on Saturday 7th February at Woodford, saw a close tussle, with the militia men playing "up the hill" in the first half, but were defeated when Will Spreckley prodded home following a goalmouth scrimmage.

Woodford Wells competed in the early years of the F.A. Cup. In 1873-4 they defeated Reigate Priory by 3-2 at home in round 1, but narrowly lost 1-2 away to the Swifts, with E. Bambridge and Nicholls scoring for the Swifts and R H Beauchamp for Wells. This was their usual team in 1874 -

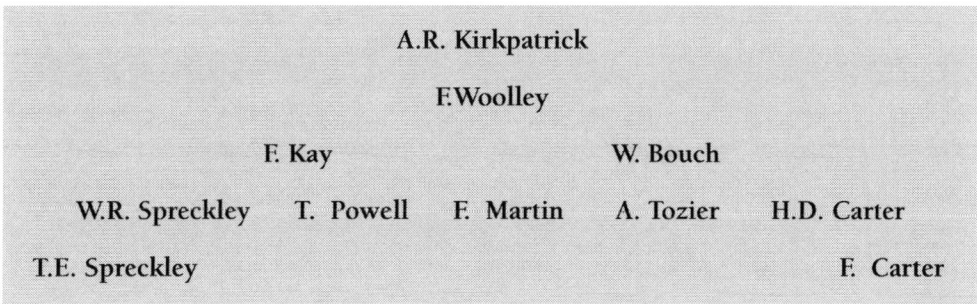

A.R. Kirkpatrick

F. Woolley

F. Kay   W. Bouch

W.R. Spreckley   T. Powell   F. Martin   A. Tozier   H.D. Carter

T.E. Spreckley   F. Carter

In the following season, they were the surprise team of the tournament when they reached the quarter-finals. Successive home wins over High Wycombe (1-0) on 31st October and Southall Park (3-0) on 5th December, saw them matched with Shropshire Wanderers, a club formed by two former Shrewsbury grammar school pupils who qualified as solicitors in London, Llewellyn Kendrick and John Hawley Edwards. Despite only being formed on 'high days and holidays' the Shropshire club were quite difficult to beat, and the cup-tie, played on the Kennington Oval ground on January 23rd immediately after the Old Etonians v Maidenhead tie had finished, ended 1-1. *The Field* newspaper remarked that "Woodford Wells had a light and fast team, but that the Salopians should have won". In the replay on 3rd February 1875 watched by 600, the Salopians took their chances on a boggy Oval turned to wintry mush by the thawing action of the players' boots on the layer of snow, and departed London as 2-0 victors to move into the semi-finals. The Wells' last attempt in the cup was November 6th 1875, when they were drawn away to Dorset side Panthers and were beaten at the first hurdle. The match was played at Winchester as a small compromise on travelling arrangements as the two clubs were 110 miles apart.

For season 1874-75, home and away fixtures were made with the following clubs - Reigate Priory, Barnes, Pilgrims, High Wycombe, Gnats (October), Clapham Rovers, Forest, Forest School, Royal Engineers (November), Crystal Palace, Gnats, South Norwood, Upton Park (December) and Swifts, Clapham Rovers, Brondesbury, Barnes and Reigate (January), Forest, Crystal Palace, Barnes, Brondesbury (February), Forest School, South Norwood and Upton Park (March), giving them a full set of weekly matches against some good quality opposition.

Woodford Wells fell off the radar after 1876, although I spotted that when the Essex team made its inter-county debut, against Bucks at the Dolphin Ground, Slough on Wednesday 19th January that year, one 'F. J. Sparkes (sic) of the Woodford Wells club' was captain of Essex, suggesting that the club was extant. I was not aware however that Francis Sparks had been their player. Only a fortnight later, for Essex's match against Surrey, F.J. Sparks was now 'of Herts Rangers' and one A.A. Robertson of Woodford Wells was also in the county team. When Wales played Scotland on 25th March 1876, G.F. Thompson of the Woodford Wells club played on the wing, partnering John Hawley Edwards of the Wanderers FC. There was no sign of Woodford Wells FC after the summer of 1876, or any announcement that they had folded, or amalgamated with another club.

Acknowledgements

With thanks to the following for their help, patience and support -

Guy Smith (Shropshire)

Christine Bevan (Dorset)

Lee Morrall Photographic Services (Staffordshire)

Dave Twydell (Middlesex)

John Griffiths (Staffordshire)

David Moor (Historical Kits)

Robin Horton (Historian who supplied several team colours)

Bibliography

Philip Sweet	*History of Merthyr Town FC*
Charles Alcock	*Football Annuals 1879-1905*
Bob Barton	*The History Of The Amateur Cup*
Richard Rundle	*Football Club History Database*
Charles Dickens	*1888 Handbook Guide To London*
Charles Murray	*1867 Guide To London*
Keith Dewhurst	*Underdogs, Randon House, London 2012*
Alan Futter	*Who Killed Cock Robin ?, London 1990*
P. C. Adams	*Little Acorns 1976*
Murray	*Guide To London 1867*
Mike Float	*Football Grounds Of South London*

References

The following newspapers were accessed or read across the Victorian and Edwardian eras:

London Standard

Bells Life

Sheffield Evening Telegraph

Bucks Herald

Morning Post

Athletic News

The Sportsman

Blackburn Standard

York Herald

Yorkshire Post

Dorking & Leatherhead Advertiser

Dover Express

Sussex Agricultural Express

Bridport News

North Devon Journal

The Penny Illustrated

Cambridge Independent Press

Lloyds News

The Graphic

Western Gazette

Western Daily Express

Chemlsford Chronicle

Pall-Mall Gazette

Portsmouth News

Dundee Courier

Hertford Mercury

Nottingham Evening Post

Hartlepool Mail

Essex Newsman

Tiverton Gazette

Surrey Comet

Surrey Mirror

Luton Advertiser

Lichfield Mercury

Herts Mercury

Kilburn Times

Windsor & Eton Times

Football Club History Database

Other titles

Lost Teams Of The South   Published by Black Country Research 2019

Lost Teams Of The Midlands   Published by X-Libris, USA, 2013

Lost Teams Of The North   John Griffiths Publishing, England, 2016

Birth Of The Saddlers   John Griffiths Publishing, England, 2014

Red Lions - Bloxwich Strollers John Griffiths Publishing, England, 2014

History of Short Heath Utd   Available from Black Country Research
19 Calstock Road, Willenhall, WV124TG

History of Darlaston All Saints Available from Black Country Research